Dental Autopsy

Dental Autopsy

William E. Silver
Richard R. Souviron

CRC Press
Taylor & Francis Group
Boca Raton London New York

CRC Press is an imprint of the
Taylor & Francis Group, an **informa** business

CRC Press
Taylor & Francis Group
6000 Broken Sound Parkway NW, Suite 300
Boca Raton, FL 33487-2742

Printed in the United States of America on acid-free paper
10 9 8 7 6 5 4 3 2 1

International Standard Book Number-13: 978-1-4200-7013-2 (Hardcover)

Library of Congress Cataloging-in-Publication Data

Silver, William E. (William Eliot), 1929-
Dental autopsy / William E. Silver, Richard R. Souviron.
p. ; cm.
Includes bibliographical references and index.
ISBN 978-1-4200-7013-2 (hardcover : alk. paper)
1. Dental jurisprudence. 2. Autopsy. I. Souviron, Richard R. II. Title.
[DNLM: 1. Forensic Dentistry--methods. W 705 S587d 2009]

RA1062.S55 2009
614'.18--dc22 2008053602

Visit the Taylor & Francis Web site at
http://www.taylorandfrancis.com

and the CRC Press Web site at
http://www.crcpress.com

Dedication

To the thousands of unidentified and missing resting in medical examiner coolers and unknown fields throughout the world.

And to our wives, Marcia (WES) and Barbara (RRS), who suffered through so many hours of our self-inflicted agony.

Table of Contents

Preface

William Gladstone, British statesman and former prime minister, once said, "Show me the manner in which a nation or community cares for its dead and I will measure with mathematical exactness the tender mercies of its people, their respect for the law of the land and their loyalty to high ideals."

The mission of this book is to educate the dental, medical, and legal professions in the conduct of a forensic dental examination of the oral structures and its many ramifications in the criminal justice system as well as in civil litigation. But it is more than that.

"Unidentified" is more than just a word. It speaks volumes of encyclopedic proportions. It implores us to continue to search for its partner, the "Missing." Together they exist somewhere in space, desperately searching for each other. As forensic odontologists, or their surrogates, we are the brokers of this union.

In the midst of this concoction one can taste the bitter flavor of a family seeking its lost one. Add to this twisted tale the individual who has not only lost his life but cannot find his past. Compounding this historic tragedy, there may be the mysterious unknown of the living culprits who are still at large and who may have caused this terrible loss by their murderous activities, still unpunished.

This is only one of an estimated 40,000 unidentified remains in this country who are held in the cool recesses of morgues since 1975. In Miami Dade County approximately 37 bodies remain unidentified each year, so now there are over 200 unidentified in this district alone. The body is normally held in the morgue cooler for six to eight months until an investigation is completed and then the body is buried in Potter's Field (Figure 1). State law forbids cremation of the unidentified remains in the event that later exhumation may be required for possible identification with a missing person. Photos, x-rays, and records are kept indefinitely for the same reason. The identified indigent is given a proper burial in the county cemetery (Potter's Field) after cremation.

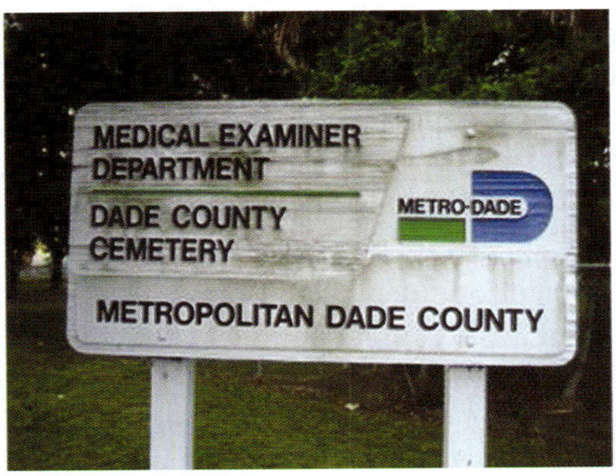

Figure 1 Potter's field.

Note: Do you know how Potter's field got its name? Judas, having been paid 30 pieces of silver for allegedly betraying Jesus in the garden of Gethsemane, returned the "blood money" to the Treasury. Not wishing to place this kind of money in the Treasury, the priests decided to purchase a burial ground for the unknown and known indigents who could not afford a burial. Living in an agricultural society they chose land that was not suitable for growing fruits and vegetables, the place which was predominantly clay, where potters sought the raw material for their crafts. And so it was that Potter's Field was named.

According to the Bureau of Justice Statistics (BJS) only 49 percent of Medical Examiner and Coroner (ME/C) offices have policies for retaining records of the unidentified. With the institution of electronic record keeping it is an easier task to retain these records indefinitely. Older records may be scanned to add to the database since "cold cases" have no limit to the time of discovery and murder has no statute of limitations. The National Crime Information Center Unidentified Persons (NCIC-UP) database contains only 15 percent of the nation's unidentified decedents. Federal mandate only requires reporting of missing persons (MP) under the age of 21 so the comparison of the unidentified is further hampered by this deficiency of a much larger population of adults who remain unreported, but may be voluntarily missing. The latest government project from the Department of Justice is the National Missing and Unidentified Persons System (NamUs; http://www.namus.gov or http://www.find-the-missing.org). This system is different from NCIC, because it will allow entry of information by the general population. NCIC (http://www.fas.org/irp/agency/doj/fbi/is/ncic.htm) has to have data entered only by qualified dental personnel in the postmortem section or law enforcement agencies in the missing person section.

Non-Governmental Organizations (NGOs) such as the National Center for Missing Adults (NCMA; http://www.theyaremissed.org), the National Center for Missing and Exploited Children (NCMEC; http://www.missingkids.com), and the DOE Network (http://www.doenetwork.org) with its sister organization the North American Missing Persons Network (NAMPN; http://www.nampn.org) have separate websites not under federal control but who work in the same fields and harvest the same information. The NGOs have an excellent record of identification enhanced by such television programs as *America's Most Wanted*, which has an audience in the millions. In addition to all the preceding is Project EDAN (Everyone Deserves A Name; http://www.projectedan.us), which is a volunteer group of forensic artists who do facial approximations and age-progression drawing as an assist to all these agencies.

Recent mass disasters of man and nature such as the World Trade Center and Hurricane Katrina have emphasized the need for coordinated resources and new technologies to assist with human identification. Federal agencies such as Disaster Mortuary Operational Response Teams (DMORT; http://www.dmort.org) have been formed and activated for this purpose. Some states have also formed disaster response teams, including Florida, with its Florida Emergency Mortuary Operational Response System (FEMORS) in place (http://www.femors.org). Development of a dental disaster response team may be found in the ASFO website (http://www.newasfo.com) and in the ABFO Manual (http://www.abfo.org).

In 1867 Oscar Amoedo, an Italian dentist, helped to identify hundreds of victims of the Great Fire of Paris. Techniques and protocols developed then are still in use today. Karl Landsteiner introduced blood typing in 1901, the same year that Sir Richard Henry adopted fingerprint identification in Scotland Yard. The fields of forensic medicine and dentistry expanded in 1984 when Sir Alec Jeffreys developed the first DNA test that is now employed to convict as well as to exonerate suspects and defendants. Using DNA, the Innocence Project (www.innocenceproject.org) has exonerated over 225 persons who had been convicted, jailed for years, or sentenced to death for crimes they did not commit. Some of these convictions were based entirely on dental evidence, such as bitemarks. Some of this evidence was poorly prepared or presented. There were always great discrepancies between prosecution and defense "expert" witnesses when the people of the jury had to make the decision of guilt or innocence. In cases of murder, this could lead to the death of those who were convicted. Even worse, this could lead to a sentence of death for a person who was innocent and the actual guilty party escaping justice.

Forensic science is essential for the existence of forensic odontology and forensic odontology is dependent upon the execution of a proper dental autopsy that is scientifically valid. The comparison of an unknown substance or set of characters against a known exemplar must be repeatable separately by a person of similar qualifications to be scientifically valid. In the case of living persons or unidentified human remains, their records would be compared to missing persons. These methods may incorporate several scientific methods including a comparison of fingerprints, DNA, and medical, anthropological, and dental characteristics.

Forensic science includes a broad spectrum of disciplines, all of which are devoted to answering questions posed by the legal system. The word *forensic* means "debate." It comes from the Latin meaning "before the forum," which places the protagonist and antagonist in an adversarial relationship for the people to decide the issues, similar to the situation in our present-day courtrooms. During Roman times, it was the open forum and today it is the defense and the prosecution or plaintiff arguing before the jury or judge, and the court decides the victor. In this forum, it may well be the forensic odontologist who is the witness of facts who provides the sword that slays the dragon or vanquishes the lion. It is important that the one who wields the sword is not the one who falls upon it. The expert witness is the provider of truth for the court and not the defender of justice for either the defense or the prosecution. It is the forensic odontologist who stands before the court to provide opinions and evidence in their simplest and purest form.

During the seventh century an Arab merchant would require a debtor's fingerprint be given to the lender to provide proof of the debt. The Chinese book *Collected Cases of Injustice Rectified*, written in 1248, was an earlier version of our present-day Innocence Project. A case of a person murdered by a sickle was solved when the people were asked to bring their sickles to one location. Flies, attracted by blood, gathered on just one sickle, which produced enough evidence to convict the murderer.

In 1784, in England, John Toms was tried and convicted for the murder of Edward Culshaw by a pistol. A pistol wad (which is crushed paper used to secure the powder and ball in the muzzle of a gun) was found in the victim's head. This pistol wad matched perfectly the torn newspaper found in John Toms' pocket.

Sherlock Holmes, Charlie Chan, and in later fiction, Dick Tracy, became the forensic forecasters of present day CSI, where every scientific solution extends beyond the bounds of present imagination only to be ensconced in the manual of a future forensic scientist.

In modern times, forensic science includes archaeology, anthropology, accounting, entomology, engineering, geology, meteorology, odontology, pathology, toxicology, questioned documents, and others. In every scientific field, whether it be bugs, bones, or bridges, there will appear an element of legal dispute that will require a forensic examination and the presentation of a witness of fact to assist the court in providing a settlement of grievances.

Figure 2 Paul Revere (John Singleton Copley, 1768). (Courtesy of the Museum of Fine Arts, Boston. Used with permission.)

History of Forensic Odontology in America

Forensic Odontology

Born in Boston in the winter of 1734, Paul Revere (Figure 2) became best known for a famous horse ride when he rode from Boston to Lexington, Massachusetts to warn the local residents of the invasion of the British troops. Of lesser interest to the general population was the fact that Paul Revere was an accomplished silversmith and a copperplate engraver of books, cards, cartoons, and bills of fare for taverns. As a silversmith, he created table settings, cups, vases, and the famous "Paul Revere Bowl."

When times got really difficult he would hang out his shingle as a dentist, clean teeth, and wire into place false teeth made from animal teeth or ivory. When Paul Revere was just 19 years old, his father died and he became the family support. In 1756, at the age of 22 he married Sarah Orne and they had eight children. His needs were very great and when Sarah died in childbirth he remarried and sired eight more children.

After the Revolutionary War he performed probably the first dental autopsy. General Warren was a prominent Boston surgeon and was conscripted into the army to tend to the troops. During the Battle of Bunker Hill he was shot and killed by the British forces and buried without his uniform or other identification as the victor was prone to do to disgrace the enemy. After the war was over, the Colonial forces sought out the grave of General Warren in order to restore his dignity and give him a proper burial. The exhumed body was identified by "Doctor" Paul Revere, the dentist, by a walrus tooth that he had wired into place to replace a missing tooth of General Warren. It was this dental skill and the comparison that made him the first forensic odontologist in North America.

On occasion, as in the case of Parkman and Webster, even if the head is missing, the dental evidence can be sufficient. Dr. Parkman and Dr. Webster were both faculty members at Harvard Medical School. Dr. Parkman made the mistake of lending Dr. Webster money, even though Dr. Webster had no means of returning it. Around Thanksgiving Day 1849 Dr. Parkman visited Dr. Webster and demanded his money. Dr. Webster became enraged and struck Dr. Parkman on the head, killing him. In a frenzy, Dr. Webster dismembered the body and burned what he could, placing the rest in a vault in his laboratory. Soon after, the janitor went exploring. He realized that the fireplace was still red hot and no one was at home. He then became suspicious and discovered human remains in the vault. Then the trial began. The head of Dr. Parkman was never found but Dr. Webster carelessly neglected to dispose of the false teeth. The most important witness at the trial was Dr. Nathan Keep, the dentist who made Dr. Parkman's false teeth. Dr. Parkman's lower jaw jutted out and Dr. Keep was able to testify that these were the dentures that he had made for Dr. Parkman. It took the jury just three hours to convict and Dr. Webster was hanged on August 30, 1850. This was the first recorded trial in the United States where dental evidence was used in the prosecution of a homicide.

There are several reasons why the dentition is especially valuable for human identification. Tooth enamel is the hardest substance in the human body and it is well protected by surrounding soft tissue. It is capable of surviving conditions that are totally destructive to other tissues in the body. Teeth can withstand temperatures in excess of 1000°F. Dental restorations are equally resistant to the same traumatic incidents. Porcelain restorations may even withstand the high temperatures (2500°F) of cremation. In the event of fire, the teeth are naturally protected by the soft tissues of the cheeks and tongue. Due to this confluence of tissues, it is usually the posterior teeth that survive the high temperatures when the anterior teeth may be carbonized. In addition, all restorations are individually created for each person in a manner that is unique to the person and yet they are consistent with standards established by the profession. Furthermore, the number, size, and shape of the teeth are finite in their anatomical configuration (see Chapter 8, Antemortem Records) making any variety of the consistent anatomical configuration a unique observation that would be available for comparison. The likelihood of making an identification is really dependent upon the preservation of the dental structures and the availability of antemortem dental records or photographs. This procedure, when compared to DNA and other techniques used in identification, is faster and far more cost effective.

The foundation of dental identification and bitemark analysis is that the total arrangement of a person's dentition creates a dental profile consisting of a certain number of units having a consistent morphology. Statistically, there are 32 teeth with five surfaces on each tooth that may be in any of 25 different combinations and restored with any of four coded types of restorative materials. Add to that the fact that each tooth may be present or missing. This is sufficient for sorting and comparing any number of dental records manually or by computer. If there is to be some order out of all the chaos, then numerical codes must be assigned to each tooth to enhance the matching systems. Because it is the responsibility of the ME/C office to enter the information for the unidentified and the parallel responsibility of the law enforcement agency to enter the information for the missing persons, then it is absolutely essential that people be properly trained to accomplish these tasks.

Acknowledgments

This has been a remarkable journey through the forensic fog where few have sought to go. We have had a lot of company assisting us with this book along the way and we want to thank all those whose help we greatly appreciate including Dr. Joe Davis, Miami Dade County chief medical examiner, emeritus, for his guidance and contribution; Lenny Wolf, director of the Forensic Imaging Bureau; and all the photographic staff. Special thanks go to Heidi Nichols, photographer, and our guide though the maze of presentations. We especially thank Dr. Bruce Hyma, chief medical examiner, for his continuing support. Among our dedicated workers who assisted us in our work at the Miami Dade Medical Examiner Department were Dr. Emma Lew, deputy chief medical examiner; Larry Cameron, director of operations; Len Sumlar, Morgue Bureau supervisor; Mandy Jackson, senior forensic technician; and in investigations, Sandy Boyd, medical examiner case facilitator.

We are grateful to Dr. Robert George, professor of anatomy at Florida International University, School of Medicine, for his advice and contribution of many drawings, and to Dr. Isaac Haber, Miami orthodontist, who contributed many photographs of the dentition.

When the idea first blossomed to do this book, it was Becky Masterman of Taylor & Francis who took our hands and shepherded us in the front door. But the nuts and bolts were left to Pat Roberson and Ari Silver who guided us through the maze of publication requirements.

About the Authors

Dr. William Silver practiced orthodontics in Boston after service in the U.S. Air Force in Japan. He received diplomate status in the American Board of Orthodontics in 1962 when he moved his family to Miami. Dr. Silver served as chief of the dental department at Miami Childrens' Hospital and held office in many organizations. After completing the Armed Forces Institute of Pathology course, he became interested in forensic dentistry and volunteered at the Miami Dade Medical Examiner Department. In 1995 he founded the Miami Dental Identification Response Team (DIRT) and in 1996 he co-directed with Dr. Souviron the dental identifications after the Valujet crash in Miami. In 2001 Dr. Silver joined the Disaster Mortuary Operational Response Team (DMORT). He participated in the dental identifications during the World Trade Center disaster in New York and a few years later he worked with DMORT on dental identifications following Hurricane Katrina. He is a member of the American Society of Forensic Odontology, a Fellow of the American Academy of Forensic Science, and in 2007 Dr. Silver achieved diplomate status in the American Board of Forensic Odontology. Working as deputy chief alongside Dr. Souviron at the Miami Dade Medical Examiner Department has become one of the great rewards of his life in retirement.

Dr. Richard Souviron received his DDS degree from Emory University School of Dentistry in 1960. He has been in the active practice of general dentistry in Coral Gables, Florida since 1960. Dr. Souviron serves as the chief forensic odontologist for the Miami Dade Medical Examiner Office, a position that he has held since 1967.

Dr. Souviron is one of the ten original founding forensic odontologists for the Odontology section of the American Academy of Forensic Sciences. He has served as chairman of the examining and credentialing committee for the American Board of Forensic Odontology and was president of the American Board of Forensic Odontology. He has also served as president of the Miami Dental Society, Coral Gables Dental Society, and the Miami Dade Dental Research Clinic.

In addition to his forensic duties and general dentistry practice, Dr. Souviron volunteers as the dentist for the animals at the Miami Dade Metro Zoo, Jungle Island, and the Miami Monkey Jungle. He has performed numerous dental procedures on lions, tigers, gorillas, and elephants.

Introduction to Forensic Odontology

1

JOSEPH H. DAVIS, M.D.
Chief Medical Examiner, Emeritus, Miami Dade Medical Examiner Department

The Dade County Medical Examiner Office opened at noon, March 15, 1956, in an unused garage across the street from the county's Jackson Memorial Hospital. The county population was about 750,000. Today the Medical Examiner Department of Miami Dade County is a modern three-building complex of 89,000 square feet located in the northeast corner of the medical center complex of the University of Miami and Jackson Memorial Hospital. It serves a population of 2.3 million not counting those who were not detected by the census.

Included within is the largest human toxicology laboratory in the State of Florida, 17,000 square feet with modern analytical equipment and headed by a Ph.D. pharmacologist. Also included is the Sterile Autopsy Suite of the Bone and Tissue Bank of the University of Miami, a large forensic imaging bureau, and a high-speed photographic range with motion picture capability of 30,000 frames per second. A separate building contains an autopsy suite for decomposed and infectious cases plus a physical anthropology suite. Three conference rooms include a large auditorium which doubles as a communication center in the event of any disasters. Dental imaging x-ray equipment is available in a separate dental room in the main autopsy suite and also in the decomposed autopsy building suite.

Within the first year of opening, dental identification confirmation of a burned body was utilized using a local military dentist in telephone communication with the chief of dental services of the U.S. Navy who compared the postmortem findings with records from the military records depository in St. Louis. The victim had a wallet with presumptive identification but good forensic practice requires confirmation by dental record comparison. Subsequent cases of skeletal material with presumptive identification, based upon circumstantial evidence were identified using local dental records. One victim had gold crowns where the treating dentist pointed out that the wear was minimal, meaning that death had occurred shortly after completion of the dental work. In another case, the skeleton of a young adult male was tentatively identified by the presence of a prosthesis in one eye. At age 11 years, several large dental amalgams had been prepared by a local dentist who made meticulous drawings of the patterns of the amalgams enough for this author to match the teeth to the records.

In February, 1963, a Northwest Airlines Boeing 720B disintegrated in rough weather killing all 43 occupants. Of interest was the pattern of distribution of the first-class passengers who fell several thousand feet striking the ground and bouncing, unless striking rock or trees. Included in the free-fallers were two occupants of Y-class seats marking the breaking away of the tail assembly while in the turbulent air. A local dentist volunteered to assist and helped to match records with those of burned bodies from the Y-class section which stayed intact and burned. Due to the rough weather the nose section with flight crew, the Y-class section, and the tail assembly plus the wings, had fallen fairly close together. Small debris and papers were scattered over an area one half mile wide and ten miles long. All parts were recovered and assembled in a hanger. Processing of bodies and identifications were completed by the small medical examiner staff within 40 hours. Interestingly, however, there were several living survivors of the free-fall. A passenger had goldfish in a plastic bag filled with water. The force of the fall ruptured the bag but the fish were found alive: the reason being that the water equally distributed the forces.

By now I was aware that Dr. Lester Luntz in Connecticut was affiliated with the police and rendering forensic dental services. I acquired and assiduously studied an excellent book by Gosta Gustafson, *Forensic Odontology*, published in 1966.

In 1967 a skeleton was found on one of the islands of the Florida Keys, in Monroe County to the south of Dade County. I was requested to examine and identify the body. We located the treating dentist, Dr. Richard Souviron, of Coral Gables, who came to the medical examiner building which was a 6000 square foot structure built for us in 1957. He matched the teeth with his patient records. He was enthusiastic and wanted to learn and experience more. I encouraged him and began to call him frequently to chart teeth of decomposed, burned, and skeletonized bodies of which we had an ample supply. He enthusiastically volunteered for several years. I arranged for him to receive a retainer which assured no limits, as would be experienced with a fee-for-service arrangement. This relationship continues to this day. When the Forensic Sciences Foundation created the concept of board certification in forensic odontology, the first examination was given in my office using specimens from my large collection. The American Academy of Forensic Sciences created a section on forensic odontology in which Dr. Souviron is still active. He was a founder of the American Board of Forensic Odontology. I chose to attend many of their section's gatherings at the annual AAFS meetings and have gained many friends in the group. Over the years Dr. Souviron has had associates work with him in our office. Dr. William Silver is currently the most active associate. He is the second board (ABFO) certified forensic odontologist in our office and serves as deputy chief in forensic odontology.

Over time, bitemark identifications entered the picture and have undergone an evolution. With the discovery of DNA application to saliva from bitemarks and semen in sexual assault cases, reliance solely upon bitemark patterns underwent a change. Cases have occurred in the United States where DNA has exonerated the presumed guilty based upon pattern injuries, and the real perpetrators have been identified. This exemplifies a principle in evidence interpretation. Some evidence trumps other evidence.

Dr. Souviron achieved considerable prominence in police circles in Florida and elsewhere. Many of his consultation cases were shared with me. I recall one in which a dentist had matched a bitemark to a suspect and Dr. Souviron was sent the materials for verification. I pointed out that it appeared that the bite had been inflicted through clothing, which was the situation apparent to both Dr. Souviron and myself but not to the initial odontologist on the case. He had not availed himself of police and scene photographs which clearly demonstrated bitemarks through clothing. Opinions based upon failure to take advantage of circumstantial evidence are prone to error.

In another case, Dr. Souviron was asked to go to Monroe County, the Florida Keys, because of what appeared to the local dentist to be possible bite patterns on a victim. He asked me to go along. The patterns were bites, but not human. Ants had created the patterns. I found a dead ant between the toes of the victim (Figure 1.1). Scalpel incisions into the bitemarks revealed no underlying reaction (see Chapter 13). This provided additional proof of lack of compressive forces, as would be expected from human bitemarks.

From 1980 to 1989, an unrecognized serial killer was suspected of leaving a total of 32 dead females. Some bodies were clearly homicides, some were still being investigated,

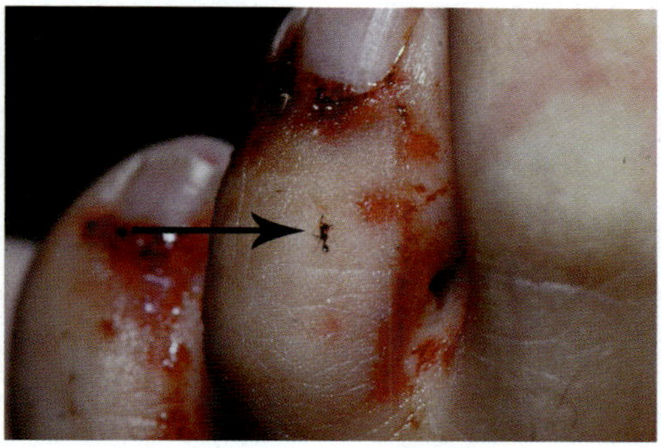

Figure 1.1 Ant on toe. (Courtesy of the Miami Dade Medical Examiners office. Used with permission.)

and a few had been called cocaine-induced deaths by staff. I became aware that something was amiss. I gathered all the case files from 1980 to 1989 into my conference room. From the first days of camera usage, we always used color transparency film because that had much greater resolution than print film. All the cases had excellent photographs with closeup views of upper and lower eyelids and upper and lower lips. Not seen, or overlooked by the staff pathologists, were minutiae documented by the camera.

For example, a 16-year-old victim was removed from an apartment and placed upon the stairs. A magnifying lens disclosed a cloth imprint upon the nose indicating pressure application. Another, with only a gross autopsy description of hemorrhage on the inner lower lip had a camera rendition of a pattern of small hemorrhages in the form of two straight lines with a connection at one end (Figure 1.2). This clearly indicated pressure of the lip against the teeth. When force is applied to skin, such as from a baseball bat, the linear pattern of hemorrhage occurs at the margin between the depressed tissue and the adjacent non-compressed tissue (Figure 1.3a,b). At the point where the depressed tissue abuts the surrounding non-depressed tissue shear stress occurs leading to the linear pattern of hemorrhage seen in such an event. The same occurred when the lower lip was pressed against a tooth or teeth. Where the tissue was displaced by the tooth the point of shear between depressed and non-displaced tissue caused the linear tooth outline.

By carefully analyzing with magnification the close-up photographs taken with color transparency film, patterns were discovered that the human eye failed to discern during

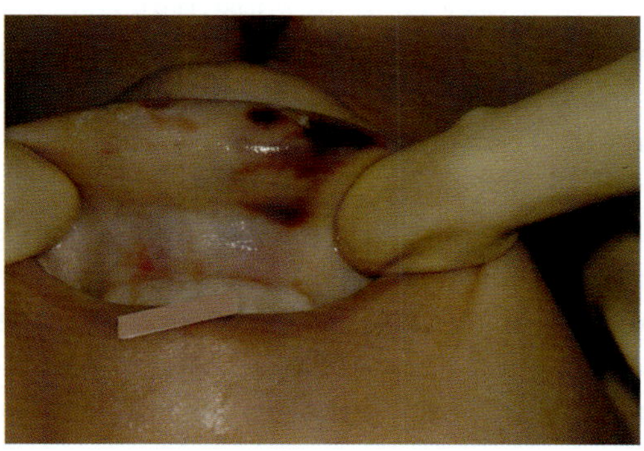

Figure 1.2 Inside lip trauma – suffocation. (Courtesy of the Miami Dade Medical Examiners office. Used with permission.)

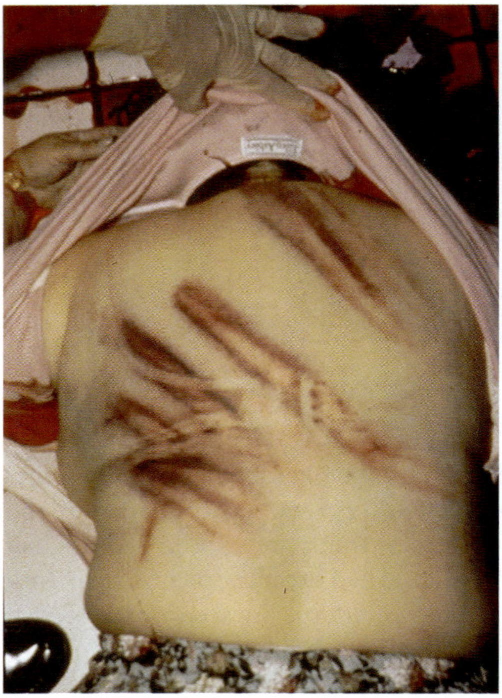

Figure 1.3a Pattern injury. (Courtesy of the Miami Dade Medical Examiners office. Used with permission.)

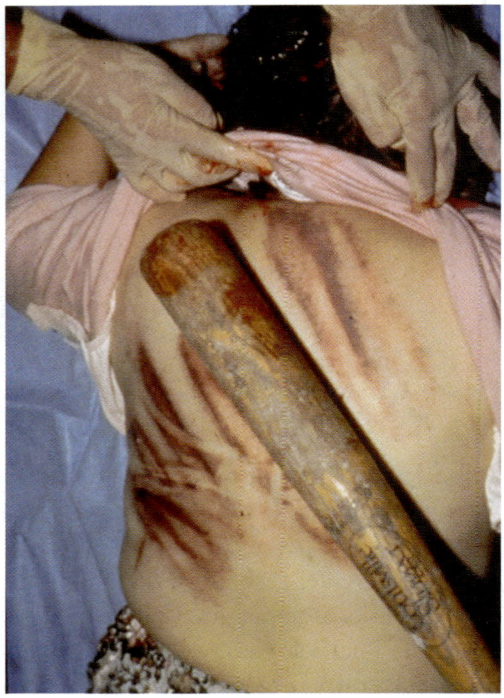

Figure 1.3b Pattern injury – baseball bat. (Courtesy of the Miami Dade Medical Examiners office. Used with permission.)

autopsy examination. Dr. Souviron concurred and identified the involved tooth. The cocaine within the bodies had nothing to do with the deaths, as they were all crack addicts and expected to contain cocaine. I met with representatives of the two major police departments involved with investigations and we set the record straight. All these cases were linked to one suspect who died of AIDS before trial.

I created a policy, agreed to by Dr. Souviron, to call him for any case involving disease or injury involving the mouth with or without tooth involvement. Medical examiners would not invite their consultant odontologists to examine a clearly evident gunshot wound of the mouth. Often, fee schedules or lack of enthusiasm would interfere. All these patterns are interesting, although not usually considered a matter for requesting a consultant forensic odontologist. Most important are those patterns, not of dental origin, which might be confused as a bitemark by someone lacking experience or with a defective thought process. By sharing all mouth injuries or injury patterns with the dental consultant, both the medical examiner and the consultant forensic odontologist become better at recognition of patterns of importance.

Today many medical examiner offices have a forensic odontologist available but, few have the volume or the fiscal arrangements and collaboration as exists in Miami Dade County.

As a result of Dr. Souviron's enthusiasm and my interests in forensic odontology, he has seen more than 2000 cases in our office since 1967. Our present medical examiner facility which we occupied in April, 1988, has ample space. One office was reserved for Dr. Souviron's use and records, now a vast resource for study and research. Our forensic imaging bureau has been available to him for preparation of Power Point presentations and preparation of illustrations for forensic odontology publications.

Animal bite patterns have been common over the years. Most involve deceased persons but some involve live persons killed by animals or living persons injured by animals, which vary from insects to land animals to marine animals.

Dogs make up an interesting pattern group. Some dog patterns involve attacks upon the living, some involve eating the flesh of deceased persons, and some involve eating of live persons. Many involve gnawing of skeletal remains and scattering of skeletons. The result is a wide variety of patterns both from teeth and from claws.

My first experience with dog nibbling and licking of blood involved a young adult man who was performing yardwork with a machete. He was found dead in the yard, the machete alongside. I was called to the scene because of a several-inch-long scalp defect, with sharp margins, which to some suggested the effect of a tangential slice by the machete. When I looked closely I saw no blood. It was clean. Even if it had been inflicted postmortem there should have been oozing and leakage of blood. I had never seen such a pattern. Later, while in the living room of the house, the pet dachshund began to retch and vomited scraps of scalp upon the rug. The history from the family indicated rheumatic heart disease in the victim. He had developed a fatal rhythm such as ventricular fibrillation, collapsed, and struck his scalp upon a small stone which I had observed. The scalp defect oozed blood attractive to the dog who licked the blood and started to nibble the scalp thus creating the sharp margins. Autopsy confirmed the heart disease.

A tragic case of false accusation of maiming of a child involved an 11-year-old girl, paraplegic from the nipple line down, mute, and mentally retarded. Her mother had cared for her since birth. Two German Shepherd dogs belonging to a male friend shared the premises, a small house near an overpass.

The weather turned cold. The only warmth was a space heater placed in the parlor. Rather than place the child into her hospital-type crib in the unheated bedroom, the mother spread a blanket on the floor near the space heater. The child was clad in a nightgown and a diaper and covered with a blanket.

During the night the mother checked on the child every hour, as was her custom. While she was asleep one of the dogs jumped on the bed and awakened her. She found the girl naked, her diaper gone, the blanket off, and the nightgown torn and punctured. The girl had long parallel scratches on her trunk. The lower abdomen extending into the pubic hair had a roughly circular defect about five inches across. The skin and subcutaneous tissue were absent down to the underlying muscle (Figure 1.4). The margins appeared sharp in some edges and small irregular defects marked the other margins. Remarkable was the

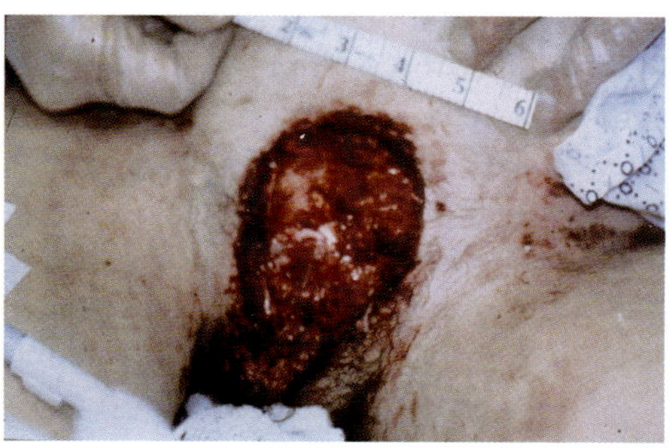

Figure 1.4 Dog bite. (Courtesy of the Miami Dade Medical Examiners office. Used with permission.)

total absence of any blood. The extensor surface of the right forearm had superficial bruising separated by lines of no bruising. Other than the scratches, the defect, and the bruises, no other injuries were apparent.

The mute and retarded girl could not relate what happened. Due to her paraplegia, the defect in the lower abdomen was in an area that lacked pain sensation.

The mother telephoned her friend, who lived nearby, and he arrived within a few minutes. The police and an ambulance were called. A deputy arrived and the ambulance transported the girl to the local hospital. Here the injuries were noted and the child was transferred to the county seat where a larger hospital existed.

The local Child Protection Team (CPT) was called and a CPT nurse immediately wrote in the record that the scratches were whip marks. She also wrote that *she did not know what made the defect but it was not dog* (emphasis supplied). The next day a CPT physician expert was summoned from a major medical center across the state who wrote that the scratch marks might be dog induced but *the defect was not from a dog although he did not know what caused it* (emphasis supplied). He noted bruises on the extensor surface of the right forearm and opined that these were self-inflicted. On the third day a local medical examiner examined her and opined in the record that the now-drying scratches were two-week-old whip marks. The defect *was cut with a curved knife like a grapefruit knife* (emphasis supplied). By now the scratch marks were dry and darkened. However, the defect had been covered and the base was still pink and moist.

The two CPT statements that the defect was not caused by dog, but the cause was unknown, lacks logic. The pathologist statement lacks understanding of the changes that scratches undergo and how a defect that is covered will remain moist. In addition, the timeframe entered for the scratches overlapped with a visit to the treating pediatrician who did not observe any injuries. The three who opined inflicted injury failed to view scene photographs and the physical evidence. The bruises on the forearm could easily correspond to the child flailing her upper extremity about during the dog attack. Chairs lined up along the small room had legs that could have been struck by the flailing forearm.

No follow-up on the possibility of a dog was done. As soon as the nurse CPT expert opined abuse, the local police were replaced by the investigator for the local assistant state attorney, who set into motion the accusatory phase with no preliminary investigative phase. The prosecutor was running for the office of state attorney and made this case his campaign issue. The prosecutor's office submitted the nightgown to the State Crime Laboratory, along with kitchen knives and scissors, with inquiry if any defects could be from the instruments. Dog was not mentioned. A single photograph of a dog paw had been taken before the state attorney's office took charge.

Subsequently, the mother was charged with aggravated child abuse. Her child was placed in foster care, protective custody. A public defender contacted the Dade County Medical Examiner for a second opinion. I advised that all the injuries were from a dog. There was no protocol followed for examination of the two family dogs (see Chapter 13). Then the deputy chief medical examiner, the chief forensic odontologist, and a forensic veterinarian reviewed the evidence and all concluded that the injuries were from a dog(s) and not from the mother. As a result, the case was dropped by the state attorney and the child was returned to the mother.

This case is an excellent example of lack of consideration of circumstances and thorough scene investigation on the part of the consultants, as well as a lack of logic. It likewise

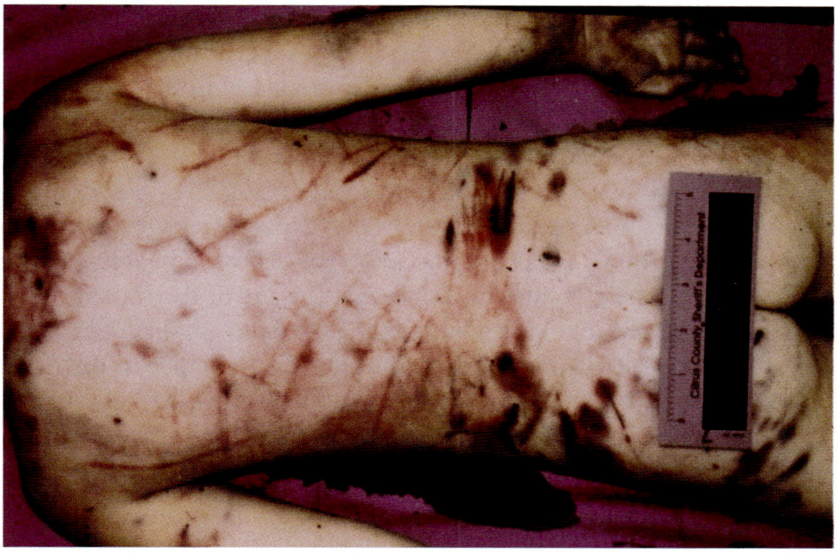

Figure 1.5 Pattern injury – dog. (Courtesy of the Miami Dade Medical Examiners office. Used with permission.)

contains the element of political ambitions which led to the accusatory phase before any adequate investigation could be completed.

Contrast this case with a dog attack in another county where the pit bull dogs' owner at the waterfront scene stated that an alligator had killed the child left alone with the dogs. The deputies at the scene called the animal control officer of their department, who took the dogs to a veterinarian that induced vomiting to examine the stomach content. A Fish and Wildlife officer was called to the scene who determined that the bite patterns were not alligator induced. After all evidence of injury had been documented, they sent the photographs and circumstances to Dr. Souviron, who shared them with me. We both opined that the bites and scratches were not alligator, but were dog induced (Figure 1.5). No false charges were made due to the proper investigation.

Anyone who has observed dogs gnawing at something knows that dogs will hold the object with paws, whose claws leave scratch marks. Dogs that attack create patterns that differ from those of gnawing or eating.

Lessons learned when I started in Miami were to visit the scenes, natural, accident, suicide, and homicide. I observed what experienced homicide detectives did. Dr. Durlacher, who brought me with him from the LSU School of Medicine, where we each had a faculty position, was 13 years my senior. I depended upon him to help me with complex cases. Unfortunately, he died after one year in office. I was on my own thereafter. I quickly learned to analyze the circumstances and learn from these. Questions from defense attorneys were superb learning exercises. I also learned that forensic pathology findings of textbooks were only a small part of the variations of different types of cases. Also, book authors tend to copy from earlier texts without criticism. Accordingly, I became adept at associating circumstances with autopsy findings. That is a lesson I taught to residents in training. Look at the circumstances and ask what autopsy findings would be expected. Then look at the autopsy findings. The chances of error are minimized by this approach.

I have published a chapter concerning the histopathologic changes in human bitemarks (*Bitemark Evidence* Dorian, 1987). One of my chapters concerns the histopathology changes of human bitemarks. I was surprised to discover that no one in the world had previously published details of human bite histology. What I noted were two patterns, a compressive force with crushing of tissue and driving of blood from the compressed tissue, plus a pattern of very early intracellular edema of basal cells of epidermis. My material was derived from bitemarks inflicted during the fatal attack.

Another chapter dealt with the estimate of aging of bitemarks based upon gross and microscopic appearances. It was quite clear from the disparate reports of color change that the variables were too great to make assumptions. For example, people do not see colors the same way. Cultural variants exist. In Botswana, the site of the Kalahari Desert, there exists the same word for blue and green but about a dozen for shades of brown. Cattle are the medium of wealth. Back in 1957 Robertson published a paper in the South African *Journal of Forensic Medicine*. An histological illustration of a five-day-old skin bruise lacks any neutrophilic reaction. What he pointed out is that neutrophilic reaction depends not on erythrocytes but upon tissue crush with escape of intracellular content. This point has been overlooked in most texts.

In another animal case a strangulation victim had been discarded in a vacant lot near the waterfront. When found four weeks later it was a skeleton. Finger bones were scattered and some missing. Forearm bones were scattered and some tiny marks at the end of some were too small and superficial to be dog and did not resemble the marks of rodents. Land crabs lived toward the rear of the vacant lot. I considered the most logical choice for the marks was land crab claw effects. It appeared that the land crabs had feasted upon the decomposing body.

The family told me that she wore rather distinctive rings, none of which were present at the scene. I reasoned that if the rings were truly gone, the suspect may have pawned them and could be traced to him. To search all pawn shops would be a waste of police resources. I contacted the lead homicide detective and we returned to the scene. I reasoned that if a swarm of land crabs were feasting upon the body and a finger was pulled off by a crab, the crab would depart to the first convenient hiding place to finish eating decayed flesh. A nearby stump of an overturned tree seemed a likely place. I crawled under, brushed aside the leaves, and found a finger bone with the ring. Using the same logic we recovered all the rings.

Another animal case involved a child who fell into a pit housing a large crocodile. The animal seized the child and pulled him underwater. The marks on the body were quite distinctive of large reptile bites and fit the teeth of the crocodile when examined by Dr. Souviron (Figure 1.6). Most commonly, we encounter postmortem disruption of flesh by alligators when bodies are discarded along the waterways of south Miami Dade County.

At the Miami Dade Metro Zoo a Bengal tiger killed an attendant. A tiger's tooth broke off and remained embedded in the face of the victim. Dr. Souviron was able to identify the tooth and later performed a root canal therapy upon the tiger. Our experience with animal marks is extensive. Both Dr. Souviron and I have published separate book chapters on the subject.

Not all cases have been initially solved in a correct manner. A Middle Eastern student was working under his car in a closed garage when a fire ensued and supposedly killed him. Earlier he had borrowed a tool from a neighbor telling him what he was doing. Police and fire personnel visited the scene. They reasoned that a bumper jack had slipped, permitting the vehicle to drop and a supporting jackstand punctured a hole in the gasoline tank. A drop-light in use ignited the fuel.

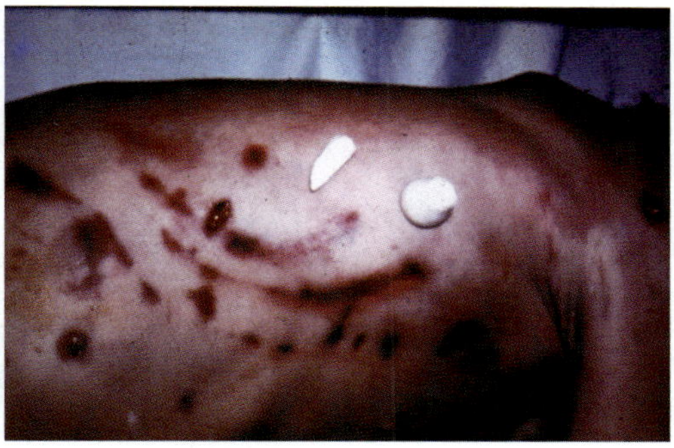

Figure 1.6 Crocodile bite with tooth. (Courtesy of the Miami Dade Medical Examiners office. Used with permission.)

At this time the police chose not to call the medical examiner to the scene, as the fire arson inspectors had already determined how the "accident" occurred. Dr. Souviron charted the teeth in the usual fashion. Autopsy disclosed a high blood carbon monoxide level but no soot particles in the airway. Based upon prior case publications that flash gasoline fires need not produce much smoke, but can elevate carbon monoxide levels, the case was certified as accident. Everyone was satisfied. However, I had a policy that when a decomposed or burned body was released, the upper and lower jaws were retained in case special dental examinations were needed. Most such bodies are cremated by next of kin, as was the case of the student.

Subsequently, it developed that he had several recently purchased large insurance policies and the sister was the beneficiary. He was a student and did not have any real insurable interests nor could he afford the policies. One company had already paid a half million dollars but the other companies were more cautious. They hired an insurance fraud investigator from New York to investigate. I had worked with him in the past and shared his caution. We asked the homicide detective to find dental records, of which there were none. We requested photographs showing teeth. Finally the detective sent us the victim's Florida state driver's license in which he was smiling. Dr. Souviron compared the license photograph with the retained jaws and noted lack of concordance. They did not match (Figure 1.7a–c). It turned out that the real person had never died and was back in the Middle East having built a large home with the proceeds from one policy. We never determined who the victim was. My opinion is that they found someone of similar age and build, killed the person with automobile exhaust, and created the false scenario.

The lesson to be learned is to save jaws when the body is burned or decomposed and no comparison records are immediately available. Subsequently photographs may be obtained. Another lesson is to beware of a person who dies under questionable circumstances and may have large insurance proceeds. Some years ago we hosted a seminar "Insurance Fraud and Murder" at which cases were presented of people who were never born, never died, yet had documents to support an accidental death for insurance purposes. The term "Nigerian Packet" has been applied to such cases.

However, insurance fraud and murder may occur anywhere. I recall reviewing summary sheets based upon accidents. When I would see one where the history seemed incomplete, I would paperclip that page and have the Records Bureau pull the case folder for me to review. One of those I marked seemed more murder than accident as I reviewed the file. The police had investigated and closed it as an accident. It was murder.

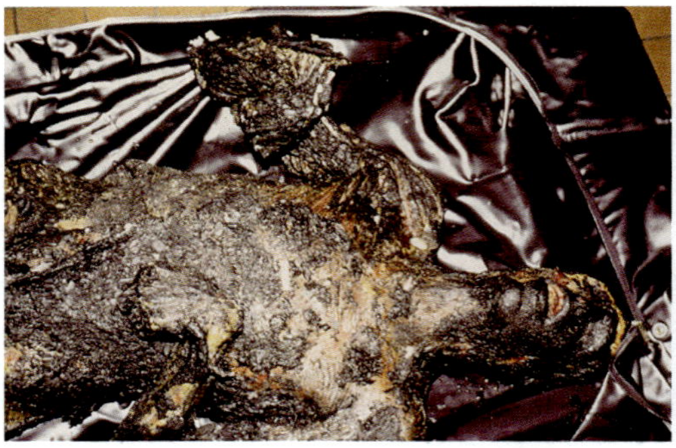

Figure 1.7a Burn victim. (Courtesy of the Miami Dade Medical Examiners office. Used with permission.)

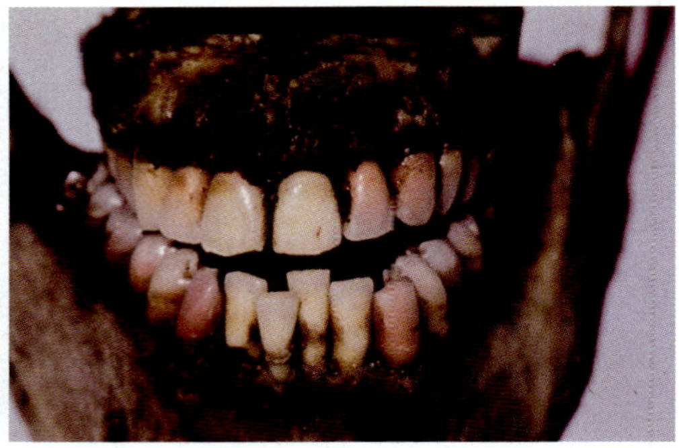

Figure 1.7b Burn victim – jaws. (Courtesy of the Miami Dade Medical Examiners office. Used with permission.)

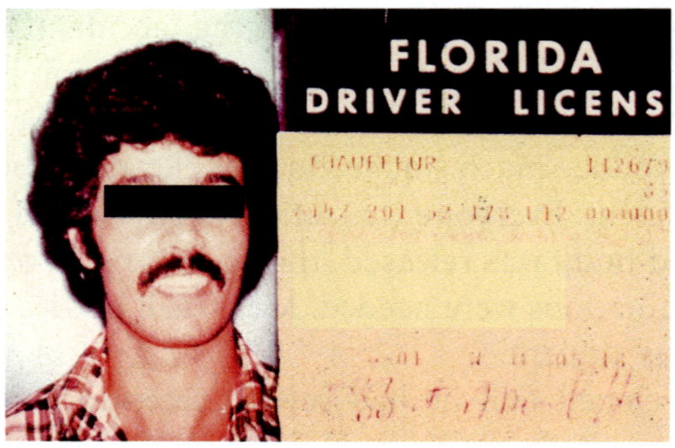

Figure 1.7c Burn victim – false ID. (Courtesy of the Miami Dade Medical Examiners office. Used with permission.)

Today the cases are subject to more critical staff review on a daily basis based upon lessons learned. Never be satisfied that the system in vogue will remain the same. It never is completely satisfactory and may always be improved.

Summary

- The early primitive facilities and methodology created a learning experience of the value of circumstances in determination of cause and manner of death.
- Initially dental identification was carried out by me with or without volunteer help from local dentists.
- Dr. Souviron's enthusiastic affiliation with the office in 1967 created a mutual learning experience for both of us.
- As he became more proficient, the Forensic Sciences Foundation created board certification programs in forensic specialties including forensic odontology.
- The first examination for forensic odontology board certification was in our office using our vast collection of specimens.
- With time, bitemarks became useful to exonerate suspects and identify perpetrators.
- With DNA saliva matching, bitemark identification has improved. There is an order of rank in evidence.

- DNA outranks patterns if the DNA is properly obtained and analyzed.
- My chapter on bitemark aging in *Bitemark Evidence* was the first-ever publication detailing the unique histological appearance of bitemarks.
- Aging of bitemarks is fraught with lack of specificity.
- The forensic dental consultant is always useful but the ultimate determination of cause and manner rests with the medical examiner who bears ultimate responsibility for every case.
- We have learned much from the more than 127,000 cases brought in for certification and the more than 81,000 autopsies performed during my 40-year tenure. We continue to learn.

Medical Autopsy

2

In biblical times any person outside of the priesthood who touched a corpse was considered "unclean" and it was necessary to take a ceremonial bath in order to cleanse himself or herself, and return to normal society. No matter the religious belief, the customs and laws regarding death are among the most stringently spelled out in whatever the religious text may be. There are as many strongly held religious beliefs about death as there are religious groups. The ceremonial passage of death is lined with graveyards, cemeteries, coffins of all designs, mausoleums, funeral pyres, crematoriums, and, more recently, cryogenic vats and undersea chambers. Tending to the needs of the deceased whether to establish identity or to determine the cause and manner of death is an authentic act of kindness which may be defined as a "good deed" to speak for those who cannot speak for themselves. Unlike in life when the recipient may acknowledge the kindness of the deed, that reciprocity is no longer available.

Autopsies performed by the forensic pathologists in the medical profession, of necessity, include the head and its masticatory apparatus with the maxilla and mandible. Physicians have performed autopsies for thousands of years (Figure 2.1). Autopsy (derived from the Greek word *autopsia* meaning "to see with one's own eyes") is also referred to as necropsy, a term primarily referred to by veterinarians for the postmortem examination of animals.

A Roman physician, Antistius, performed a forensic examination in 44 BCE on Julius Caesar, documenting 23 stab wounds. In 1410 the Catholic Church ordered an autopsy on Pope Alexander V to determine if he was poisoned by his successor, but no evidence was found. During the nineteenth century family members often objected to the performance

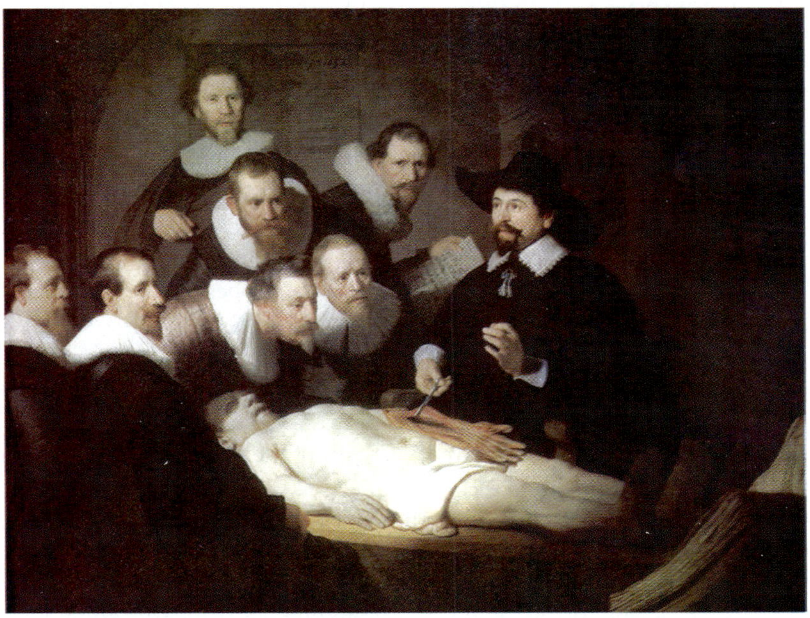

Figure 2.1 The Anatomy Lesson of Dr. Tulp. (Rembrandt van Rijn, 1632.) (Courtesy of the Mauritshuis Royal Picture Gallery, The Hague. Used with permission.)

of an autopsy citing desecration of the body and religious reasons, but doctors in search of the cause and manner of death would hurry to perform an autopsy before the family decision was made. Ambrose Bierce in his *Devils' Dictionary* of 1881, defined the grave as "a place in which the dead are laid awaiting the coming of the medical students." In fact, families would place guards over the gravesite during the night hours to protect the bodies from theft, which is where we get the term "graveyard shift".

Near the end of the nineteenth century prominent physicians, such as William Osler of Baltimore, led the fight to reveal the true nature of the autopsy and to share the results with the family and the doctors in an effort to discover the cause of death. Thus, this effort to defeat the fear of what was believed to be the desecration of the human body actually led to a better understanding of tuberculosis, appendicitis, and many iatrogenic errors thus informing the physicians of their missed diagnoses. Today, autopsies are granted in 80 percent of the cases when requested. In many cases the autopsies are mandated by law. In that case there is no choice for the family or the medical examiner or coroner. Any autopsy requires a full examination of the body as well as full investigation of the circumstances surrounding the death.

When a person dies in the State of Florida the following statute (#406) applies:

> In any of the following circumstances involving the death of a human being, the medical examiner of the district in which the death occurred or the body was found, shall determine the cause of death and shall, for that purpose, make or have performed such examinations, investigations and autopsies as s/he shall deem necessary or shall be requested by the State Attorney:
>
> When a person dies in the State of Florida
>
> - Of criminal violence
> - By accident
> - By suicide
> - Suddenly, in apparent good health
> - Unattended by a practicing physician or other recognized practitioner
> - In any prison or penal institution
> - In police custody
> - In any suspicious or unusual circumstance
> - By criminal abortion
> - By poison
> - By disease constituting a threat to public health
> - By disease, injury or toxic agent resulting from employment
> - When a dead body is brought into the state without proper medical certification
> - When a body is to be cremated, dissected or buried at sea
>
> The medical examiner shall have the authority to perform, or have performed, whatever autopsies or laboratory examinations s/he deems necessary and in the public interest to determine the identification and cause or manner of death of the deceased or to obtain evidence necessary for forensic examination.
>
> The Medical Examiners Commission shall adopt rules providing for the notification of the next of kin that an investigation by the medical examiner is being conducted. A medical examiner *may not retain or furnish any body part of the deceased for research or any other purpose which is not in conjunction with a determination of the identification of or cause or manner of death of the deceased or the presence of disease without notification of and approval of the next of kin.*

The dental postmortem examination of the deceased person is an integral part of the medical autopsy. When called for, it may be the determining factor in the identification of the unknown deceased and it may also assist in the identification of a suspect involved in the death.

The primary purpose of the medical autopsy is to determine the cause and manner of death. The dental autopsy may assist in that determination but its primary purpose is to establish the identification of the remains. This involves the comparison of antemortem and postmortem records and sometimes the comparison of the dentition to a pattern injury, such as a bitemark, in order to identify the individual who may have created the mark. Some autopsies have legal or criminal implications and then the manner of death and the identification of the remains becomes even more significant. Insurance claims, return of remains to family, and identification of victims of crime, are all matters of great importance in this process. There are many instances of insurance claim fraud and mixup of identity.

It is important to distinguish between "cause of death" and "the manner of death." There are a multitude of causes of death. Death may have been caused by loss of blood from a knife wound to an artery, or from a gunshot wound, or poison, or even a fall from heights. The question then arises: what was the manner of death? Did the individual trip and fall by accident or maybe was pushed, as in murder? Was the bullet wound self-inflicted, as in suicide? This is usually determined by the medical examiner working in concert with the investigative staff. Naturally, the crime scene, as well as the careful examination of the body, would make a significant contribution to this determination. The death certificate will always ask the question of the medical examiner as to the manner of death, and it may not be possible to answer this question immediately, even though the cause of death is known. And then, the answer may very well be that the manner of death is undetermined—at least at this time—pending further investigation, including toxicology and other tissue tests.

There are only four classifications for the manner of death until a final designation has been established, the manner of death will be listed as undetermined:

- Natural
- Accidental
- Suicide
- Homicide
- (and undetermined)

Photos or visitation to the crime scene are very helpful as is the investigator's report of the circumstances surrounding the death. Cause of death may be blunt trauma to the head. Was this as a result of an accidental fall, an automobile accident, or the blows of a baseball bat during a brawl? Poisons and drugs may be an accident, suicide, or homicide. Very often, the cause may be determined even though the manner may not be known.

Establishing the time of the injury in relation to the time of death is an important function of the medical examiner and the odontologist, especially in the case of a bitemark. In the case of a bitemark, the time of the bite—antemortem, perimortem, or postmortem—may be determined by the condition of the pattern injury. Was the victim bitten days before death or at the time of death? Perhaps, it was after. This is an important question that may be answered by the odontologist and could possibly exonerate or incriminate the perpetrator (see Odontoglyphics—Bitemarks, Chapter 13).

Time of Death

Three terms can be referred to in an attempt by the medical examiner to determine the approximate time of death: algor mortis, livor mortis, and rigor mortis.

Algor mortis occurs as body temperature changes after death occurs. There is usually a steady decline in temperature until the body reaches the ambient temperature. According to the seasons and the geographical area, the ambient temperature may vary widely and should be a consideration. Using the Glaister equation:

36.9°C (98.6°F) minus the rectal temperature divided by 1.5

will give the approximate hours elapsed since death. Then, as decomposition occurs, the temperature of the body tends to increase. The rate of decomposition will depend upon the local conditions, for example, sun, water, or ice.

Livor mortis or postmortem lividity accompanies death due to a settling of the blood in the most dependent portions of the body after death occurs. This causes a purplish red discoloration of the skin due to the red blood cells sinking through the serum as a result of gravity. This discoloration is missing from any portion of the skin that may be in contact with the ground where the blood vessels would be compressed. (Figure 2.2) Therefore, it is possible to determine if the body had been moved from the original position depending upon the location of the area with no discoloration. When used to help determine the time of death one can state that livor mortis starts about 20 minutes to 3 hours after death and is congealed in the blood vessels in 4 to 5 hours. Maximum lividity occurs within 6 to 12 hours subject to many variables such as location, temperature, and so on.

Rigor mortis is a condition that occurs a few hours postmortem. Physiologically, what happens is that the muscle fibers become more permeable to calcium ions. Normally, muscle fibers ratchet together becoming shorter and shorter (muscle contraction) as long

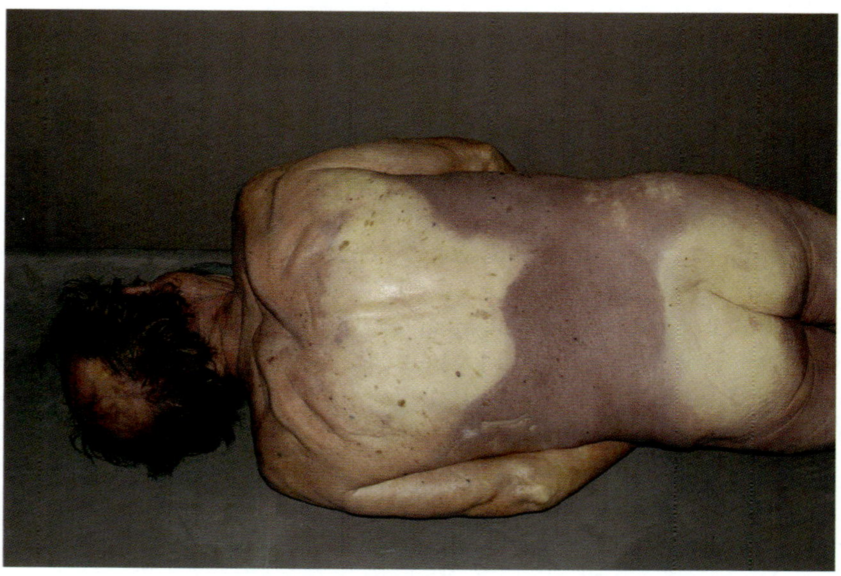

Figure 2.2 Livor mortis. (Courtesy of the Miami Dade Medical Examiners office. Used with permission.)

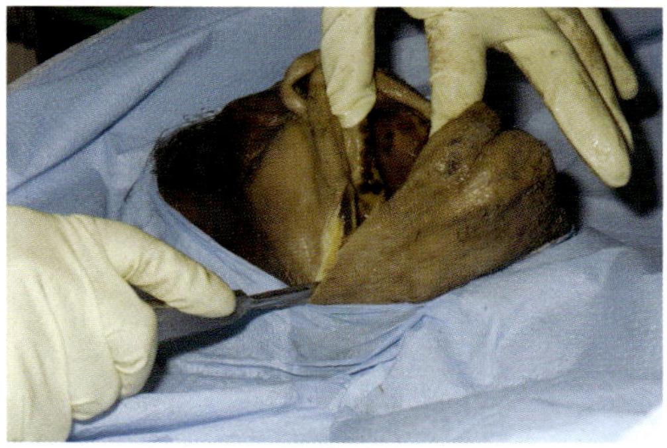

Figure 2.3 Dissection of soft tissue. (Courtesy of the Miami Dade Medical Examiners office. Used with permission.)

as the neurotransmitter acetylcholine and adenosine triphosphate (ATP) are present. However, muscles need ATP in order to be released from a contracted state. Because the ATP reserves are quickly depleted along with other cellular elements, the fibers remain locked in their ratcheted position until the muscles begin to decompose. Rigor mortis may be used to establish the approximate time of death. The onset of rigor mortis may range from 10 minutes to several hours and the maximum stiffness is usually reached about 12 to 24 hours after death, depending upon the ambient temperature and circumstances. The forensic odontologist will have to deal with rigor mortis because it manifests itself by stiffening all the joints of the body and therefore the mandible will become locked in place. The muscles of mastication are affected first and then rigor mortis spreads to the rest of the body. Depending upon the surrounding conditions, the joints may be stiff for up to three days, but then decomposition will cause the muscles to unlock or relax.

Practical applications to this condition which may impair access to the oral cavity for proper examination may be:

1. Manual application of force to open the jaws (see Chapter 9) by placing one hand on the anterior teeth of the upper jaw and one hand on the anterior teeth of the lower jaw and physically, slowly, pulling them apart. This may be accomplished better if a lever is first inserted between the posterior teeth (*see* Chapter 9) with tongue blades in place over the occlusal surfaces of the posterior teeth to protect the tooth cusps.
2. Dissection of the muscles in soft tissue between the commissure of the lips and the tragus of the ear (Figure 2.3) will help to obtain access and eliminate areas of muscle tension that prevent opening. This procedure is limited to the non-viewable remains, usually in the decomposed area. Permission of the ME/C should be obtained before proceeding with this operation. Special consideration should be given to the family, who would be very disturbed by any change from viewable to non-viewable by a disfiguring procedure that could have been avoided.
3. Removal of the jaws provides the ultimate access, especially in badly decomposed remains, and is necessary in cases when the jaws must be retained for the purpose of evidence. Jars containing formalin are best suited for this purpose to preserve the jaws after charting, radiographing, and photographing the jaws separately.

Guidelines for the Medical Examiner Identification Procedures

The following procedures should be completed in the identification process:

- The body shall be identified as soon as possible.
- The method of identification shall be recorded on the first autopsy report.

- Detailed physical description including height and weight, skin, hair, and eye color.
- Clothing and personal effects.

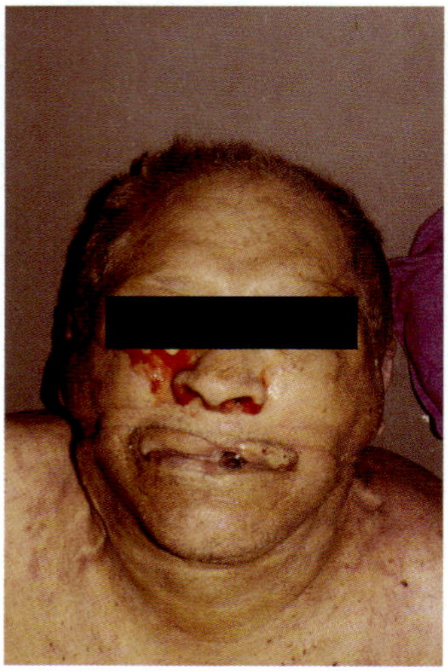

Figure 2.4a Before cleaning. (Courtesy of the Miami Dade Medical Examiners office. Used with permission.)

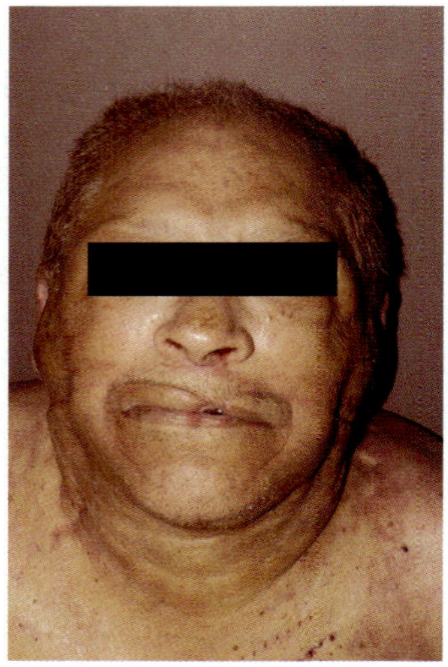

Figure 2.4b After cleaning. (Courtesy of the Miami Dade Medical Examiners office. Used with permission.)

Photography

At least two digital facial photographs (before and after cleaning; Figure 2.4a,b) are required in order to evaluate the presence of evidence and then to be able to present the face to next of kin for identification, without any distractions. Views of the face may be taken from different angles (Figure 2.5a–c). A view of the anterior dentition is also helpful in identification.

Photographs of clothing, tattoos, jewelry, and other features (Figure 2.6a–c) serve to assist in identification. Tattoos are unique and easily recognizable by family members after presumption of name has been achieved. The clothing provides clues as to size—height and weight—as well as gender and community placement. Depending upon the time between death and discovery, the clothing may supply information regarding the season during which the death occurred. For instance, if the deceased was wearing heavier clothing in northern climes it might indicate that the death had occurred during the winter months even though the body was found in the summertime. Jewelry with engraving or antemortem photographs of the person wearing the item not only demonstrates identity but ownership for valuable pieces.

Photo documentation of pertinent wounds and any pattern injuries (Figure 2.7a–c) should be made as soon as possible before fading. Correct lighting or the use of alternate light sources, such as ultraviolet or infrared, of these areas might disclose additional information. For instance, the use of infrared light photography will usually disclose tattoos that were hidden by severe burning of the skin. In addition, the use of proper measuring guides, such as the ABFO#2 ruler, is strongly recommended. All pictures are taken both with the ruler and without the ruler in order to observe the complete field. Pattern injuries such as a chain, knife wound, bullet wound, or bungee cord are very distinctive and revealing as to evidence.

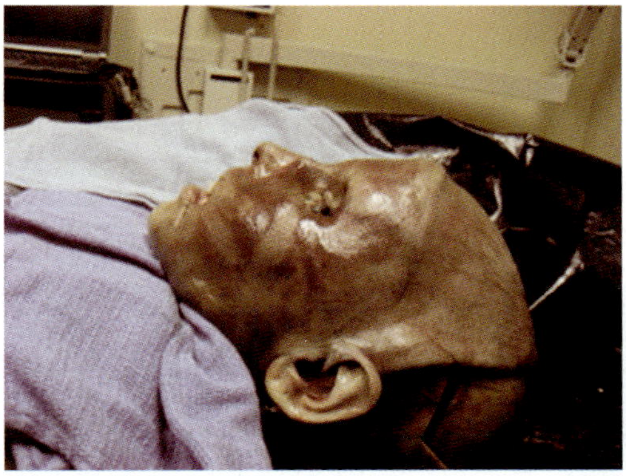

Figure 2.5a Profile. (Courtesy of the Miami Dade Medical Examiners office. Used with permission.)

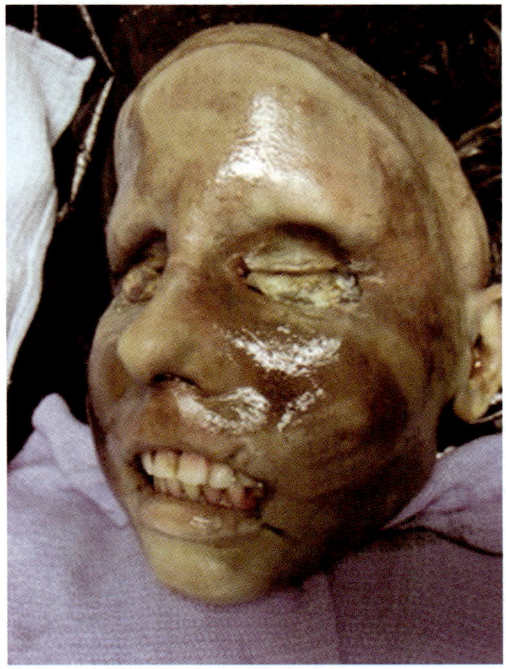

Figure 2.5b Front. (Courtesy of the Miami Dade Medical Examiners office. Used with permission.)

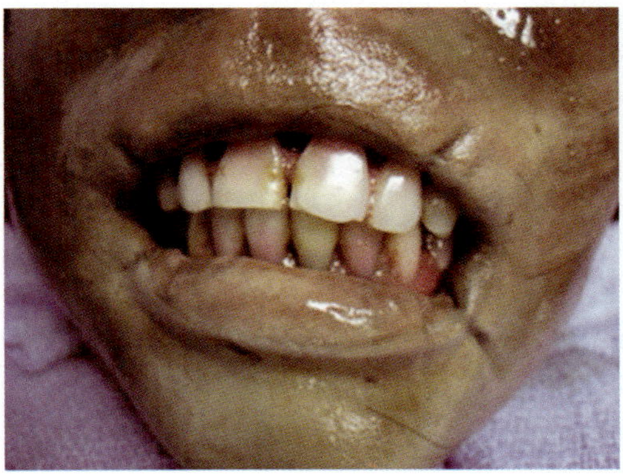

Figure 2.5c Teeth. (Courtesy of the Miami Dade Medical Examiners office. Used with permission.)

Family photographs of a smiling (Figure 2.8a,b) individual before death are extremely valuable when they show upper front teeth. In this case there was a significant chip on the corner of the upper front tooth which the parent confirmed. It was not immediately observed because the tooth had been repaired subsequent to the photo. It was only through the diligent use of good lighting and a magnifying glass that the former chip was observed and then the positive identification was made. That one chipped tooth was sufficient, when the postmortem record and the antemortem photo were compared, to make the identification.

Chipped teeth, malocclusion (bad bite), and unique restorations such as gold caps, grilles, and braces (Figure 2.9a–c) are unique characteristics that are extremely valuable in the antemortem–postmortem matching process to arrive at an accurate identity, especially when the usual dental records may be missing or unobtainable at the moment. The unidentified may not have even had a dentist, as is often the case, or the dentist has lost the records.

Upon entry into the morgue, full body photos are taken while still on the gurney and fully dressed. There is a scale platform built into the floor for determining weight, and a camera is permanently mounted overhead (Figure 2.10). Personal effects are retrieved and placed in a proper safe after recording all items and then the body is undressed and

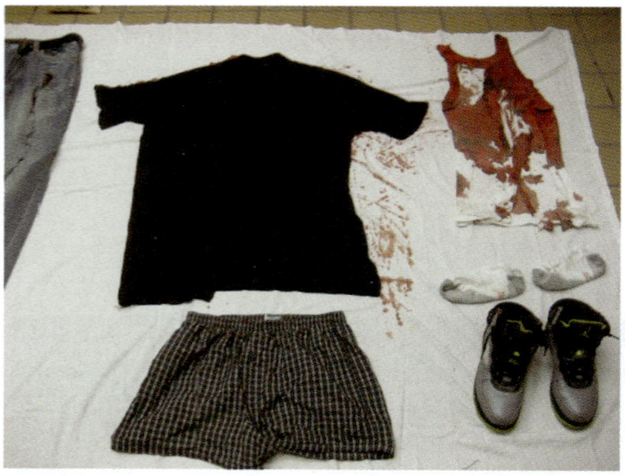

Figure 2.6a Clothing. (Courtesy of the Miami Dade Medical Examiners office. Used with permission.)

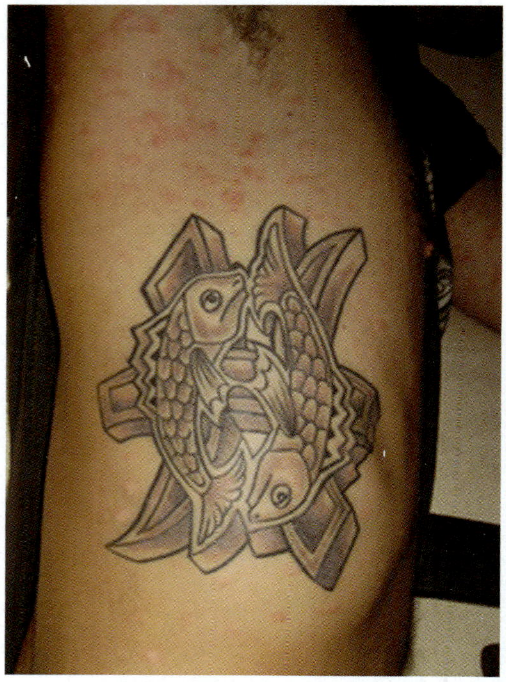

Figure 2.6b Tattoo.

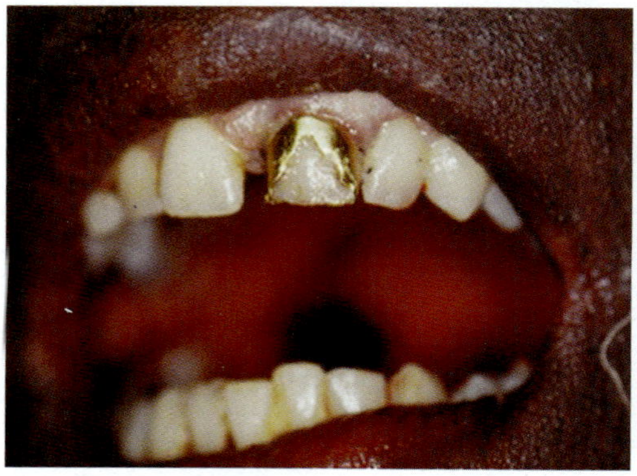

Figure 2.6c Gold cap. (Courtesy of the Miami Dade Medical Examiners office. Used with permission.)

photographed again. After this, a full body radiograph (Figure 2.11) is taken to discover any unseen or undetected material such as bullets, teeth, and so on. Teeth sometimes have a tendency to disappear, mostly because they are not recognized as such. This is may be due to severe trauma or in the skeletal remains when the soft tissue of the periodontal membrane has been lost, the teeth are no longer attached. They may be lost in the body cavity or in the body bag. It has been suggested in times of mass disaster, or other critical situations, that the head be "bagged" until arrival at the morgue in order to protect against the postmortem loss of teeth. On occasion, condoms filled with drugs may be found in the intestinal tract of "body packers" who use this method to transport drugs. A full body radiograph will help in the disclosure of these matters.

Dental radiographs, photographs, and charts (Figure 2.12 a–c; Appendix, Figure A.2) are accomplished by a forensic dentist. It is the responsibility of the medical examiner/coroner to see that a proper dental examination is conducted. It is advisable to have this done by an American Board of Forensic Odontology (ABFO) dentist or by one who has been recommended by an ABFO dentist. Dental radiographs of high quality are essential for purposes of comparison with antemortem records. Photographs will record details that are often lost

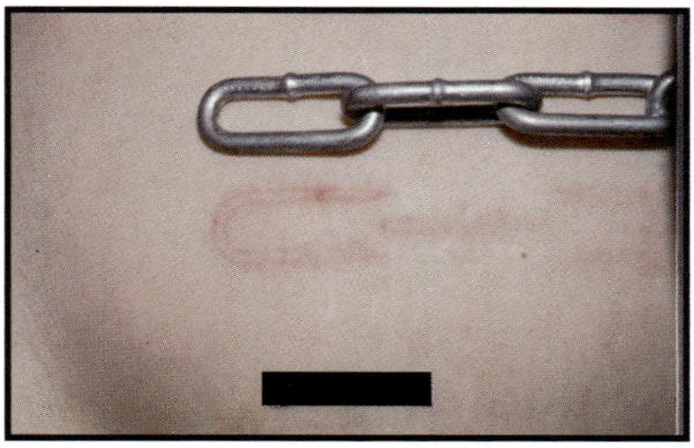

Figure 2.7a Pattern – chain. (Courtesy of the Miami Dade Medical Examiners office. Used with permission.)

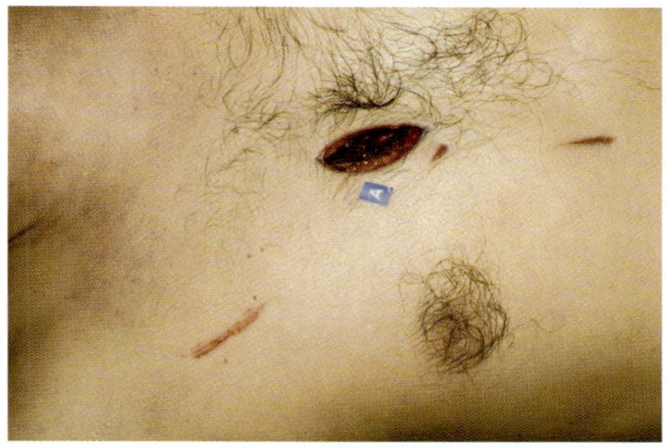

Figure 2.7b Pattern – stab. (Courtesy of the Miami Dade Medical Examiners office. Used with permission.)

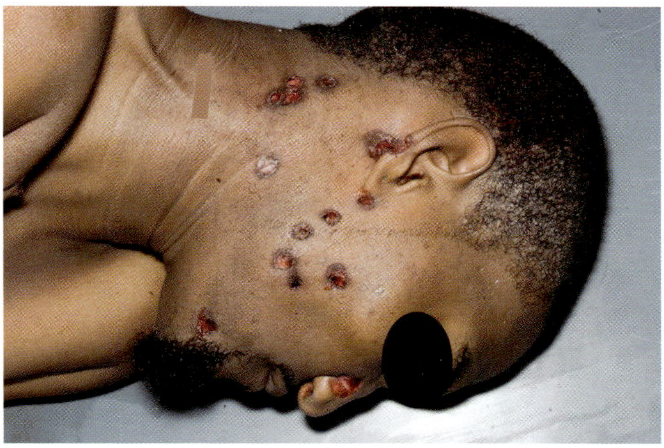

Figure 2.7c Pattern – bullet. (Courtesy of the Miami Dade Medical Examiners office. Used with permission.)

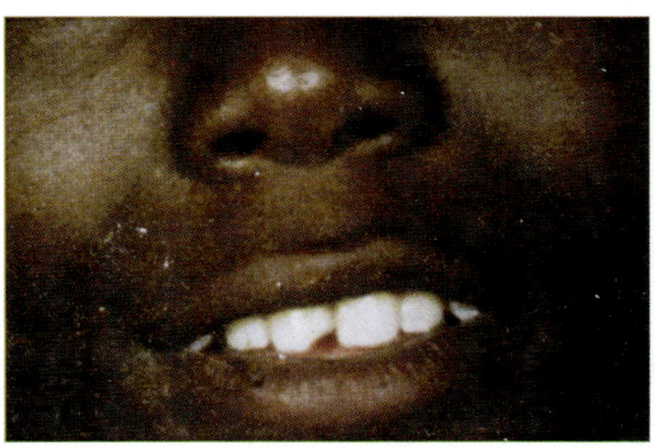

Figure 2.8a Chipped tooth. (Courtesy of the Miami Dade Medical Examiners office. Used with permission.)

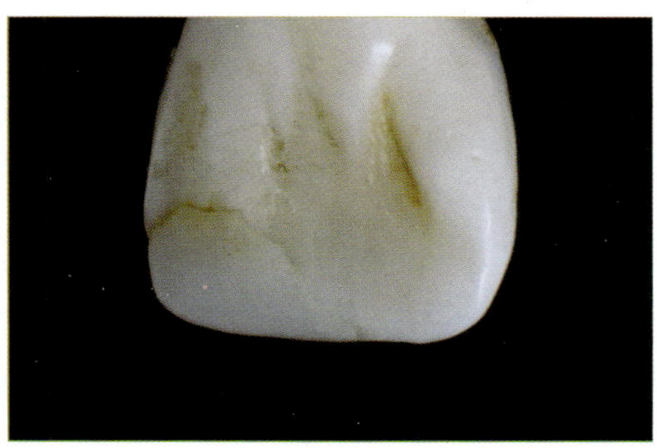

Figure 2.8b Chip repaired. (Courtesy of the Miami Dade Medical Examiners office. Used with permission.)

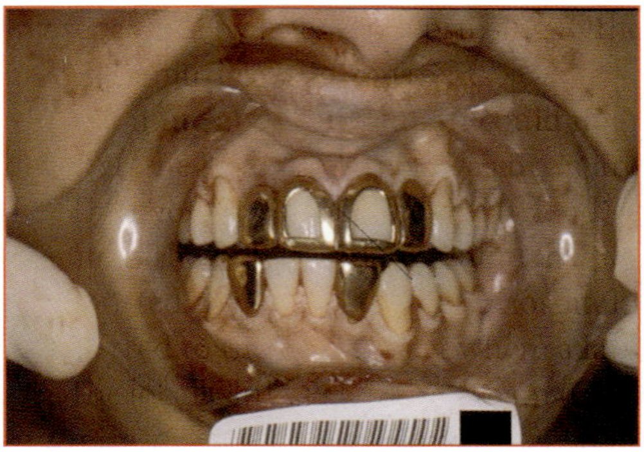

Figure 2.9a Gold caps. (Courtesy of the Miami Dade Medical Examiners office. Used with permission.)

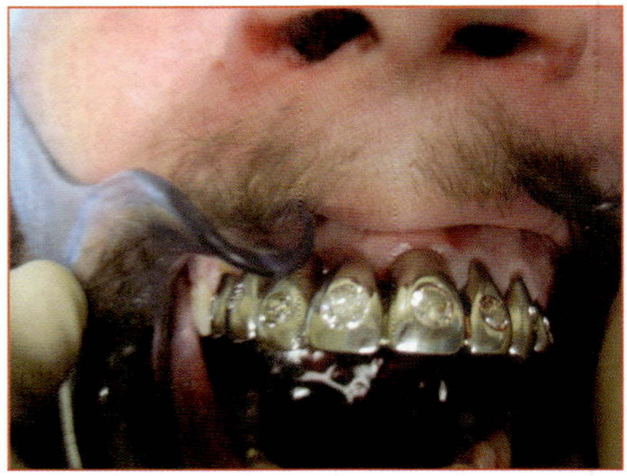

Figure 2.9b Removable grille. (Courtesy of the Miami Dade Medical Examiners office. Used with permission.)

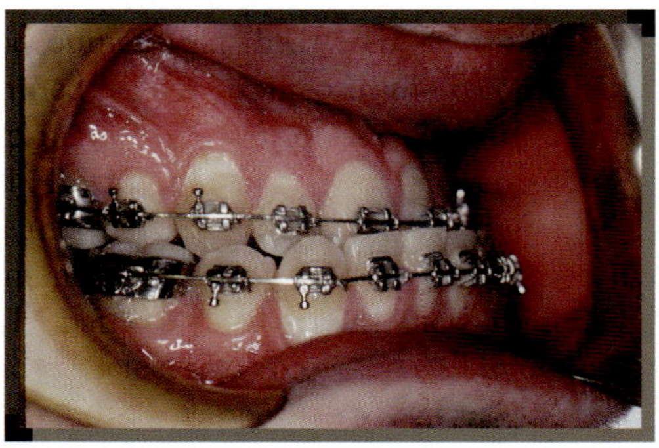

Figure 2.9c Malocclusion with braces.

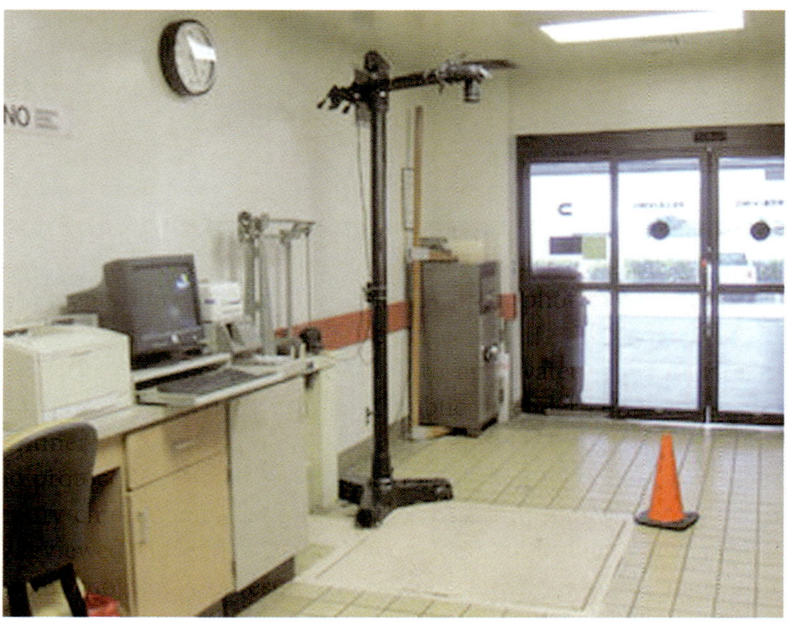

Figure 2.10 Miami Dade morgue entry. (Courtesy of the Miami Dade Medical Examiners office. Used with permission.)

Figure 2.11 Full body x-ray. (Courtesy of the Miami Dade Medical Examiners office. Used with permission.)

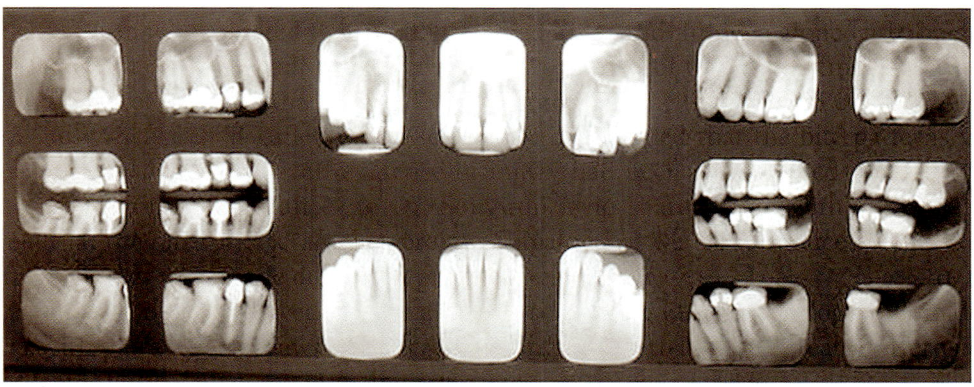

Figure 2.12a Full mouth x-ray series.

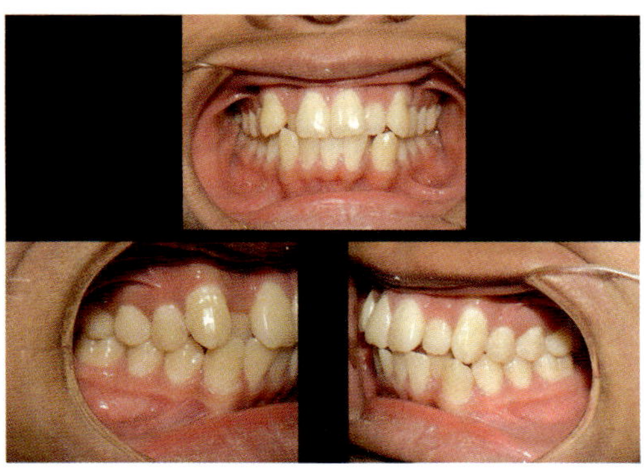

Figure 2.12b Photos of dentition.

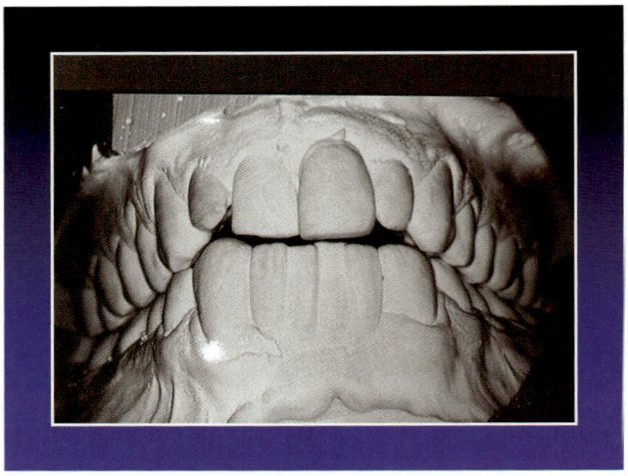

Figure 2.12c Stone model.

in the menial manipulations of the examiner. The dental chart will supply the hardcopy and data to be placed into the National Crime Information Center (NCIC) network for comparison with antemortem records of thousands of missing persons.

Antemortem dental charts, photographs, and radiographs from a dentist or hospital related to the presumptive remains should be obtained in their original state. The dentist may make a copy of the record before forwarding it to the requesting agency and these original records may be returned to the dentist or hospital later if requested.

Photographs, impressions of the teeth, and models are made in the case of possible bitemarks. In certain cases, it is necessary to make models of the victim's and the suspect's teeth when the circumstances of the event are not clear. It should also be a part of standard procedure to make a swab of the area in order to obtain sample DNA. If the suspect is in custody, then the impressions of the teeth may have to be taken within the confines of the corrections facility at a later date. It may be necessary to obtain permission from the suspect or a court order in order to proceed with the gathering of evidence.

Jaw removal (see Chapter 9) may be done by a tree limb lopper or a Stryker saw, according to one's preference. In any event, the evidence must be preserved, properly labeled, and placed in a secure location. It is stored in an appropriate solution (formalin) and at a proper temperature (refrigerator). When removing the jaws, it is important not to cause injury to the teeth. Be sure that the instrument is placed midway up on the ramus during a horizontal cut of the ramus, and well above the roots of the maxillary teeth in a similar position to what would be the cut in a LeForte I surgical procedure. Always be sure to obtain permission from the medical examiner/coroner before removing the jaw(s).

Blood, tissue, or marrow samples should be obtained on all unidentified remains for blood group and typing and for potential DNA analysis. These are also maintained in proper storage for any future use.

All bodies should be fingerprinted for possible matching with AFIS (Automatic Fingerprint Identification System). CJIS (Criminal Justice Information System) is open 24/7 for this purpose. Matching is possible from criminal, military, or employment records in their database, which is quite extensive. If, in the event that the body has been discovered after immersion in water, the skin on the hands may be removed in its entirety like a "glove" and placed over the operator's hand so as to produce an accurate recording of the fingerprints.

Figure 2.13a Skin glove. (Courtesy of the Miami Dade Medical Examiners office. Used with permission.)

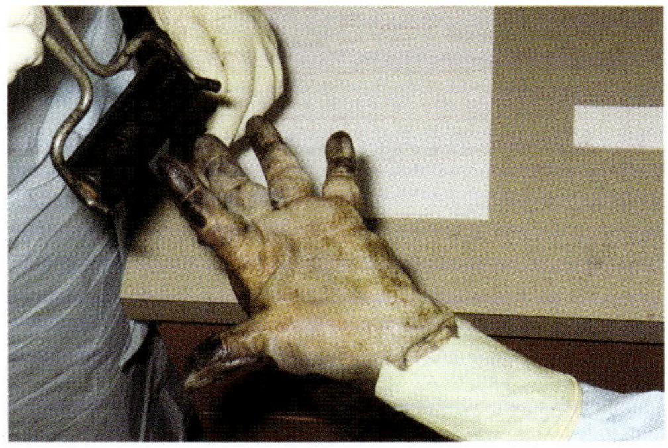

Figure 2.13b Fingerprint glove. (Courtesy of the Miami Dade Medical Examiners office. Used with permission.)

Infants under one year of age are footprinted and airline cockpit personnel are footprinted and fingerprinted (Figure 2.13a,b). All homicides should be palmprinted, in addition to fingerprints of the victim and suspect (if available).

The final and most important step in seeking to identify the unidentified is to enter the information into the National Crime Information Center (NCIC 2000) record (Figure 2.14a–c; Appendix, Figures A.3 and A.4). It is only in this way that the unidentified can be compared with the missing. The information on missing persons should already have been entered into NCIC by a law enforcement agency. The unidentified person data is entered through the ME/C office.

It is the primary responsibility of the medical examiner department (ME/C) to enter all the information obtained on the unidentified person. And it is the responsibility of the law enforcement agency to enter the information on the missing person. Either one without the other is just useless information. There are two separate books for recording this information: *Unidentified Persons* and *Missing Persons*. NCIC booklets are available free of charge from FBI/CJIS, 1000 Custer Hollow Road, Clarksburg, WV 26306.

The identified remains may then be released for burial to the family or local funeral home in the county in which death occurred. If indigent, at the family request, the remains will be placed in the county cemetery, Potter's Field (Figure 2.15), by a funeral home who has the county contract.

At some time in the future there may arise a clue as to the identity of the unidentified and exhumation may be required, therefore, cremation of unidentified remains is not allowed. The case must be reviewed by the chief medical examiner/coroner before release, and the time for storage is also determined by the chief medical examiner. Thereafter all unidentified persons are buried in their natural state.

All records are then delivered to permanent storage, physical or electronic.

Note: The Earnhardt Family Protection Act in Florida (Appendix, Figure A.5a,b) deemed Florida's medical examination autopsy photographs, video, and audio recordings exempt from public inspection without the expressed permission from applicable next of kin.

However, the medical examiner department may receive approval by going to the courts to provide autopsy photos, videos, and audiovisual materials for use in education, medical training, medical peer review, research, teaching, and training programs subject to written confirmation that the identity of all deceased shall be maintained confidential.

NCIC Missing Person File
Data Collection Entry Guide

Agency Case #______________

NCIC Missing Person Dental Report

SECTION 1

Patient's Name: ______ __________ ________ Age at Disappearance: ______ NCIC #: __________ ____

Completed by: __________ __________ __________ ________ Date Completed: ______ ______

Address: __________ __________ __________ __________ __________ __________ ______

Telephone #: ____ __________ ________ Email Address: ____ __________ __________ __________

X-Rays Available? ☐ Yes ☐ No Dental Models Available? ☐ Yes ☐ No Dental Photographs Available? ☐ Yes ☐ No

SECTION 2 ***DENTAL CHARACTERISTICS***

Upper Right

01 (18)__________
02 (17)__________
03 (16)__________
04 (15)__________(A)
05 (14)__________(B)
06 (13)__________(C)
07 (12)__________(D)
08 (11)__________(E)

Upper Left

09 (21)__________(F)
10 (22)__________(G)
11 (23)__________(H)
12 (24)__________(I)
13 (25)__________(J)
14 (26)__________
15 (27)__________
16 (28)__________

(Numbers in parentheses represent FDI System.)

(Letters in parentheses represent deciduous dentition.)

Lower Right

32 (48)__________
31 (47)__________
30 (46)__________
29 (45)__________(T)
28 (44)__________(S)
27 (43)__________(R)
26 (42)__________(Q)
25 (41)__________(P)

Lower Left

24 (31)__________(O)
23 (32)__________(N)
22 (33)__________(M)
21 (34)__________(L)
20 (35)__________(K)
19 (36)__________
18 (37)__________
17 (38)__________

SECTION 3 ***DENTAL CODES***

X = Tooth has been removed or did not develop
V = Tooth is unrestored or no information (Default Code)
M = Mesial Surface Restored
O = Occlusal/Incisal Surface Restored
D = Distal Surface Restored
F = Facial or Buccal Surface Restored
L = Lingual Surface Restored
C = Lab Processed or Prefabricated Restoration
R = Endodontic Treatment
/ = Tooth present but clinical crown missing (i.e., fractured)*

(*The codes V and / are used differently in the Missing Person Dental Report than in the Unidentified Person Dental Report.)

SECTION 4 ***DENTAL REMARKS***

☐ **ALL** (All 32 teeth are present and unrestored) ☐ **UNK** (No dental information available)

____
____
____
____

Rev 2/06 30

Figure 2.14a NCIC missing person dental report. (Courtesy of the U.S. Department of Justice.)

NCIC Unidentified Person File
Data Collection Entry Guide

Agency Case #________________

NCIC Unidentified Person Dental Report

SECTION 1

ME/Coroner Case #: ____________ ____________ NCIC #: ____________

Completed by: ______ ____________ ________ Date Completed: ________

Address: ____________ ____________ ____________

Telephone #: ____________ Email Address: ____________ ____________

X-Rays Available? ☐ Yes ☐ No Dental Models Available? ☐ Yes ☐ No Dental Photographs Available? ☐ Yes ☐ No

SECTION 2 ***DENTAL CHARACTERISTICS***

Upper Right		Lower Right
01 (18)______		32 (48)______
02 (17)______		31 (47)______
03 (16)______		30 (46)______
04 (15)______(A)	(Numbers in parentheses	29 (45)______(T)
05 (14)______(B)	represent FDI System.)	28 (44)______(S)
06 (13)______(C)		27 (43)______(R)
07 (12)______(D)		26 (42)______(Q)
08 (11)______(E)		25 (41)______(P)
Upper Left		**Lower Left**
09 (21)______(F)	(Letters in parentheses	24 (31)______(O)
10 (22)______(G)	represent deciduous	23 (32)______(N)
11 (23)______(H)	dentition.)	22 (33)______(M)
12 (24)______(I)		21 (34)______(L)
13 (25)______(J)		20 (35)______(K)
14 (26)______		19 (36)______
15 (27)______		18 (37)______
16 (28)______		17 (38)______

SECTION 3 ***DENTAL CODES***

X = Tooth has been removed or did not develop
V = Tooth is present and unrestored
M = Mesial Surface Restored
O = Occlusal/Incisal Surface Restored
D = Distal Surface Restored
F = Facial or Buccal Surface Restored
L = Lingual Surface Restored
C = Lab Processed or Prefabricated Restoration
R = Endodontic Treatment
/ = Postmortem Missing or Not Recovered (Default Code)

(*The codes V and / are used differently in the Unidentified Person Report than in the Missing Person Dental Report.)

SECTION 4 ***DENTAL REMARKS***

☐ ALL (All 32 teeth are present and unrestored) ☐ UNK (No dental information available)

____
____
____
____

Rev 2/06 30

Figure 2.14b NCIC unidentified person dental report. (Courtesy of the U.S. Department of Justice.)

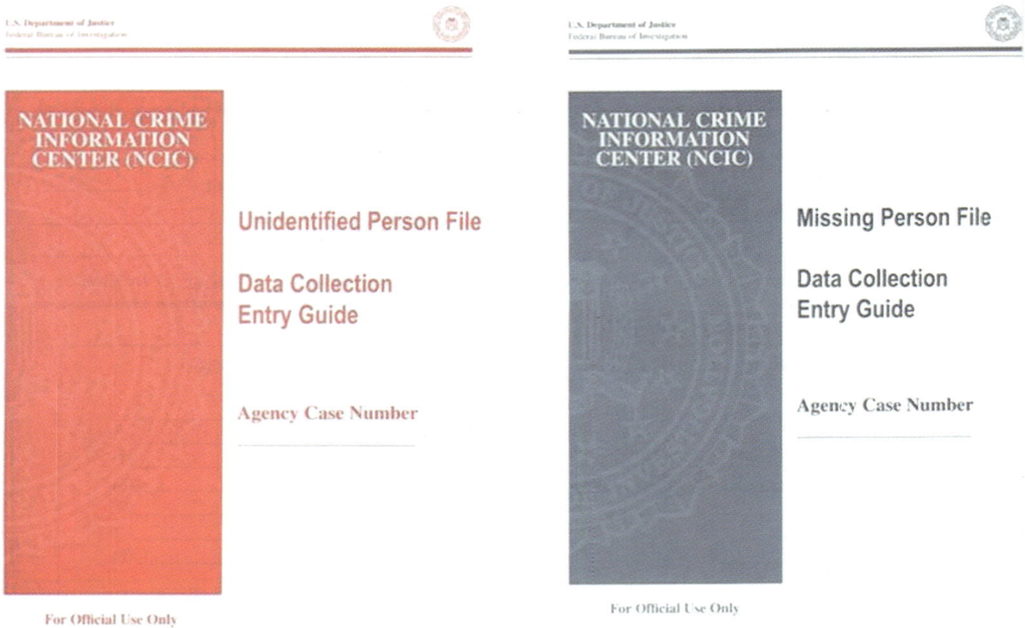

Figure 2.14c NCIC booklets.

Figure 2.15 Potter's field gravestones.

Forensic Odontology

3

Variability is the law of life.

Sir William Osler, MD, founder of modern medicine

The mission of forensic odontology involves criminal, civil or family, and dental practice matters. The forensic odontologist is critical in making the identification of unknown remains. The odontological process is fast, accurate, and inexpensive compared to all other methods. For that reason alone, no medical examiner's or coroner's office should be without a forensic odontologist on staff or on call. More important, when it comes time to go to court and testify, all credentials should be in order for a qualified expert witness to assist the court in reaching an intelligent decision. That begins when the decision is made as to who will be called to properly gather and process the evidence and make the identification, as well as the presentation, of that evidence in court (see Chapter 14).

Civil or family matters often involve mistakes and confusion. This is but one example of the importance of the forensic odontologist in avoiding confusion and making a speedy and accurate identification. A tragic example of the lack of forensic identification recently made national news. For over a month the Van Ryn family were telling friends and family how their daughter Laura was recovering from an automobile accident that had killed five people including her friend, Whitney Cerak. The Van Ryn family maintained constant vigil at the hospital attending their daughter's recovery. Shortly after the horrible accident 1400 people attended a funeral service for Whitney Cerak.

Whitney E. Cerak　　　　Laura VanRyn

Figure 3.1 Two girls – mixed-up identification. (Used with family permission.)

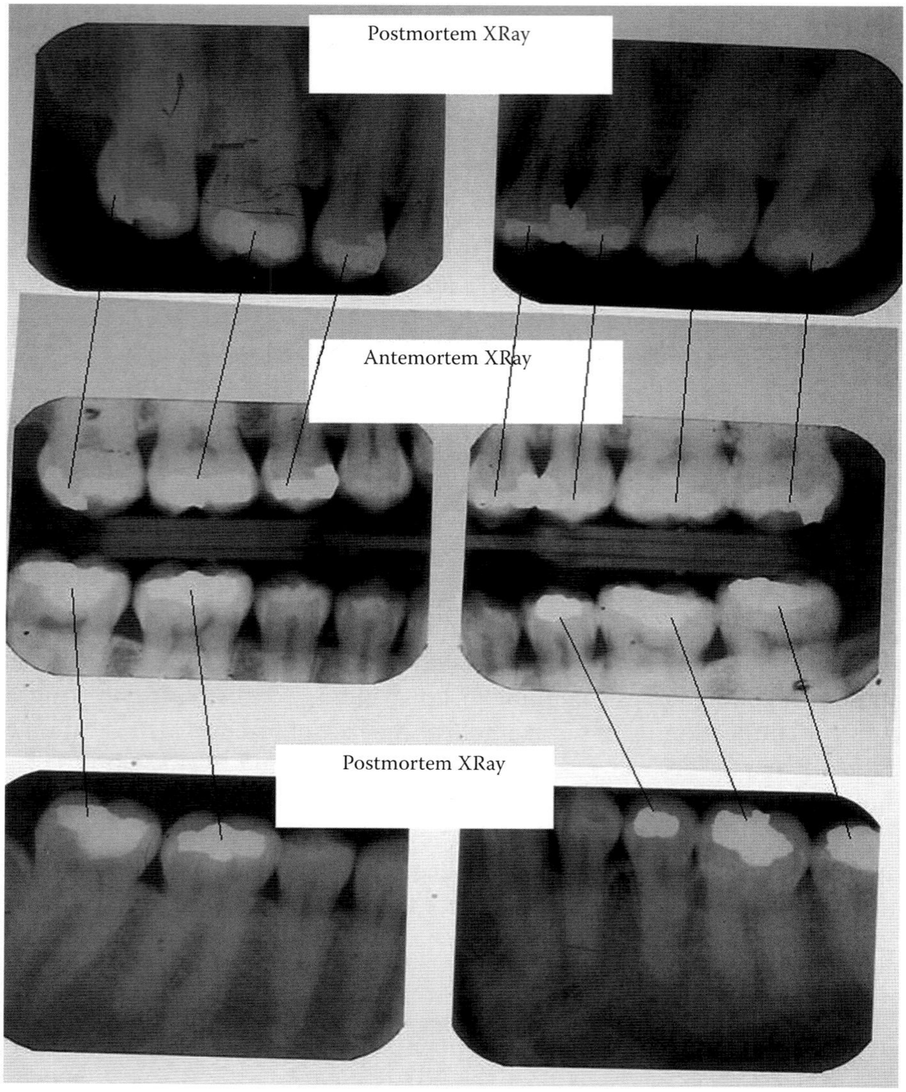

Figure 3.2 Antemortem/postmortem x-ray comparison. (Courtesy of the Miami Dade Medical Examiners office. Used with permission.)

After the tracheotomy was capped, and the bandages were removed, and the swelling went down, the young blonde girl in the bed began to speak and asked for her parents, stating that her name was Whitney, and she asked what happened to Laura, her blonde-haired friend (Figure 3.1).

There was unbelievable shock to both families. Why? The mistakes began at the accident scene when Whitney was placed in the helicopter with Laura's identification. Then the Cerak family declined to view what they thought was their daughter Whitney Cerak's body. Most importantly, no autopsy was done, especially a dental examination, which would have properly identified the deceased and prevented the disaster that struck both families in such an unusual manner. This is a real-life example of the importance of a dental ID. If the next of kin is unwilling or unable to confirm the identity of an individual, or if the facial disfigurement is so great, then it is the obligation of the medical examiner or

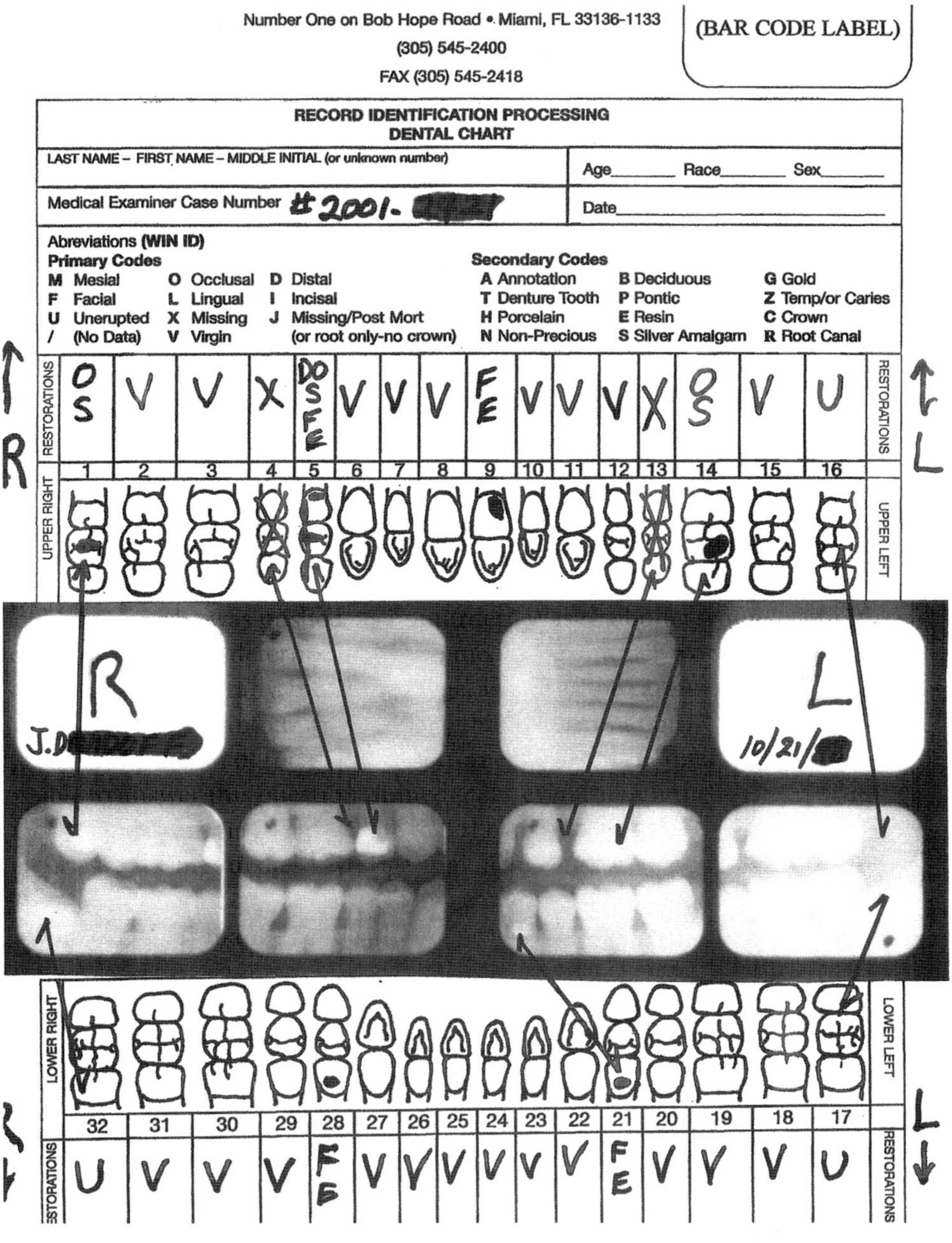

Figure 3.3 Court identification.

coroner to obtain the services of a forensic odontologist to make a positive identification. This is the simplest, fastest, and least expensive course of action that will alleviate much grief and confusion.

Criminal investigation involving the forensic odontologist can range from simple battery to murder. It is the task of the forensic odontologist to assist in the identification of the victim as well as the perpetrator. In the first instance, identification can be achieved by comparison of antemortem and postmortem radiographic records (Figure 3.2). In courtroom procedures the parties will usually stipulate as to the identity of the deceased. However, in some cases the defendant may present their own defense and decide to challenge the

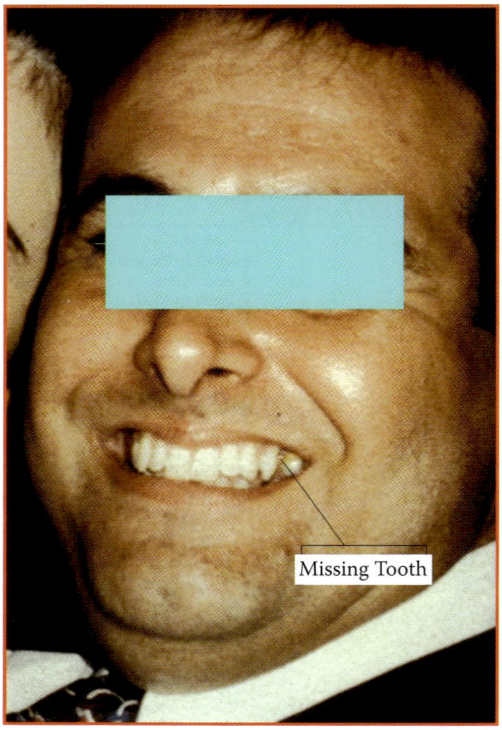

Figure 3.4 Smiling face. (Courtesy of the Miami Dade Medical Examiners office. Used with permission.)

identification of the deceased and not stipulate. Therefore it may be necessary for the forensic odontologist to appear in court and demonstrate the fact that the body was, in fact, that of the suspected decedent. No other evidence is usually necessary to support the identification (Figure 3.3). Figure 3.3 illustrates the comparison of antemortem radiographs with the postmortem chart. Each arrow indicates an item of concordance. There being no areas of conflict, the identification is positive for the presumed victim.

In the absence of dental records, smiling photographs can be very helpful (Figure 3.4). In any case it is the expert witness testimony of the forensic odontologist that may provide the essential forensic evidence in obtaining a conviction or an acquittal. Men and women have been convicted and sent to prison or death row on the basis of forensic odontological testimony only to discover later that some are innocent. The identity of the perpetrator may require bitemark analysis as well as DNA (see Chapter 13).

Dental is a seemingly easy term to describe. The general dentist does not limit the area of practice just to the teeth. Nor is the forensic dentist limited to the teeth alone. The surrounding soft tissues and supporting bone are essential to the practice of dentistry as well as forensic odontology. Beyond that we encounter the sinuses and the bones of the maxilla and the mandible. Gingival conditions, tongue shape and function, lips, cheek, and palatal rugae may be factors in identification. Even this is not a static relationship. The function of these parts may be critical in identification and in the analysis of possible bitemarks as well as the differentiation of these alleged bitemarks from other injury patterns. The dynamic relationship of the various elements will often lead to the identity of the unidentified person, who may be the victim or the suspect.

Why is it important for non-dentists to understand odontology?

1. There may be no dentist available to call.
2. Better communication with members of the dental profession.
3. Use of dental records as a means of identification.
4. Other disciplines may contribute essential information (e.g., genetic variation, ritual dental practices, ballistics, decompositional changes, and statistical variation).

Because this book has as part of its mission the education of non-dentists, such as medical examiners, coroners, lawyers, and other lay people, it is important to take time out to discuss basic dental anatomy. This is important as well for the forensic dentist who may find a single tooth lying on the ground and attempt to place it in its proper order in the dentition or for the scene investigator to identify the item as a tooth at all. It is well to remember that finding a tooth at the scene is important, but just as important is not to place the tooth or teeth back in the jaw but to place it into an evidence bag to travel with the body until a qualified dentist is available to determine its proper place in the jaw.

Dental Anatomy

Each tooth is covered on its crown with enamel and filled with dentin and pulp. It is lined with cementum along the root surface and the root is attached to the socket by the periodontal ligaments. DNA and characteristics of age, diet, level of dental care, and community placement or racial origins may be found within the area of the tooth and its supporting structures. Each tooth has its own individual characteristics that would allow the trained professional to discern the proper placement of that tooth in the dental arch (Figure 3.5).

Tooth Surfaces

Mesial, occlusal, distal, facial, and lingual (MODFL) are the basic five surfaces of any tooth (Figure 3.6). There are duplications; certain surfaces have different names. That may be confusing. So read carefully and follow the diagram.

Mesial is always the portion of a tooth facing towards the midline of the dental arch.
Occlusal is the biting surface of the back teeth.
Incisal is the term referring to the biting surface of the front teeth.
Distal is always the portion of the tooth away from the midline, towards the back of the dental arch.
Facial is the front surface of the front tooth.
Labial is the term referring to the front surface of the front teeth (same as facial).
Buccal is the front surface of the back teeth.
Lingual is the inside surface of the teeth which is next to the tongue, usually on the lower, but may also be on the upper.
Palatal is the inside surface of the upper teeth next to the palate.
Gingival or *Cervical* refers to that portion of the tooth that is adjacent to the gingiva (gum) or neck of the tooth, all around the tooth.

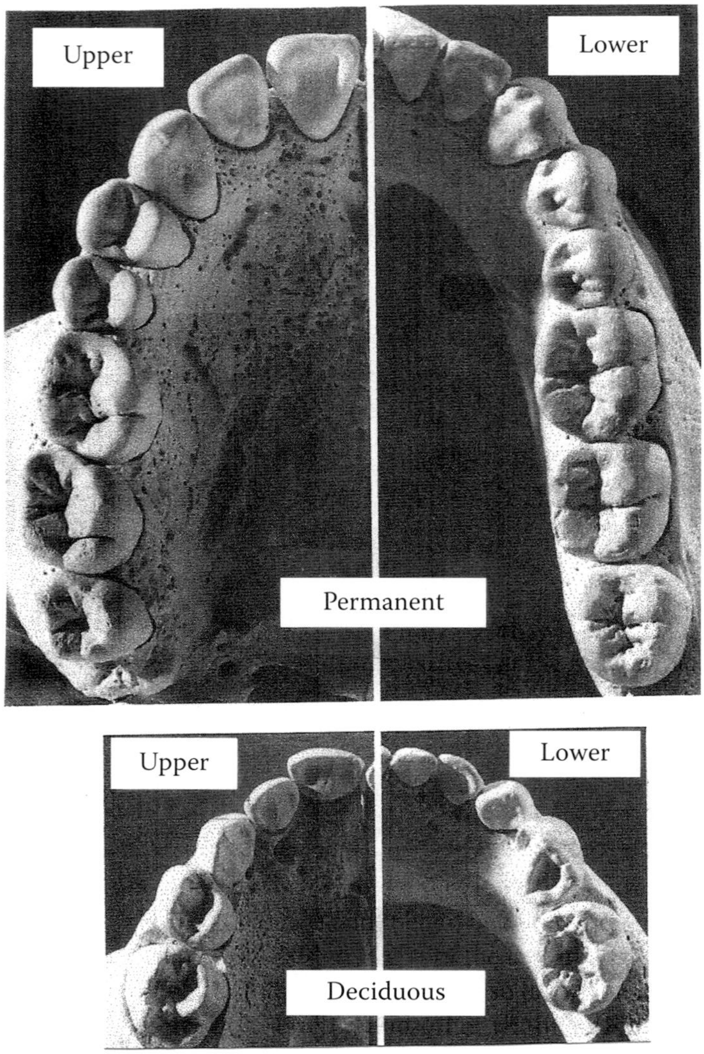

Figure 3.5 Dental anatomy. (From *The Human Bone Manual*. Reprinted with permission, Elsevier.)

A cross-sectional diagram of a single molar tooth and surrounding structures is shown in Figure 3.7.

1. *Enamel:* Outer covering of the tooth crown. It is crystalline in structure with no living cells and no way to repair itself. It is the hardest substance in the body and most resistant to change. It is 98 percent inorganic material.
2. *Dentin:* Main component of teeth just below the enamel with organic and inorganic elements. It is tubular in structure with tubes running from the dentin–enamel junction to the pulp. It is approximately 40 percent organic.
3. *Cementum:* Hard, porous substance covering the dentin on the root section of the tooth. It provides the surface for the attachment of the periodontal ligaments which run from the root to the tooth socket.

4. *Pulp:* Tissue contained within the root and crown of a tooth which consists of nerve, blood vessels, and lymphatics providing nutrients and sensitivity to the tooth.
5. *Periodontal ligament:* Surrounds the root surface and provides the attachment between the root and the surrounding socket of bone and acts as a shock absorber for the protection of the tooth.
6. *Alveolar bone:* Cancellous bone in which the teeth are set surrounded by cortical bone of the mandible and maxilla.
7. *Gingiva:* The "gums" are the soft connective tissue covered by mucous membrane which surrounds the tooth and covers the alveolar bone.
8. *Crown:* Natural enamel or artificial restoration "cap" of the tooth.
9. *Cusp:* Raised portion of the crown forming the varied anatomical landscape of the biting surface.
10. *Root:* Portion of the tooth normally below the crown and contained within the alveolar bone socket. Formed as the tooth develops and erupts into the oral cavity, it is subject to exposure in later life by recession of the gingiva and bone.
11. *Neck (Cervix):* Where the root and the crown meet. Also called the CEJ (Cemento–Enamel Junction). This is the area where the gingiva normally attaches to the tooth and may vary according to age and dental health.
12. *Apex:* Root end of a tooth.
13. *Occlusal plane:* Level to which a tooth normally erupts to form the biting surface.

The most common type of restorations ("fillings") found in the teeth are those made from silver amalgam, a pasty substance of metallic particles mixed with mercury which is packed into the prepared space after the decay has been removed. This "amalgam" is allowed to harden and it is usually polished to a shiny silver surface. Aesthetics and science have combined to develop plastic/resin substances that may be dispensed in tooth colors to fill the spaces left by removal of decay in the front or back teeth. This has become very popular but has presented a problem of detection in postmortem examination. These restorations are so well matched in color that only a magnifying glass or ultraviolet light will detect them. Gold is the sturdiest of all the restorative materials. It is a cast restoration when used to replace the area of the tooth destroyed by dental decay, but it is also used as a "cap" on normal or artificial teeth, sometimes just for decoration.

When some or all of the teeth are lost, then a removable partial (Figure 3.8a) or full denture (Figure 3.8b) is inserted in the mouth to replace the missing teeth. These dentures may be constructed of all plastic or a combination of metal and plastic. In either case, they may rest directly on the tissue or they may be anchored in place with metallic implants set under the gingiva and into the jawbone with metallic anchors above the gingiva for stabilization. Fortunately, due to the plastic construction and the removable nature, these appliances may even assist the forensic odontologist in postmortem identification if the name of the patient is inserted into the plastic of the denture. This procedure is mandatory in 21 of the United States.

If a tooth has lost its vitality—the nerve and blood vessels within the pulp chamber have become infected—then it is necessary to remove the debris and fill the canal with an inert

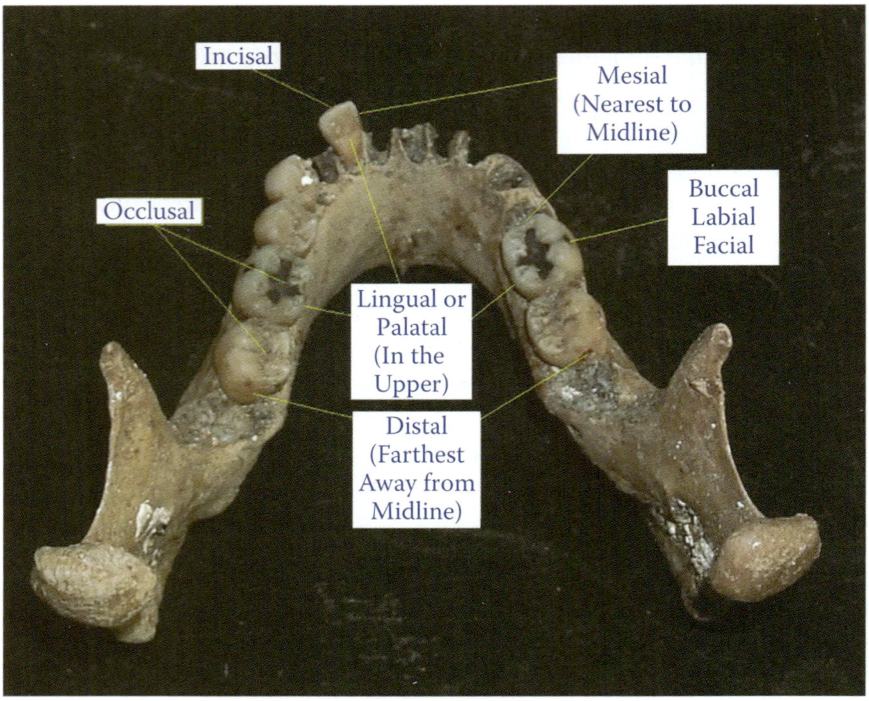

Figure 3.6 Tooth surfaces. (Courtesy of the Miami Dade Medical Examiners office. Used with permission.)

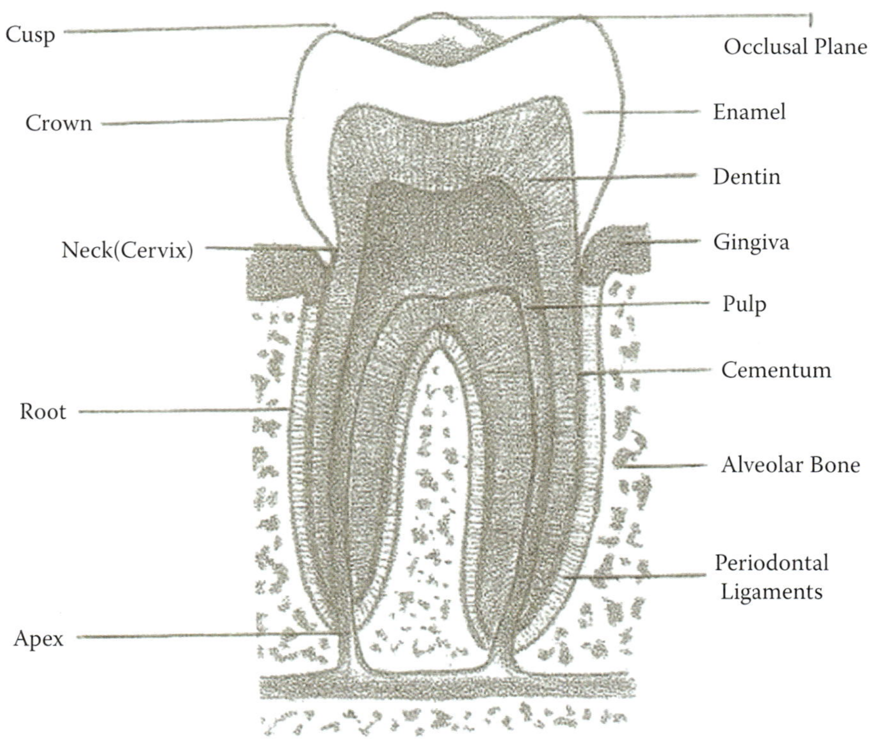

Figure 3.7 Tooth cross-section. (Courtesy of Dr. Robert George. Used with permission.)

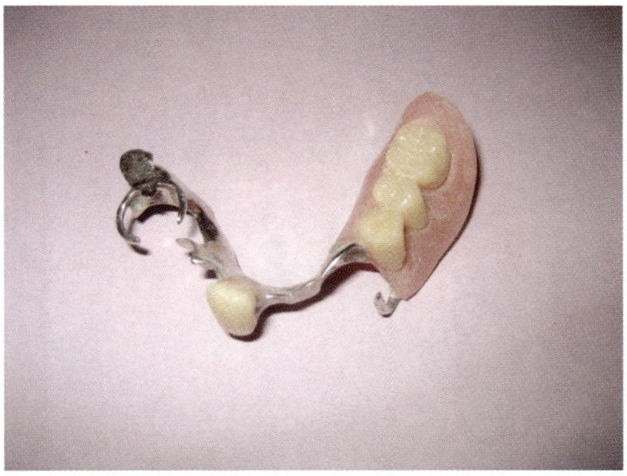

Figure 3.8a Partial denture. (Courtesy of the Miami Dade Medical Examiners office. Used with permission.)

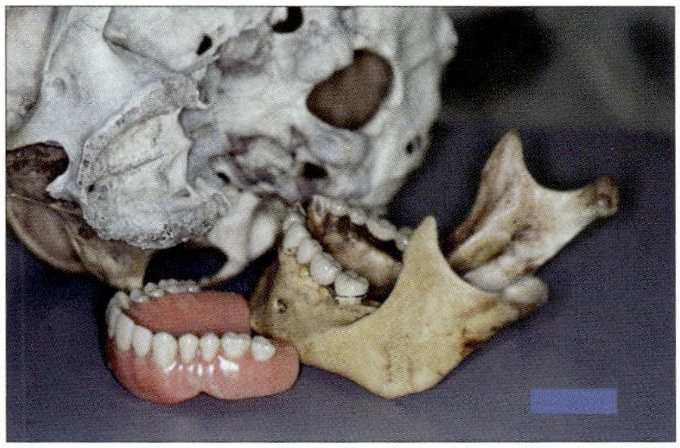

Figure 3.8b Full denture. (Courtesy of the Miami Dade Medical Examiners office. Used with permission.)

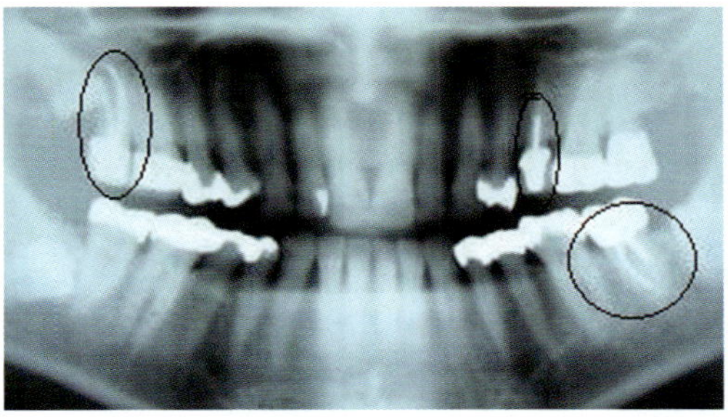

Figure 3.9 Crown with root canal (circled).

substance, such as a silver point or cement. Entrance to the root canal is gained through the crown and if the integrity of the crown is compromised, then it will be necessary to build a new crown on the tooth, of either ceramic or gold (Figure 3.9).

Although dental implants have been in use for a long time, they are becoming more prevalent in ordinary dental practice. Basically, the metallic implant is a substitute for the root of a lost tooth upon which a new crown will be set. One distinct advantage is that it is not necessary to prepare the surrounding teeth in order to replace the missing tooth (Figure 3.10a,b).

With a fixed bridge it is necessary to prepare the teeth (abutments) on either side of the missing tooth for crowns, in order to support the bridge, and to permanently fix it in place. These implants are very helpful in identification by their presence, configuration, and location, but lack serial number identification at the present time, when they are discovered postmortem (Figure 3.11).

Tooth Numbering Systems

FDI—Federation Dentaire International

Shown in Figure 3.12, this is the most widely used system in the world, even though it is not commonly used in the United States. It is the system of choice, notably by our

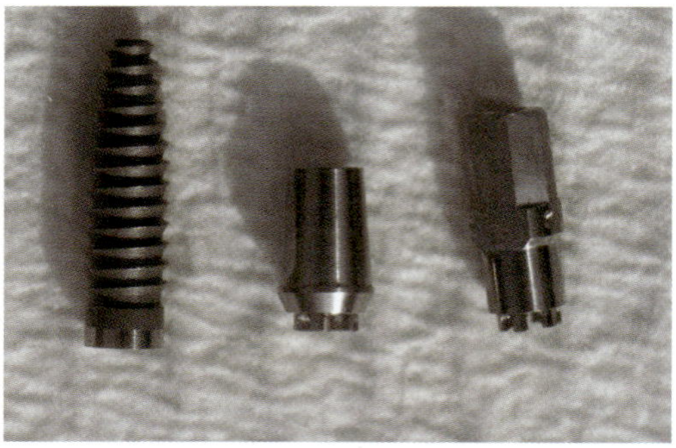

Figure 3.10a Dental implants.

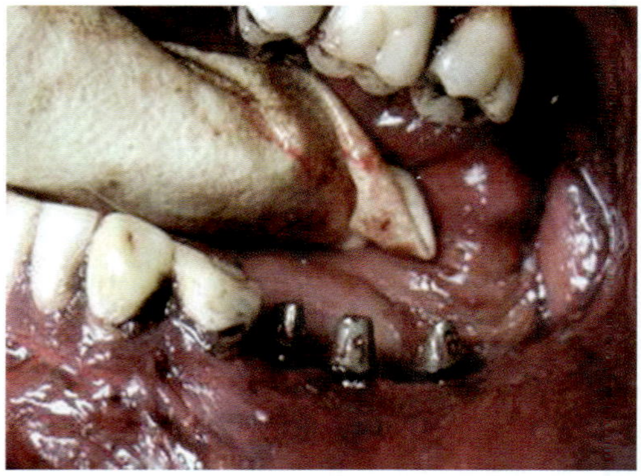

Figure 3.10b Implant in place. (Courtesy of the Miami Dade Medical Examiners office. Used with permission.)

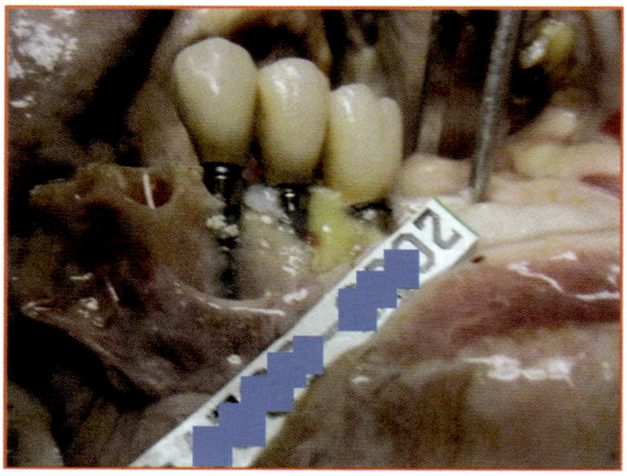

Figure 3.11 Implants with crowns. (Courtesy of the Miami Dade Medical Examiners office. Used with permission.)

Canadian and European colleagues. This is the only other system available in WINID and the forensic odontologist should be familiar with it and its conversion to the Universal System.

Universal

The United States is relatively alone in its use of this system of tooth numbering (see Figure 3.13). However, this system has been integrated into NCIC which still appears to be the best system for computer matching of missing and unidentified persons. The WINID software system enables the operator to switch between the FDI and Universal systems with one click of a button.

FDI/Universal Deciduous

The deciduous dentition has a separate system for the numbering (lettering) of teeth (see Figure 3.14). This is of assistance in the charting of teeth but it is of little importance to

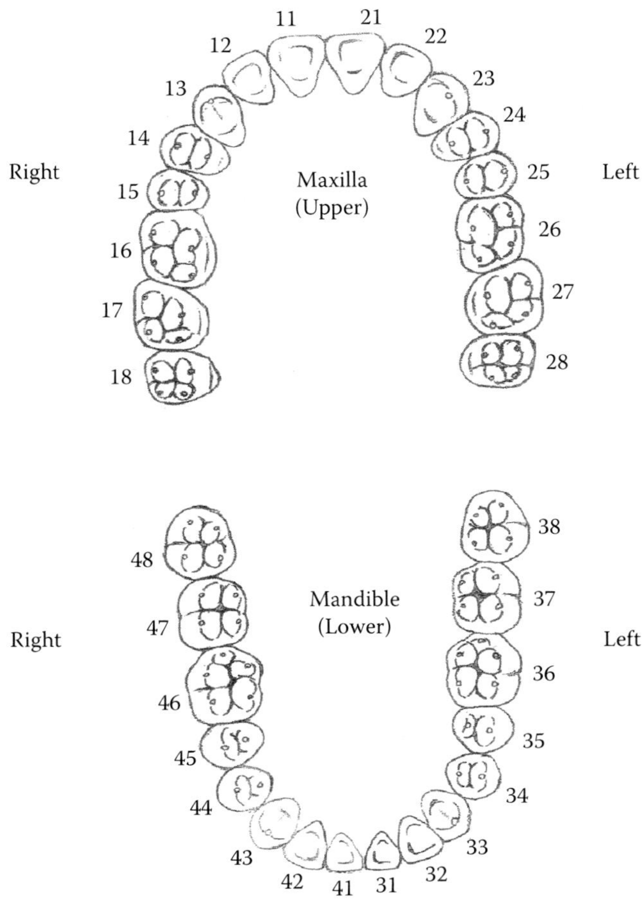

Figure 3.12 FDI tooth-numbering system (permanent).

most computer systems that do not take deciduous teeth into consideration due to their temporary nature. Unerupted permanent teeth beneath the deciduous teeth are charted as "Virgin" which describes their presence as well as their condition.

Nomenclature and Eruption Patterns (Permanent and Deciduous)

Incisor is the nomenclature employed to describe the four front teeth in the upper or lower arch of the permanent and deciduous dentition. These are the teeth that maintain the aesthetic appearance of the person.

Cuspid, canine, or *eye tooth* all refer to the same tooth, upper or lower, whether permanent or deciduous. This is the strongest tooth and often the last tooth to be lost.

First bicuspid/second bicuspid or *first premolar/second premolar* refer to the two teeth between the cuspid and the first molar. These teeth are found only in the permanent dentition. They erupt from beneath the first and second deciduous molars and are referred to as bicuspid due to the presence of a lingual and a buccal cusp, or they are called premolars because of their location in front of the molars.

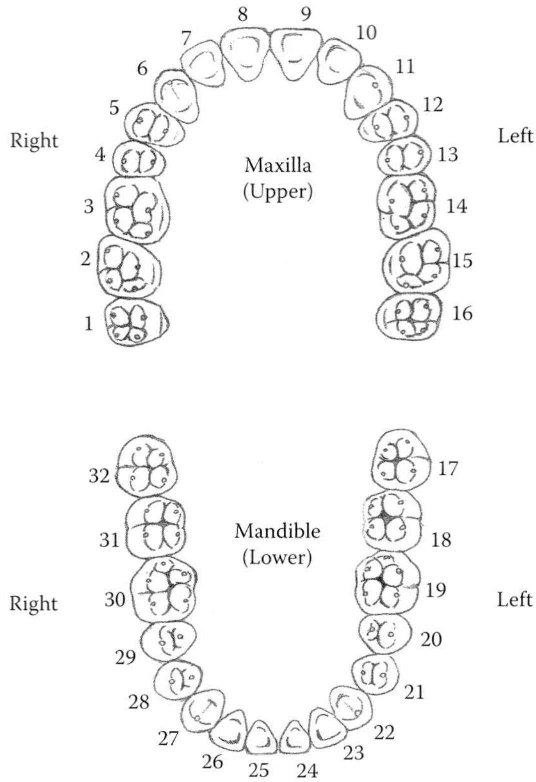

Figure 3.13 Universal tooth-numbering system (permanent).

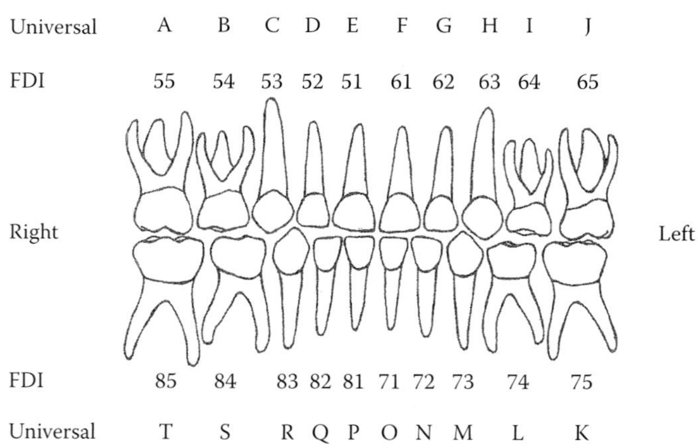

Figure 3.14 FDI and universal tooth-numbering systems (deciduous teeth).

First molar, or sometimes referred to as the six-year molar, is often the first of the permanent teeth to erupt into the mouth and therefore subject to the most decay and early loss. The first molar erupts distal to (behind) the last deciduous tooth in the arch and may be confused as being an additional deciduous tooth, which it is not. On occasion this tooth may get caught under the distal of the second deciduous molar during its course of eruption, preventing its further eruption. In the event

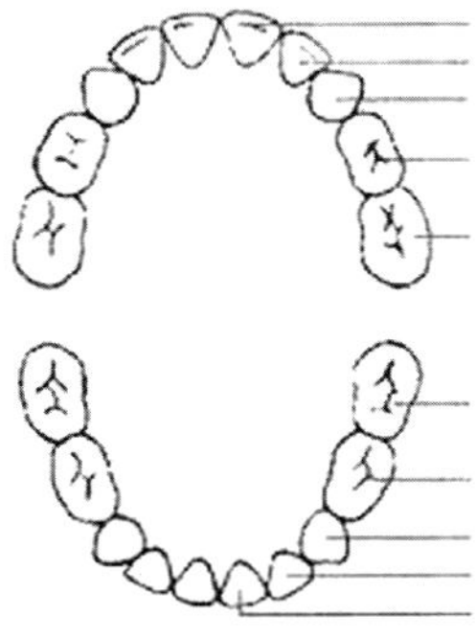

Primary (Deciduous) Teeth — Upper Teeth	Eruption	Shed
Deciduous Central Incisor	8–12 Months	6–7 Years
Deciduous Lateral Incisor	9–13 Months	7–8 Years
Deciduous Cuspid (Canine)	16–22 Months	10–12 Years
First Deciduous Molar	13–19 Months	9–11 Years
Second Deciduous Molar	25–33 Months	10–12 Years
Lower Teeth	**Eruption**	**Shed**
Second Deciduous Molar	23–31 Months	10–12 Years
First Deciduous Molar	14–18 Months	9–11 Years
Deciduous Cuspid (Canine)	17–23 Months	9–12 Years
Deciduous Lateral Incisor	10–16 Months	7–8 Years
Deciduous Central Incisor	6–10 Months	6–7 Years

Figure 3.15a Nomenclature: eruption and shedding (deciduous teeth). (Primary tooth eruption chart is copyright of the American Dental Association. This chart has been modified with permission by Dr. William Silver for the exclusive purpose of this publication.)

Permanent Teeth — Upper Teeth	Eruption
Central Incisor	7–8 Years
Lateral Incisor	8–9 Years
Cuspid (Canine)	11–12 Years
First Bicuspid (Premolar)	10–11 Years
Second Bicuspid (Premolar)	10–12 Years
First Molar	6–7 Years
Second Molar	12–13 Years
Third Molar (Wisdom Tooth)	17–21 Years
Lower Teeth	**Eruption**
Third Molar (Wisdom Tooth)	17–21 Years
Second Molar	11–13 Years
First Molar	6–7 Years
Second Bicuspid (Premolar)	11–12 Years
First Bicuspid (Premolar)	10–12 Years
Cupsid (Canine)	9–10 Years
Lateral Incisor	7–8 Years
Central Incisor	6–7 Years

Figure 3.15b Nomenclature and eruption (permanent teeth). (Permanent tooth eruption chart is copyright of the American Dental Association. This chart has been modified with permission by Dr. William Silver for the exclusive purpose of this publication.)

that the second deciduous molar is lost prematurely, space maintenance would be required to hold the space for the second premolar by preventing the first molar from drifting forward.

Second molar is known as the 12-year molar and erupts distal to the first molar.

Third molar (*wisdom tooth*) is a reluctant relic of a tooth that appears as the last tooth along the dental arch and is often absent. It erupts at various stages and ages and often fails to erupt at all due to its impacted status. On rare occasions there may even be a fourth molar present.

Figure 3.15a shows the deciduous dentition, eruption, and shedding schedule and Figure 3.15b shows the permanent dentition and eruption schedule.

Miscellaneous Dental Anatomy

Torus/mandible/maxilla are bony extrusions usually found on the midline of the hard palate or the inner surface of the mandible. It is important to note that they are benign. Their greatest significance is that they will interfere with the design and construction of dentures that may be required in the same area and may have to be removed for that reason. They also may become irritated as a result of trauma from food.

Condyle/ramus are the vertical components of the mandible making the lower jaw the only "double-jointed" bone in the body. The condyles articulate on both sides with the cranium through the condylar fossa and are cushioned by the meniscus of the temporomandibular joint. This joint has been the focus of much attention in the dental community and remains an enigma with regard to treatment of various symptoms associated with its function.

Tongue function, size, and shape have been variously discussed as the cause of everything from malocclusion and speech defects to snoring and sleep apnea. The tongue has been pierced and surgerized for reasons ranging from sexuality to somnambulism. It is an organ of taste and sexual prowess. Its protrusion may be an indication of anything from disdain to thirst. In any case, it would be very difficult for us to do without it.

Palatal rugae (Figure 3.16) may be significant in the identification process. In cases where there are no teeth present or the teeth have been lost or destroyed, if a previous work or study model is available, the pattern of the palatal rugae may be the basis for comparison and therefore identification.

Malformation There are many genetic and unknown causes of dental-oral malformations, from lip pits to bilateral cleft of the lip and palate (Figure 3.17). Development of the mandible may be affected by everything from fetal position, genetics, and ankylosis, to trauma of the temporomandibular joint. In some cases the jaw will be too small, micrognathia (Figure 3.18). Also, in some cases the jaw may be too large to fit with the opposing jaw, prognathia (Figure 3.19). Individual teeth may be affected as well as the jaw.

Figure 3.16 Palatal rugae.

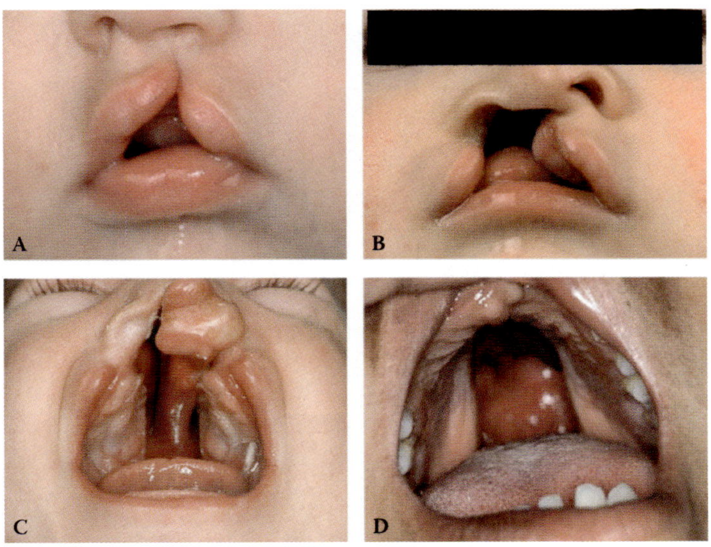

Figure 3.17 Clefts of lip and palate.

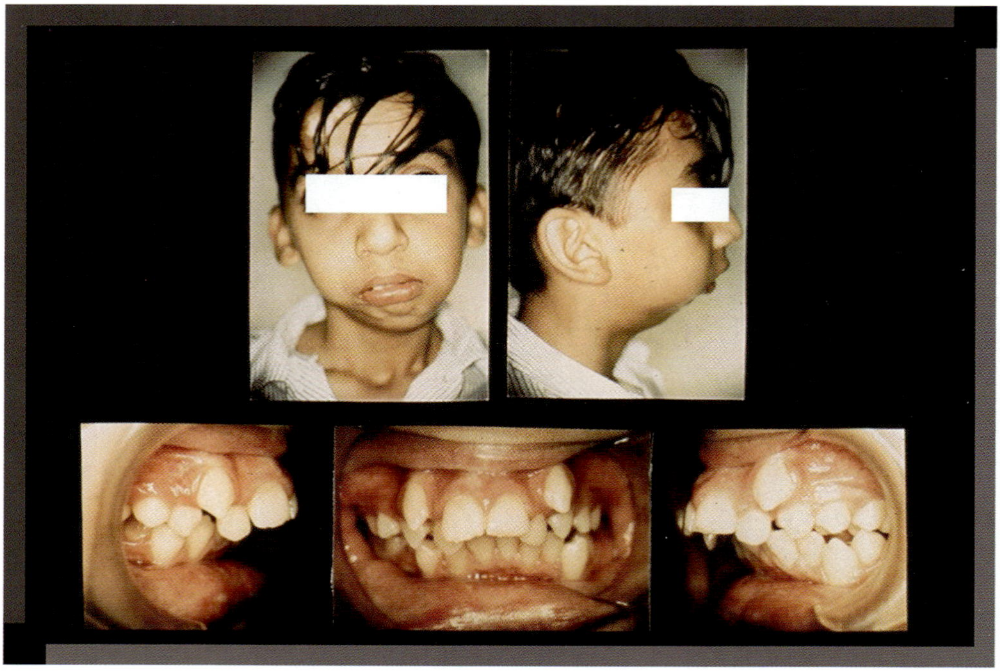

Figure 3.18 Micrognathia.

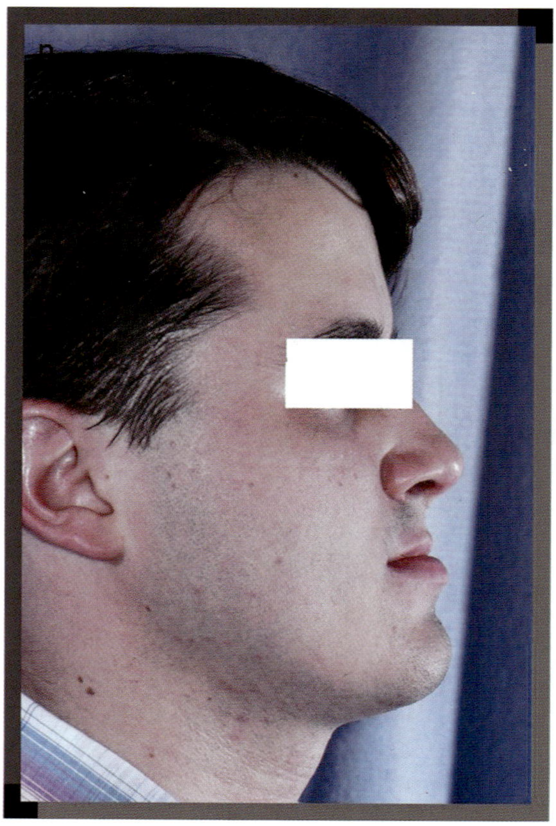

Figure 3.19 Prognathia.

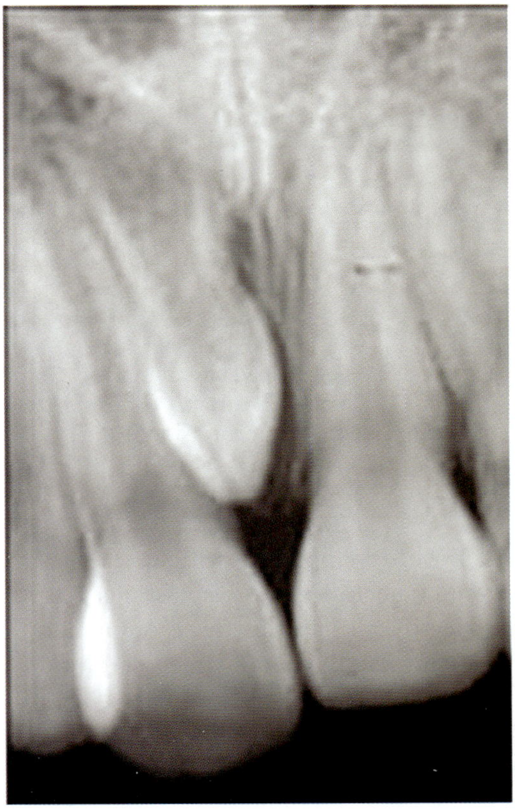

Figure 3.20 Mesiodens. (Courtesy of Dr. Charles Dunlap, *Abnormalities of Teeth*. Used with permission.)

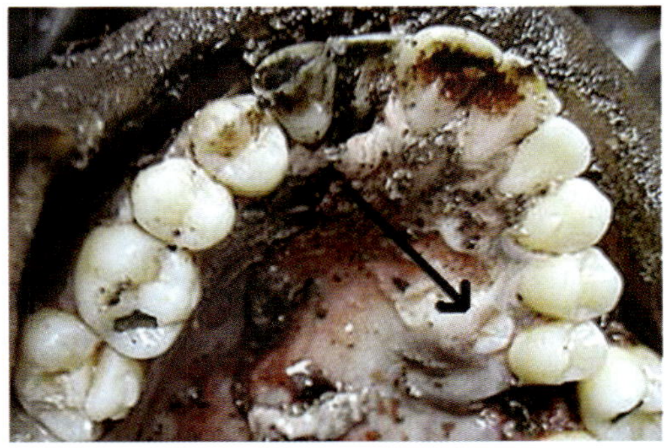

Figure 3.21 Supernumerary bicuspid (post-mortem). (Courtesy of the Miami Dade Medical Examiners office. Modified with permission.)

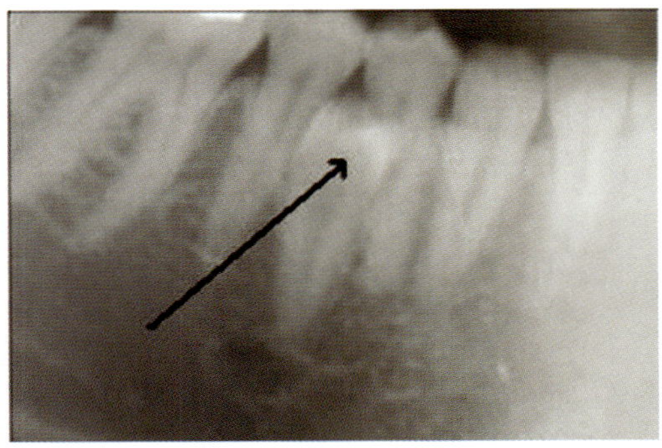

Figure 3.22 Supernumerary bicuspid x-ray. (Courtesy of Dr. Charles Dunlap, *Abnormalities of Teeth*. Used with permission.)

Supernumerary Teeth

Inherited developmental anomalies may alter the size, shape, and number of teeth. They are truly a reflection of Mendelian inheritance. The most common forms of supernumerary teeth (hyperdontia) are (in order of their occurrence):

Mesiodens, is a single tooth located in the midline between the upper central incisors (Figure 3.20).

Fourth molar, is an extra molar which is located in the area behind the "wisdom" tooth.

Bicuspid tooth, is usually found between the permanent first and second bicuspid teeth. This may be discovered after the jaw has been removed and the tissues are thoroughly cleaned (Figure 3.21) or only after the radiographs have been taken and carefully examined (Figure 3.22).

Lower anterior teeth are also prone to produce an extra tooth on occasion. The condition known as cleidocranial dysostosis will produce hyperdontia of great magnitude (50+ teeth) in addition to missing clavicles and short stature.

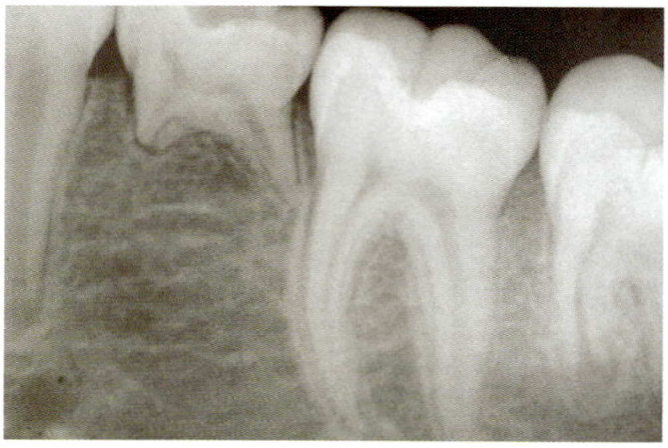

Figure 3.23 Congenitally missing bicuspid. (Courtesy of Dr. Charles Dunlap, *Abnormalities of Teeth*. Used with permission.)

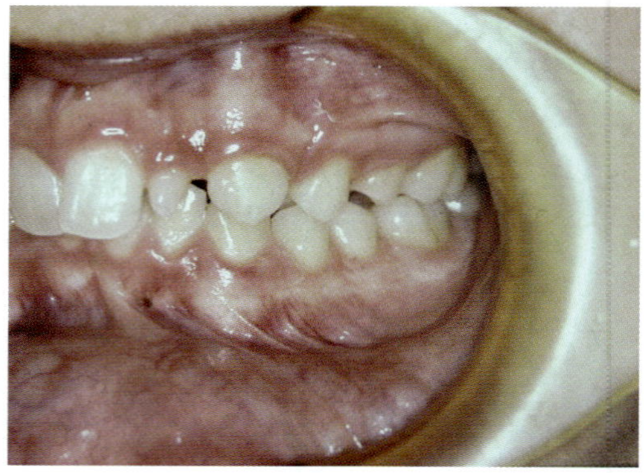

Figure 3.24 Peg-shaped lateral incisor. (Courtesy of Dr. Charles Dunlap, *Abnormalities of Teeth*. Used with permission.)

Congenital Absence of Teeth

Anodontia is the total congenital absence of tooth development, which is a very rare occurrence usually related to other systemic ectodermal dysplastic conditions. Ectodermal dysplasias will also produce dysplasia of teeth accompanied by malfunction of sweat glands, malformed fingernails, and sparse head hair, brows, and lashes.

Hypodontia (partial anodontia) is the congenital absence of six or fewer teeth.

Oligodontia is the congenital absence of more than six teeth.

Lower second bicuspid is usually accompanied by the overretention of the second deciduous molar (Figure 3.23). Often there is a "submerged" deciduous second molar present. This condition is unrelated to the absence of the permanent successor. Submerging teeth (usually deciduous molars) may occur even if the permanent tooth is present. The deciduous tooth is not submerging; actually, the surrounding teeth and alveolar bone continue to erupt leaving behind the ankylosed deciduous tooth that is anchored to the bone. This can become so exaggerated that the deciduous tooth will disappear below the gingiva and the teeth on either side will collapse towards each other.

Upper lateral incisor can be missing either unilaterally or bilaterally. Sometimes this condition will appear in a lesser form as a "peg-shaped" (microdontia) lateral incisor (Figure 3.24). This condition has a strong familial tendency and one should examine other family members for a similar condition.

Third molars (*wisdom teeth*) are commonly congenitally absent, which is usually of little concern because their presence typically causes more problems than solutions. If present, they are often impacted and require surgical removal.

Malformations

Fusion is the joining of two tooth germs during development to form one large tooth. This is discernable by counting the number of teeth in the group. Are there four lower anteriors or three? If there is a large tooth and two others then it is fusion.

If there is a large lower anterior tooth and three others, then it is *gemination* which occurs when one tooth attempts to form two teeth during development.

Age Changes in Natural Teeth

What happens to teeth during our lifetime will sometimes indicate a lifestyle or it may be symptomatic of various pathological conditions. All of these conditions may lead to a unique discovery in the comparison of missing and unidentified persons, which may result in a dental identification. In the formative years, age is more easily determined due to the formation, eruption, and shedding pattern, previously noted. However, the variety of development is so widespread that it is still difficult to establish a specific age, only a range. As a forensic odontologist we are often asked to make an estimate of age. This may be for purposes of immigration, criminal activity, or just in reference to the remains of an unknown person presented to us.

Remember: the younger, the easier and the older, the more difficult. So, when it comes to estimating age, you should adopt a narrow range in the younger and a wide range in the adult.

Attrition is the normal wear of the tooth surface. This may be caused by "grinding" of the teeth or the contact between natural tooth substance and the harder surface of porcelain restorations, such as crowns. In some instances the entire enamel surface will be worn enough to expose the underlying dentin.

Erosion is the chemical dissolution of tooth structure due to excessive acid such as in the regurgitation of gastric contents in bulemia (Figure 3.25) or the excessive intake of acidic foods such as lemon juice or cola drinks.

Abrasion describes beyond normal wear caused by mechanical forces such as a toothbrush. The term is usually applied when loss is on a non-biting surface, such as the gum line.

Internal resorption is an iodiopathic condition where one or more teeth may be involved and the resorption extends outward from the pulp chamber. The cause of this activity which invades the dentin from within the pulp chamber is unknown.

External resorption progresses from the outer surface of the apical or lateral surface of the tooth root. The cause is unknown but is often related to pressure from an adjoining (erupting) tooth or the excessive pressure of orthodontic movement. Root

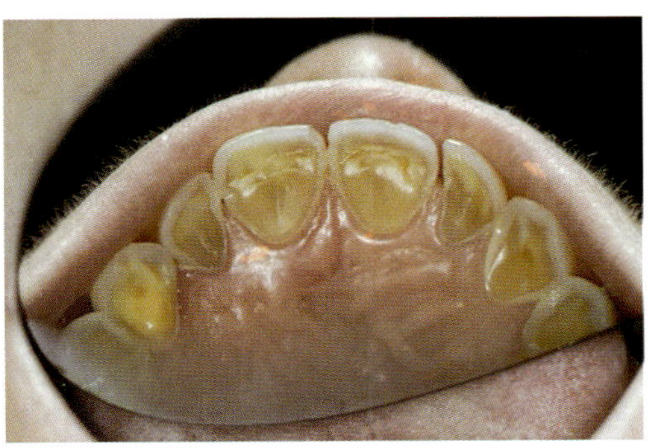

Figure 3.25 Bulimic erosion. (Courtesy of Dr. Charles Dunlap, *Abnormalities of Teeth*. Used with permission.)

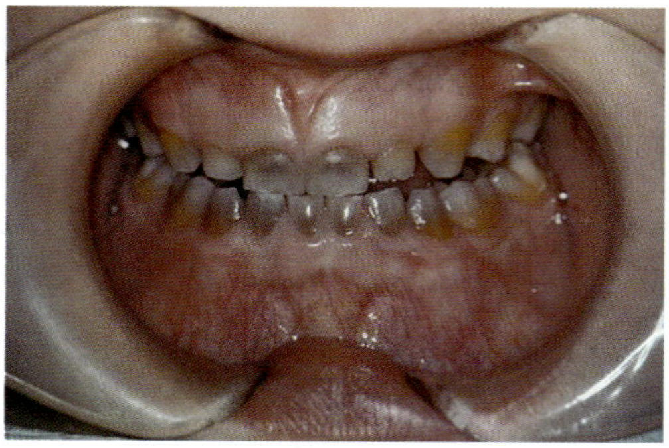

Figure 3.26 Tetracycline staining. (Courtesy of Dr. Charles Dunlap, *Abnormalities of Teeth*. Used with permission.)

tips may be shortened. Entire roots may be lost or there may just be cupping along the root surface invading the cementum and dentin. This may lead to ankylosis of the tooth which impedes further orthodontic movement and also any extraction.

Staining. Tetracycline may cause staining of all the teeth at a certain level depending upon the stage of tooth formation at the time of administration of the drug (Figure 3.26).

Positional relationships. Malocclusion is the relationship between the upper and lower jaws and/or teeth that if not treated orthodontically or surgically, will remain basically the same throughout life, thereby making a dependable mark of distinction for comparison and identification. For example, if you observe the absence of four first bicuspids and the presence of uncrowded Class I occlusion you may assume that the person had been treated by an orthodontist and you may wish to seek out these records for identification. If surgical bars or screws are in place in the jaw, you would search for the oral surgeon to obtain further records regarding a repair subsequent to an accident or perhaps orthognathic surgical procedures to correct jaw relationships.

Note: *Overbite* is the vertical component or the distance that the upper front teeth overlap the lower front teeth. A negative overbite would indicate an open bite relationship when the back teeth contact but the front teeth are apart. *Overjet* is the horizontal component or the distance that the upper front teeth protrude beyond the lower front teeth. A negative overjet would be used to describe the upper teeth as being behind the lower teeth instead of in front of the lower teeth.

Classification of Maloclusion

Class I (Figure 3.27a)

The upper cuspid and first molar occlude distal to its lower protagonist. There is no overjet but may have deep overbite or open bite and there is an irregular tooth arrangement.

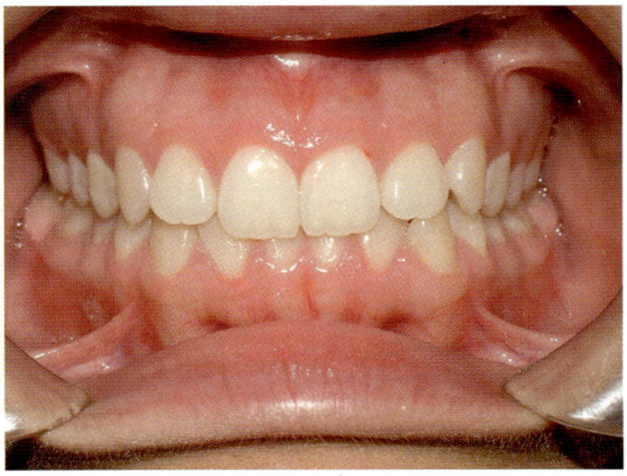

Figure 3.27a Class I occlusion. (Courtesy of Dr. Isaac Haber.)

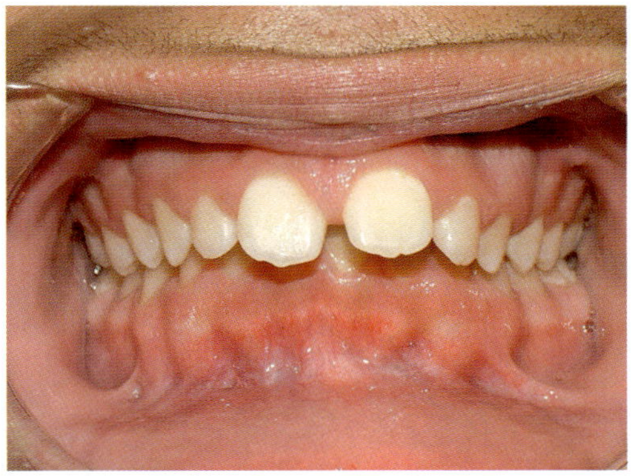

Figure 3.27b Class II malocclusion. (Courtesy of Dr. Isaac Haber.)

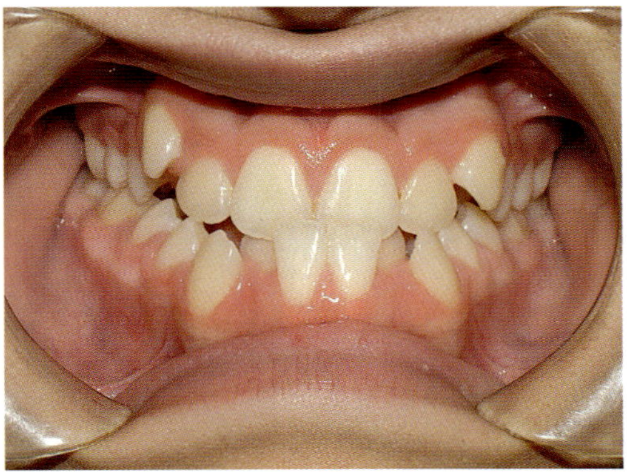

Figure 3.27c Class III malocclusion. (Courtesy of Dr. Isaac Haber. Used with permission.)

Class II (Figure 3.27b)

The upper cuspid and first molar are forward of their lower counterparts. There is an excessive overjet (protrusion) with either a deep or open vertical bite. In some cases there is a lingual version of upper centrals and protrusion of upper lateral incisors. This protrusion is commonly referred to as "buck teeth".

Class III (Figure 3.27c)

Upper cuspid occludes with lower first bicuspid. Upper first molar occludes with lower second molar. Lower jaw and anterior teeth protrude beyond upper anterior teeth. Commonly referred to as "lantern jaw".

The combination of dental characteristics is almost unlimited. If you take the number of surfaces (MODFL) on each tooth and the type of common (four) restorations (silver, gold, resin, porcelain), times the number of teeth (32) either present or absent it would equal possibilities in the billions.

Classification of Dental Remains

4

It is important that all professionals have a language that is common to their task. To someone on the outside it may appear as a foreign language, so the compromise is numbers. In forensic odontology the remains are presented in only three conditions: fresh, decomposed, or skeletal. Each of these conditions may be whole or fragmented. Thus we have a "Classification."

Class I Fresh
- A. Whole
- B. Fragmented

Class II Decomposed/Incinerated
- A. Whole
- B. Fragmented

Class III Skeletal
- A. Whole
- B. Fragmented

Class I Fresh

A. Whole

This is when the face and dental structures are intact and viewable (V); (Figure 4.1). The cause of death may be unrelated to the facial area and therefore the face is in its normal state, and may be viewed by the next of kin. Severe trauma to other parts of the body,

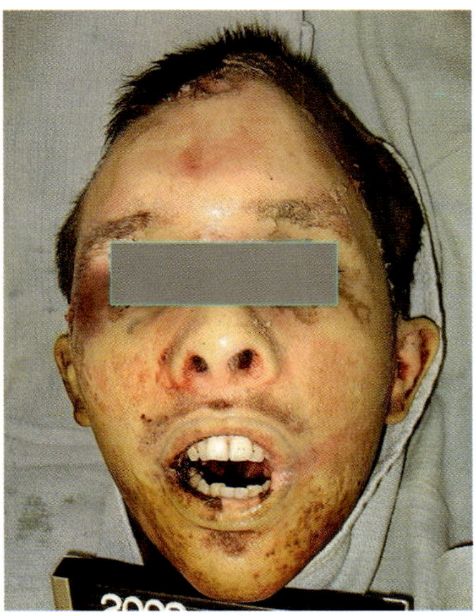

Figure 4.1 Class I(A): fresh/whole. (Courtesy of the Miami Dade Medical Examiners office. Used with permission.)

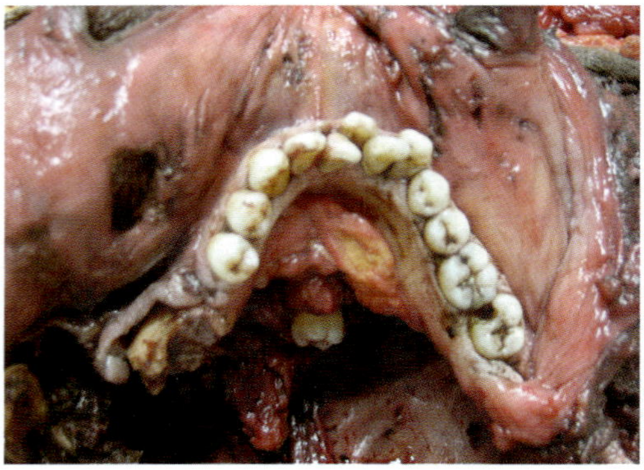

Figure 4.2a Class I(B): fresh/fragmented (jaw). (Courtesy of the Miami Dade Medical Examiners office. Used with permission.)

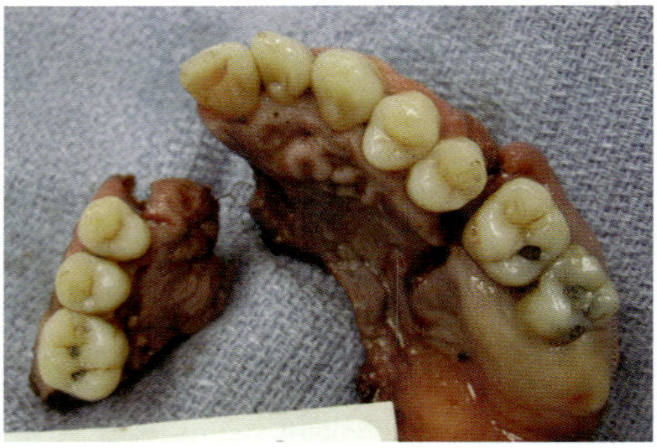

Figure 4.2b Class I(B): fresh/fragmented (jaw pieces). (Courtesy of the Miami Dade Medical Examiners office. Used with permission.)

bullet or knife wounds, and introduction of substances, such as drugs, that would affect the integrity or function of the body, may be involved. In Class I, A the forensic odontologist must not apply any procedure that would affect the integrity of the facial appearance. Examination of the dentition must proceed with normal manual retraction for viewing the dental arches so that all facial features will remain intact.

Non-viewable (NV) Class I A instances would not allow viewing of the deceased by the next of kin. Mutilation of the facial features by gunshot without damage to the oral structures or blunt force trauma to the head by physical battery or automobile accident without destruction of the dentition, would be in the same Class I A category because the skin is fresh and the dentition is intact. Surgical intervention by the forensic odontologist in these cases is warranted for disclosure of the dentition and full examination.

B. Fragmented

In mass fatality incidents such as an airline crash, bombing, or train wreck, when there is no fire or immersion in water for a period of time, the tissues may be fresh but the dental arches have been fragmented into many pieces and scattered over a large area. This may also be true for the individual involved in an automobile accident or one who fell or jumped from a great height when the only destructive force is blunt force trauma brought on by the accident or another individual. In either case the dental arch is fragmented and at times some portion of the dental arch may be entirely missing. Every attempt should be made to discover the missing parts in the body bag, the body cavity, or the crime scene. However, many identifications have been made just on the basis of one or two teeth when the population of suspects is limited, as in an airplane disaster with a passenger list (Figure 4.2a,b).

Class II Decomposed/Incinerated

A. Whole: Fire, water, time, temperature, insect, or animal destruction

Immersion in water is destructive by virtue of the bloating and distension of the tissues (Figure 4.3a). Time and temperature are also factors because higher temperatures will cause greater destruction of the tissues within a shorter period of time. Surgical removal of overlying tissue, is usually necessary and at times jaw removal is also required.

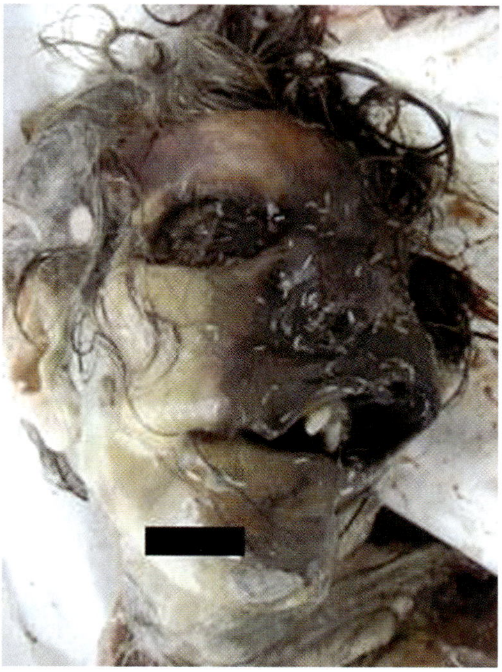

Figure 4.3a Class II(A): decomposed/whole. (Courtesy of the Miami Dade Medical Examiners office. Used with permission.)

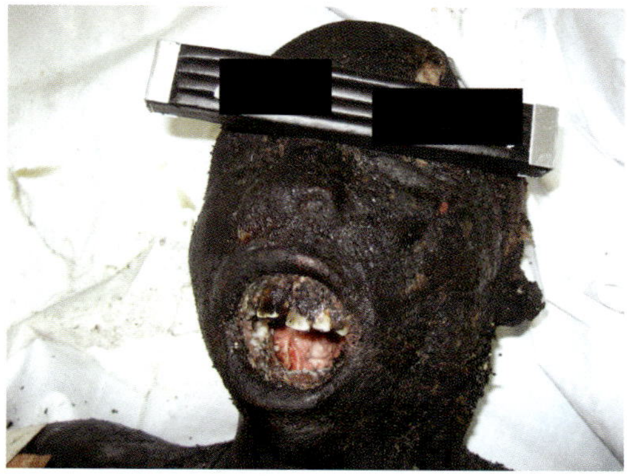

Figure 4.3b Class II(A): incinerated/whole. (Courtesy of the Miami Dade Medical Examiners office. Used with permission.)

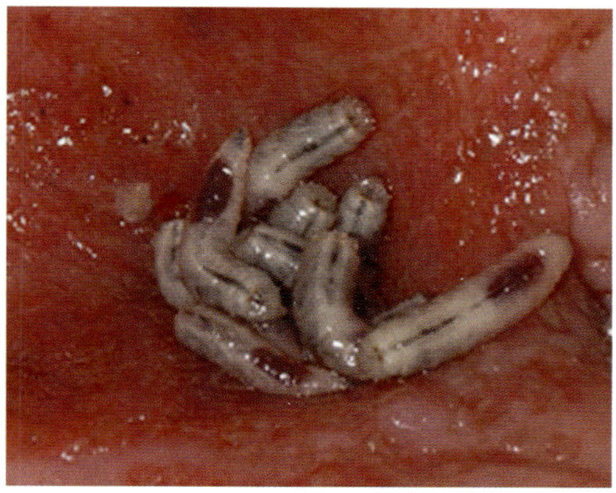

Figure 4.3c Class II(A): maggots. (Courtesy of the Miami Dade Medical Examiners office. Used with permission.)

Fire is the most common destructive force (Figure 4.3b). In automobile accidents, airline crashes, house fires, and mass disaster situations, all soft tissue features are destroyed. If the fire is intense, the anterior teeth are often carbonized and useless for identification. However, the posterior teeth, which are well protected by the buccal fat pad and the cheeks, are usually available in decent condition for examination. In this instance, surgical removal of tissue surrounding the teeth is required. If jaw removal is desired, then removal of the mandible alone should be sufficient for a clear examination of upper and lower teeth. Sometimes removal of both jaws is required as evidence or previous to burial with cremation. In any case, removal of jaws requires the prior approval of the medical examiner/coroner in charge.

After the body has been exposed to the air for a period of time it is subject to deterioration by insects, such as flies and maggots. The giant maggots eat necrotic tissue and then turn into flies again, only to repeat the life cycle and continue the deterioration of the exposed remains. This ingestion of necrotic tissue has been advantageous to the medical profession by employing the disinfected maggots in Maggot Debridement Therapy (MDT) for the treatment of nonhealing wounds (Figure 4.3c).

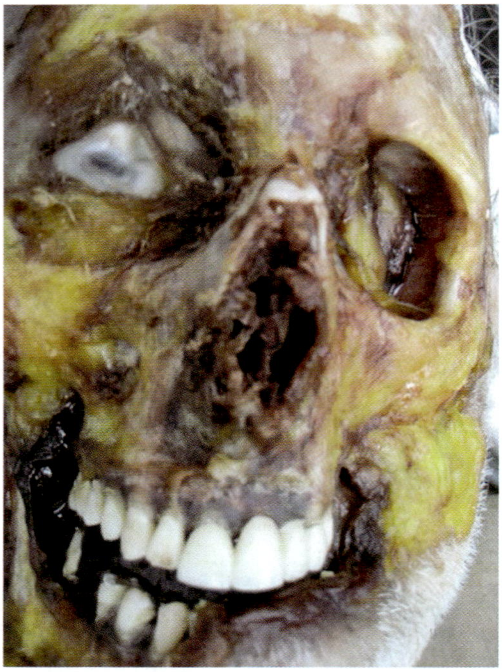

Figure 4.3d Class II(A): decomposed/whole (animal feeding).

Animal activity will cause the destruction of soft tissue. Human remains that are left undiscovered in a space shared by a pet or left in the open field will soon be devoured (Figure 4.3d).

Once the human body has been buried, the natural process of decay takes place subject to body preparation and internment, according to customs of various cultures. Embalming will assist in only slowing the process. The absence of a concrete vault in which the coffin is contained will usually allow the invasion of insects. Contact with the soil will change the chemical balance and sometimes produce mummification or saponification.

This only becomes evident when it is necessary to exhume the body for further examination or, in the case of area flooding during Hurricane Kartrina, the body comes out of the ground or out of the aboveground crypts (Figure 4.3e) and has to be retrieved and examined for reburial. Mummification will cause the skin to become almost leatherlike and the body will appear more lifelike. Examination of Egyptian mummies will verify this process. Saponification involves the conversion of fatty tissue. This process occurs only weeks after burial where the burial ground is particularly alkaline. It is a white waxy substance and is produced when bacteria and enzymes break down these fats into fatty acids and soaps. Corpses kept in plastic bags will undergo the same adipocere formation and the outer layers of the skin will slough off.

B. Fragmented

The fragmented decomposed remains are usually the result of trauma. The fragmentation or scatter may take place prior to or subsequent to the decomposition. The force of an automobile or airplane crash, explosives, or bombing, and the ensuing fire will cause vast destruction of tissue and the explosion of body parts (Figure 4.4a,b). Gunshot wounds to

Figure 4.3e Class II(A): Hurricane Katrina-exhumed crypts.

Figure 4.4a Class II(B): incinerated/fragmented. (Courtesy of the Miami Dade Medical Examiners office. Used with permission.)

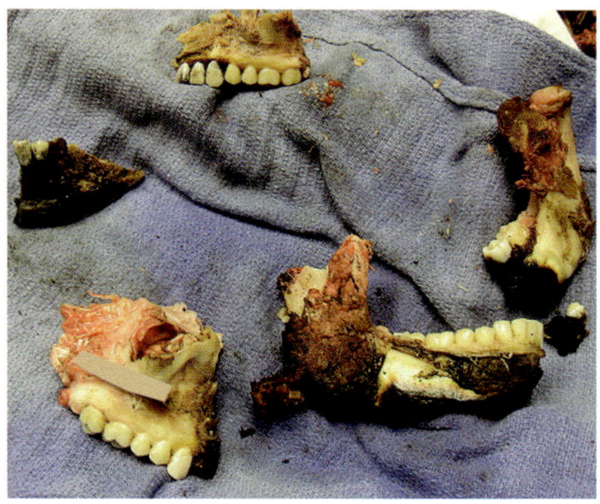

Figure 4.4b Class II(B): incinerated/fragmented (jaw pieces). (Courtesy of the Miami Dade Medical Examiners office. Used with permission.)

the oral cavity, by choice or by chance, will have similar results. Human remains left in the presence of animals, at home, or in the wild, will be subject to marauding and scattering which causes the fragmentation. Marine animals, such as sharks or alligators, may cause similar damage to bodies that remain immersed for periods of time.

Class III Skeletal

A. Whole

An entire skeleton is an interesting find (Figure 4.5). The time of death may vary widely depending upon the local climate. A body left out in the warmth and moisture of the Florida Everglades will be skeletonized in a month, long before a body found during the winter in Wyoming. In fact, a body left out in the open in Alaska or in a dry desert may

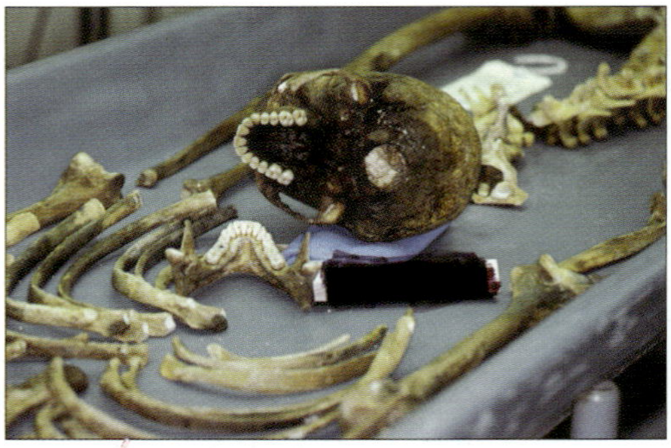

Figure 4.5 Class III(A): skeletal/whole. (Courtesy of the Miami Dade Medical Examiners office. Used with permission.)

only mummify and never skeletonize. Popular understanding is that all bodies become skeletons, but exhumation of ancient tombs and aboveground crypts in Louisiana belie that assumption. Processing of remains as well as climatic circumstances of time and temperature will produce different results. The whole skeleton will read like a book to one who is skilled in anthropology and osteology. The forensic odontologist should easily read these chapters related to the skull to determine age, gender, community placement, or ancestry, and proceed to full examination of the dental arches for comparison of unidentified and missing persons. Perhaps the singular problem with skeletal remains is the lack of soft tissue components to keep the teeth in place. If not handled in a careful manner, teeth may be lost, greatly hindering the comparison procedure. Any individual teeth that may be found should be placed in an evidence bag and should travel with the body. These teeth should be set in their proper place by a competent forensic dentist. Sometimes it is advisable to place a plastic bag over the head at the scene to prevent the loss of any loose teeth or removable prostheses during transportation to the morgue.

B. Fragmented

Fragmented skeletal remains may be produced by mechanical, animal, or premeditated human behavior (Figure 4.6). Construction sites and woods are the most popular habitats for fragmented remains. Discovery of a mandible and a cranium do not necessarily

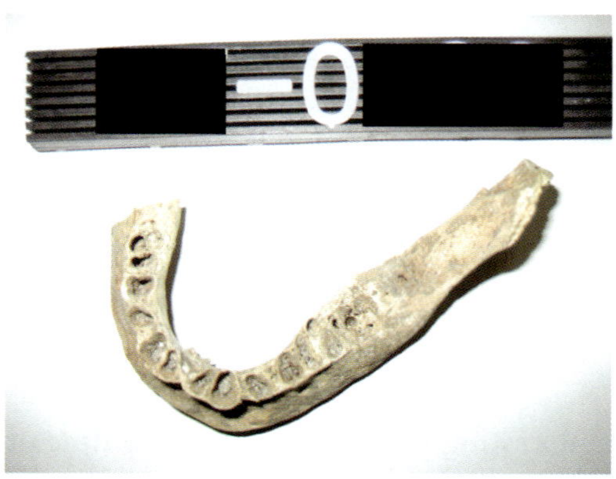

Figure 4.6 Class III(B): skeletal/fragment. (Courtesy of the Miami Dade Medical Examiners office. Used with permission.)

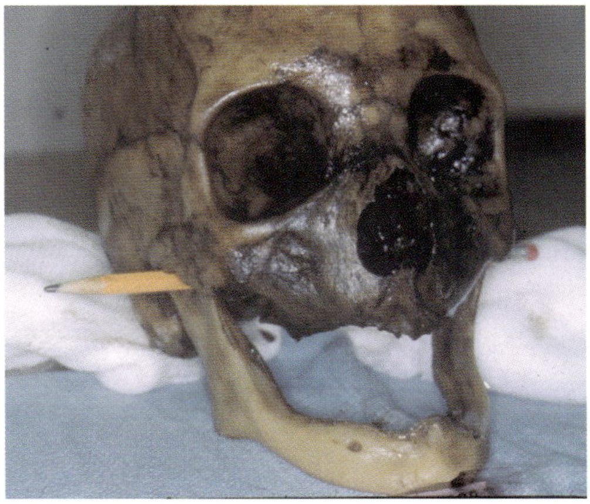

Figure 4.7 Edentulous jaws with pencil. (Courtesy of the Miami Dade Medical Examiners office. Used with permission.)

indicate the presence of one body until the jaws are matched. Any mismatch will only lead to the conclusion that there may be two bodies, not one, and the search will continue. Fragmented skeletal remains must be examined even more closely due to lack of clues as to the presumptive identity and the lack of supporting evidence. Unique features of root and alveolar bone formation or sinus anatomy may all be applicable features used in comparison.

At times the discovery may be of an edentulous person, which presents problems of orientation as to the true relationship of the jaws. One method recommended to orient edentulous jaws is by passing a pencil across the mandibular notch (Figure 4.7).

Dealing with family is a delicate issue which is best left to the investigative and administrative staff of the medical examiner or coroner department. Fresh remains may be viewable (V) or may not (NV) be viewable by NOK (Next of Kin), depending upon the condition of the remains. That is a decision that is made by the medical examiner or coroner and the investigative staff. In most cases a photographic presentation is sufficient and less traumatic. Funeral directors and mortuary staff are quite skilled in restoration of facial features that may have been destroyed or altered. This is accomplished for viewing the decedent at the time of a funeral. Naturally, decomposed, fragmented, and skeletal remains are not viewable by the next of kin.

Role of Dental Professionals

5

The general dentist has a principal role in the antemortem and postmortem phases of identification as custodian of the patient records (Figure 5.1a,b). Unfortunately, some dentists are under the false impression that all original dental records must remain in his or her custody and control. It is true that the records must be retained by the practicing dentist and then passed on to another custodian of records. This is for the protection of the dentist in the event that there is any question regarding treatment procedures, or medications prescribed, and also would protect the dentist against any accusation of malpractice. This is also of benefit to the patient, especially in the realm of identification and also for the transfer of records if the patient chooses to go to a new dentist or if the dentist ceases to practice. The dentist may preserve the patient record by copying the record but according to state law the dentist must provide the original patient record to the requesting agency, whether it is the medical examiner/coroner (ME/C) or a law enforcement agency.

With regard to unidentified persons, it is the ME/C who requests records for identification. For the missing person, it is usually the law enforcement agency who requests records in order to enter them into the NCIC database for possible matching. It is important for the family of the missing person to submit these records as soon as possible, so that law enforcement will have these on file and they will not have to remind the family again whenever there is a possible identification. The original records may be returned to the dentist if requested by the dentist or by the family, after the dental identification is completed or, in the case of a criminal trial, adjudication has been made. It is usually advisable for the forensic odontologist or ME/C to retain these records indefinitely, especially in cases when the remains are still unidentified or if there is any indication that there will be a trial. In the event that the dentist refuses to deliver the records promptly, a subpoena would be served and any failure to obey would then result in a contempt of court citation (Appendix, Figure A.6).

Role of Dental Practitioner
Antemortem

Maintain complete record of existing conditions

Chart all existing restorations and unusual conditions

Note missing, unerupted and supernumerary teeth

Add all new restorations, including material

Maintain records indefinitely–digital

Figure 5.1a Role of a dental practitioner (antemortem).

Role of Dental Practitioner
Postmortem

Maintain complete record of existing conditions

Chart all existing restorations

Note missing, unerupted and supernumerary teeth

Chart all new restorations, including materials

Maintain records indefinitely–digital systems

Figure 5.1b Role of a dental practitioner (postmortem).

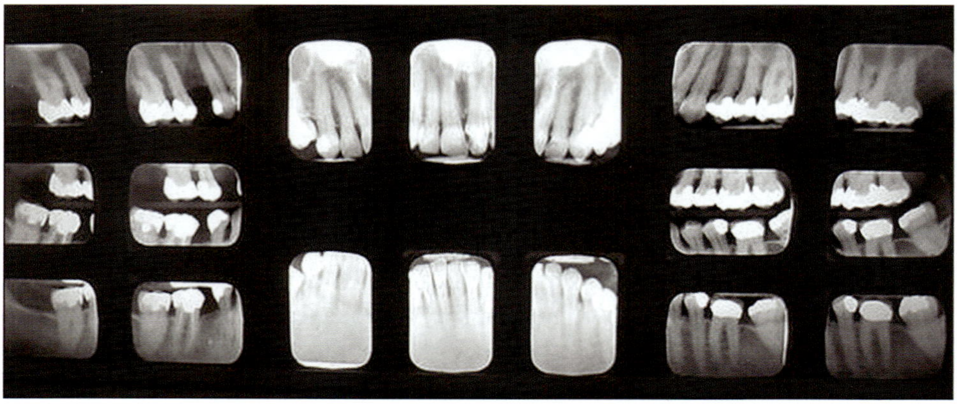

Figure 5.2a Full mouth series of radiographs.

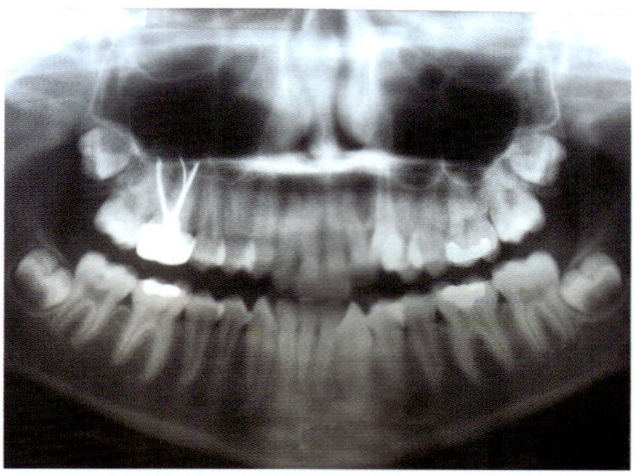

Figure 5.2b Panoramic radiograph. Note: three lower anteriors.

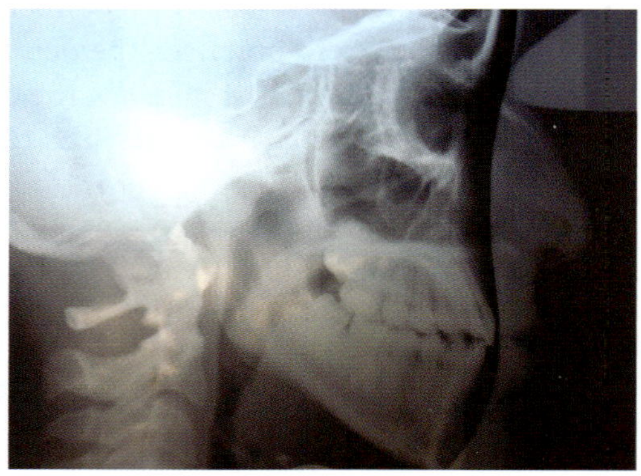

Figure 5.2c Cephalometric radiograph with soft tissue outline.

Records may be gathered from dentist, especially in the event that there were multiple procedures performed and specialty referral was made to an endodontist, oral surgeon, or orthodontist. A complete set of records would consist of:

1. Periapical and bitewing radiographs and, if available, panographic and cephalometric radiographs (Figure 5.2a–c)
2. Models, laboratory or diagnostic (Figure 5.3)
3. Photographs, face and/or dentition (Figure 5.4)
4. Dental charts and/or narrative reports locating all restorations, position, and material

This may include planned as well as actual treatment (Figure 5.5). Do not be confused by charts that may contain both. And be aware that there are times when restorations are inaccurately recorded or not recorded at all in the haste of the dentist's daily operation. On the other hand, writing in restorations and making charges for work not received may be just plain fraud, or maybe it was meant to be in the area of planned work. Be very careful and be understanding as well.

The dentist, together with the family, can be essential to the entire investigation of the unknown person. The investigative staff of the ME/C office should be aware of the

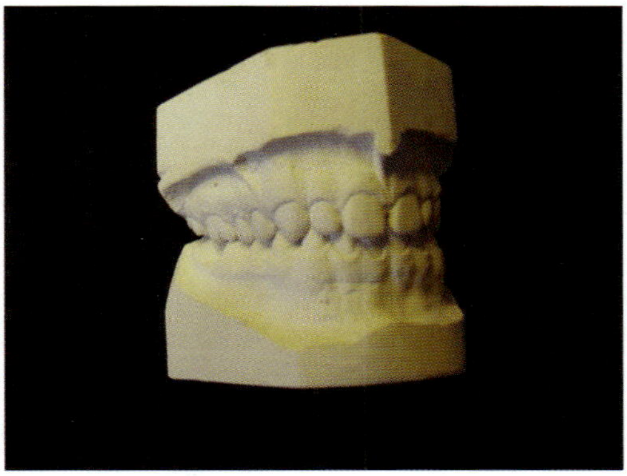

Figure 5.3 Stone model.

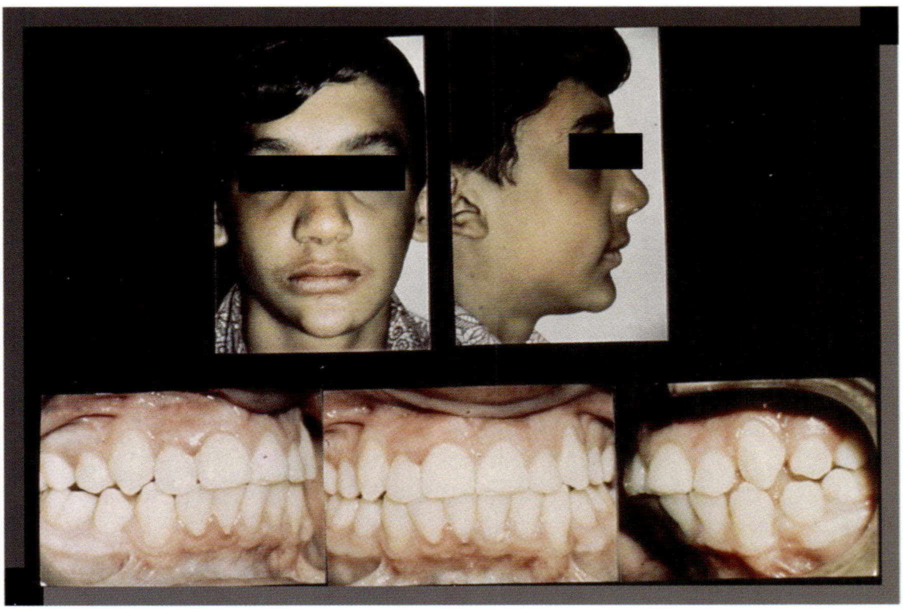

Figure 5.4 Facial and dental photographs.

tremendous contribution that is made by the dental profession. Dental identifications are accurate, less time consuming, and inexpensive. Notations of unique dental findings, for example, "grilles" (Figure 5.6) or anterior teeth mutilations and unique gold crowns as well as simple chips can be sufficient identification when dental records are not available or not of evidentiary quality.

Often the identity is only presumed and it is necessary to confirm the identity to satisfy the needs of the family, the insurance company, or other interested parties. Sometimes the person does not have a dentist or the dentist is unknown by the family. If the dentist does not have the dental record, then photographs of the decedent, in wide smile, are very helpful as are tattoos; body, tongue, and lip piercings; or dental mutilations (Figure 5.7a–d). Records of referrals to specialists (orthodontists, oral surgeons, endodontists) could provide further information. The presence of orthodontic

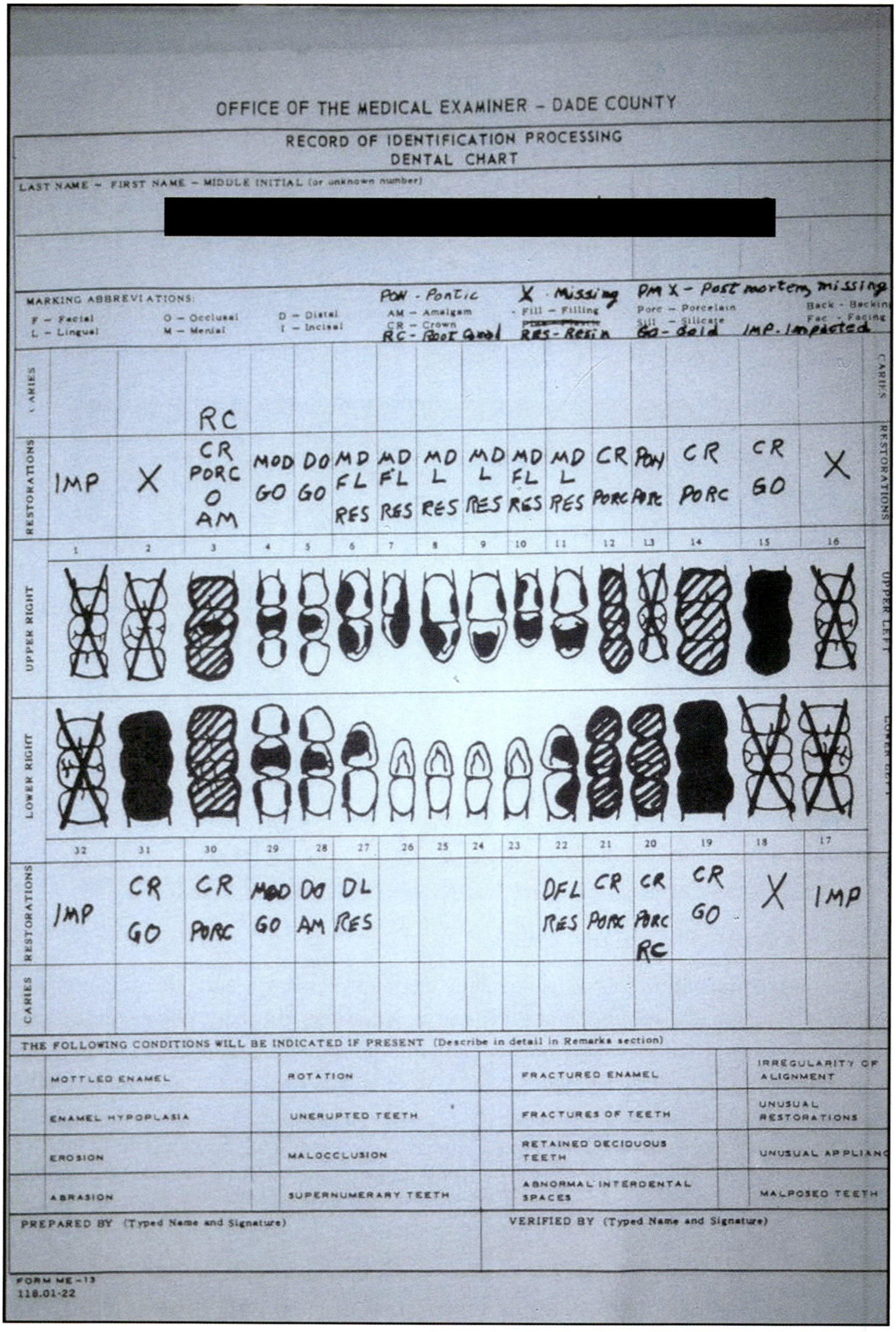

OFFICE OF THE MEDICAL EXAMINER - DADE COUNTY

RECORD OF IDENTIFICATION PROCESSING

DENTAL CHART

LAST NAME - FIRST NAME - MIDDLE INITIAL (or unknown number)

[redacted]

MARKING ABBREVIATIONS:
F - Facial
L - Lingual
O - Occlusal
M - Mesial
D - Distal
I - Incisal
PON - Pontic
AM - Amalgam
CR - Crown
RC - Root Canal
X - Missing
Fill - Filling
RES - Resin
PM X - Post mortem missing
Porc - Porcelain
Sili - Silicate
GO - Gold
Back - Backing
Fac - Facing
IMP - Impacted

Upper	1	2	3	4	5	6	7	8	9	10	11	12	13	14	15	16
CARIES																
RESTORATIONS	IMP	X	RC CR PORC O AM	MOD GO	DO GO	MD FL RES	MD FL RES	MD L RES	MD L RES	MD FL RES	MD L RES	CR PORC	PON PORC	CR PORC	CR GO	X

UPPER RIGHT — UPPER LEFT

LOWER RIGHT — LOWER LEFT

Lower	32	31	30	29	28	27	26	25	24	23	22	21	20	19	18	17
RESTORATIONS	IMP	CR GO	CR PORC	MOD GO	DO AM	DL RES					DFL RES	CR PORC	CR PORC RC	CR GO	X	IMP
CARIES																

THE FOLLOWING CONDITIONS WILL BE INDICATED IF PRESENT (Describe in detail in Remarks section)

MOTTLED ENAMEL	ROTATION	FRACTURED ENAMEL	IRREGULARITY OF ALIGNMENT
ENAMEL HYPOPLASIA	UNERUPTED TEETH	FRACTURES OF TEETH	UNUSUAL RESTORATIONS
EROSION	MALOCCLUSION	RETAINED DECIDUOUS TEETH	UNUSUAL APPLIANC
ABRASION	SUPERNUMERARY TEETH	ABNORMAL INTERDENTAL SPACES	MALPOSED TEETH

PREPARED BY (Typed Name and Signature)

VERIFIED BY (Typed Name and Signature)

FORM ME-13
118.01-22

Figure 5.5 Dental chart (filled in).

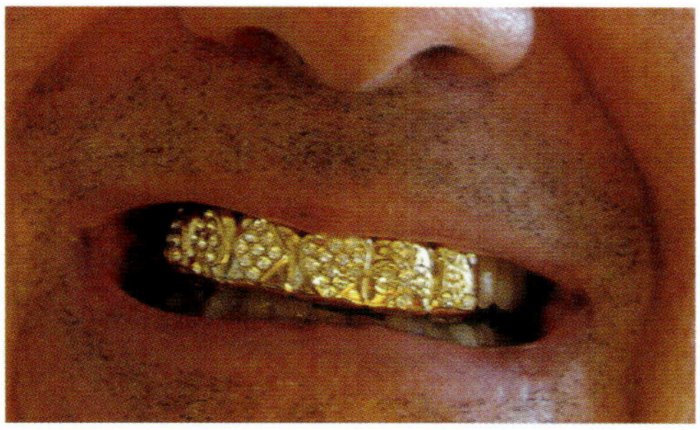

Figure 5.6 Removable grille.

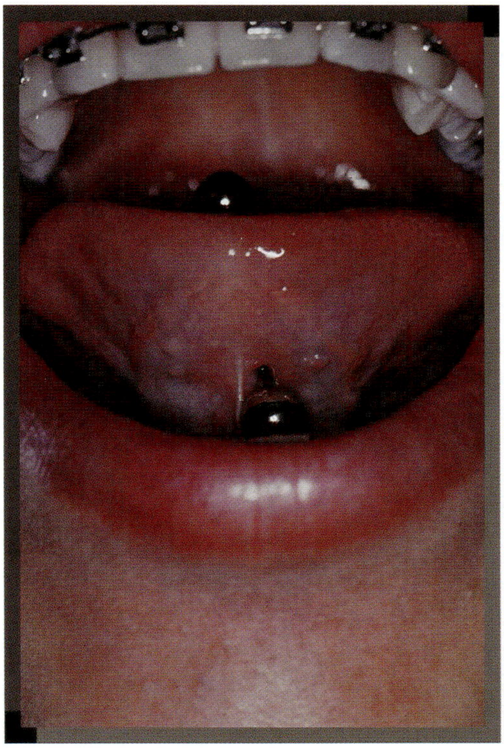

Figure 5.7a Tongue piercing.

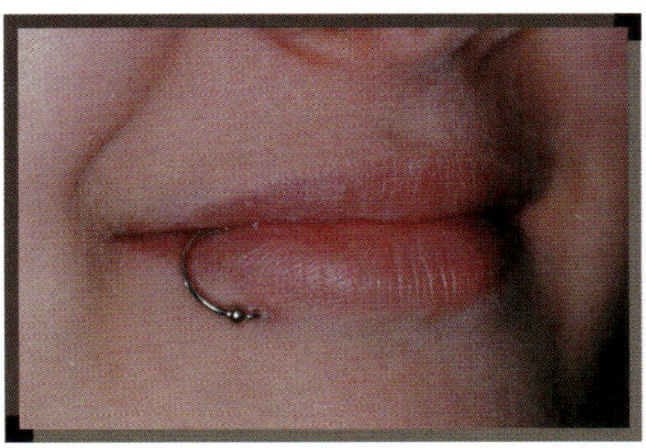

Figure 5.7b Lip piercing.

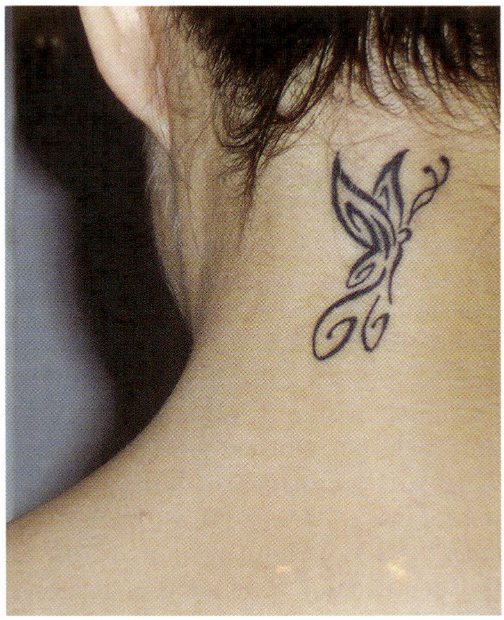

Figure 5.7c Small tattoo.

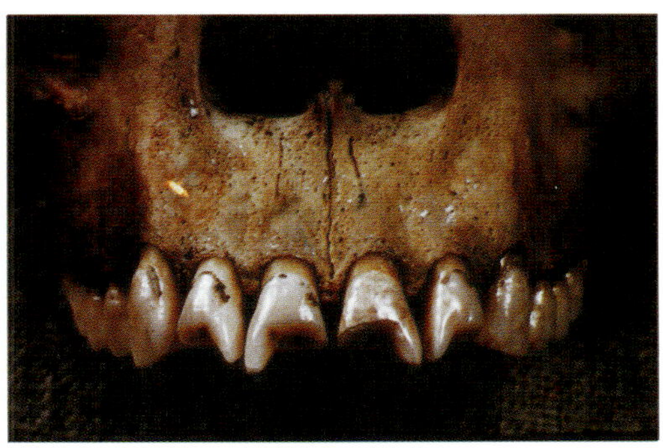

Figure 5.7d Mutilation. (Courtesy of the Miami Dade Medical Examiners office. Used with permission.)

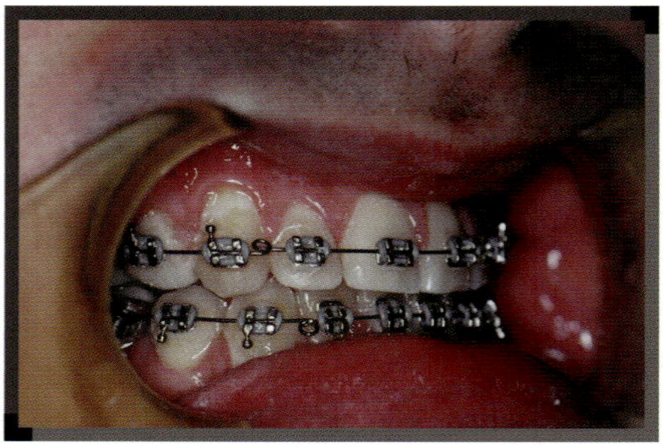

Figure 5.8 Braces.

appliances, "braces" (Figure 5.8), will provide good clues to further investigation in the dental community.

The general dentist and staff of the decedent are usually excluded from the postmortem examination due to the close relationship established between them and their patient. Upon interview, they will supply vital information regarding the dental condition of their patient. The dental hygienist and the dental assistant play a very important role in the identification process.

Evidence obtained from dental hygienists can be very important. Records of periodontal conditions, staining, and good charting of all teeth are critical. Records of prophylactic cleaning sessions are related to the patient history. Frequently the dental hygienist will be able to provide more information than the dentist because of the close relationships that have been established over the years. There are many opportunities for the dental assistant to record the procedures accurately on the patient's chart at chairside. Good records depend upon good recording. Good identification depends upon good recording. Not only do dental assistants work in the office, but they and the dental hygienists are invaluable during the postmortem procedures. They are skilled in taking radiographs and charting, which are essential parts of the autopsy procedure. They are often called upon to assist the forensic odontologist at the morgue. They are especially valuable during times of mass disaster when many more hands and minds are needed. The dental team is vital in the identification of remains and in the collection of evidence during the investigation of death.

The forensic odontologist is obliged not to work alone. All recording should be done in pairs—one looking over the shoulder of the other—to prevent mistakes. The task of radiography cannot be accomplished alone. It is essential to have "shooters" who take the x-ray, " locators" who set the recording film or sensor, and the "recorder" who fills out the chart. These positions do not necessarily have to be filled by forensic odontologists. Dental assistants and dental hygienists are skilled in these everyday tasks. This rule applies, especially in bitemark cases, when all opinions should be blind-reviewed by other forensic odontologists before making a final report.

Instrumentation

6

Before we enter the building where the morgue is located all must be in readiness. Either we bring the essential instruments and supplies with us in the ubiquitous "ready bags," (Figure 6.1a,b), or they must be immediately available, clean, and properly set out at our facility. There are two basic setups: first and most frequent are the means for identification. Second, and less frequent, are the supplies for bitemark examination.

The morgue in Miami Dade County is basically divided into two sections, the regular morgue (Figure 6.2a) and the "decomp" area which is set up the same as the morgue but only has two autopsy stations compared to about 12 in the main area. Each section has its own entry area, its own coolers for body storage (Figure 6.2b), and work areas. The area for decomposing bodies has extra air conditioning and ventilating systems, and

Figure 6.1a Ready bag.

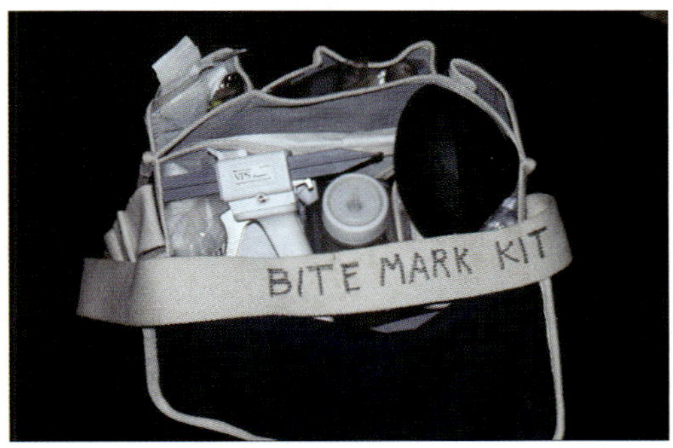

Figure 6.1b Bitemark ready bag.

Figure 6.2a Miami Dade Medical Examiner morgue. (Courtesy of the Miami Dade Medical Examiners office. Used with permission.)

Figure 6.2b Miami Dade Medical Examiner morgue (main cooler/body storage). (Courtesy of the Miami Dade Medical Examiners office. Used with permission.)

a wall-mounted dental x-ray unit is available. A separate dental room is adjacent to the main morgue work area and is fully equipped with fixed and portable x-ray machines, lights, all instrumentation, and a computer and scanner mounted on a cart that can be moved to the decomp area, if necessary. In addition, there is a portable high-intensity lamp and an eyewash station for emergencies. Of course, there is sufficient room for a body on a gurney to be rolled into the dental room area for examination.

It should be noted that access to the morgue facility is limited to those who have reason to be there and have been properly cleared. Persons under 18 years of age are not permitted. For the purpose of security, a magnetic card system may be employed that would open access to everything from the parking lot gate to the morgues and every door in the building. There is much sensitive material present, and unauthorized persons may attempt entry for any nefarious purpose. Photographs and other evidence have great value within the morgue area and the chain of evidence must be well protected. Unfortunately, their monetary value may increase a hundredfold on the outside. Passage of the Earnhardt Law (Appendix, Figure A.5) in Florida was essentially for the purpose of preventing any information from leaving the precincts of the medical examiner/coroner (ME/C) department. Individuals, as well as media, are prevented from obtaining access to this information without reason—approved by the courts—and may not distribute this to the public.

To begin, every set of remains will have a toe tag (Figure 6.3a) which contains the identification, if available or presumed, and also the case number assigned by the medical examiner department. Every set of remains would be in a body bag (Figure 6.3b), mounted on a portable plastic gurney with room for clothing and other effects to be carried below. The ME/C numbers will be matched to labels (Figure 6.3c) created by a label machine for use on rulers, charts, photos, x-rays, and digital cards, if any. The numbers may come in different sizes according to their application, particularly in photography, and the labels are self-adhesive. It is critical that every photo be identified within the photographic frame

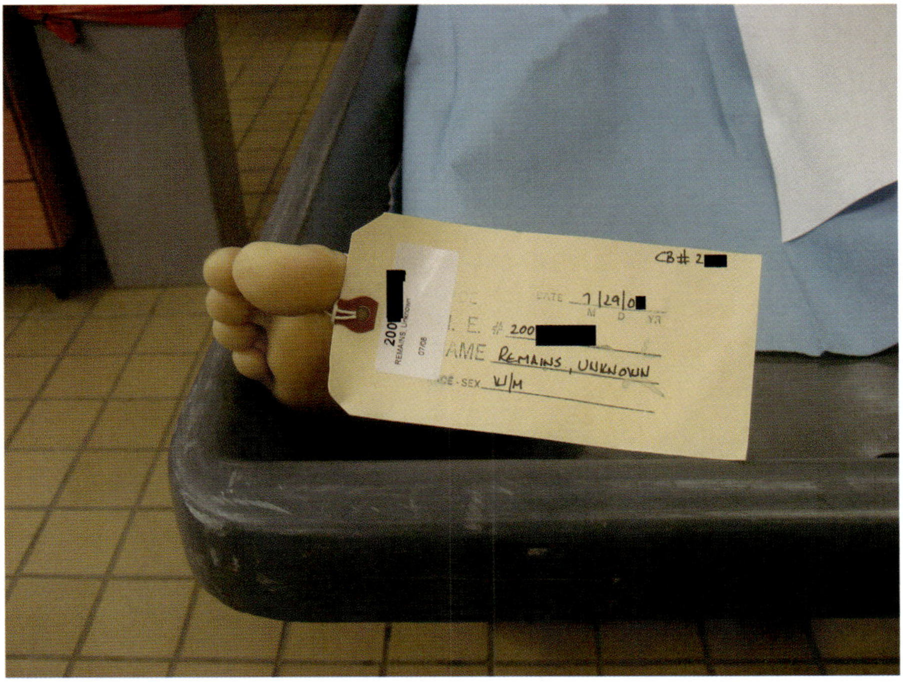

Figure 6.3a Toe tag. (Courtesy of the Miami Dade Medical Examiners office. Used with permission.)

and that the number correspond with the ME/C number on the toe tag. The ruler, usually an ABFO#2, is important for the purpose of creating an accurate 1:1, lifesize, photographic representation of the evidence at a later date. When the body arrives at the entry point there is a platform (Figure 6.4) where the remains are photographed and the height and weight are taken. The clothing is removed and any valuables are properly recorded and secured. The body is then placed in the cooler until the medical examiner is ready to perform the autopsy.

Note: A medical examiner is an MD or DO who performs the autopsy, whereas a coroner may be an MD, DO, or a lay person who is elected to that office and then appoints a medical examiner to perform the autopsy.

The dental autopsy is usually performed by the forensic odontologist, after the medical autopsy, but may be performed before the medical autopsy, if scheduling permits.

When the forensic odontologist arrives everything is ready. The high-intensity light (Figure 6.5) is properly positioned. The fixed, wall-mounted dental x-ray machine (Figure 6.6a) is properly adjusted for suitable radiographs and double-packet x-ray film is available. Radiographs may be developed at the dentist's office, as most ME/C offices do not maintain x-ray developing tanks and chemicals, due to the infrequent occasions when they may be needed. This is one of the strongest imperatives for the institution of digital radiography for the forensic odontologist in the ME/C office, especially with the NOMAD portable x-ray machine (Figure 6.6b,c; see http://www.aribex.com). Instead of waiting to develop the film at the ME/C office, or bringing the film back to the dental office only to discover that the image is not satisfactory, the digital x-ray image is produced in seconds on the

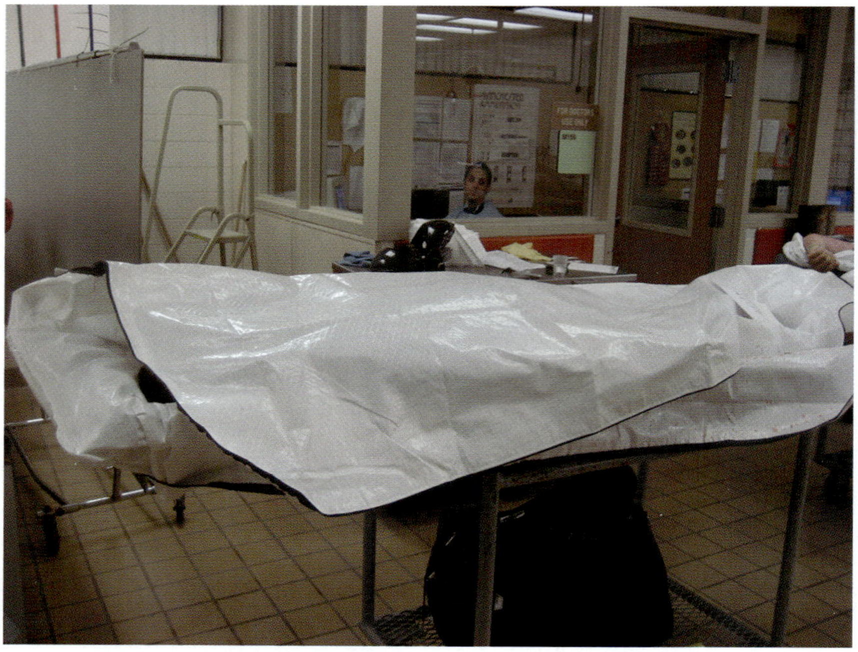

Figure 6.3b Body bag. (Courtesy of the Miami Dade Medical Examiners office. Used with permission.)

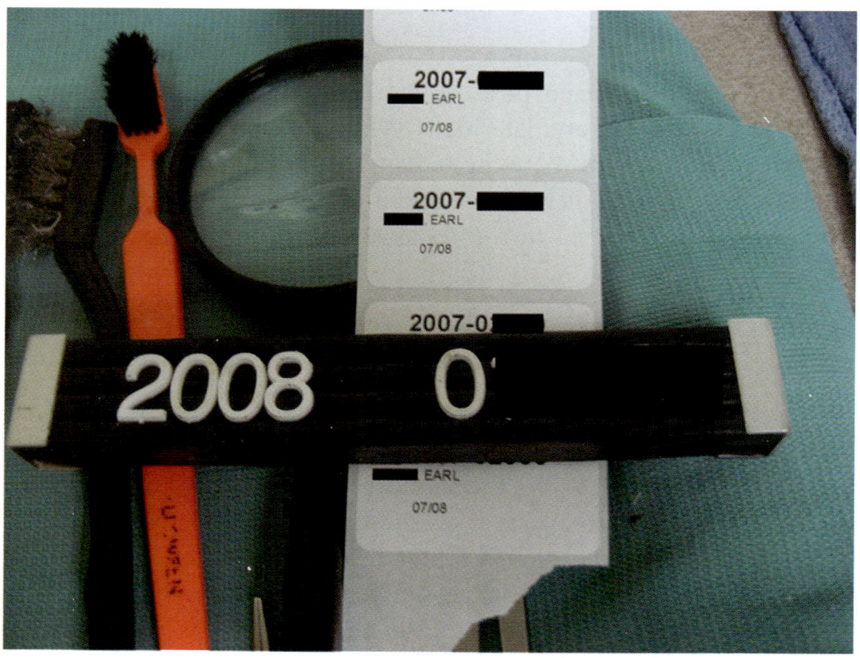

Figure 6.3c Labels. (Courtesy of the Miami Dade Medical Examiners office. Used with permission.)

computer screen. If the image is not satisfactory, it may be manipulated electronically (e.g., brightness, contrast, etc.) or it may be repeated instantly while the subject is still present.

For the sake of convenience, the sensor, which is the picture-capturing element shaped like a periapical film (Figure 6.6d,e) is attached directly to a laptop computer. The computer

Figure 6.4 Miami Dade Medical Examiner morgue (entry - platform, camera, and scale).

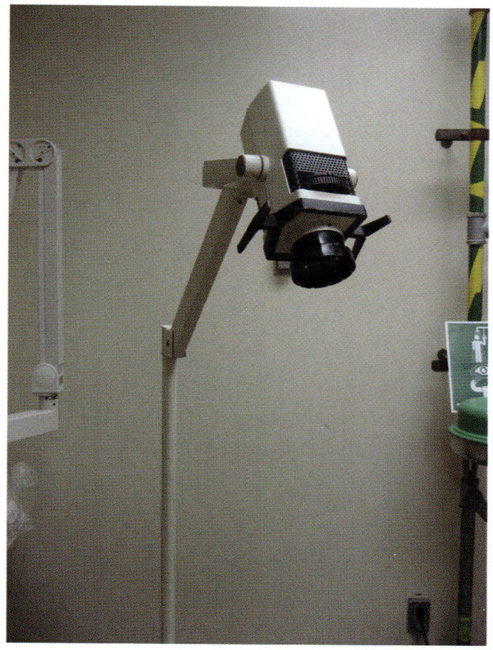

Figure 6.5 Miami Dade Medical Examiner morgue (lamp stand).

contains the proper software (DEXIS-FORENSIC; http://www.dexis.com) installed for recording the radiographs. The computer also contains the WINID software program (http://www.winid.com) for storing information and for the comparison of antemortem and postmortem information. The scanner, with transmissive and reflective capability completes the elements on the dental room cart (Figure 6.6f). The transmissive phase, where the light in the scanner comes from above the item to be scanned, will allow the entry of radiographs into the WINID system. The reflective system, where the light comes from below, as in most typical scanners, produces regular copies of documents that can be scanned for entry into the WINID software. The scanner is principally used for entry of antemortem data and the digital x-ray system for the entry of postmortem data.

Instruments are an important element in a proper dental examination. They must be clean, sharp, well maintained, and available. A simple tray setup (Figure 6.7a,b) consisting of mirror and explorer, tweezers, hemostats, bristle and wire brushes, scaler, tongue blades, forceps, scalpel (blade and holder), identification labels, magnifying glass, and scissors is essential. In addition, it is advisable to have x-ray sensor holders, battery charger, cheek and lip retractors, ratchet jaw openers, holding jig, gauze, clipboard for chart, pens, and pointers, in addition to double-packet film or digital memory cards. The full complement of barrier items including rubber gloves and plastic aprons is discussed below.

Accurate photography via a Single Lens Reflex (SLR) camera (Figure 6.8a,b,c) with film or digital camera with digital card is necessary. The same advantages that applied to radiographs also apply to photography. In digital photography it is possible to view the images immediately and to repeat if necessary, whereas with film it is necessary to have

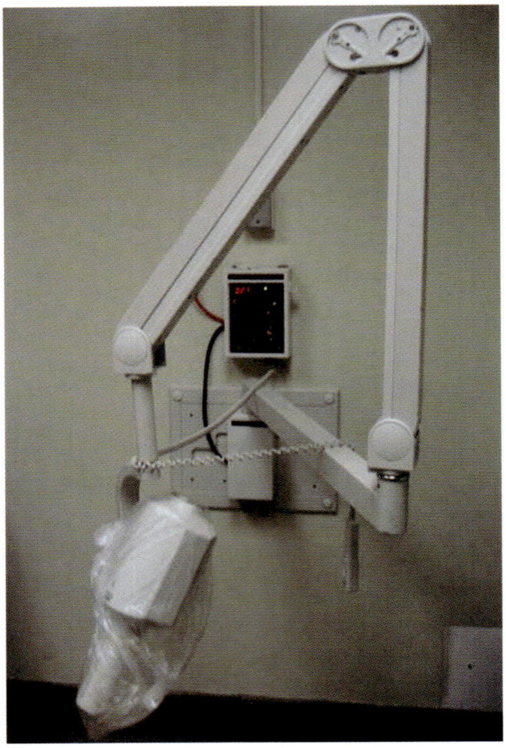

Figure 6.6a Fixed dental x-ray.

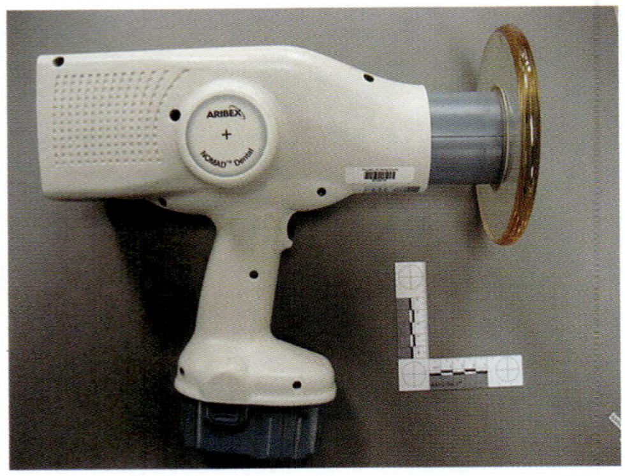

Figure 6.6b Portable Nomad dental x-ray.

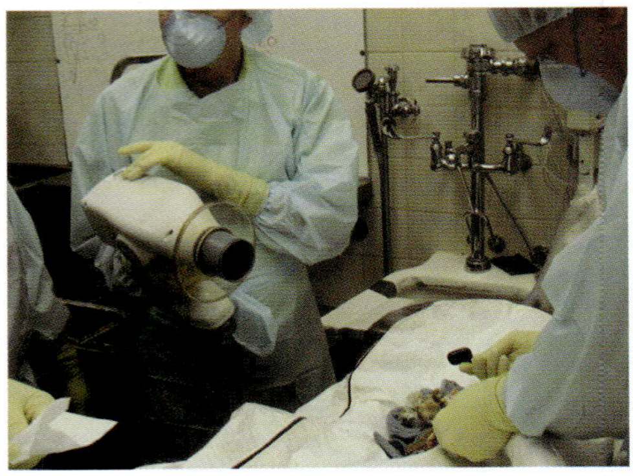

Figure 6.6c Portable Nomad dental x-ray in use.

the film developed and too much time elapses between the image taking and the viewing. In any event, the camera is our vision, permanently recorded. No bias, no personal prism of subjective analysis, the unretouched photograph is the final judgment for presentation of evidence. It records every detail for later examination and evaluation, and it must record those details with a high degree of accuracy for focus, dimension, and color. Creation of the original scene is essential. Never be concerned with how many pictures are taken. This is particularly advantageous with digital photography, when the digital recording device (card) can hold hundreds of photos without changing cards, and the card can be reused after downloading the photographs to the computer.

The forensic odontologist should always have available the ABFO#2 ruler, electronic flash and battery pack (fully charged), large metal mirror, and greyboard for background in photographing specimens. Alternate Light Sources (ALS) are desirable, but not always available, due to special expertise required in their use and the high cost of equipment. However, a small ultraviolet (UV) flashlight (Figure 6.8d) is very handy and inexpensive for disclosing tooth-colored filling material or other artificial tooth replacements such as ceramic or plastic pontics and crowns.

Jaw removal, which usually takes place in the decomp area, is a serious matter. Less is better. If access can be obtained by removal of the mandible only, then the procedure should be limited to that jaw. In all cases, permission must be obtained from the depart-

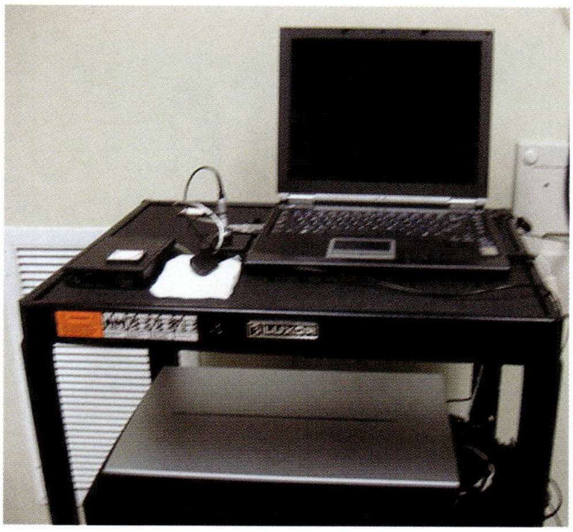

Figure 6.6d Computer and x-ray sensor.

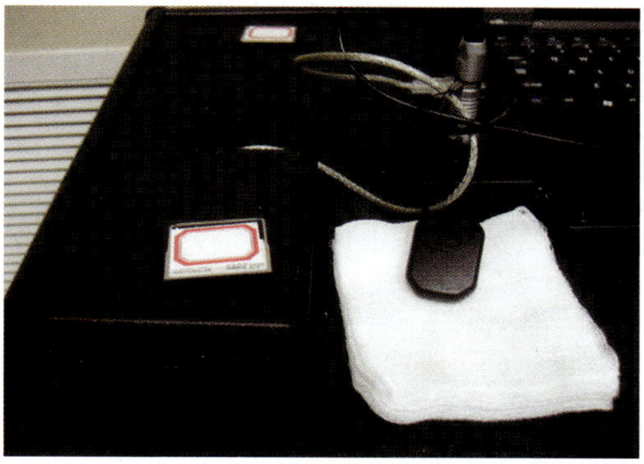

Figure 6.6e X-ray sensor and card reader.

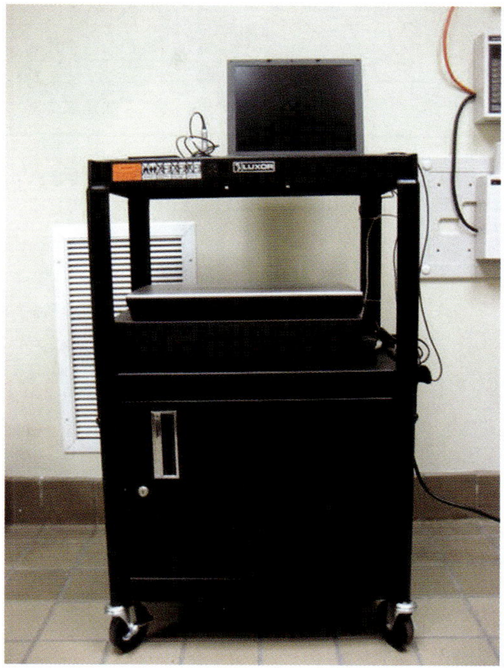

Figure 6.6f Equipment cart.

ment head or medical examiner before proceeding. Upper and lower jaw removal can be accomplished with either lopper or Stryker saw instrumentation (Figure 6.9,b) depending upon the operator's experience and preference.

Radiation control badges are advisable, if required by the local authorities. The use of the NOMAD portable x-ray machine does not require these radiation badges if instructions for its use are properly observed, due to the low level of radiation and the design of the machine.

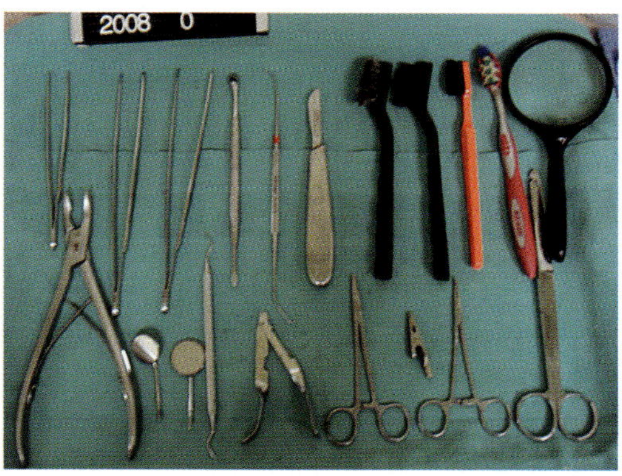

Figure 6.7a Basic instrument tray.

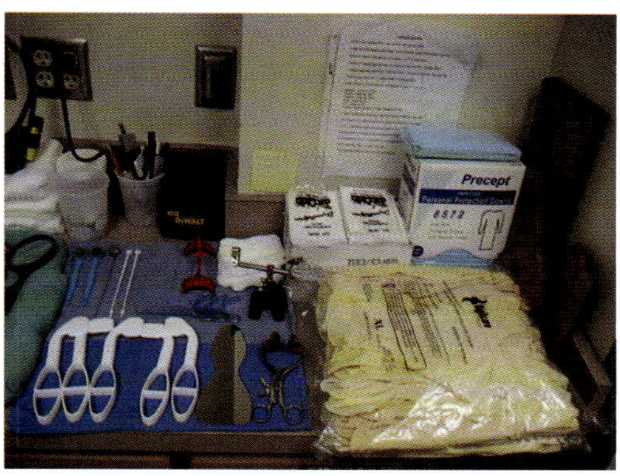

Figure 6.7b Basic equipment setup.

Figure 6.8a Camera bag setup. (Courtesy of the Miami Dade Medical Examiners office. Used with permission.)

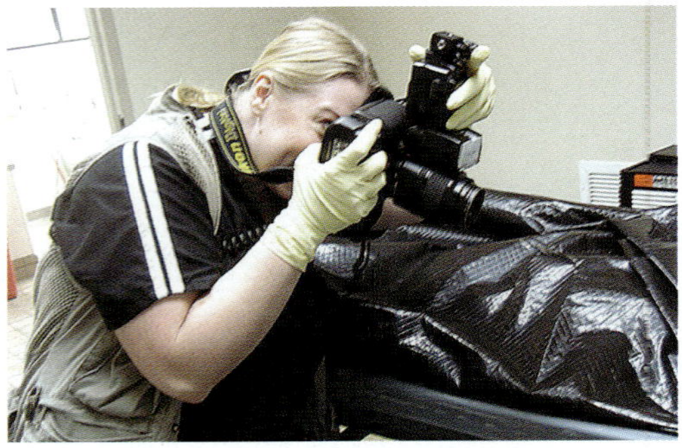

Figure 6.8b Morgue photography.

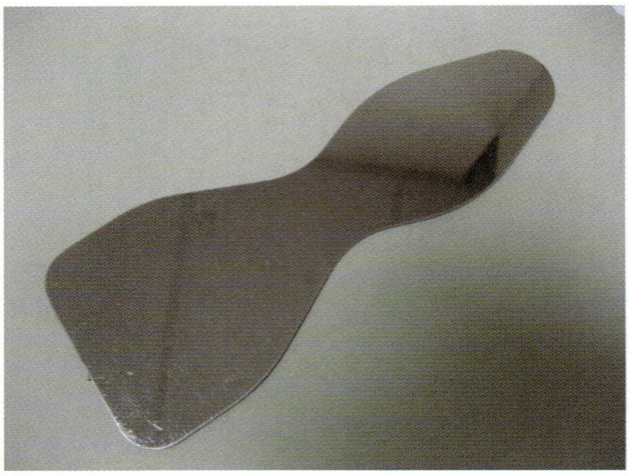

Figure 6.8c Intraoral mirror.

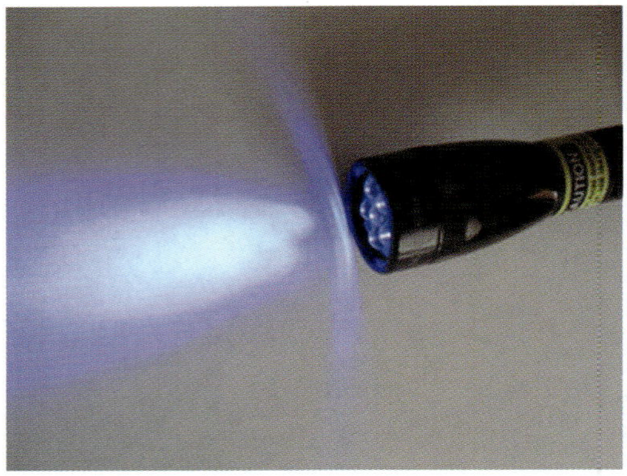

Figure 6.8d Ultraviolet flash light.

Barrier Techniques

Masks, soft and molded (with or without face shield), gloves (latex and nonlatex, vinyl, in sizes S, M, L, and XL), and plastic aprons or gowns (Figure 6.10a,b) should be available at all times.

Plastic aprons to cover street clothing are acceptable but may not provide complete protection. Head cover and shoe covers as well as arm protection are necessary when wearing only an apron or plastic gown. Plastic gowns covering arms and body sides are better but not quite as complete as the bodysuits. The bodysuit covers feet, head, and full body. That is the most complete protection and is usually constructed of Tyvek material to protect against tears and water intrusion (Figure 6.11a–c).

Head covers and eyeglasses (plain or prescription with side splash protectors) are needed, as well as soap and water and sterilizing lotions. Plastic (Saran) wrap is used as a cover to protect the keyboard on the computer, and a large plastic bag is used over the head of the x-ray machine.

Plastic sleeves are available from the manufacturer for the x-ray sensor and its connecting cable to the computer. When finished with your dental examination be sure to remove all clothing and place it in the special receptacle for soiled materials. Wash hands thoroughly before departing the morgue.

Figure 6.9a Lopper. (Courtesy of the Miami Dade Medical Examiners office. Used with permission.)

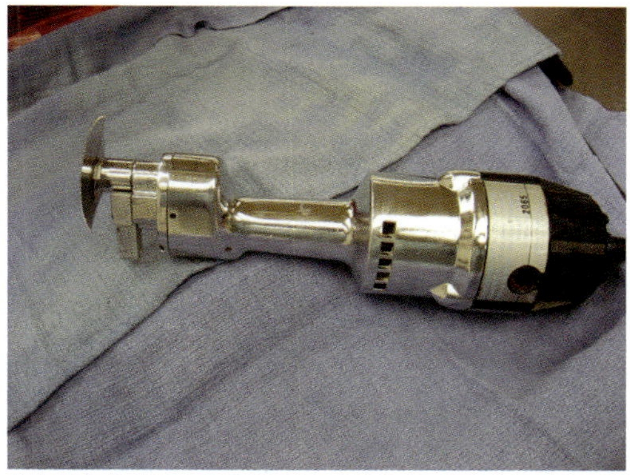

Figure 6.9b Stryker saw. (Courtesy of the Miami Dade Medical Examiners office. Used with permission.)

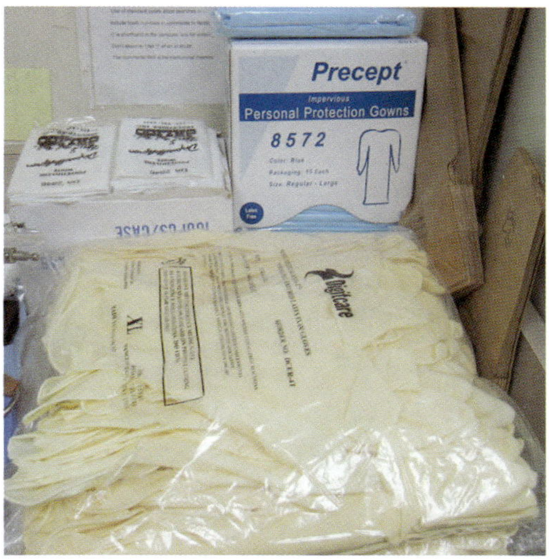

Figure 6.10a Barrier equipment: gloves and aprons. (Courtesy of the Miami Dade Medical Examiners office. Used with permission.)

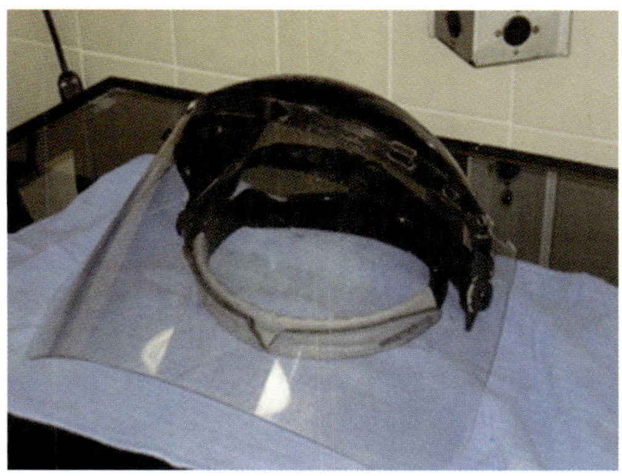

Figure 6.10b Barrier equipment: face shield. (Courtesy of the Miami Dade Medical Examiners office. Used with permission.)

Note: It is always a good idea to double-glove especially when proceeding from the body to a camera, the x-ray machine, or a chart. This makes it easier to remove and replace the second glove without touching your skin or fighting the accumulation of sweat on your hands. More important, this also prevents contamination of the camera, chart, or x-ray machine.

Figure 6.11a Barrier equipment: full-body suit.

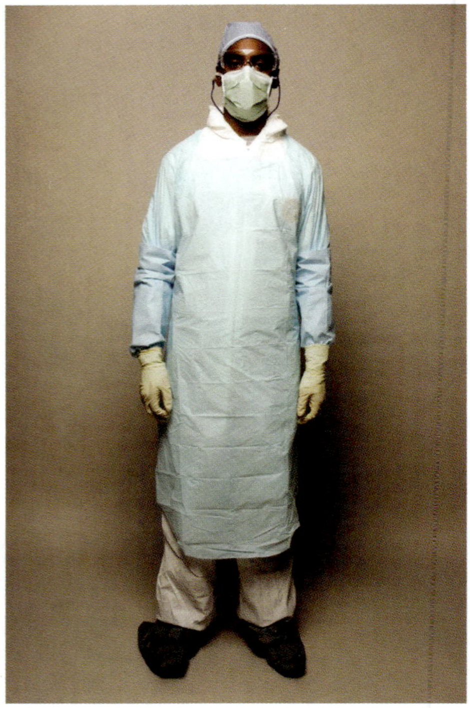

Figure 6.11b Barrier equipment: full plastic apron. (Courtesy of the Miami Dade Medical Examiners office. Used with permission.)

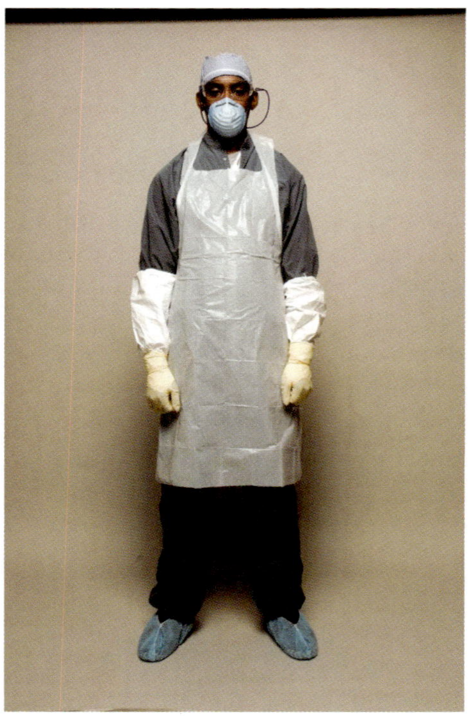

Figure 6.11c Barrier equipment: small plastic apron. (Courtesy of the Miami Dade Medical Examiners office. Used with permission.)

Crime Scene

7

The forensic odontologist does not get invited to the crime scene very often. After all, it is an "invitation only" event. In the case of individual deaths, it is usually the appearance of a possible bitemark that creates the first call. Unless it's a mass disaster, and then everybody is in! It is important that the medical examiners and coroners become knowledgeable concerning these pattern injuries and also aware of the availability of the forensic odontologist to assist at these crucial times, naturally, the sooner, the better when it comes to bitemarks. If the dentist is not present, then the photographer should be there; even better would be both. The medical examiner should be knowledgeable enough to swab for DNA on those occasions when there may even be a suspicion of a bitemark, and perform the procedure before the body is removed and washed during the morgue entry. Another possibility, particularly during times of mass disaster, is the scattering of body fragments and the ability to recognize teeth and other dental parts, such as crowns, dental fragments, bridges, or dentures, especially in high-trauma incidents. These fragments must not only be sorted out from various debris but they need to be identified and preserved properly for further analysis back at the morgue (Figure 7.1a).

Upon arrival at the scene the forensic odontologist should establish contact with the medical examiner at the crime scene. Every scene should be considered a crime scene in order to preserve the integrity of the area and any evidence that may be present. There is great need for proper protocol with which the dentist should become familiar. We only walk in certain areas established as entrances and exits. Rubber gloves are mandatory at all times and any physical evidence should remain undisturbed.

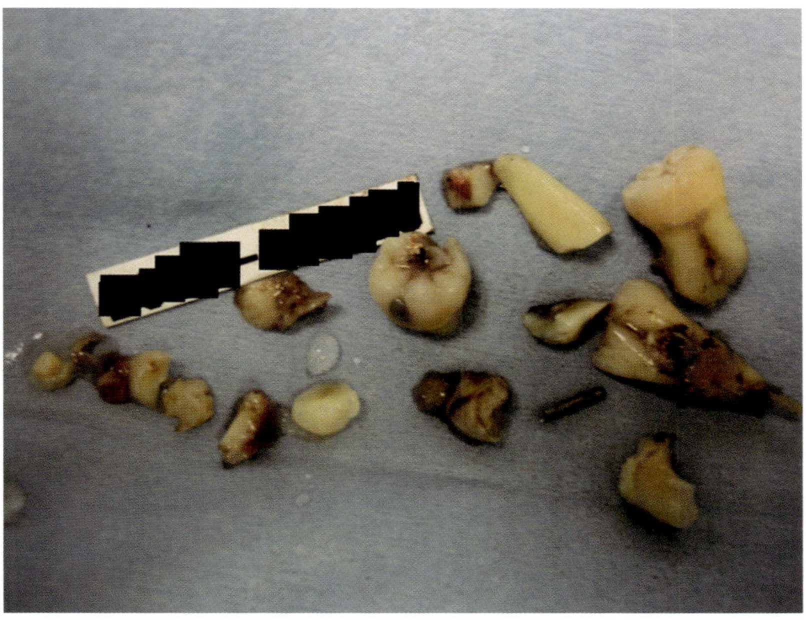

Figure 7.1a Tooth fragments. (Courtesy of the Miami Dade Medical Examiners office. Used with permission.)

Figure 7.1b Crime scene. (Courtesy of the Miami Dade Medical Examiners office. Used with permission.)

When entering the area, and all the time while present, proper identification by badge or card should be clearly visible. This usually consists of plastic cards worn on neck chains. Sometimes hats, fluorescent vests, and T-shirts are almost as important in sorting out the various players at the scene. Most important, of course is eliminating the incursion of strangers or media who should not be present. Before proceeding to the vicinity of the scene, request a review of the circumstances and the local environment.

Weather reports, ground conditions, access by road, water, or trail, and a determination of the immediacy of your service, would all be critical. In these days of possible terrorism, you should be aware of any contamination by nuclear, biological, or chemical agents.

Shortly after arrival you want to establish the appearance, location, and condition of the affected body or bodies. Position of the body may be very important in determining the amount of distortion that may be applied in creating the original position of the body when a bitemark was made. Livor mortis will usually tell us if the body had been moved from its original position, and may also be an indicator of the time of death. In any event, never disturb the body on the scene without permission from the crime scene investigators, and always do so in their presence.

Make note of the time of your arrival and departure from the scene. A quick sketch or a few panoramic photographs, followed by close-ups of the scene and the body, are important for effective recall of the event, especially if you are called some time later — sometimes years later—to testify as to your participation in this event. Re-create the scene as best you can (Figures 7.1b,c).

As you observe the scene, note the clothing or lack of clothing. Attempt to independently determine the gender and possible age of the decedent, and any bitemarks or other pattern injuries about the body. There will be other persons present and note should be taken regarding who these people are. It is a good idea to have your own professional cards available and to obtain those of others who are present for future contact. Make personal

Figure 7.1c Crime scene closeup. (Courtesy of the Miami Dade Medical Examiners office. Used with permission.)

notes of any other observations from the scene. Always remember that these notes may be open for examination at some future date in a trial proceeding. In the case of bitemarks, or possible bitemarks, always ask if any swabs were taken for possible DNA analysis.

In the event that you do not have a camera or may not be allowed to photograph the scene, contact the crime scene photographer and request the photos that you wish to have taken. The use of a digital camera is emphasized again because of its instantaneous capabilities. Anything can be retaken if not entirely satisfactory, and photographic enhancements are possible as long as the original image is saved. Electronic storage of all images is not only possible but space-saving, inexpensive, and easily retrievable. If the photographer is from the ME/C office, the task will be much easier. We assume that the Crime Scene Investigator (CSI) will have a proper ABFO#2 ruler, but it is a good idea to carry one with you at all times when approaching the crime scene. Sorry to say, but experience has taught us that police departments still have more to learn when taking photographs of importance to the forensic odontololgist. Make sure that you have all the contact information regarding the crime scene photographer for follow-up to obtain the requested photos at a later date. Finally, if advisable, bag the head to prevent further loss of teeth.

Chain of Custody

All evidence must be identified and preserved. Evidence containers that may be appropriate include plastic and paper bags (Figures 7.2a,b). Handling of the evidence is critical so as not to contaminate the material and at the same time to maintain the chain of custody. The use of tweezers and rubber gloves to place the evidence in containers is advised. Teeth and other dental parts as well as personal items should travel with the remains. Special attention must be taken with foodstuff. Preservation is critical when time may cause the deterioration of the substance that contains the clues for identification, for example, apple (Figure 7.3), cheese, and so on. Photography, with the appropriate ruler, is

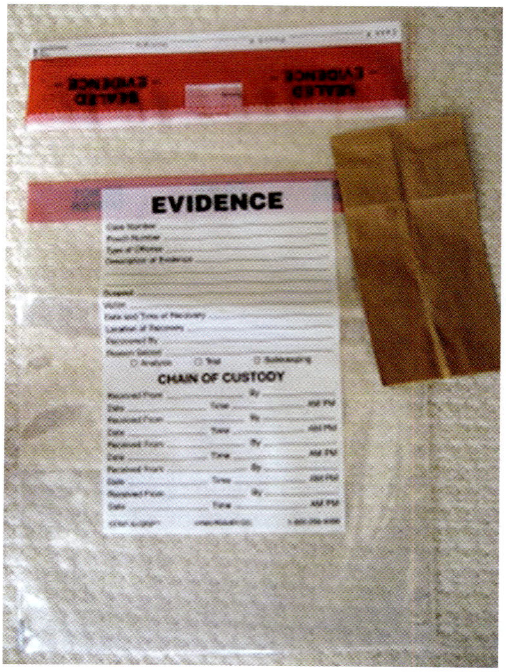

Figure 7.2a Miami Dade Medical Examiner plastic evidence bags. (Courtesy of the Miami Dade Medical Examiners office. Used with permission.)

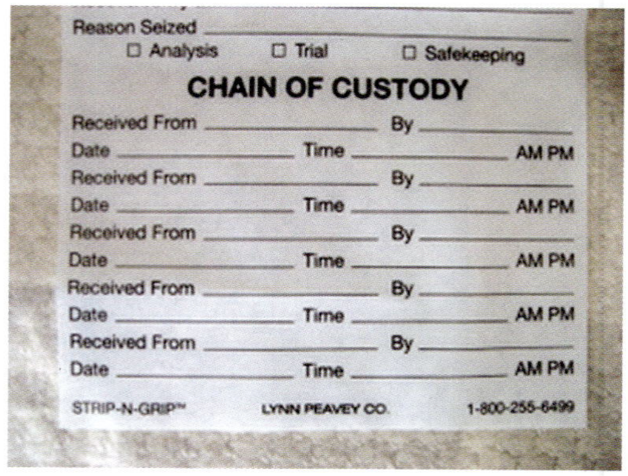

Figure 7.2b Miami Dade Medical Examiner chain of custody form on plastic evidence bag. (Courtesy of the Miami Dade Medical Examiners office. Used with permission.)

Figure 7.3 Apple bite registration. (Courtesy of the Miami Dade Medical Examiners office. Used with permission.)

essential followed by possible use of impression material to form casts. Then refrigeration for longer-term preservation is advisable. Tissue specimens may have to be preserved in a formalin solution.

As the evidence passes from the scene to the transport vehicle to the morgue, there must be a record trail to establish a continuing custody of the evidence. This is the "paper trail" or chain of evidence. Every person who sends or receives such evidence must record that transaction with an initial, a date and time, and full name.

Film and digital cards (Figure 7.4a) that have been used for photography or radiography are placed in a safe for collection with the proper label (Figure 7.4b), and recorded in a log book above the safe with the date, ID number, and person (DDS) who created the information. The safe preserves the integrity of the material and the labels preserve the information and the chain of custody.

Film is best developed and printed in-house. But, unfortunately, not all ME/C offices have the expensive equipment to handle this, which is another good reason to use digital systems that can be recorded and reproduced on any ordinary computer and printer and then later preserved on digital disc. Simple! When sensitive medical examiner information is sent to outside facilities it may be subject to "leakage." Under these circumstances, this

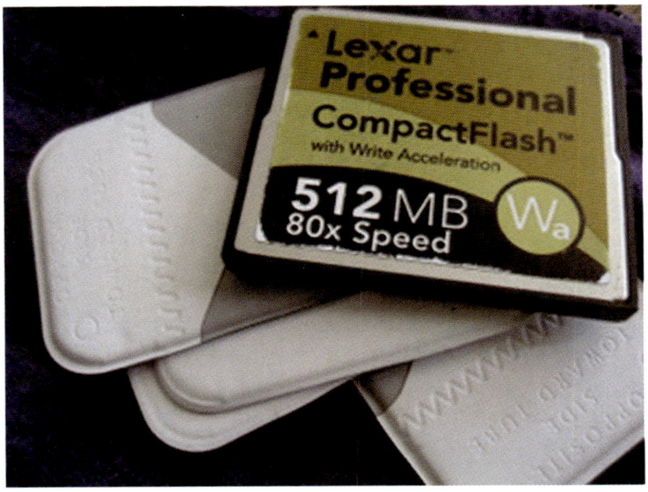

Figure 7.4a X-ray film packet with digital memory card.

Figure 7.4b Digital media protection safe.

material could easily be disclosed to outside sources or viewed by unauthorized personnel. The film and any hardcopies are stored for future use, but this material, by its very composition, could be subject to deterioration due to chemical or environmental conditions. Archiving is a vexing problem because, in some cases, there may not be any statute of limitation, as in murder cases. Furthermore, the appearance of unknown remains may be matched to a missing person only after decades. The use of digital imaging allows for electronic storage which is less costly in terms of space or funds, and the preservation of imagery is better protected from unauthorized use. There is also the advantage that electronic imagery is not subject to deterioration, and search for specific files is fast and easy. As far as we know, at this time, electronic images have no storage time limitations, although erasure problems may exist from magnetic fields and tampering (hacking). Whether by film or digital, court acceptance has been universal as long as the integrity of the evidence has been maintained.

Antemortem Records

8

In many instances there may only be a presumptive identification. The person was driving a car registered in their name. Or was another person driving? Who was the passenger and when was that person last seen? Someone has reported a missing person that same day. Perhaps it was an airplane accident, and there is a list of passengers. Which one? Or was it just a small plane with a few passengers, and a flight plan was filed? Did a fire occur in an apartment where one person was known to live, or was somebody else murdered and placed in the apartment? In the crash of Valujet flight 592 in Miami, not all passengers were accounted for. One unaccounted-for passenger was scheduled to be indicted for murder. Did she give her ticket to another passenger? When the plane went down? She was now free because it was assumed that she died in the plane crash. But did she? Or is she walking the malls of some city with a new identity. A more imaginative script writer might have had her place an incendiary device on board the aircraft. In another instance there was only one tooth (Figure 8.1) that made the identification. With a closed population, as in an airplane crash, this was the only passenger whose antemortem record showed this exact configuration in a filling in an upper second molar. The clues are many—and sometimes few—so the opportunity for error is great, which is all the more reason to proceed cautiously.

First contact would ordinarily be by the investigative staff to the family who could provide the sources of dental treatment. That is, assuming that there is a family and that the person had a dentist. It is important, in the case of missing persons, that the dental records of the missing person be transmitted to the local law enforcement agency as soon as possible. In the identification of unknown remains the investigative staff will attempt to contact the general dentist and request all records of the presumptive person (Appendix, Figure A.6). Usually, this is the private practice dentist, but otherwise, if there has been military service, then the search will extend to the military dental facility. In some cases, if it has been determined that the decedent/missing person received hospital treatment then the hospital will be a good source of records of other surgical procedures including

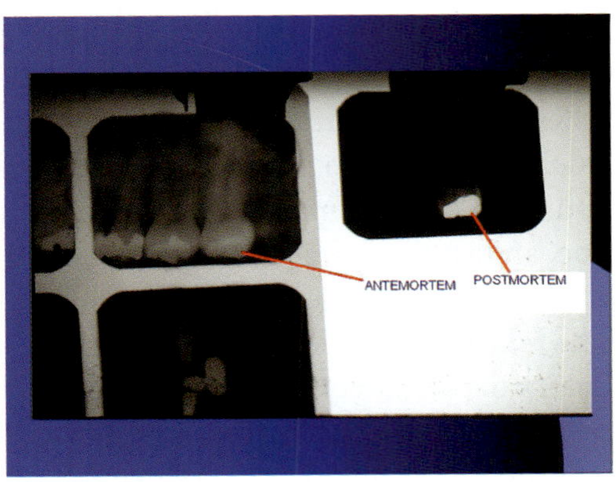

Figure 8.1 Single tooth identification. (Courtesy of the Miami Dade Medical Examiners office. Used with permission.)

Figure 8.2 Serial number on a hip implant. (Courtesy of the Miami Dade Medical Examiners office. Used with permission.)

appendectomy, loss of kidney, but more especially operations or diagnostic procedures that may have involved the skull and the dental apparatus.

Plastic surgical operations, that may explain facial changes, should not be overlooked. Even breast implants will contain serial numbers that can be traced. Surgical bars and other body or dental implants, that may contain serial numbers (Figure 8.2), will provide clues leading to the identification of the unidentified by disclosing the manufacturer and, subsequently, the doctor who will have a log of patients who have received the implant. All this can be accomplished without even knowing or making a family contact. Unfortunately, dental implants as yet do not provide these important serial numbers.

Employment history, birth records, citizenship, medical and dental insurance, marital status (spouse, ex-spouse, and children), and auto registration are other possible sources. If there is a record of incarceration, then a corrections institution may have prison dental records as well. Any of these sources may also provide further clues regarding referral to specialists such as orthodontists, oral surgeons, endodontists, periodontists, or prosthodontists. Every area should be explored.

A family photograph with a smiling face may be critical (Figure 8.3a,b). The photograph, supplied by the family, is enlarged to focus on the teeth when smiling and it is hoped that there may be some distinguishing feature. In this particular case, the upper right lateral incisor (#7) demonstrated a significant rotation, and all the rest of the teeth were well aligned. Comparison with the postmortem remains revealed a perfect match (Figure 8.3c), which was sufficient to declare a positive identification. We are not always so fortunate to have excellent antemortem photographic records, but even non-smiling photos may assist in the identification if no other dental records are available. Nose, eye, ear, and other facial patterns may also be employed in the identification process by virtue of their unique color, shape, and size. In some areas the popularity of tattoos, piercing of the tongue, lips, and cheek, as well as the dental application of various shapes of gold to natural teeth, have facilitated the identification process (Figure 8.4a,b).

In 21 states it is mandatory to place identification in a removable partial or full denture (Figure 8.5) as well as in other removable appliances, such as an orthodontic retainer. This is important, not only in the identification process, but many elderly persons who are confined to a hospital or nursing home will misplace dentures. Without identification, it is unfortunate and it is expensive to replace these dentures or to do without, just because the dentist did not place the patient's name in the removable appliance. When the time comes

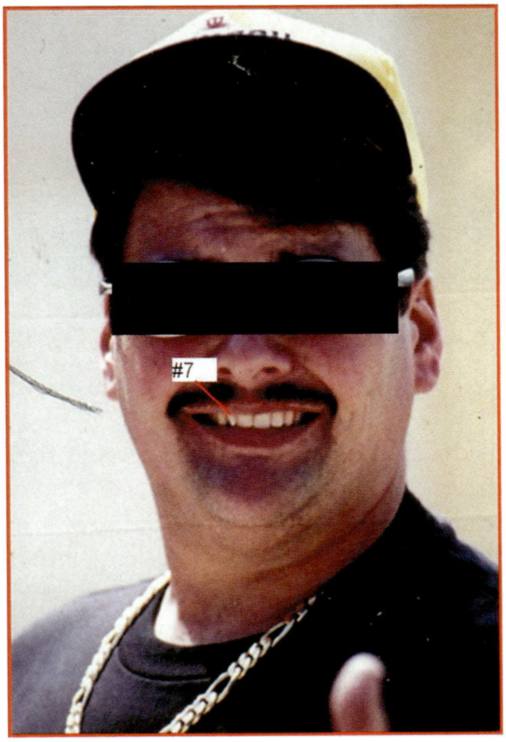

Figure 8.3a Smiling photo. (Courtesy of the Miami Dade Medical Examiners office. Used with permission.)

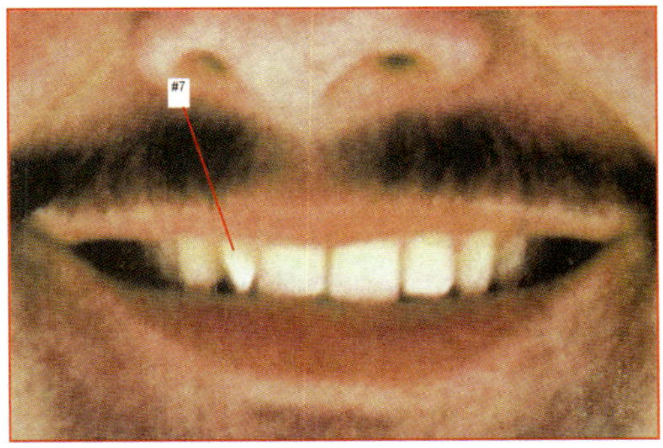

Figure 8.3b Closeup of teeth. (Courtesy of the Miami Dade Medical Examiners office. Used with permission.)

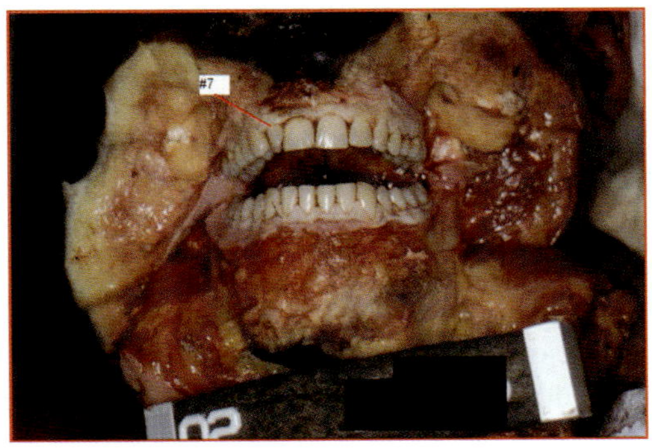

Figure 8.3c Postmortem fragment. (Courtesy of the Miami Dade Medical Examiners office. Used with permission.)

Figure 8.4a Grilles.

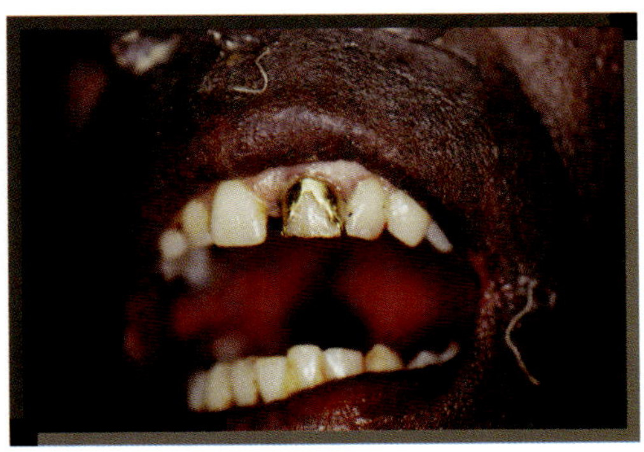

Figure 8.4b Gold caps. (Courtesy of the Miami Dade Medical Examiners office. Used with permission.)

for the forensic odontologist to go to work, discovery of this identification in the morgue makes the ID easier and positive.

Personal effects are reliable if accompanied with the correct remains. On occasion, the personal effects of one person are mixed with those of others, especially in the trauma or chaos of a disaster or individual loss of life. Items such as wallets and purses, credit cards,

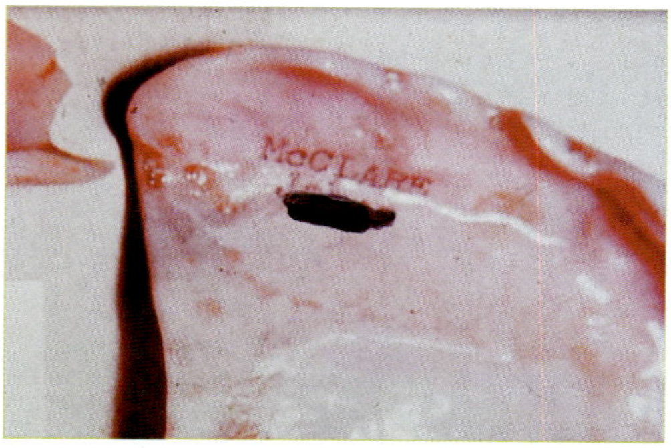

Figure 8.5 Denture identification. (Courtesy of the Miami Dade Medical Examiners office. Used with permission.)

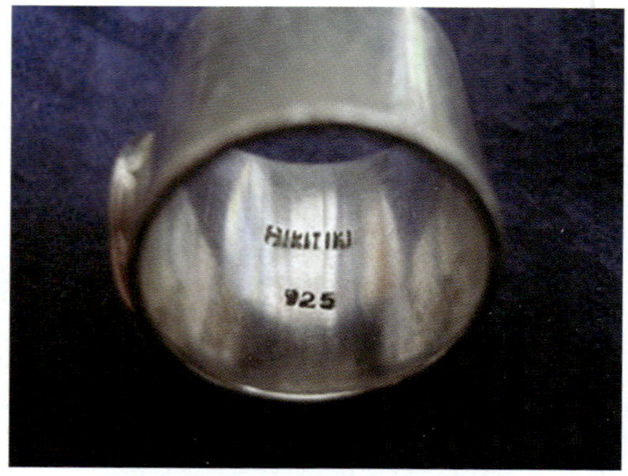

Figure 8.6 Ring with initial.

and driving license are easily misplaced and are subject to destruction in the event of an accompanying fire or long immersion in the water.

Finger rings (Figure 8.6) are more reliable as they are less subject to destruction or loss because of their attachment to the hand. In addition, the ring may even have engraving, as in this example, "HINTITIKI", or other lettering, such as names or initials, to assist in identification. Family members may supply antemortem photos of the jewelry being worn by the deceased.

Clothing (Figure 8.7) will establish gender, size, season of the year at time of death, and possible DNA or other material evidence collected from the area of the unknown remains. Manufacturer labels and point of sale may also add to the investigative effort. In this illustration, the remains were skeletonized, but the clues were intact. The wool cap with

Figure 8.7 Facial reconstruction with clothing.

a "NIKE" symbol, the aviator goggle glasses, and the necklace with a Swiss Army knife and a medallion were all helpful clues in the reconstruction of the antemortem appearance.

Fingerprints are very fragile, and their preservation is difficult at times. The AFIS (Automatic Fingerprint Identification System) database is very accurate. FBI/CJIS maintains a 24/7 examination mode for all law enforcement to check identity. Unfortunately, fire, water, and natural decomposition are prone to degrade any fingerprints over a period of time. However, even when this occurs, the print that is left behind will be as valuable as the finger itself to point to the unknown suspect or the victim.

The airplane manifest listing all passengers and crew, employee lists, residents, tax rolls, auto license and registration, or resident directory may be available as a source of antemortem data. Even the report of a single missing person, closely related, will provide an excellent clue to the investigator to seek the appropriate family and dental records.

DNA samples (usually buccal swabs which are now required in the U.S. military) have become the gold standard in the identification of victim and suspect among the unidentified. However, this takes weeks and sometimes months to process, and is a very costly laboratory procedure.

In the final analysis, what is left is the most reliable, least expensive, fastest, and enduring data: the teeth!

Dental Records

All records must be original, no copies (Figure 8.8a–c).

HIPPA (Health Insurance Portability and Accountability Act) Privacy Rule and Release of protected health information has been cited as a reason for not releasing records. However, dentists who are covered under the HIPPA privacy regulation generally may release dental records or make disclosures from the record to law enforcement officials under the regulation without patient authorization provided they present a valid, properly served warrant, court order, subpoena, or administrative request. In the case of an administrative request, two conditions generally must be met: the information must be related to a legitimate law enforcement inquiry and it must be reasonably limited to the scope of the inquiry. The HIPPA privacy regulations also permit dentists covered by the rule to release patient records and make disclosures to a coroner or medical examiner for the purpose of identifying a deceased person, determining a cause of death, or other duties as authorized by state law.

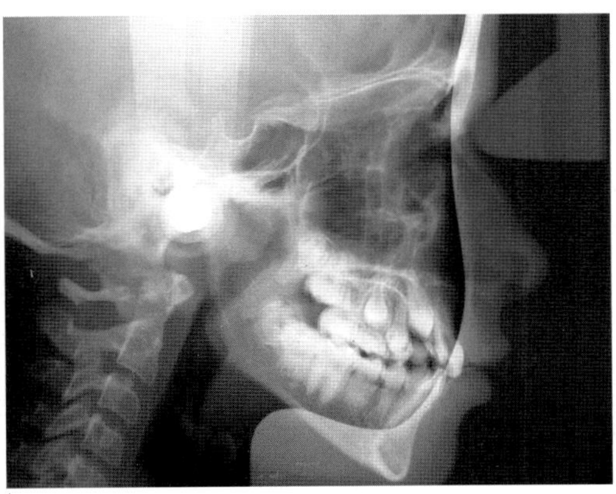

Figure 8.8a Cephlometric radiograph.

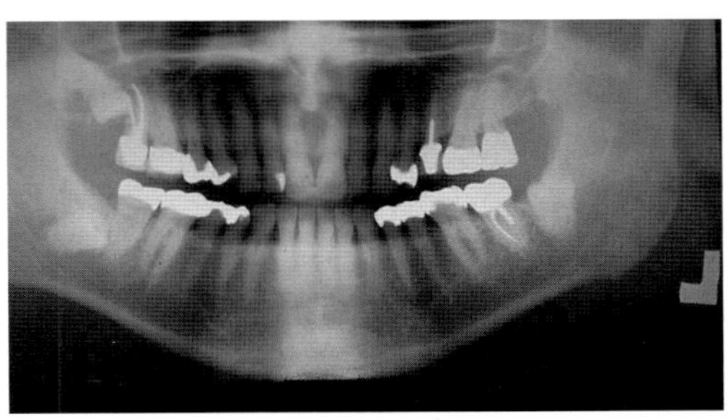

Figure 8.8b Panoramic radiograph.

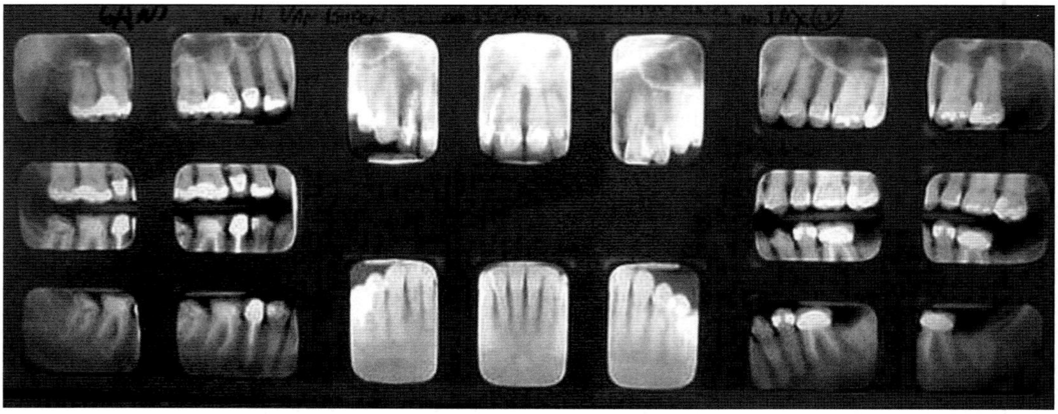

Figure 8.8c Full mouth radiographic series.

Under HIPPA the dentist may use his or her judgment regarding when it is appropriate to release the records to a family member. Usually it is more prudent to release the records directly to the law enforcement officer and to obtain a receipt denoting all the records produced. In all instances it is advisable for the dentist to make copies of the original records. In the reproduction of radiographs, the right and left sides must be noted as well as the date the films were taken and the patient's name.

Place the dentist's name, address, and phone number on all records, as well as the name of the patient, in the event that the investigator may wish to contact you with any questions regarding the record.

Depending upon the circumstances of the request, or perhaps the celebrity of the deceased, the dentist may wish to seek permission from the person named in the record as next of kin or consult with his or her own attorney.

A dentist who refuses to comply with a final, valid, properly served warrant, court order, subpoena, or administrative request for records could be found in contempt of court.

Don't

- Write in pencil.
- Attempt to erase or white-over.
- Change the original record in any way shape or manner.
- Allow staff to write record without checking or supervision.
- Use too many abbreviations, acronyms.
- Scribble.

Do

- Write in permanent ink.
- Cross out with a single line and initial where struck; never erase.
- Check all staff entries.
- Use standard forms and nomenclature (Universal numbering system).
- Make all notes brief and thorough.
- Chart all teeth before proceeding.
- Label "Treatment Plan" separately.
- Chart all work accomplished (standard codes).

- Note all referrals.
- Label all dentures with patient name.

The general dentist is the prime source of all such records. However, in many cases it is the specialist, such as the orthodontist, who will likely take models, photographs, and additional radiographs of measurable characteristics. It is important to track all referrals, no matter at what age. The endodontic radiograph of a single tooth may be critical to the entire identification. Periodontal charting could also be relevant. Certainly, a surgical procedure would have required a radiograph by the oral surgeon.

Hospital records of medical/surgical procedures involving the head and neck would also be important as would be dental and medical insurance company records. Records may be faxed or e-mailed, subject to clarity and registration of sidedness. If time is of the essence, USPS, UPS, DHL, and FedEx are available.

In all cases the dentist maintains status as custodian of records and that is why they must maintain a chain of custody receipt to establish the location or disposition of the records. It is also suggested that a copy of the records should be made and kept in the dentist's possession.

9 Postmortem Records—The Dental Autopsy

Order of Reliability of Identification Methods

1. Dental Records—x-rays, charts, and photos
2. Fingerprints
3. Laboratory tests—DNA
4. Surgical evidence
5. Footprint
6. Skin, scars, and tattoos
7. Personal effects
8. Visual

Essential Elements of the Dental Autopsy

Things to Do

Take complete records: x-rays, photos, chart, and models (if necessary).
Consult with scene doctors and investigator. Get scene photos.
Treat every set of remains as if it had a communicable disease.
Wear full barrier clothing including mask, boots, gloves, gown, and glasses.
Treat every set of remains with due respect.
Wash thoroughly before departing the autopsy area.
Check for instruments and supplies in the body and in the bag.
Clean all instruments thoroughly.
Change clothes if necessary due to splatter, odor, or contamination.
Note location of eyewash station and exit doors.
Dispose of all barrier clothing in proper place.
Preserve all evidence and maintain chain of custody.
Use correct identification on each photo, chart, x-ray, impression, or model.
Identify the digital card in camera or computer.
Maintain photo log: time, place, ID, conditions.
Record serial number, lot number, manufacturer, name, and expiration date of material.
Obtain medical examiner permission for jaw removal.

Don't

Jump to conclusions.
Work alone.
Speak to the press or family members.
Display photos outside of the morgue.

The Autopsy—Activation

It all begins with a simple phone call.

"Hi, it's Sandy." That call from the chief investigator in the Miami Dade medical examiner office almost always tells us that there is a body in need of dental identification waiting for us.

As soon as I heard the phone ring again, I had a premonition. It was Dick and it was time to go downtown. "We got a case," he declared. " I'll meet you at the morgue at 5:30." Like it was 4:30 now and how did he know I had nothing else to do? It was lucky for him because it is not convenient or advisable to do a dental autopsy alone.

I still beat him to the morgue because he had to finish taking care of the last patient, which is always the stumbling block of the day. Naturally, I had already showered after my tennis game. The traffic was easy because I was running against the flow of everyone homebound from work at the end of the day. I turned off the Interstate only 15 minutes after leaving home and headed into the "medical district." There was the VA Hospital, the immense county-run Jackson Memorial Hospital, University of Miami Hospital, and the University of Miami Medical School. Then there was the state attorney office, the public defender, and the Miami Dade Criminal Justice Building. I turned the corner onto Northwest 10th Avenue, past the National Parkinson Institute and Bascom Palmer Eye Institute and rolled up to the Joseph Davis Center for Forensic Pathology, otherwise known as "the morgue," appropriately across the street from the Ryder Trauma Center with its constantly whirling helicopter blades depositing a multitude of maimed on its busy rooftop.

I passed my cherished plastic card against the slot at the entrance to the building and the traffic arm opened giving me privileged entrance to another world. Then another security slot to open the door into the Miami Dade medical examiner facility and I was on my way upstairs where I picked up the "Request for Forensic Odontology Service" (Appendix, Figure A.1). I checked the name of the referring associate medical examiner, the case investigator, and the morgue number of the remains. After that, I read the report on the circumstances where this body was found and in what condition, which might lead to the correct cooler depending upon whether it was fresh (Class I), decomposed (Class II), or skeletal (Class III). In that separate "decomp" area, with its special air circulation and separate cooler, I would have to bring a few things from the main autopsy suite to perform the dental autopsy.

Fortunately the body was in the main morgue cooler. So, I made my way through the half dozen tables adorned with bodies in various poses and states of disassembly, and then waded through the chill of cooler #2 to find the gurney with the correct body bag. As I rolled out the gurney to the dental autopsy room I thought to myself about my mission. Whenever I come to this place where the unknown reside, I wonder if I will be able, not just to identify a body, but to establish the existence of a life: a life that once was lived, with family and friends, with success and failure. A name is not just a conglomeration of letters. Right now that identity is just a number, but a name is more than that. It is a reputation. It is a person who belonged to the community. A name, given with diligence and care by its parent, describes what has existed from its birth to the present, and maybe beyond. It is a ticket to some form of immortality to avoid falling into the abyss of mortality that we all must face. Every life must have a name and that is what we were seeking as Dick came into the room with a hearty, "C'mon, let's do it!"

Figure 9.1 Floater/decomposition. (Courtesy of the Miami Dade Medical Examiners office. Used with permission.)

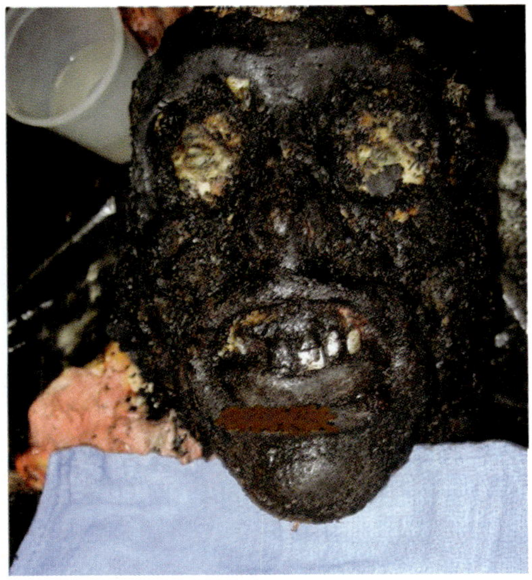

Figure 9.2 Incinerated. (Courtesy of the Miami Dade Medical Examiners office. Used with permission.)

There are always the questions. Is it a "decomp," a body in some state of decomposition? Perhaps it is a "floater" (Figure 9.1) who has been in the water for a while, so the color has changed to gray and the skin has begun to peel away? Or is it incinerated remains (Figure 9.2), a person caught in the flames at home in bed or in the instant of an automobile accident. Perhaps it is a "jumper" (Figure 9.3) from a nearby tall building?

Maybe it is fresh, recently discovered. Or maybe it is a skeleton (Figure 9.4a,b) that has languished out in the Everglades for weeks or has just been discovered buried in the woods or uncovered at a construction site after many years. Each body that arrives at the medical examiner door has a story to tell. The ones that we see need to have the last chapter of their lives written because they are unknown, known only to their own family as missing.

The questions continue. Is there a presumptive identification indicated by some item found on or near the body? Maybe there is a license plate for the car or an address where a person lived. Is there a dentist available with antemortem records available for comparison?

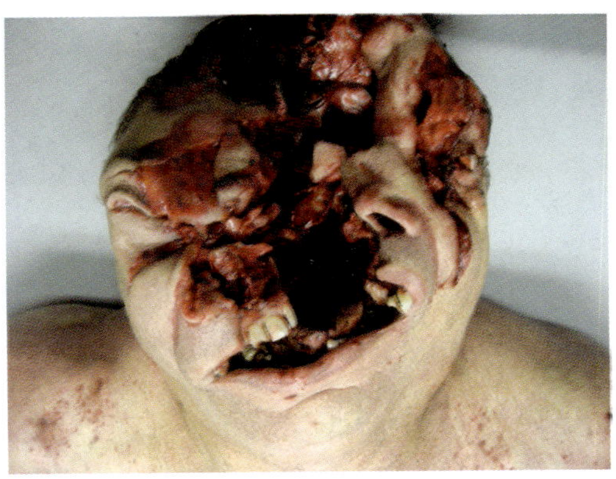

Figure 9.3 Jumper. (Courtesy of the Miami Dade Medical Examiners office. Used with permission.)

Figure 9.4a Field excavation. (Courtesy of the Miami Dade Medical Examiners office. Used with permission.)

Figure 9.4b Recovered bones. (Courtesy of the Miami Dade Medical Examiners office. Used with permission.)

Can you believe that some people never went to a dentist, or that the dentist did not take x-rays, or that the records are now missing or misplaced? Perhaps there was work billed that was not accomplished. Impossible? Not!

Did the presumptive person live in this local area? Are there any clues as to age, gender, ethnicity, or physical character such as height and weight, eye, skin, or hair color? Is there a family waiting for their loved one to grieve for? Do they have any smiling photographs

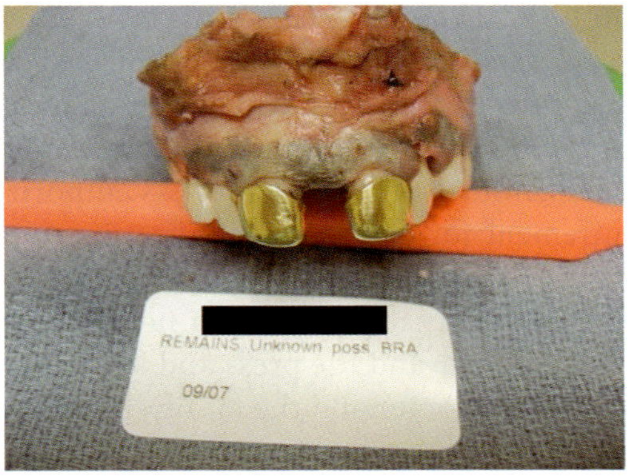

Figure 9.5 Gold crowns on teeth. (Courtesy of the Miami Dade Medical Examiners office. Used with permission.)

that might be helpful? What was the manner of death? What was the cause of death? Is this a criminal case and might it be necessary to appear in court at some time? Will the police investigator and the crime scene report add any pertinent information? Where were the remains found and when? What was the position of the body? Had the body been moved from another location? Are there any photographs of the crime scene? Are there any bitemarks requiring a much more time-consuming set of procedures, or are there identifying marks such as scars and tattoos, including obvious unique dental characteristics such as gold crowns, missing teeth, or large spaces between the teeth (Figure 9.5)? These two gold crowns in the front of the mouth and a large diastema (space) between the two front teeth are excellent means of identification. The questions are endless, but they all must be asked and, hopefully answered, in our endless search for identity.

As consultants we are "on call." We spend our days in more productive ways than sitting at the ME/C office waiting for that rare unidentified body to appear. It is difficult to contemplate that there are tens of thousands of unidentified who lie in coolers and graves throughout the country quietly awaiting their return to the world of the known. According to CJIS (Criminal Justice Information Service) latest estimates, there may be more than 40,000 unknown remains lingering in coolers or boxes in the morgues of this country, and about 1000 unidentified persons are added every year. If there is a waiting family, we will respond immediately, otherwise we will set a specific time with the morgue personnel to examine the remains during regular working hours. Examination of the remains after hours makes it difficult for the staff as well as the doctors, but it can be accomplished if necessary.

Then there is a matter of great present interest, when one body is magnified to become hundreds or even thousands, the mass disaster: where, when, and what? Explosive, nuclear, biological, or chemical? A ship, plane, subway, building, or stadium? No one knows when or where, so we must be prepared for any eventuality. We must be prepared for the single unidentified person as well as for the multitudes, whether it is a single location or a multitude of locations, and whether it is over a short period of time or an extended period of time. We must also consider whether it directly affects our personal space and residency, or it is far away. Chemical, nuclear, and biological considerations require special decontamination procedures. Compared to these situations a single body looks easy, but it is not always. Even in a mass disaster, every body is treated individually, as a single body, with the same full expert examination and respect.

Entrance to the morgue is through strict security. Because of the sensitive nature of observing the deceased's remains, access to the facility is limited to those who have need to be there. Magnetic cards or similar means are employed in limiting access. And what happens in the morgue, stays in the morgue. No pictures, no specimens, no information leaves the medical examiner department unless authorized by the chief medical examiner or it is a requirement for court or identification purposes. There is also an exemption when there is a need to use these photos for the purpose of education and training (Appendix, Figure A.7). It is important to note that there should not be any communication between the doctor and the press and it is unlikely that there would be any communication between the doctor and the family, but this also should be avoided.

The Autopsy—Methodology

Gender

In the absence of genitalia, for example, head only or skeletal remains, an anthropological examination/confirmation may be necessary. Clothing, jewelry, and remnants of hair may also be helpful but not necessarily definitive due to many transgender appearances.

Table 9.1 shows various features according to the University of Toronto Forensic Anthropology Laboratory.

Note: In postmortem skeletal cases the sex may be determined through laboratory test by the presence in the male of heterogametic chromosomes XY and the absence of the Y-chromosome in the dental pulp of the female with homogametic chromosomes XX.

Table 9.1 Various Gender Features

Feature	Male	Female
Size	Big and rugged	Small and smooth
Forehead	Low, slopes posterior	Rounded, full, vertical
Frontal eminence	Small, double-bossed	Large, single-bossed
Supraorbital ridge	Medium to large, thick	Small to medium, thin
Orbits	Squared, low	Rounded, high
	Rounded margins	Sharp margins
Nasal aperture	High, thin, sharp margins	Lower, wider, rounded margins
Nasal Bone	Large	Small
Malar bone	Posterior–lateral	Anterior–lateral
Zygomatic	Extends	Does not extend
Parietal eminences	Small	Large
Mastoid	Medium–large	Small–medium
Occipital	Well-muscled, rough	Not marked, smooth
Occipital condyles	Large	Small
Palate	Large, U-shape	Small, parabolic
Tooth size	Large, M1 5cusp	Smaller
Mandible	Large, high symphysis	Small, low symphysis
	Broad ascending ramus	Small ascending ramus
	Gonial angle <125	Gonial angle >125
	Gonial angle flares	Gonial angle does not flare
Chin	Square–two point	Rounded–1 point

Source: Modified from Krogman, 1962.

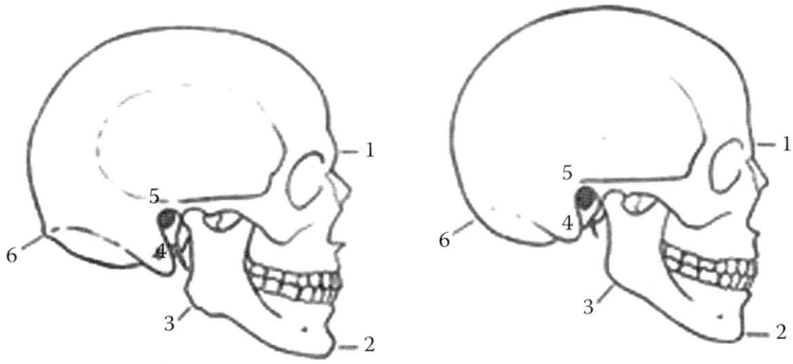

(a) Male (b) Female

1. Superciliary arch
2. Mental protuberance
3. Angle
4. Mastoid process
5. Temporal line
6. External occipital protuberance

Figure 9.6 Skulls (male/female). (Courtesy of Dr. Robert George. Used with permission.)

European Ancestry

1. Sharp nasal sill
2. Retreating zygomatics
2. Little or no prognathism (orthognathous face)
4. Long narrow face
5. Narrow nasal opening
6. Narrow nasal bridge
7. Angular orbits
8. Triangular palate

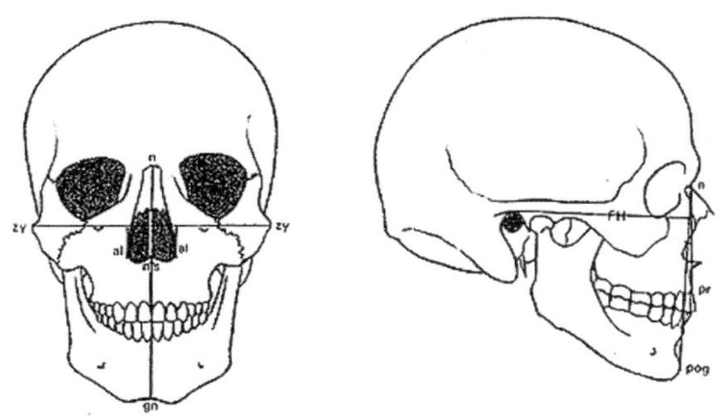

(a) (b)

Figure 9.7a Skull (European ancestry). (Courtesy of Dr. Robert George. Used with permission.)

Figure 9.6 shows the difference in skulls by gender and Figure 9.7a–c shows skulls of African, European, and Asian ancestry.

Asian Ancestry

1. Projecting zygomatics
2. Edge to edge bite (I wearing)
3. Shovel-shaped maxillary incisors
4. Face width may exceed cranial width
5. Flaring gonial angle
6. Extreme narrowing of the nasal bones
7. Rounded orbits
8. Horseshoe shaped palate

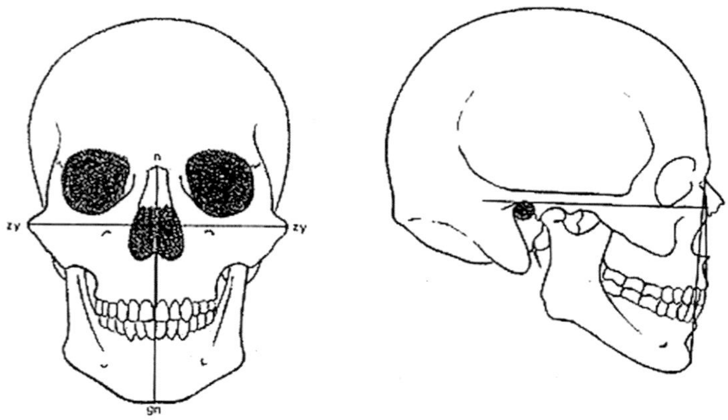

(a) (b)

Figure 9.7b Skull (Asian ancestry). (Courtesy of Dr. Robert George. Used with permission.)

African Ancestry

1. Nasal guttering (no sill)
2. Marked prognathism
3. Wide nasal opening
4. Bregmatic depression
5. Wide nasal bridge (thus wider interorbital distance)
6. Rectangular orbits
7. Rectangular palate

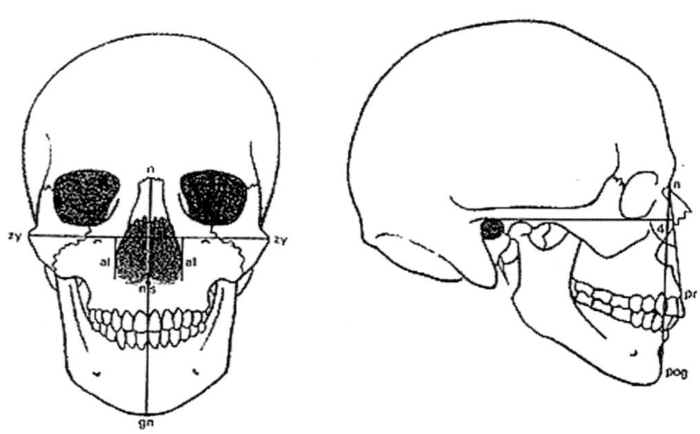

(a) (b)

Figure 9.7c Skull (African ancestry). (Courtesy of Dr. Robert George. Used with permission.)

Table 9.2 Ancestral Skull Analysis

	Nordic	Alpine	Mediterranean	African	Asian
Skull length	Long	Short	Long	Long	Long
Skull height	High	High	Middle	Low	Middle
Sagittal contour	Rounded	Arched	Rounded	Flat	Arched
Facial breadth	Narrow	Wide	Narrow	Narrow	Very Wide
Facial height	High	High	Mod. High	Low	High
Orbital opening	Angular	Rounded	Angular	Rectangular	Rounded
Nasal opening	Narrow	Mod. Wide	Narrow	Wide	Narrow
Lower nasal margin	Sharp	Sharp	Sharp	Guttered	Sharp
Facial profile	Straight	Straight	Straight	Down-slant	Straight
Palate shape	Narrow	Mod. Wide	Narrow	Wide	Mod. Wide
General impression of skull	Massive, Rugged, Elongate	Large, Mod. Rugged, Rounded	Small, Smooth, Elongated	Massive, Smooth, Oval	Large, Smooth, Rounded

Age Estimation

Franklin and Cardini, in 2007, measured ramus height in subadults of African ancestry and concluded that ramus height can be used to predict age in the subadult skeleton with accuracy closely approaching that of standards based upon the dentition.

There are many systems to determine age based upon the development of the dentition. According to work done at the Forsyth Dental Infirmary, there is a significant difference between boys and girls as demonstrated on the chart shown in Figure 9.8.

Other methods of age estimation by Mincer, Harris, and Berryman use the third molar as an estimator of age. Mincer et al. concluded that maxillary M3 formation was slightly advanced over mandibular M3, and root formation developed earlier in males than in females. M3 formation was tabled using Demirjian's eight-grade classification. In this manner, information may establish whether an individual is 18 years of age, a medico-legal question that may determine majority, and according to government guidelines it may decide whether a person is allowed to remain in this country or be returned to their country of origin.

The age of redemption at 18 years can establish adulthood, but dental evidence, unfortunately, is not sufficiently accurate to make that determination with great accuracy, except when no other evidence is available.

Demirjian's eight stages of tooth development (2047 boys/2349girls) demonstrate one method of determining age according to the developmental stages of the third molars (Figure 9.9).

Note: Studies by Moorees, Fanning, and Hunt (Harvard study, N = 134) are similar, with five stages of development.

Contrast all this with the popular 1941 *Development of the Human Dentition* by Schour and Massler, which was based on a much smaller population (Figure 9.10) and is still used in the popular American Dental Association chart for guidance. The development of young people is a combination of physical events. Dental age is only one biological event in the assessment of age. Equal weight must be given to skeletal age, secondary sexual characteristics, and morphology of the individual. Once maturation has occurred, we lose this sequencing of events, which is a more reliable indicator. Even these events are but moments in time and not fixed milestones in the progression of age.

When the dentition is complete, the task of determining age becomes more difficult. Functional and degenerative changes start to take place, such as attrition, dentin

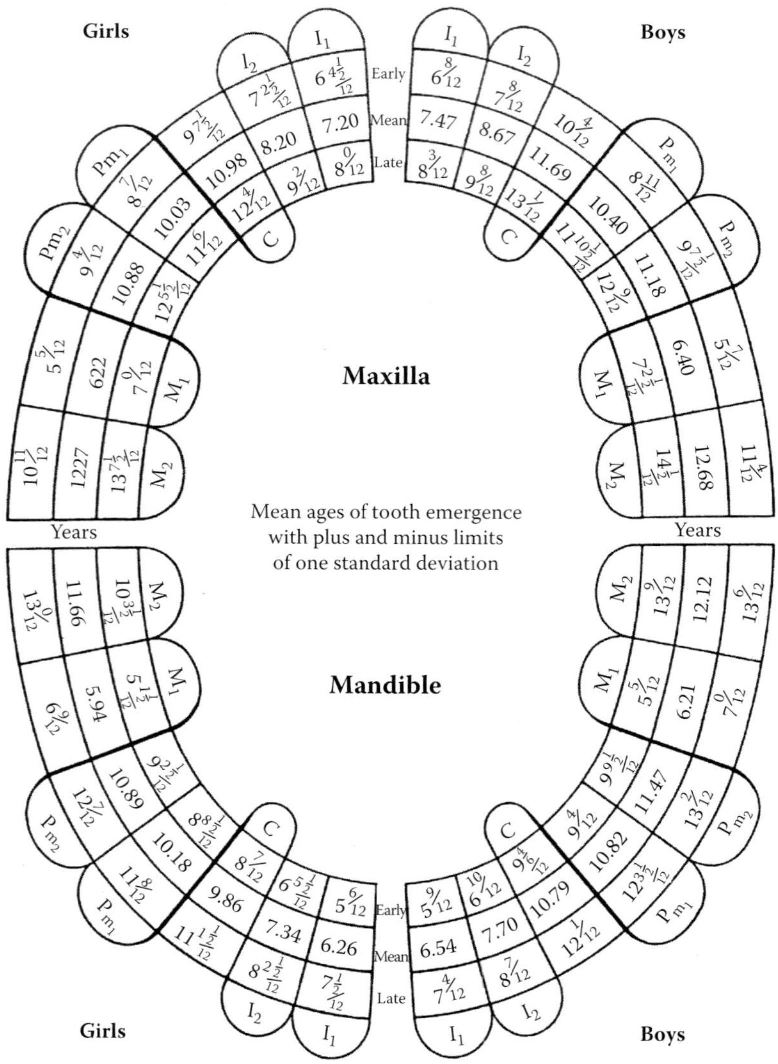

Figure 9.8 Forsyth dental chart. (Designed by V.O. Hurme, D.M.D., for the Forsyth Dental Infirmary for Children.)

deposition, and root transparency. Aspartic acid recemization and pulp/tooth area ratio are all considerations when determining age during adulthood. The range of age estimation becomes wider as the individual becomes older. Dental care, nutrition, habits, and environment are factors that may affect age indiscriminately. Therefore it is incumbent upon the forensic odontologist to be extremely conservative and wide ranging in endeavoring to establish age.

Community Placement

Community placement is a subjective analysis of the dentition which would lead the operator or investigator to a determination of the social or economic environment in which the subject may have lived. A full mouth rehabilitation with multiple crowns and implants is significantly different from a dentition consisting of rampant caries, root fragments, and no

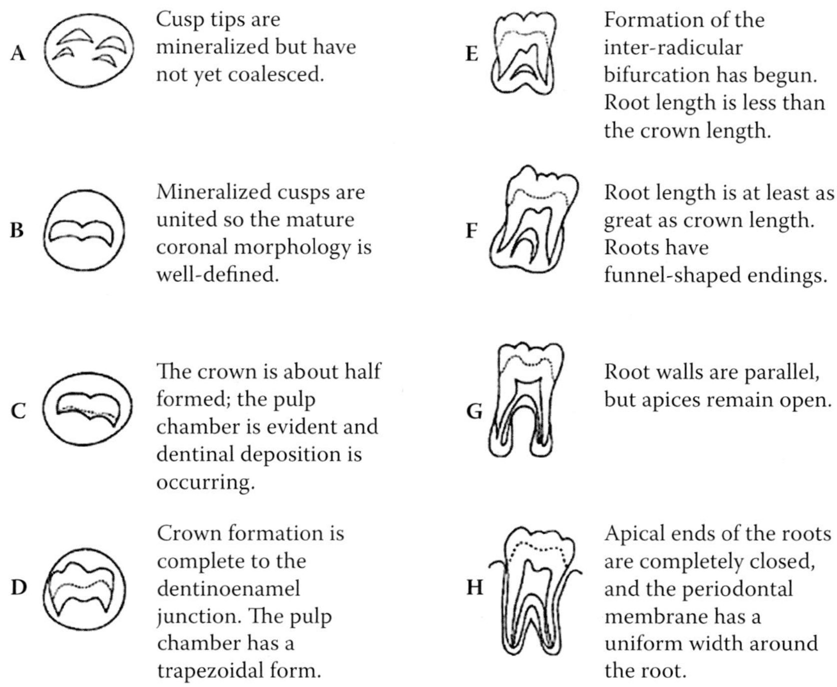

Figure 9.9 Demirjian's eight stages of tooth formation.

evidence of dental care. Poor personal hygiene, disheveled clothes, and present life style—even homelessness—can hide the true identity of a past existence that teeth will disclose.

Sometimes, the presence of dentistry peculiar to another country will be revealing, such as the presence of stainless steel crowns as a permanent restoration.

Other Considerations

The outline of the different sinus cavities may be available in panographic films from a dental office or full skull Waters projection, taken in a hospital environment that may have been taken for diagnostic purposes, can be the basis of comparison.

Root morphology, in the absence or presence of teeth, is available from typical periapical x-rays as well as panographic films and may prove to be distinctive enough to provide an identification. In the event that the teeth are missing postmortem, the use of radiopaque material injected into the sockets of lost teeth may reveal the anatomy of the lost root.

Alveolar bone pattern adjoining the tooth socket may be unique as well, with areas of radiopacity or radiolucency. The healing pattern of a socket from an extracted tooth may indicate the time of extraction or the callous formation in the jaw, subsequent to a fracture, may produce unique patterns. There are many opportunities for comparison in normal alveolar patterns, because all cancellous bone is not the same.

This leads to the next pattern available in the area of the mandible which is the inferior alveolar canal. This structure, containing the nerve and blood supply to the lower teeth, flows like a river from the lingual surface of the mandibular ramus through the body of the mandible to exit at the mental foramen on the external surface on the anterior body of the mandible. By virtue of its size and location of its entrance, pathway, and exit, the

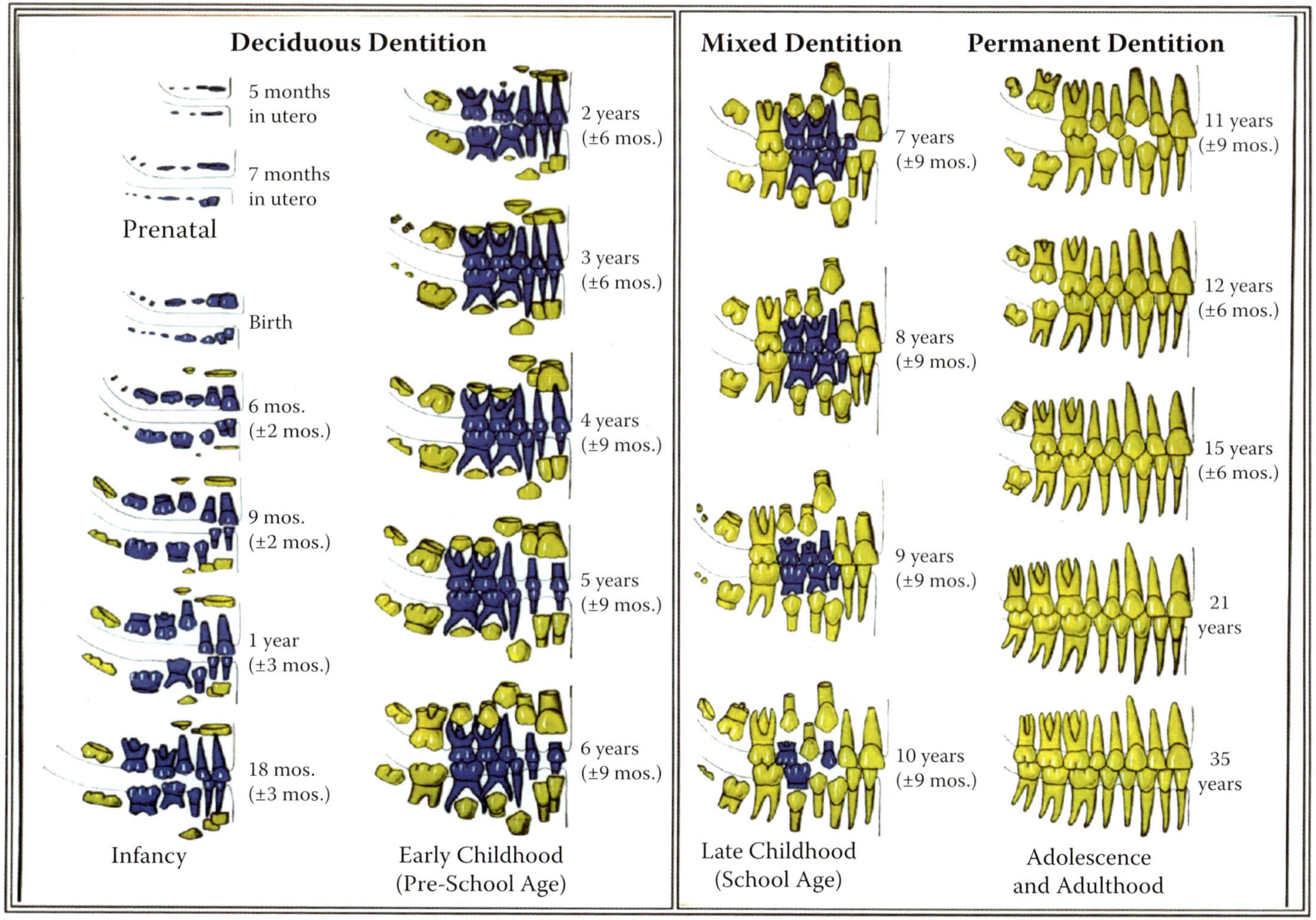

Figure 9.10 Schour and Massler dental development diagrams. (From Ash, M. *Wheeler's Dental Anatomy, Physiology and Occlusion, 7th Edition*, W.B. Saunders (Ed.), 1992. Used with permission from Elsevier.)

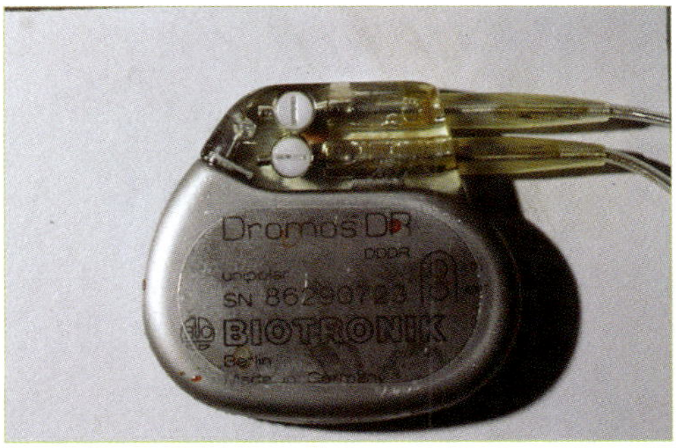

Figure 9.11 Serial numbers on implant.

inferior alveolar canal creates its own unique pattern which presents another opportunity for comparison.

Palatal rugae behind the upper anterior teeth also present a unique geographic landmark. They are not always available except in models taken from impressions of the maxillary hard palate. This may be available from orthodontic models or models used in constructing prosthetic appliances such as dentures, crowns, bridges, or bite guards in that area. If a night guard is available, then this may be used to make a model of the entire arch.

Serial numbers on dental implants remain in the future. It is hoped that someday we may see serial numbers on dental implants as there are presently on other body implants. Serial numbers are present now on some breast implants, surgical bars and plates, cardiac pacemakers (Figure 9.11), defibrillators, and joint replacements. Why not on dental implants which are becoming so prevalent in dentistry today? In 21 states it is mandatory for dentures to have identification placed within the appliance.

The Morgue

- Request for Forensic Odontology service.
    - Written form with duplicates for reporting results.
        - Phone—establish source of request.
            - Determine the individual and the investigating agency.
        - Standard form.
            - Medical Examiner/Coroner ID (M.E. # 2008-09999).
            - Agency ID of Police Dept., FBI.
- Barrier clothing in place.
    - Gown, eyeglasses, mask, gloves, shoe cover, head cover.
- Location of the body.
    - Building (Miami Dade Medical Examiner Department; Figure 9.12).
    - Cooler (Figure 9.13).
        - Number on toe tag; match to request (Figure 9.14).
        - Classification of the Body I, II, or III (fresh, decomposed, or skeletal).
        - Receiving area—Garage (Figure 9.15).
            - Entire automobiles and small planes have been accommodated in this area for the convenience of the medical examiner staff when they make a thorough examination, which may not be possible at the actual scene.

Figure 9.12 Miami Dade Medical Examiner building.

Figure 9.13 Miami Dade Medical Examiner morgue (cooler). (Courtesy of the Miami Dade Medical Examiners office. Used with permission.)

The garage doors can be closed for complete security, if necessary. Deliveries to funeral homes and body recovery is handled in this area of the morgue.

Entry Station

Height and weight, personal effects (Figure 9.16).

Photography and full body x-ray.

Registration area for all remains.

- Remove body to dental working space.

  Regular morgue (Figure 9.17).

  Dental space adjacent to regular morgue area (Figure 9.18).

Figure 9.14 Toe tag. (Courtesy of the Miami Dade Medical Examiners office. Used with permission.)

Figure 9.15 Miami Dade Medical Examiner morgue (receiving area). (Courtesy of the Miami Dade Medical Examiners office. Used with permission.)

X-ray and computer, camera, lights, charts, instruments.

Decomp area.

Same equipment and supplies.

Body remains on gurney in body bag (Figure 9.19) accompanied by odontologist in full barrier attire.

- Open body bag.

  Re-check for correct M.E. #.

  Check gender, race, age (estimate), and condition.

- Establish protocol for Class I, II, III (condition, fragmented or whole).

  Visual.

  Do not disturb the integrity of the facial features. Examination is made by routine mirror and explorer and high-intensity light.

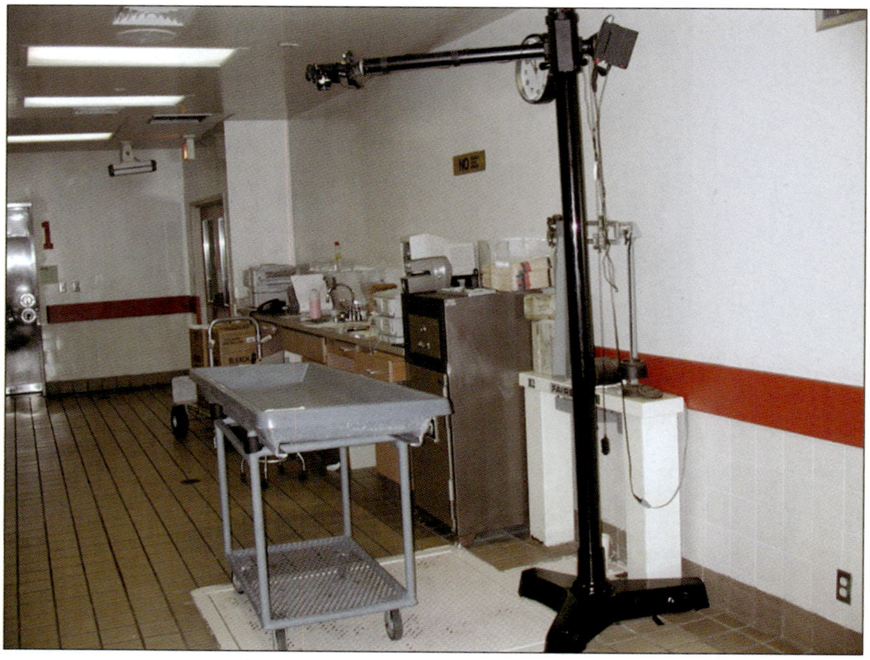

Figure 9.16 Miami Dade Medical Examiner morgue (entry area with gurney). (Courtesy of the Miami Dade Medical Examiners office. Used with permission.)

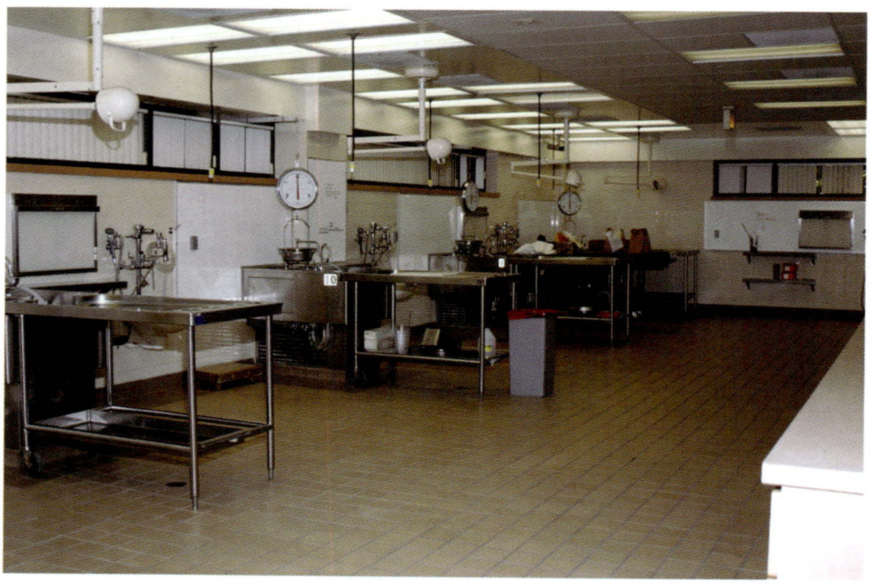

Figure 9.17 Miami Dade Medical Examiner morgue (autopsy table). (Courtesy of the Miami Dade Medical Examiners office. Used with permission.)

Non-visual.

The soft tissue surgical exposure consists of a horizontal cut from the commissure of the lips to the tragus of the ear on both sides, then a vertical cut in the philtrum of the upper lip and in the midline of the lower lip. It may be necessary to make a circumferential cut in the mucobuccal fold

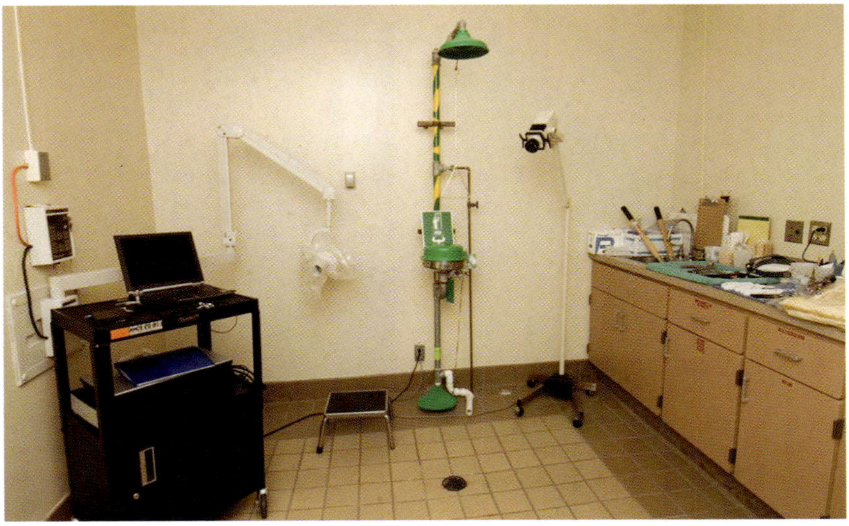

Figure 9.18 Miami Dade Medical Examiner morgue (dental room). (Courtesy of the Miami Dade Medical Examiners office. Used with permission.)

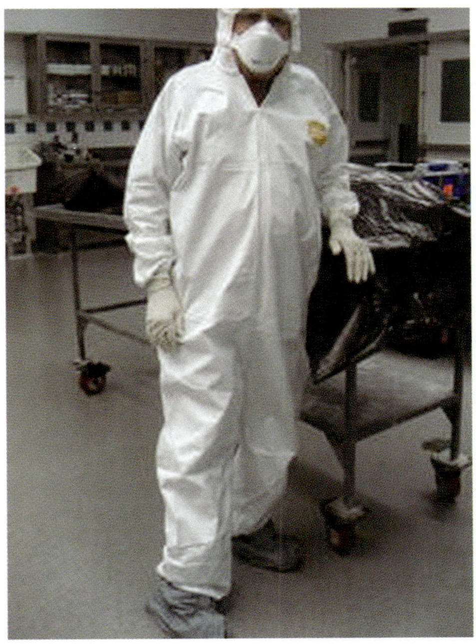

Figure 9.19 Palm Beach Medical Examiner morgue (examiner, body bag, and gurney).

from molar to molar to properly reflect the soft tissue (Figure 9.20a,b). This will allow full access to the upper and lower teeth.

Surgical exposure: permission from medical examiner applies only to jaw removal (Figure 9.21a–d). In cases of severe burn to the jaws it is necessary to remove the mandible for access (Figure 9.22a). Oftentimes, when the identification may not be made until much later, it will be necessary to remove the maxilla as well (Figure 9.22b) and preserve it for future investigation.

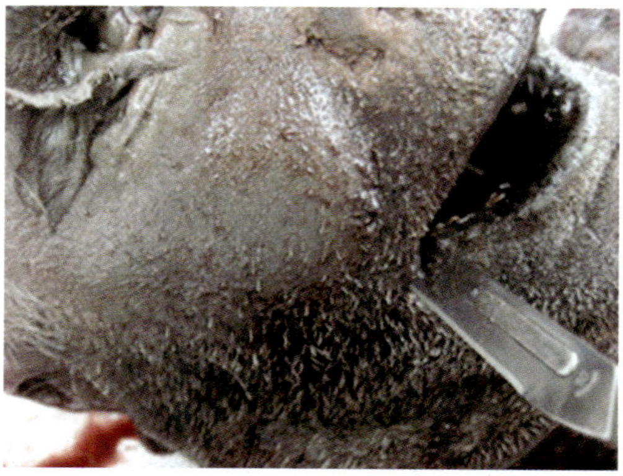

Figure 9.20a Initial dissection of non-viewable body. (Courtesy of the Miami Dade Medical Examiners office. Used with permission.)

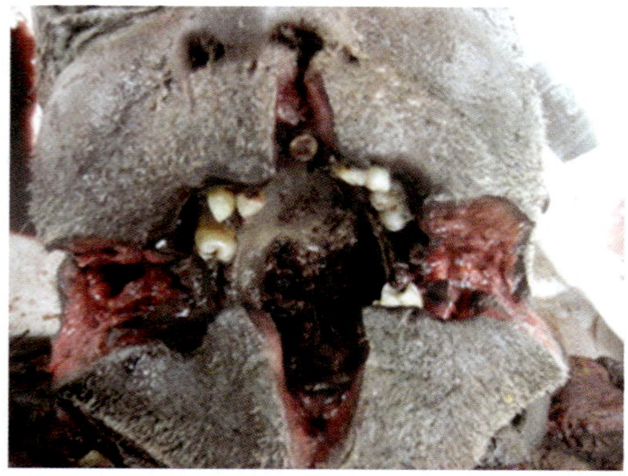

Figure 9.20b Complete dissection of non-viewable body. (Courtesy of the Miami Dade Medical Examiners office. Used with permission.)

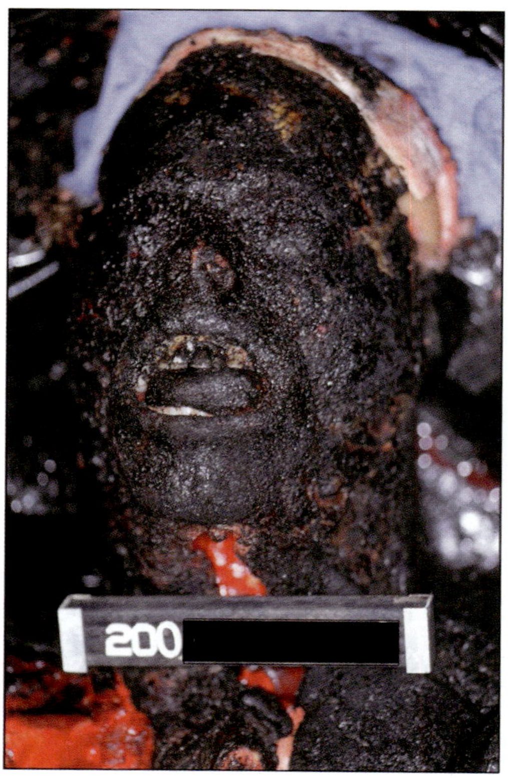

Figure 9.21a Burn victim, non-viewable. (Courtesy of the Miami Dade Medical Examiners office. Used with permission.)

Figure 9.21b Dissection of burn victim, non-viewable. (Courtesy of the Miami Dade Medical Examiners office. Used with permission.)

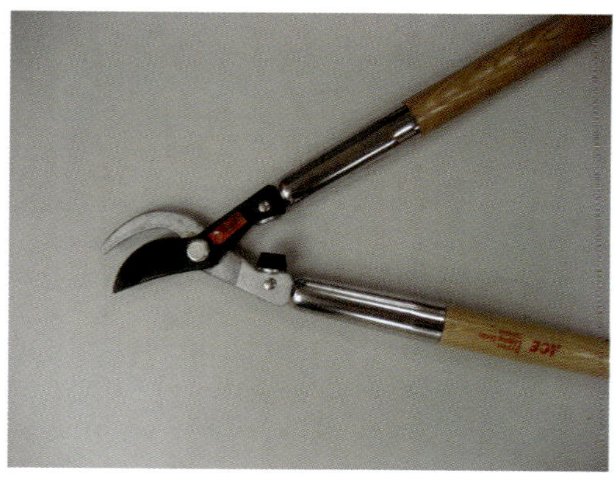

Figure 9.21c Lopper. (Courtesy of the Miami Dade Medical Examiners office. Used with permission.)

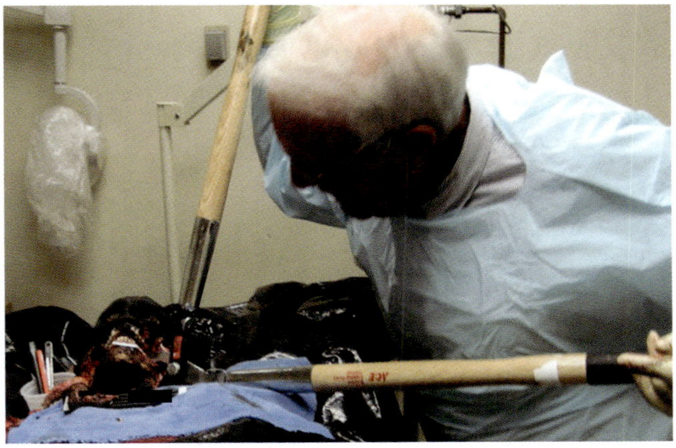

Figure 9.21d Lopper – jaw removal. (Courtesy of the Miami Dade Medical Examiners office. Used with permission.)

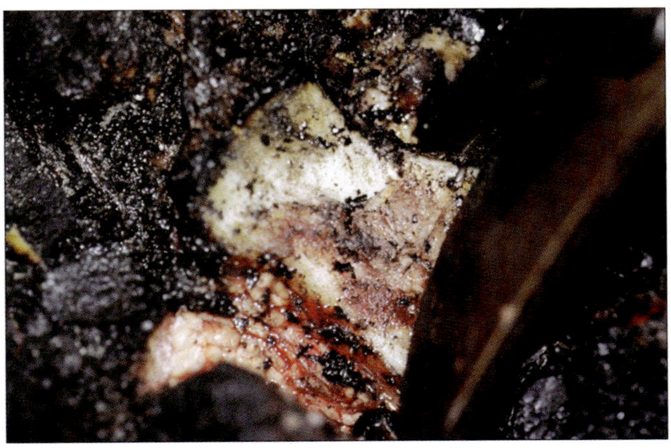

Figure 9.22a Mandibular ramus jaw cut. (Courtesy of the Miami Dade Medical Examiners office. Used with permission.)

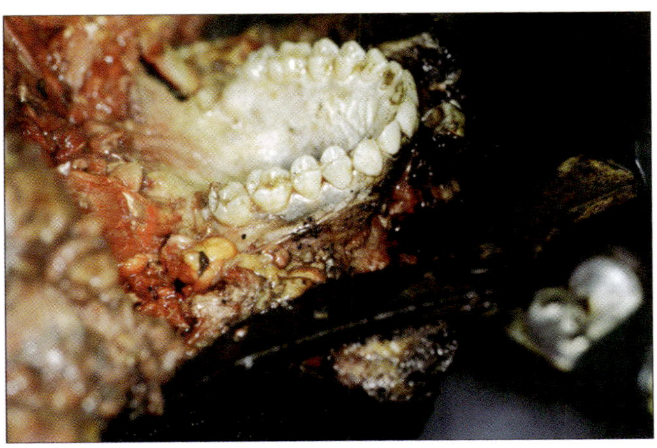

Figure 9.22b Maxillary lateral sinus jaw cut. (Courtesy of the Miami Dade Medical Examiners office. Used with permission.)

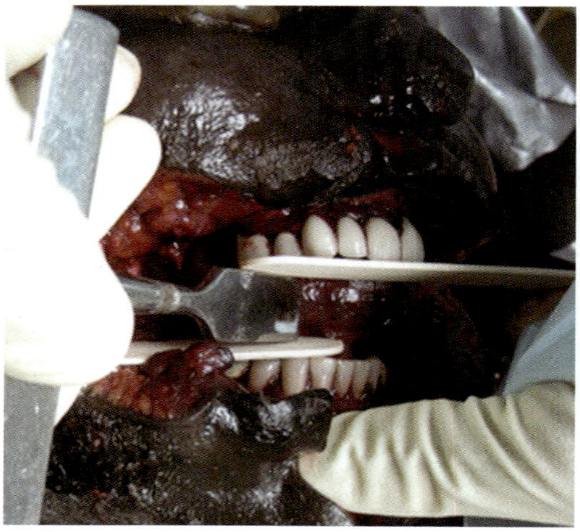

Figure 9.23a Jaw opening (lever). (Courtesy of the Miami Dade Medical Examiners office. Used with permission.)

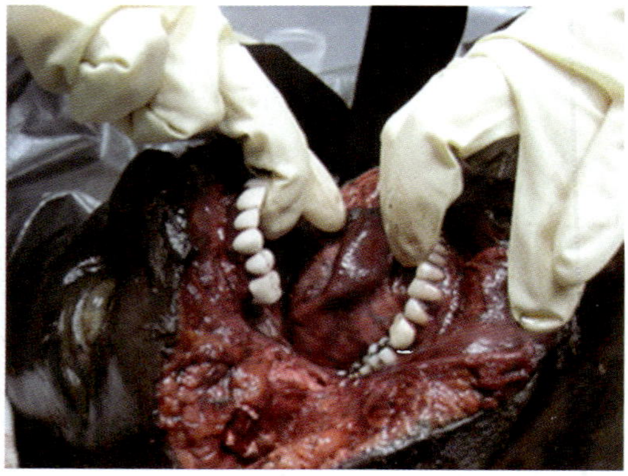

Figure 9.23b Jaw opening (manual). (Courtesy of the Miami Dade Medical Examiners office. Used with permission.)

After soft tissue has been removed and the jaws exposed, the lopper is placed at a right angle to the ramus, about halfway up. The small beak of the lopper is placed on the lingual side of the ramus, and a quick hard closure of the lopper should sever the ramus. In the maxilla, the small beak of the lopper is placed inside the lateral wall of the nasal cavity with the outer beak at a right angle to the bony surface. Then the lopper jaws are quickly and forcefully closed. This same procedure is repeated on the opposite side in the maxilla and the mandible. Subsequently soft tissue and nasal septum may have to be severed for the final removal of the jaws.

Depending upon the amount of time that has passed since the time of death, rigor mortis may still be present. The jaws are "locked" shut and we need access. The practical solutions to rigor mortis, which may impair access to the oral cavity, may involve.

1. The application of a lever to the posterior teeth, which are protected by wooden tongue blades (Figure 9.23a,b) followed by manual opening: placing the hands carefully over the upper and lower anterior teeth and slowly pulling them apart.
2. Dissection of the muscles of mastication which close the jaw, for example, internal and external pterygoids, masseter, and temporal will assist in this procedure.
3. Surgical revelation through removal/reflection of overlying soft tissue.
4. Jaw removal (mandible only) which will then allow full access to the maxillary arch (Figure 9.24).

This should be sufficient to clearly observe all mandibular and maxillary teeth. The removal of the maxilla, in addition to the mandible, would be necessary only to preserve evidence, and all tissues would be placed in formalin in the event of burial or cremation of the body.

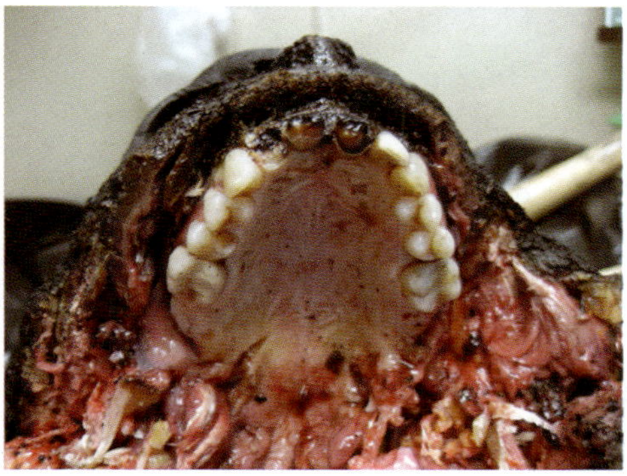

Figure 9.24 Maxillary arch. (Courtesy of the Miami Dade Medical Examiners office. Used with permission.)

Photography

Photography is a language just as English and French. It is a reliable means of communication. It is also an unflinching eyewitness with total memory recall. It is the only way to document what the mind and eye forget.

When you arrive at the scene you only begin to tell the story. When the body presents at the morgue you are working on the final chapter and hope that you will have the solution: identification.

Find a camera with which you are comfortable. It may be film (Ektachrome) or digital. Today, digital is the standard. A single lens reflex, Nikon D100 or similar camera, with 28–70-mm zoom and 105-mm macro lenses would be basic. In addition, you need an off-camera flash unit with cord and battery case. We recommend a camera case to keep all the equipment together (Figure 9.25). Be sure to test the equipment before venturing out.

Figure 9.25 Single lens reflex camera setup. (Courtesy of the Miami Dade Medical Examiners office. Used with permission.)

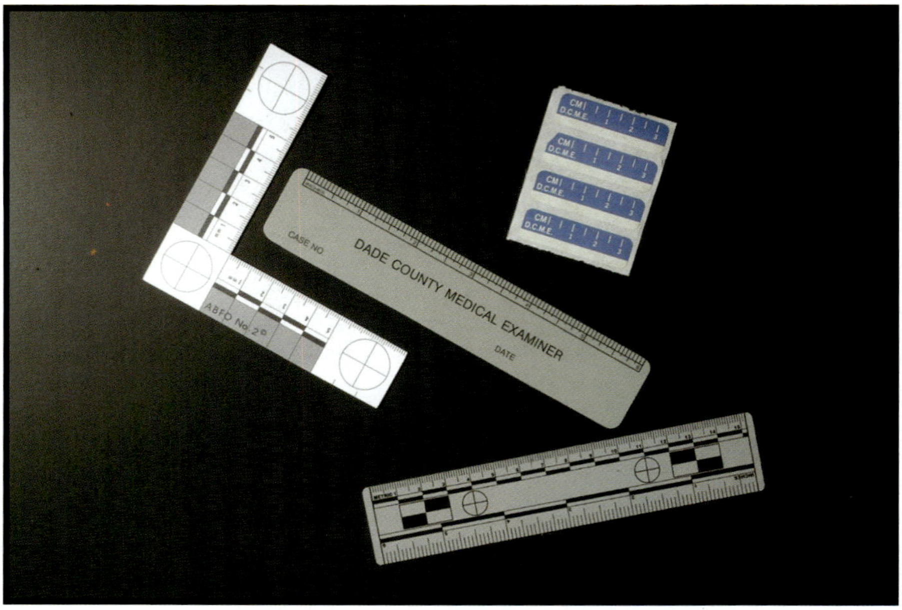

Figure 9.26 Rulers. (Courtesy of the Miami Dade Medical Examiners office. Used with permission.)

One of the principal advantages of the digital mode is that you see the picture immediately and can retake it if necessary. In addition, there are no chemicals or darkroom necessary for development.

When using the flash always consider the angle for proper illumination, and try to eliminate reflections. At times, an angle is recommended to accentuate depth. If it ever becomes necessary to create a 1:1 image, then it is critical to include an ABFO#2 ruler (Figure 9.26) in the field. In addition, the same photo should be taken without a ruler to demonstrate that no evidence has been obscured by the ruler. It is always better to take more pictures than you think you need. That is much easier to do using digital format.

Note: Never move or change any part of a scene until it is photographed. In bitemark cases, be sure to photograph the subject in the position in which he or she was found. Taking photos of a bitemark (see Chapter 13) over a period of time is also beneficial to proper documentation. Then attempt to photograph the subject in other positions. If it is at all possible that the bitemark was self-inflicted, then photograph the teeth of the victim as well as the suspect. Be sure that all pictures are sharp, clear, and properly exposed so that you will be confident that they will be well accepted in court.

All photos must contain identification so as to ensure integrity (Figure 9.27).

Do

Take front and profile facial photos.
Take photos of the dentition: front, side, and occlusal.
Maintain clean surrounding field.
Photo(s) with the lips apart or teeth apart.
Close-up of unique characteristics.

Figure 9.27 Labels. (Courtesy of the Miami Dade Medical Examiners office. Used with permission.)

Gold crowns, grilles, overretained deciduous teeth, and so on.
Maintain clean clear background.
Hardcopy all photos and place in case file.
Maintain electronic record.
Keep photo log with picture number, date, time, place, exposure, type of film or digital card.
ALS (Alternate Light Source) when available.
    UV ultraviolet for natural or artificial teeth and restorations.
    IR infrared.

Radiography

It is essential that radiographs be taken before charting so that undisclosed areas will be recorded in the chart, for example, root canal, posts, implants, retained roots, impacted teeth, and so on.

It is also critical that all evidence be photographed and then thoroughly cleaned before being radiographed (Figure 9.28a,b). This is also critical in reading the details contained in the evidence.

One distinct advantage of the digital x-ray is the immediate availability of data. Film is still a popular method of radiography. This medium may be employed with a fixed,

Figure 9.28a Fragment before cleaning. (Courtesy of the Miami Dade Medical Examiners office. Used with permission.)

Figure 9.28b Fragment after cleaning. (Courtesy of the Miami Dade Medical Examiners office. Used with permission.)

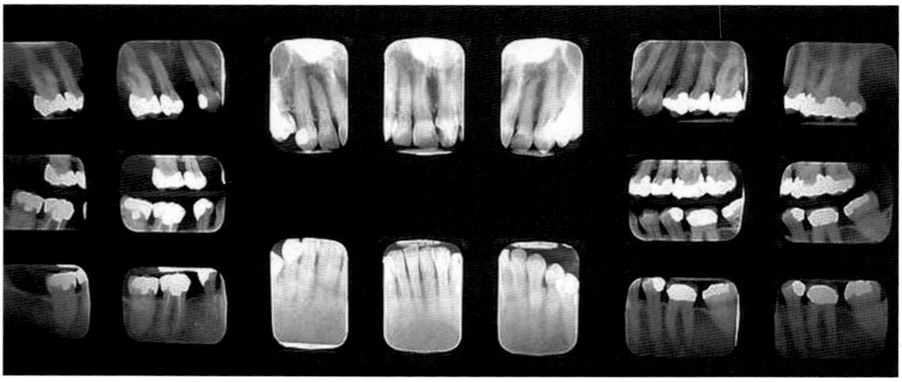

Figure 9.28c Full mouth radiographic series.

wall-mounted x-ray or portable x-ray apparatus. However, there is a serious time lapse involved between the exposure and the viewing of the radiograph when using film. It should be noted that all film must be in double packets.

With the use of digital x-ray sensors, the time lapse to view x-rays has diminished to seconds. The sensor delivers the image to the laptop computer for immediate viewing. The picture can be repeated, if it is not satisfactory, and all elements of the area will be seen and properly recorded. This system also provides for electronic storage and retrieval at any future date.

Guide for a full mouth radiographic survey (18 films) film or digital (Figure 9.28c)

- Film and portable x-ray machine (NOMAD)
- Digital and wall-mounted x-ray machine
- Digital and portable x-ray machine (NOMAD)
- Laptop and software (DEXIS) for recording radiographs
- Radiation protection apron (not required for NOMAD)
- Radiation monitoring badges
- Printout of hardcopy/mount films

Charting and Recording

Medical examiner dental chart (Appendix, Figure A.2)
Auxiliary charts for bitemarks, pathology, and other characteristics (Appendix, Figure A.8)

The forensic odontologist should be familiar with many different systems, the most important are:

DEXIS, a commercial software program for the recording of charts and x-rays with the use of intraoral sensors (http://www.dexis.com)

WINID, software program developed by Dr. Jim McGivney for the purpose of recording and comparing dental charts (http://www.winid.com)

NCIC 2000, Federal program (National Crime Information Center) for matching Unidentified and Missing persons as well as Wanted persons (http://www.fas.org/irp/agency/doj/fbi/is/ncic.htm)

Autopsy—The Report

(See Appendix, Figure A.19)

Report date
Address to agency/person requesting forensic odontology service
Agency/medical examiner/coroner identification number
Name of medical examiner/coroner and investigator
Date and time of notification
Date, time, and place of examination; persons present at examination
Evidence collected
Dental chart: intraoral and extraoral examination (soft and hard tissues) results
Photographs: number and type (film or digital)
Impressions and models: material, type, and number
Radiographs: number and type (film or digital)
Race, gender, and age (estimation)
DNA, if available
Comparison procedures: antemortem/postmortem
Procedures utilized to compare data
Points of concordance: number and type
Points of non-concordance with explanation
Description of the degree of certainty using ABFO guidelines
Appropriate embedded images whenever possible
Description of method (digital and hardcopy) and location of records to be retained
Signature, degree, title, and license of examining dentist

Terminology for Body Identification

ABFO Guidelines

Positive Identification

The antemortem and postmortem data match in sufficient detail to establish that they are from the same individual. In addition, there are no irreconcilable discrepancies.

Possible Identification

The antemortem and postmortem data have consistent features, but due to the quality of either the postmortem remains or the antemortem evidence, it is not possible to positively establish dental identification.

Insufficient Evidence

The available information is insufficient to form the basis for a conclusion.

Exclusion

The antemortem and postmortem data are clearly inconsistent. However, it should be understood that identification by exclusion is a valid technique in certain circumstances.

Note: The forensic dentist is not ordinarily in a position to verify that the antemortem records are correct as to name, date, and so on; therefore, the report should state that the conclusions are based on records, which are purported to represent a particular individual.

Custodian of the Records

All records must be preserved for a certain period of time according to the law of the agency that ordered the autopsy. It is advisable to retain all records for an indefinite period of time which becomes easier today in light of scanning and electronic storage methods. What happens in the morgue, stays in the morgue.

The burial or cremation protocol will differ according to the jurisdiction. If the remains are identified within a reasonable time after discovery, and next of kin are available, the family will be notified and the body will be released to the designated funeral home. If the next of kin are not available or choose not to claim the remains, for personal or financial reasons, the body is cremated and buried in Potter's Field.

When no identification is possible, after many attempts over a period of time, the remains are kept in the morgue coolers and then the body is buried in Potter's Field. It is not embalmed or cremated. In the event that any further evidence leads to an identification in the future, the body can be exhumed for further examination. If the jaws were removed during dental autopsy, then the evidence will have been preserved in formalin and kept securely in the morgue refrigerator for an indefinite time or defleshed and stored in the bone room.

Exhumation and Taphonomy

Taphonomy is the study of decaying organisms and, in this case, human remains. Experimentation usually consists of burial of the remains under varying conditions for different lengths of time. Non-human remains are sufficiently available but not of direct concern to the medical–dental profession. What is of concern is the preservation and the ability to make later identification of remains after varying periods of burial. The condition of the remains is critical. Discovery in the realm of anatomical remains is limited by the degree of preservation. Ground conditions, time, and temperature may result in preservation of the integumental elements. Artifacts of clothing, jewelry, religious, and personal items will assist in identification. Some coffin identification may be available with information residing in coffin identification glass tubes placed in the coffin by the funeral home. Then there is the possibility of matching the headstone, plaque, or crypt inscription.

Water is not compressible, and when water comes into a cemetery in a flood, and burial has taken place aboveground, the coffin or crypt is exposed and may be transported miles in any direction. During Hurricane Katrina, many coffins were exposed and remains were strewn over a wide area. It was necessary to identify these remains and return them to their proper resting place. Tidal water and flood are the culprits then, but sometimes it is the sole grave robber seeking valuables, or the fraudulent cemetery caretaker who has decided to make room for more remains by removing the previous remains.

When all is lost there is still one remaining anatomical portion that has not been affected by the ravages of decay: the teeth. Teeth may decay while residing in the living person but do not decay when life has been lost. This is often the one remaining clue that will make identification possible.

Whether the body has been encased in cement inside an old oil drum for criminal purposes, secretly buried in the woods, weighted down to the bottom of the ocean, or frozen solid with liquid nitrogen, the teeth will be intact and available for forensic odontological examination leading to the identification of those remains.

Methods of Comparison and Identification

10

Local and Worldwide

> The human features and countenances, although composed of some ten parts or a little more, are so fashioned that among thousands of men there are no two in existence who cannot be distinguished from one another.
>
> **Pliny the Elder, 23–79 C.E.**

There exist many and varied systems of comparison for identification of dental remains. It is inevitable that some are old and some are new. Some are accepted and some are rejected. It is fortunate that some are valuable because they employ standard procedures and charts, and it is unfortunate that others have chosen to re-create a separate language or a duplication of another system. In most industries or professions there is a gold standard. This is what the forensic odontology profession seeks as more systems blossom and fade.

CAPMI (Computer Assisted Post Mortem Identification) is an older system created by the military. We used CAPMI during the dental identification of passengers on the Valujet disaster, and it has worked well in many other times and places. But now, the principal problem with CAPMI is that it is DOS-based, which is no longer the most prevalent computer system. It is not Windows and it is not Apple, neither fish nor fowl. It is not available for updating although it is still in limited use even though it was basically replaced by WINID, which is the coding system in antemortem and postmortem DMORT forms. NCIC (National Crime Information Center) has been in existence for many years for matching missing and unidentified persons. Now, NCIC has been updated and replaced by the NCIC 2000, especially in the dental section. The latest version of NCIC 2000 employs the WINID nomenclature and coding, but has reduced the number of WINID codes considerably. NamUs (National Missing and Unidentified System), sponsored by CJIS (Criminal Justice Information System), chose to take another path with its own coding system thus creating a measure of incompatibility.

It is important to note differences between these systems, each of which do contain advantages. NamUs is designed for non-professionals to access the program input data and search for matches. WINID and NCIC are restricted to qualified professional use only.

The following are systems and outside agencies that may be employed in making comparisons:

Systems:

- CAPMI: Computer Assisted Post Mortem Identification
- WINID: System for matching missing and unidentified persons
- NCIC2000: National Criminal Information Center
- NDIR: National Dental Image Repository
- NamUs: National Missing and Unidentified System

- VICTIMS: Victim Information, Catalog, Tracking and Image System
- NAMPN: North American Missing Persons Network
- DOE: Missing persons network
- EDAN: Everyone Deserves a Name
- FLUIDDB: Florida Unidentified Deceased Data Base
- IDIS: Intelligent Dental Identification System
- CAMP: California Missing Persons
- ADIS: Automatic Dental Identification System
- LOCATOR
- INTERPOL DVI: Disaster Victim Identification
- CPIC: Canadian Police Information Centre

Outside Agencies

- NCMA: National Center for Missing Adults
- NCMEC: National Center for Missing and Exploited Children

CAPMI (Computer Assisted Post Mortem Identification System)

CAPMI was developed at the U.S. Army Institute of Dental Research to facilitate rapid identification of human remains. Dental-based identification of unknown postmortem remains and comparison with antemortem records of missing persons or victims of high energy incidents required the introduction of computer technology, in order to facilitate the process. CAPMI was developed because of the need to replace the repetitive chart-by-chart screening characteristic of traditional identification tasking, which was outmoded and time consuming. CAPMI software is available to governmental, civic, or humanitarian organizations at no cost.

Operating on a DOS-based system, and without current IT (Information Technology), has caused the decline in the use of CAPMI and the rise in application of WINID. In the technological age in which we live less has become better. There is an abundance of codes in CAPMI, which has been proven to be unnecessary for the purpose of computer matching. This is especially true because secondary codes (filling materials) are not even used in the computer matching system. The few primary codes that are available, are sufficient to make "possible matches." There is nothing that will replace the human eye and brain to make the final sort. Although some jurisdictions makes effective use of this program, it no longer has any application on a national or federal level. In order to understand records that may be using CAPMI we have included the Dental Coding System. This system was in use in 1996 when it assisted in making identifications in the Valujet air disaster in Miami, Florida.

Coding for CAPMI

AM	Amalgam	CF	Crown Full
GI	Gold Inlay	CP	Crown Partial
GF	Gold Foil	CV	Crown Veneer
SS	Any other metal restoration	FP	Fixed Partial
CO	Composite Resin	RP	Removable Partial

JM	Jaw Fragment Missing	CD	Complete Denture
TA	Traumatic Avulsion	M	Mesial
FX	Fractured Crown	D	Distal
RT	Root Tip	O	Occlusal
PN	Present. Not Restored	I	Incisal
RO	Rotated	F	Facial
RF	Root Canal Filling	L	Lingual
AP	Apicoectomy	C	Caries
IR	Intermediate Restoration	U	Unerupted
CT	Crown Temporary	X	Extracted

Copies of CAPMI software and instructions can be obtained free of charge from The Director, Armed Forces Institute of Pathology, 14th and Alaska Ave, NW, Washington, DC 30306-6000.

WINID

WINID was developed by Dr. James McGivney as a dental computer system that matches missing persons to unidentified human remains. It is incident-specific in that the comparative database is composed of known persons (missing persons, disaster victims) who are entered into the WINID database which stores the data in a Microsoft Access Database. This provides extensive data filtering and data sorting capabilities. The unknown person is only being compared to the database of missing persons or the passenger list involved in that particular incident or event. It is local—not global. WINID was used successfully in the World Trade Center identification process and in other incidents, large and small, because the unknown remains were compared to a known list of missing persons provided by the community.

WINID uses dental characteristics to rank all the possible matches, even though anthropometric notations are recorded. Even then, it only matches the primary codes. WINID is used by forensic odontologists, pathologists, medical examiners/coroners, and law enforcement agencies whose mission it is to bring the missing person and the unidentified remains together again. The program is made so that the operator can switch among English, Italian, Portuguese, and Spanish. At the touch of a button it will convert Universal Tooth Numbering systems to Federation Dentaire Internationale (FDI). An odontogram is automatically created when data is entered and request for "best matches" is immediately available.

There are only 10 primary codes and 12 secondary codes in WINID. A dash is placed between the primary and secondary code, but this is automatically recorded when using the computer for entry. If you are unsure of the secondary code (restorative material) then leave it out. The computer does not search secondary codes. The entire program and manual may be downloaded online at www.winid.com.

WINID Primary Codes

(Note the close relationship between NCIC2000 and WINID codes.)
All codes must be entered in proper sequence: MODFL, for example, "OD" not "DO".

Caries (decay) is never coded.

M Mesial surface of the tooth is restored.
O Occlusal surface of the tooth is restored.
D Distal surface of the tooth is restored.
F Facial surface of the tooth is restored (buccal or labial: use the same code).
L Lingual surface of the tooth is restored (palatal: use the same code).
U Tooth is unerupted.
V Virgin tooth, unrestored.
X Tooth is missing, extracted.
J Tooth is missing postmortem or the clinical crown is not present for examination. The root or open socket remains.
/ No information about the tooth is available. No records or missing fragment.

WINID Secondary Codes

A An anomaly is present; details in the comments section.
B Tooth is deciduous.
C Crown.
E Resin filling.
G Gold restoration.
H Porcelain.
N Non-precious filling or crown.
P Pontic, primary code must be X.
R Root canal filled.
S Silver amalgam.
T Denture Tooth. Primary code must be X.
Z Temporary filling.
A Annotation, standard comments, may be used to filter records.

Abrasion	Resorbtion	Pedo
Apico	Retainer	Torus
Cong Miss	Retrofill	Pin
Cyst	Root Tip	Post
Hemisect	RPD	Written Record Narrative
Impaction	Sealant	Date of Xrays
Implant	Silver Point	Orthodontics
Opacity	Supernum	Temporary

NCIC 2000 (Also Known as NCIC)

The National Crime Information Center is the United States' central database for tracking crime-related information. The NCIC is maintained by the Federal Bureau of Investigation (FBI) Criminal Justice Information Services Division (CJIS).

The CJIS system was established in 1992 to serve as a focal point and central repository for criminal justice information services in the FBI. Programs consolidated under CJIS included NCIC as well as the Integrated Automated Fingerprint Identification System

(IAFIS) and others. NCIC is interlinked with similar systems that each state maintains. Most data is received from federal, state, and local law enforcement agencies and non-law enforcement agencies for missing persons, and from medical examiner/coroner offices for the unidentified persons.

The NCIC database was created in 1967 under FBI director J. Edgar Hoover. The purpose of the system was to create a centralized information system to facilitate information flow between various law enforcement branches. Its principal mission was (and still is) the identification of criminal activity, and persons by distribution of crime information, as the title suggests. In the mid-1990s the program went through an upgrade from the legacy system to the current NCIC2000 system. The current version of NCIC2000 serves criminal justice agencies in all 50 states, the District of Columbia, the Commonwealth of Puerto Rico, the United States Virgin Islands, and Canada. Canada has a separate system, CPIC (see below), that interfaces with NCIC and is presently under study to make it more compatible with NCIC by using Universal Tooth Numbering, rather than the FDI tooth numbering system.

The NCIC2000 has had a dramatic effect upon the dental information section. The number of codes went from 56 to 10 and the number of items for coding went from 256 to 32. This simplification of the entry system is expected to increase the rate of utilization of the former system. The entry of data on missing persons is the responsibility of law enforcement, and the entry of information on the unknown is the responsibility of the ME/C departments. The institution of a more simplified system should be of assistance to both entryways and increase the number of files with dental records.

NCIC Files with Dental Records (January 2009)

Unidentified		Missing	
Number of records	7147	Number of records	99778
With dental records	4738	With dental records	8201
66.3%		8.2%	

The Missing Person and the Wanted Person files include dental characteristics for purposes of matching information against records in the NCIC2000 Unidentified Person File.

There are three sections:

1. Administrative information and evidence available
   a. Radiographs
   b. Models
   c. Photos
2. Dental Characteristics
   a. DCH
3. Acceptable Dental Codes (completed by a trained dental professional)
   a. Dental Remarks

Note: Whenever a Supplemental Dental Record is entered or modified, NCIC automatically compares Missing Person (MP), Unidentified Person (UP), and Wanted Person (WP) records against each other and produces a report called a Dollar M ($.M) to determine possible matches.

Note: A "$.N" message denotes no matches. To assist in reading these messages it is important to understand the codes and the body parts (Appendix, Figure A.9) to which they may be referred.

NCIC2000 Codes

All codes must be entered in proper order: ("MODFLCR," e.g., usual "DO" is entered as "OD").

Note: There is no code for deciduous teeth or for caries.

Unidentified persons

One or more codes must be entered for each tooth.

Primary Dental Codes

- / (Default code for unidentified persons) Used when the tooth is not recovered or it is impossible to determine if the crown has been restored; also, postmortem loss.
- V Virgin. Tooth is present and unrestored including unerupted teeth, for example, wisdom teeth.
- X Missing. Tooth has been extracted or is congenitally missing.
- M Mesial surface of the tooth has been restored.
- O Occlusal or incisal surface of the tooth has been restored.
- D Distal surface of the tooth has been restored.
- F Facial, buccal, or labial surface of the tooth has been restored.
- L Lingual or palatal surface of the tooth has been restored.

Secondary Dental Codes

(Cannot be used independently. Must be used in conjunction with Primary Dental Codes. These are not used in computer comparison.)

- C Any laboratory-processed restoration including crowns, inlays, onlays, and veneers.
- R Root canal. Endodontic procedure has been started or completed.

Missing Persons

All dental codes are the same as for unidentified persons, **except**:

- / A portion of the tooth is remaining and treatment may have been accomplished, but it is impossible to determine which surfaces have been restored, for example, pit filling on x-ray; cannot determine which surface.
- V Virgin. (Default code for missing persons) Tooth is unrestored, or no information is available, including unerupted teeth. Also, when a tooth has been restored but it is not possible to determine the surfaces restored. False or incorrect information might cause a mismatch, whereas "V" avoids any conflict for the discovery later of restorations in unidentified remains.

FAQ (Frequently Asked Questions)

Q. Why only Primary Codes for ranking?
A. Secondary Codes are only descriptors.
Secondary Codes are not necessary for ranking.
Secondary Codes are more subjective for MP and WP recording.
Q. Why not codes for ortho, implants, and the like?
A. Not necessary for ranking.
Sufficient codes exist; may use filter. K.I.S.S.
Q. Why is "V" the default code for MPs and WPs?
A. Because all teeth are unrestored (Virgin) when they erupt.
Program logic assumes that the dental records may not be the most recent.
"V" presents a no-conflict statement with any other subsequent condition.
Q. Why is "/" the default code for UPs ?
A. If a tooth is not available because it fell out after death or the crown has been lost or that fragment of the jaw is missing, we cannot assume that any treatment was or was not accomplished. No information is a no-conflict statement with any other previous condition.
Q. Why not a code for primary teeth?
A. Only 0.3% of MP records are 12 years old or under.
Only 3% of UP records are 1 year old or under.
Remark section available for notation.
Unerupted permanent teeth may be coded as "V".
Q. Why not code pit and fissure sealants?
A. They are easily lost, fall out, and wear out.
Difficult to detect in postmortem examination.
Progression may be false, filling to no filling.
May cause a mismatch when there is none.
Remark section available for notation.
Q. Why not use "U" or "I" for unerupted/impacted teeth?
A. Importance is not condition but whether they are present.
Erupted or unerupted may be subjective.
Difficult to determine whether skeletal or tissue-related conditions.

In addition, NCIC makes available a variety of records to be used by law enforcement:

Active arrest warrants
Gang membership
Sex offenders
Firearms records, lost or stolen
Stolen vehicles and boats
Jewelry

When requests are made for comparison of a missing or unidentified person the reports are transmitted by messages that advise the inquiring department as to a "Match" ($.M) or "No Match" ($.N).

In order to read the $.M messages the following codes are used:

Dollar M Codes

BLT	Blood type	MAN	ME/C agency name and case number
BPS	Body part status (see body part diagram)	MAT	ME/C telephone number
BXR	Body x-rays available	MIS	Miscellaneous
CDA	Cause and manner of death	MKE	Message key
CMC	Caution and medical condition	MNU	Miscellaneous number
CRC	Circumcision	MNP	Missing person record type
DBF	Date body found	MPA	Dental models/photographs available
DCH	Dental characteristics	MPC	Missing person circumstances
DLC	Date last contacted	NAM	Name
DLO	DNA location	NIC	NCIC number
DNA	DNA profile indicator	NOA	Notify originating agency flag
DOB	Date of birth	OCA	Originating agency case number
DOE	Date of emancipation	OLN	Operator's license number
DRE	Dentist remarks	OLS	Operator's license state
DTE	Date and time of entry	OLY	Operator's license year of expiration
EDD	Estimated date of death	ORI	Originating agency identifier
EYB	Estimated year of birth	POB	Place of birth
EYE	Eye color	RAC	Race
FBI	FBI number	SEX	Sex
FPA	Footprints available	SKN	Skin tone
FPC	Fingerprint classification	SMT	Scars, marks, tattoos, and other characteristics
HAI	Hair color	SOC	Social Security number
HGT	Height	VCO	Vehicle color
JWL	Jewelry description	VIN	Vehicle identification number
JWT	Jewelry type	VMA	Vehicle make
LIC	License plate number	VMO	Vehicle model
LIS	License plate state	VRX	Corrective vision prescription
LIT	License plate type	VST	Vehicle style
LIY	License plate year of expiration	VYR	Vehicle year
LKA	Linking case number	WAC	WACIC number
LKI	Linking agency identifier	WGT	Weight or approximate weight
MAL	ME/C locality		

Descriptors

DXR = Dental x-rays
- M = Match
- P = Possible
- N = No Match
- U = Unknown

BPS Field (see body parts diagram, Appendix, Figure A.9)
- N = Not recovered
- F = Fresh — Class I
- D = Decomposed — Class II
- S = Skeletal — Class III

There are two books for NCIC recording: *Missing Persons* (Blue), Appendix, Figure A.3 (Dental Section), and *Unidentified Persons* (Red), Appendix, Figure A.4 (Dental Section).

These booklets are available at no cost from the FBI/Department of Justice, 1000 Custer Hollow Road, Clarksburg, WV 26306.

NDIR (National Dental Image Repository)

In May of 2005, the FBI's Criminal Justice Information System (CJIS) management approved the creation of the NDIR to facilitate the identification of missing, unidentified, and wanted persons. The NDIR is housed on Law Enforcement Online (LEO) and will permit LEO members to store, access, and supplement dental records in the NCIC system.

CJIS advises that the NCIC system does not have sufficient image capability for dental radiographs, models, and photographs. However, the NDIR will provide users with direct access to digital images of these dental records.

Agencies digitize their supplemental dental images and e-mail images to ndir@leo.gov. A member of the NDIR review panel is contacted to review the NCIC dental record.

Review panel member reviews and confirms or corrects the coding.
Information is posted to the NDIR on LEO.
NDIR field added to NCIC.

What Is LEO?

LEO is an acronym for Law Enforcement Online. It is a controlled access website for law enforcement, criminal justice, and public safety employees. It is a secure e-mail, chat, special interest group (SIG) with libraries, and contains the National Dental Image Repository (NDIR).

How Do I Qualify and Get on LEO?

NDIR Review Panel members qualify as well as dentists who work in conjunction with law enforcement officials or ME/C departments. Complete an application and receive a user name and password (approximately three weeks; ndir@leo.gov).

NamUs

The National Missing and Unidentified System is made up of the Endangered Missing Persons Reporting System (EMPRS; http://www.find-the-missing.org) together with the Unidentified Decedent Reporting System (UDRS; http://www.identifyus.org).

In 2003, the President's DNA initiative was launched. The Office of Justice Program's (OJP) National Institute of Justice began funding to maximize the use of DNA technology in the criminal justice system. The work of NIJ has focused on developing tools to investigate and solve the thousands of cases of missing and unidentified persons.

The NamUs databases of missing and unidentified persons are just one element of a broader program to improve the nation's capacity to address these problem cases. NIJ also funds free testing of unidentified human remains and provides family reference sample kits. They include training law enforcement officers, medical examiners, forensic odontologists, judges, and attorneys on forensic DNA evidence. As a result of a meeting in 2005 of federal and state law enforcement officials, ME/C, forensic scientists, key policy makers, victim advocates, and families, the deputy attorney general created the National Missing Persons Task Force and charged the U.S. Department of Justice with identifying every available tool to solve these cases.

The National Missing Persons Task Force identified the need to improve access to database information by people who can help solve missing and unidentified deceased persons cases. NamUs was created to meet that need.

NamUs was launched in July 2007 as the first national online repository for missing and unidentified persons. It brings together two innovative programs and their online searchable databases for access by professionals as well as the general public. It is this access to the general public that distinguishes NamUS from NCIC.

http://www.IdentifyUs.org is the website for information on unidentified human remains.
http://www.Find-The-Missing.org is the website for information on missing persons.

The national database entry system for unidentified decedent records has been completed. This will allow searches based on characteristics such as demographics, anthropological analysis, dental information, and other body features.

In 2009, a fully searchable NamUs system was released which can search cases in its missing person database against cases in the unidentified decedent database in an effort to identify unidentified human remains and solve missing person cases.

The present coding system for NamUs consists of a Universal Tooth Numbering system and nine (9) codes with 13 check boxes and a box for comments:

N = Natural tooth, no filling	A = Antemortem loss (healed socket)
F = Filling, inlay, onlay, or veneer	P = Postmortem loss (open socket)
C = Crown or cap	I = Impacted
B = Part of a bridge	O = Other features (see Dental Comments)
R = Root canal	

Dental summary (Check all that apply)

One or more teeth present	Implants	Upper jaw present
Baby/primary teeth present	Braces	Upper jaw had no teeth during life
Filling or crown present	Retainer	Lower jaw present
Removable dentures	Root Canal	Lower jaw had no teeth during life
Cemented bridge		

Dental comments

This project has been designed to be available online principally for the development of a database of missing persons, but also for the unidentified, in addition to the NCIC, which is available only to law enforcement agencies, and ME/C offices.

The addition of a different coding system may cause confusion; however, the present NamUs system will convert NCIC codes as necessary, within the program. It is important for all systems to adhere to the same gold standard and, at least in dental identification, we should all speak the same language.

Interpol

The Interpol system (http://www.interpol.int/public/disastervictim) has a more international appeal because it does employ the FDI tooth numbering system. However, it has developed its own coding, with the addition of color coding:

M = Mesial
O = Occlusal
D = Distal
V = Vestibular
L = Lingual
Black = Amalgam
Red = Gold
Green = Tooth-colored material

X = Tooth missing antemortem
Encircle tooth number = Tooth missing postmortem
Leave unmarked = Sections not recovered

Living and working in a global environment today has made it essential to coordinate our coding language for dental identification. One glaring example of this problem would be the use of the "V" code for vestibular when "V" is used predominantly referring to a Virgin or natural unrestored tooth. Postmortem loss and unrestored teeth in this system, lack any code. The use of colors in place of codes precludes the use of facsimile (fax) transmission of data, computer data entry, or copying records in many venues.

It is important to note that the forms for dead body (unidentified) and missing persons are the same except for the page color: dead body (pink) and missing person (yellow).

CPIC (Canadian Police Information Center)

The Canadian Police Information Centre (http://www.cpic-cipc.ca) is a computerized system similar to NCIC. It is an integral part of the Royal Canadian Mounted Police (RCMP), National Police Service (NPS), and it is the only national information-sharing system in the same way that NCIC is in the United States. The CPIC system has four databanks: Investigative, Identification, Intelligence, and Ancillary, which includes files and information on dental characteristics. The individual dental records assist police in identifying human remains or comatose and amnesia victims.

CPIC is presently operating under the FDI tooth numbering system and uses the following system of codes:

M = Mesial
O = Occlusal
D = Distal
F = Facial
L = Lingual
C = Crown
R = Root canal
U = Unknown
X = Missing
V = Virgin

This coding is practically the same as NCIC and in the future it is hoped that the tooth numbering system will also conform to the Universal Tooth Numbering, system used in NCIC, in order to establish complete across the border compatibility (Appendix, Figure A.11).

NAMPN (North American Missing Persons Network)

This site (http://www.nampn.org) is dedicated to all missing persons in North America. It is the "sister" site to the DOE Network (http://www.doenetwork.org). It is not necessary to be a law enforcement person to enter or modify the case information. Family members can enter full information including photographs and pertinent medical or dental history. It is devoted to both child and adult missing persons in the United States and Canada. Directors link NAMPN to local law enforcement agencies. They are responsible for validating cases and relaying information they receive from the general public to the proper agencies in their area.

DOE Network

The DOE Network (http://www.doenetwork.org) is an international database for unidentified and missing persons covering the United States, Canada, Australia, Europe, and Mexico. It is a sister organization to NAMPN (North American Missing Persons Network). The DOE Network is a volunteer organization devoted to assisting law enforcement agencies in solving cold cases, where a person may have suffered an unexplained disappearance or is an unidentified victim. Their method is to give cases exposure through their website, attempt to obtain media exposure, and for volunteers to search for clues in order to make possible matches between missing and unidentified persons. The unique element of this organization is the ability of non-professionals to access the website and search for clues, faces, or other paraphernalia such as watches or clothing that might lead to an identification. Many of the cases have little evidence available.

EDAN (Everyone Deserves A Name)

EDAN cooperates with the DOE Network. It consists of a group of volunteer forensic artists who donate their time and skills to create reconstructions and age progressions of the Missing and Unidentified Persons (MUPS). This work is offered to law enforcement agencies and is also featured on their website (http://www.projectedan.us).

FLUIDDB (Florida Unidentified Deceased Data Base)

This site (http://www.fluiddb.com) is a clearinghouse containing information about those found dead in Florida whose identities remain unknown. Family as well as medical examiners/coroners may enter this site to provide information or to search through the unidentified or missing persons. The database is formed by medical examiners in Florida who enter the information on unidentified human remains found in their jurisdiction. Other persons from out of state may query the database and find a match.

In October of 2005, a detective in Cleveland, Ohio, searching for an individual who was reported missing in March of 1986, found similarities with an unidentified decedent listed on FLUIDDB. The decedent was a victim of a homicide in Jacksonville, Florida in November, 1986. After reviewing the information and the available sketch, and contacting the District Four Medical Examiner Office, the detective from Cleveland was able to establish a positive identification.

Many other states, including California, have such databases.

California Missing Persons

The website for California is http://www.ag.ca.gov/missing where you will find the Missing and Unidentified Persons Unit of the California Department of Justice. Their mission is to assist law enforcement and criminal justice agencies in locating missing persons and identifying unknown live and deceased persons through the comparison of physical characteristics, fingerprints, and dental/body radiographs. In California, a missing person is someone whose whereabouts is unknown to the reporting party. This includes any child who may have run away, been taken involuntarily, or may be in need of assistance. It includes a child illegally taken, held, or hidden by a parent or non-parent family member or non-family member. In California there is no waiting period for reporting a missing person.

The State of California maintains a searchable database of missing persons which allows anyone to look for a missing person by name, description, county, and many other categories. The number of missing person cases in California averages around 25,000. The clearinghouse provides a nationwide, toll-free hotline to receive tips and provides awards of up to $500 for information leading to the recovery of the missing person (1-800-222-FIND).

VICTIMS (Victim Information, Catalog, Tracking, and Image System)

The mission of the FBI Laboratory VICTIM System is to accumulate records from all available sources related to unidentified human remains only and to provide a software system for orderly access to the records for the purpose of assisting law enforcement, ME/C offices, and the public, in the identification of the remains. The VICTIMS System is actually a group of research projects and development efforts sponsored by the FBI Laboratory.

These projects are designed to bring technology to bear on the problem of identification of unknown human remains. Currently, there are many groups attempting to bring closure to an estimated 40,000 unidentified human remains nationwide, but VICTIMS intends to produce a comprehensive approach to the problem. With 1000 new unidentified victim cases in the United States each year, deployment of tools useful to the law enforcement community and medical examiner and coroner's offices is critical.

IDIS (Intelligent Dental Identification System)

In recent studies this system (Figure A.17) resulted in 82–100% identification when applied to permanent, mixed, and deciduous dentition. It is based upon guidelines of ABFO and Interpol, but codes for missing and impacted teeth are confusing.

ADIS (Automatic Dental Identification System)

In 1997 the Criminal Justice Information Services Division (CJIS) of the FBI created a Dental Task Force (DTF), whose goal was to improve the utilization and effectiveness of the National Crime Information Center's (NCIC) Missing and Unidentified Persons (MUP) files. The DTF recommended the creation of a National Digital Image Repository (NDIR) and an Automated Dental Identification System (http://www.csee.wvu.edu/adis) with goals and objectives similar to the Automated Fingerprint Identification System (AFIS), but using dental characteristics instead of fingerprints.

Owing to their survivability and diversity, dental features are widely accepted among forensic scientists as reliable characteristics for establishing positive postmortem (PM) identification. Modern materials, used in filling, and restoration, possess poor radiographic characteristics, and it is expected that contemporary generations will have less dental decay than their predecessors. Therefore, there appears to be a need to shift towards comparison based on inherent tooth and bone characteristics.

The goal of ADIS is to automate the process of dental identification using image processing and pattern recognition techniques. Given a postmortem radiograph, the antemortem database would be searched in order to retrieve the closest match using the contours of the teeth as one feature among others. Unfortunately, poor image quality is a major deterrent as is orientation of radiographs. Both problems are prevalent among antemortem and postmortem radiographs, which makes for great difficulty in establishing reliable databases. Large discrepancies exist when comparing radiographs of the same teeth when vertical and horizontal beams are varied, for example, elongation, foreshortening, overlapping, and so on. This system is still in development.

Outside Agencies

Missing Children

NCMEC (National Center for Missing and Exploited Children)

Founded in 1984 by John Walsh after the tragic loss of his own son, Adam, the National Center for Missing and Exploited Children (http://www.missingkids.com) has as its mission the prevention of child abduction and sexual exploitation, as well as providing assistance in finding missing children. It serves as a clearinghouse for information about missing children, distributes photographs and descriptions of missing children worldwide, and networks with non-profit service providers and state clearinghouses about missing person cases. Input is accepted from the general public by Internet or phone (1-800-THE LOST).

According to NCMEC, one in six missing children is recovered as a result of someone recognizing his or her photo and notifying the authorities.

Note: The Adam Walsh Act requires law enforcement, within two hours of notification of a missing person (under 21 years of age), to enter this person into NCIC.

Missing Adults

NCMA (National Center for Missing Adults)

The National Center for Missing Adults maintains a national database for information pertaining to adults. It is accessible to law enforcement agencies, medical examiners/coroners, and the general public. There are online support groups for individuals and families in similar situations, and personal profiles are regularly included on the website (http://www.theyaremissed.org). Photographs and personal data may be entered at any time and the database may be searched by any registered member. According to the NCIC/FBI there are 50,930 active missing adult cases in the United States as of January 31, 2007. In examining adult cases there are many voluntary, as well as involuntary, instances among the missing.

In 1994 the Nation's Missing Children Organization (NMCO) was founded and it was well noted, at that time, that missing adults were a segment of the population that lacked adequate resources. The focus was on adults (over the age of 18) who were at risk due to diminished mental capacity, physical disability, or suspicion of foul play. In an effort to educate the population, Robert and Deborah Modafferi shared the painful story of the disappearance of their daughter, Kristen, who mysteriously vanished in June, 1997. In October, 2000 Kristen's Act was passed unanimously by Congress. This authorized the U.S. attorney general to provide grants for organizations to find missing adults. As a result the NCMA was created and now serves the public under the auspices of the NMCO and the U.S. Department of Justice as a national clearinghouse for missing adults in the United States.

Mass Disaster

11

The definition of a mass disaster has been rewritten since the events of September 11, 2001 at the World Trade Center in New York City (Figure 11.1). It is no longer a single incident but may be a series of related incidents occurring about the same time, at the same or different locations, when there are more fatally struck victims than can be accommodated and processed by the usual personnel at the local medical examiner/coroner facility, within an acceptable period of time. It may also involve the threat of more similar activity in the area. In addition to trauma, there may be nuclear, biological, or chemical hazards which are actual or threatened, perceived, or clandestine. "Terrorism" has been added to the mass disaster vocabulary.

Mass disasters usually occur suddenly and cause loss of human life, ecological damage, and a deterioration of health and supporting health services, as well as loss of essential infrastructure. There are natural disasters such as flood, hurricane, or earthquake, and there are manmade disasters, intentional acts of terrorism, and unintentional disasters such as airplane disasters or major building and ship fires. Each of these may take place in a single location (Valujet plane crash) or in multiple locations (Hurricane Katrina) and may occur within a limited time or extended time periods (ethnic conflicts). Acts of terrorism are particularly disastrous because they encompass all three elements. They may take place in one or more sites at once , over a short or extended period of time, and they are intentional and therefore subject to repetition.

In different locations, this definition has great flexibility due to the wide range of personnel and facilities. Storage capacity for remains may be as few as four or as many as four

Figure 11.1 World Trade Center.

hundred, depending upon the district in which the event occurs. Not all facilities have a dental x-ray machine and there may be a limited number of forensic odontologists and medical examiners available.

Whether it is an airplane, ship, highrise building, manmade, or natural disaster, the National Transportation Safety Board (NTSB) has the primary responsibility for the recovery, identification, and processing of the fatalities in any mass disaster involving U.S. citizens or property. They will investigate the site, and they will determine if the local authorities have the capability to deal with the incident. Large or small, it may be necessary for the local ME/C to rely upon federal assistance. This assistance will come at the direction of the National Transportation Safety Board.

Aviation Disaster Family Assistance Act of 1996 (702b)

The National Transportation Safety Board (NTSB) shall have the primary federal responsibility for facilitating the recovery and identification of fatally injured persons.

If the local facilities are not sufficient and the needs are overwhelming, the NTSB will act accordingly with the cooperation of the local ME/C. This usually involves the National Disaster Medical System (NDMS) and the activation of one or more Disaster Mortuary Operational Response Teams (DMORT), who will supply all the necessary equipment, personnel, and supplies. There are ten DMORT teams located around the country (Figure 11.2). These teams are activated to federal duty as the occasion demands.

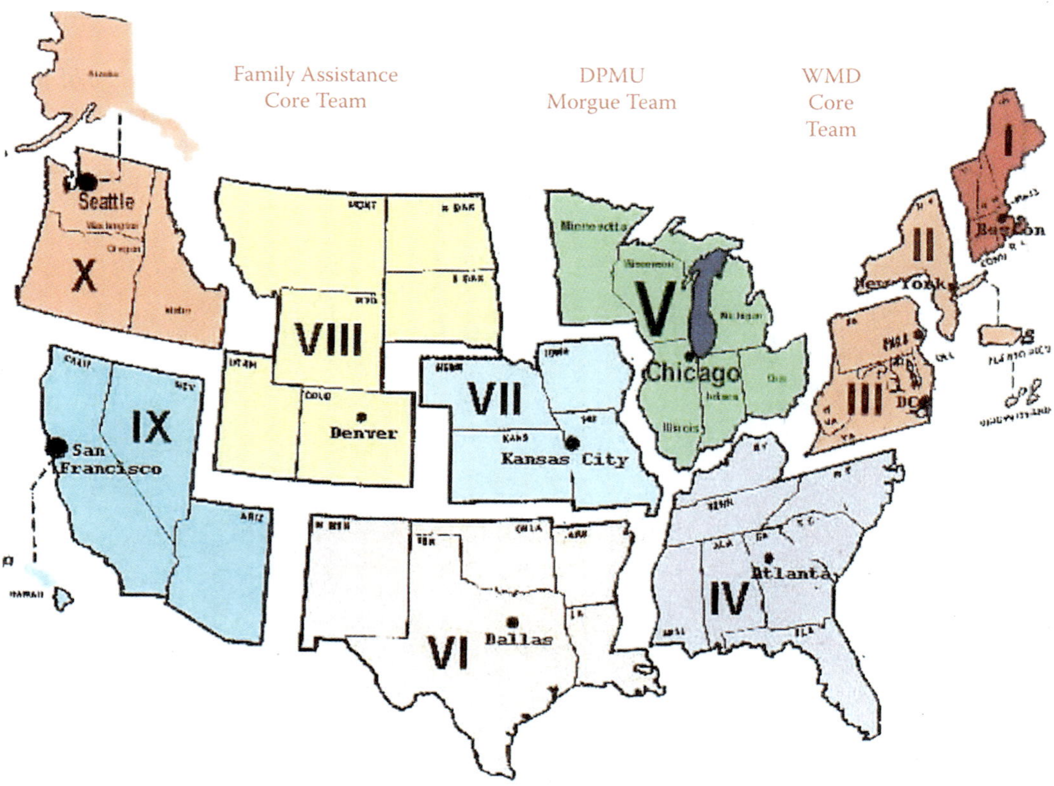

Figure 11.2 DMORT teams. (Courtesy of the National Disaster Medical Service.)

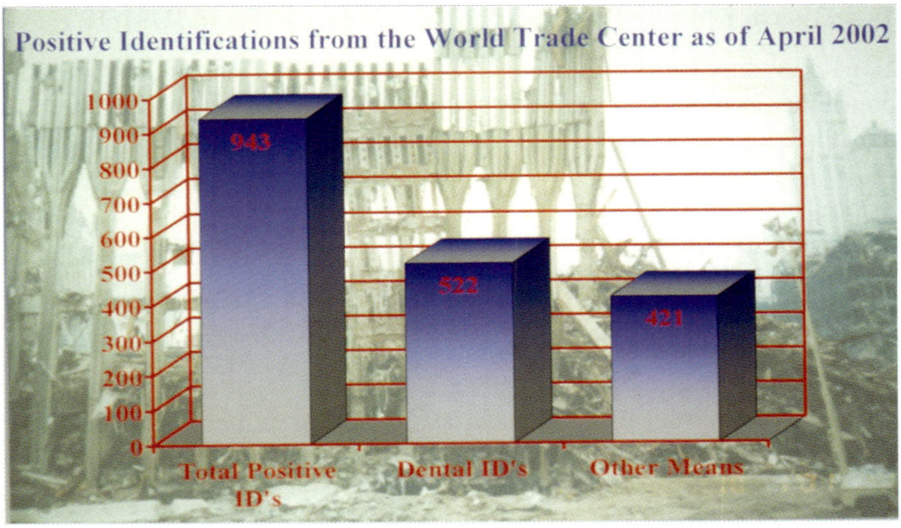

Figure 11.3 Dental identifications at World Trade Center.

World Trade Center data reveals (January 2004) that among 2749 total fatalities, 2029 had dental records (720 had no dental records). Among the first 1000 victims, 50 percent were identified by dental evidence (Figure 11.3). Immediately upon notification on September 11, 2001, the author (WES) proceeded to New York by auto with other DMORT members. All air traffic had been halted that day and there was great unease in the country. Organizational preparedness stemmed the tide of emotional panic. Housing and work assignments were made and, as usual, it was a few days before the actual work began on the identification of the remains. This activity was centered at the morgue of the New York City Medical Examiner facility. The size of the facility was sufficient, but the personnel had to be increased to accommodate the work to be done. The disaster site was sufficiently far enough away not to allow any distraction from the mortuary work. All remains were transported from the disaster site to the morgue and held in refrigerator trucks parked on location. The DMORT dentists, and others, were transported from motels in the suburbs by bus every morning and evening.

In the beginning there were two shifts of 12 hours each every day. After a period of two weeks on duty, teams were replaced by new teams from different parts of the country, different DMORT regions. This rotation went on for many months. Even after the disposition of the remains to the morgue was complete, all material was collected at a separate site in Staten Island to be combed further by personnel in order to discover any forgotten remains. The postmortem team collected data in the morgue. At a separate location, in a nearby building, the antemortem team collected data, together with the Family Assistance Center, from persons all over the world who reported missing relatives, friends, employees, or visitors thought to be at that location. The dental information from dentists came in from all over the world and presented many challenges to decipher the data for entry into WINID. Then it was the task of the comparison team to match the missing and the unknown and to pass this information to the medical examiner and chief forensic odontologist for confirmation, death certification, and transmission to the Family Assistance Center for notification of Next of Kin (NOK).

What Is a Disaster Mortuary Operational Response Team (DMORT)?

The National Response Plan assigns the National Disaster Medical System (NDMS) section the responsibility to provide victim identification and mortuary services. These responsibilities include:

- Temporary morgue facilities
- Victim identification
- Forensic dental pathology
- Forensic anthropology methods
- Preparation and disposition of the deceased

In order to accomplish this mission, Disaster Mortuary Operational Response Teams (DMORT) were developed. DMORT is composed of private citizens, each with a particular field of expertise, who are activated in the event of a disaster involving U.S. citizens or property. DMORT members are required to maintain appropriate certifications and licensure within their discipline. When members are activated, licensure and certification is recognized by all states, and the team members are compensated for their duty time by the federal government as temporary federal employees. During an emergency response, DMORT works under the guidance of local authorities by providing technical assistance and personnel to recover, identify, and process the deceased remains.

DMORT is directed by the NDMS. Teams are composed of funeral directors, medical examiners, coroners, pathologists, forensic anthropologists, medical records technicians and transcribers, fingerprint specialists, forensic odontologists, dental hygienists and assistants, x-ray technicians, mental health specialists, computer professionals, administrators, security and investigative personnel, as well as social service workers for family assistance.

The Department of Homeland Security (DHS) Federal Emergency Management Agency (FEMA), in support of the DMORT program, maintains two Disaster Portable Morgue Units (DPMU). Both DPMUs are stored at FEMA logistic centers. The DPMU also acts as a repository of equipment and supplies for deployment to a disaster site. It contains a complete morgue, with designated workstations for each processing element, and prepackaged equipment and supplies (http://www.dmort.org).

In addition to the federal response, many states have their own organization, which is prepared to act in the event of a disaster that falls below federal guidelines and is beyond the capacity of the local medical examiner/coroner. For example, in Florida, we have the Florida Emergency Mortuary Operations Response Team (FEMORS, http://www.femors.org). This team is conducted under the supervision and sponsorship of the Florida Department of Health in conjunction with the Florida Department of Law Enforcement (FDLE), and the Florida Medical Examiners Commission (FMEC). On occasion, the local dental society may train dentists in forensic odontology procedures and techniques, in order to prepare them for the occurrence of a disaster in their own backyard. In Miami, we have a Dental Identification Response Team (DIRT), the members of which may partake of training and may be called upon to assist the local forensic odontologist at the medical examiner department with a dental autopsy. In case you are confused by the plethora of acronyms, consider the following and the fact that you are in good company.

You are in a FOG about the latest CEMP and need to get in touch with the DOH about the NIMS so that you can join either FEMORS or DMORT, and then you can work in a

DPMU. Maybe you ought to go to your local FAC and check out DIRT in order to defend yourself against the NBCs of WMD.

You thought that life was as simple as an MOD filling. Well, life is getting more complicated and we are facing crucial times when our lives and the world itself is filled with disasters of all kinds. Hurricanes and floods are natural disasters that we are almost accustomed to. But Mother Nature has to take a back seat to disasters that are manmade. Weapons of Mass Destruction (WMD) may not have been found in Iraq but they are everywhere else. Nuclear, Biological, and Chemical (NBC) weapons abound and we must be prepared to deal with them.

The federal government (U.S.) has a Comprehensive Emergency Management Plan (CEMP) to provide Emergency Support Functions (ESF-8) for health and medical services. Of course, that all comes under the National Incident Management System (NIMS). Naturally, that has led to the establishment of the Disaster Mortuary Operational Response Team (DMORT) on a national level and on a local level such teams as the Florida Emergency Mortuary Operational Response System (FEMORS). Then, if you are inclined to be more local, the individual dental societies may become organized such as in Miami with the Miami DIRT (Dental Identification Response Team). You could meet in the Disaster Portable Morgue Unit (DPMU) which was just flown in from Arizona. And the Family Assistance Center (FAC) is just around the corner

Had enough? Every one of these groups needs dentists. The forensic odontologist is the backbone of the mass disaster identification system and every dentist has the basic knowledge to accomplish this task, with the proper training. During the World Trade Center disaster dental identifications were responsible for over 500 of the first 1000 unidentified persons. Before that, local dentists were responsible for many of the identifications in the Valujet crash, without the assistance of any outside dentists.

All you have to do is follow the Field Operational Guide (FOG) and educate yourself about the dentist's role in mass disaster. It's very simple—one tooth at a time—and a few lectures on the subject at your local dental society! Because, if you don't know what to do about WMD there won't be any MOD in your life anymore.

There is a system in the organization of the morgue as well as for each team. This is practiced well in advance by annual exercises in mock disaster operations. Tents may be set up and walkthroughs designed in preparation for the real thing. The body proceeds through the morgue facility on a wheeled gurney, and each body is accompanied with an escort. It is the responsibility of the escort to get each station signed off and covered. The sequence is strict, in order to maintain complete coverage for each body (Figure 11.4 and Appendix, Figure A.13 [full-sized]).

Each station is staffed by the members of the applicable specialty, and each specialty may have several teams to provide relief when the task extends over many days or weeks. The standard time for assignment is about two weeks before deploying another team.

The Dental Team (Figure 11.5) Dental Organizational Chart (Appendix, Figure A.14) is unique for its autonomous organizational scheme. No other team has such requirements. There are three dental teams required:

- Antemortem
- Postmortem
- Comparison

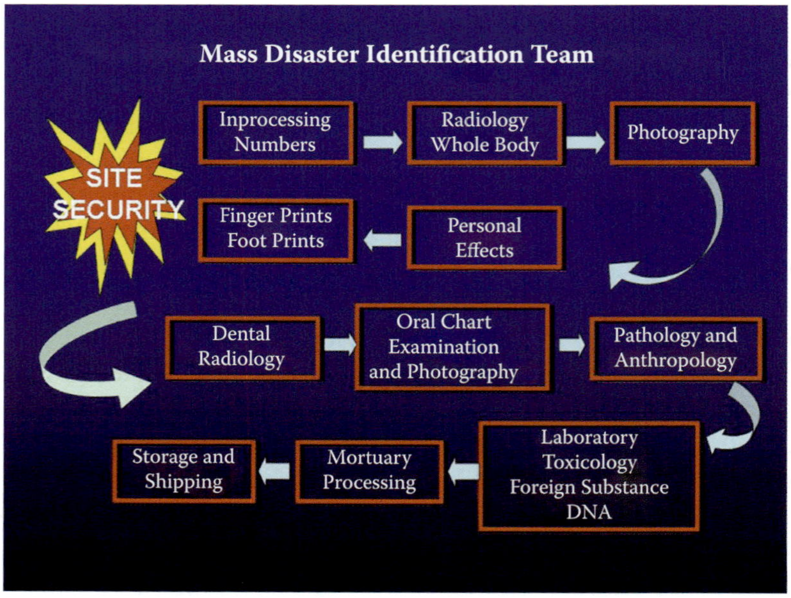

Figure 11.4 Mass disaster identification team flowchart.

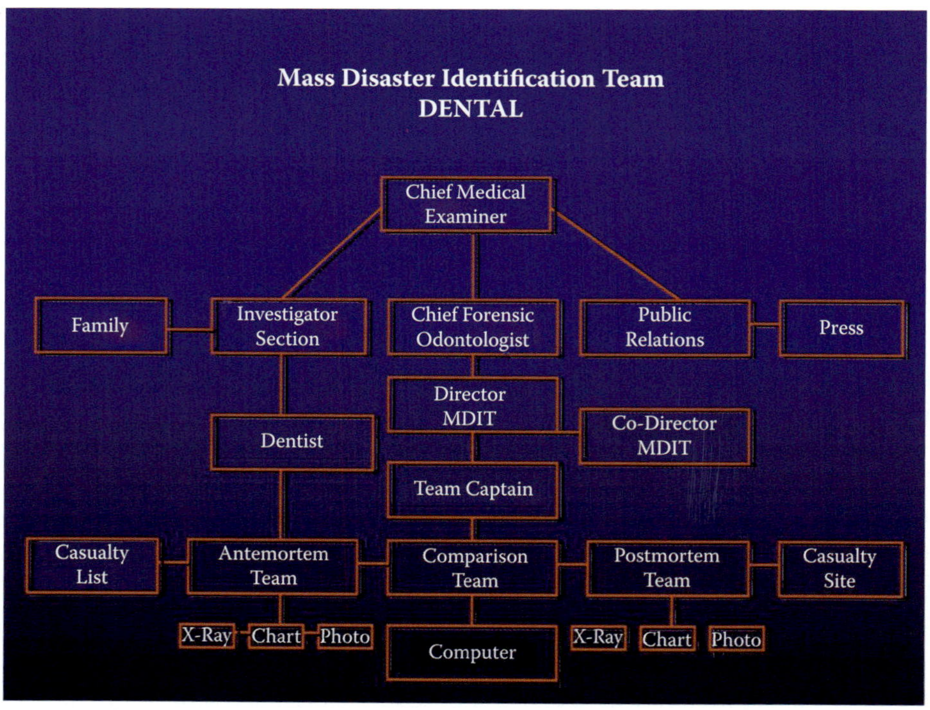

Figure 11.5 Mass disaster dental identification team flowchart.

Each team has a captain and is responsible for the x-rays, photos, and charts related to their area of concern. The antemortem team receives its information from the casualty source and secures all records from the treating dentist. The postmortem team receives its information from the remains of the disaster site or morgue autopsy. In some instances it is important that the forensic odontologist examine the scene. Often dental items are missed at the scene and would only be recognized by a skilled odontologist. Each of these teams sends their data to the comparison team, who attempt to make the identification using computer or hand-sorting techniques (Locator). During Katrina and the World Trade Center all data was entered and compared using WINID because of the large numbers of remains to be identified. The paperwork required in all systems has been adopted by DMORT from the WINID coding. In order to avoid confusion, the antemortem sheet is printed on yellow paper and the postmortem sheet is printed on green paper. The codes entered are on columns that face each other for easier comparison (Appendix, Figures A.15 and A.16).

In small events, and in the absence of computers or limitations of power in remote locations, the LOCATOR system may be depended upon to produce accurate results and sometimes just as quickly. This system was developed by Dr. Cheri Lewis to run "by hand". The sorting method is manual so as to reduce the time required to match records without the use of computers. Postmortem records are placed in stacks according to the presence of dental characteristics. Then upon receipt of the antemortem record the comparison person goes directly to the appropriate record stack, rather than sorting all records. Records are sorted in stacks accordingly:

- NO RESTORATIONS PRESENT
- CLASS I OCCLUSAL, FACIAL, OR BUCCAL PIT
- CLASS V FACIAL OR LINGUAL
- CROWNS PRESENT WITH OR WITHOUT ROOT CANAL
- CROWNS WITH BRIDGES, WITH OR WITHOUT IMPLANTS
- LARGE EDENTULOUS AREAS AVAILABLE FOR PROSTHESIS
- ROOTS PRESENT WITHOUT CLINICAL CROWN/RESTORATIONS UNKNOWN
- DECIDUOUS TEETH PRESENT

Upon identification or non-identification, the comparison information is sent to the team captain, and then to the director of the MDIT and to the odontology chief at the local ME/C department to confirm the identification. This operation is supervised by the chief or deputy chief of the forensic odontology staff. After the final determination has been made, the death certificate is signed by the chief medical examiner. The family is notified and funeral arrangements are made through the FAC (Family Assistance Center).

It should be noted that there are no lines of communication between the dental teams and the press. It is a strict rule that there should be no communication between these elements. Only the chief medical examiner or odontology chief will speak to the press, and then only through the public relations staff. Also, the relationship between the antemortem team and the family is through the dentist or the investigations staff.

The autopsy procedure at a mass disaster site is the same as any individual autopsy, multiplied many times. One significant difference may be the multitude of charting methods and tooth numbering systems. It is advantageous to become familiar with the major systems which we have described in previous chapters, for example, Universal, FDI, DVI.

Usually, due to federal assistance, there is a high degree of organization and a large support staff that only enhances the work of the odontologist. Portable equipment is standard as is electronic compilation of all data. It is incumbent upon the odontologist to become familiar with the various forms of electronic record taking, radiography, and photography in order to accomplish this task. DMORT participants are paid at federal salary levels during their activation period, which is usually limited to two weeks in a disaster zone. In addition there are annual training sessions during which all the latest techniques are developed.

The Valujet airplane disaster in 1996 had 110 persons on board, of whom only about 80 were positively identified, mostly due to the scattering of the remains after the aircraft hit coral rock bottom in the Everglades outside of Miami, Florida. In this particular case the local DIRT group of dentists developed by the local South Dade District Dental Society was able to accomplish the task without any federal assistance. The author (WES) was on a plane to Denver the same day that Valujet crashed in Miami. Because the team had been organized and trained previously, he was able to complete the meeting in Denver and return to Miami a few days later. The team, under co-author RRS, set up headquarters in the auditorium of the Miami Dade Medical Examiner department, loaded CAPMI into the computers and, as would be expected, the remains to be examined began to arrive after a few days of searching the waters of the Everglades. Due to the poor conditions at the crash site and the close proximity of the Miami Dade Medical Examiner morgue all remains were transported from the crash site to the local morgue for examination (Figures 11.6a,b).

One of the most incredible results of Hurricane Katrina and Hurricane Ike were the number of bodies that were spontaneously exhumed from aboveground and crypt burial sites (Figures 11.7a,b) in addition to the number of unknown from among the victims of this natural catastrophe. Unless there was evidence of personal artifacts contained within the coffin or on the remains, identification of the exhumed bodies presented problems that were previously unknown. Identification of unknown remains from the present community was complicated by the destruction of the dental offices where the residents received their dental care and where we would expect to find the antemortem records. The intensity of the storm and the subsequent damage can be seen in what was a local gas station (Figure 11.8). This effort took months and thousand of hours under strenuous conditions

Figure 11.6a Valujet crash in Florida Everglades. (Courtesy of the Miami Dade Medical Examiners office. Used with permission.)

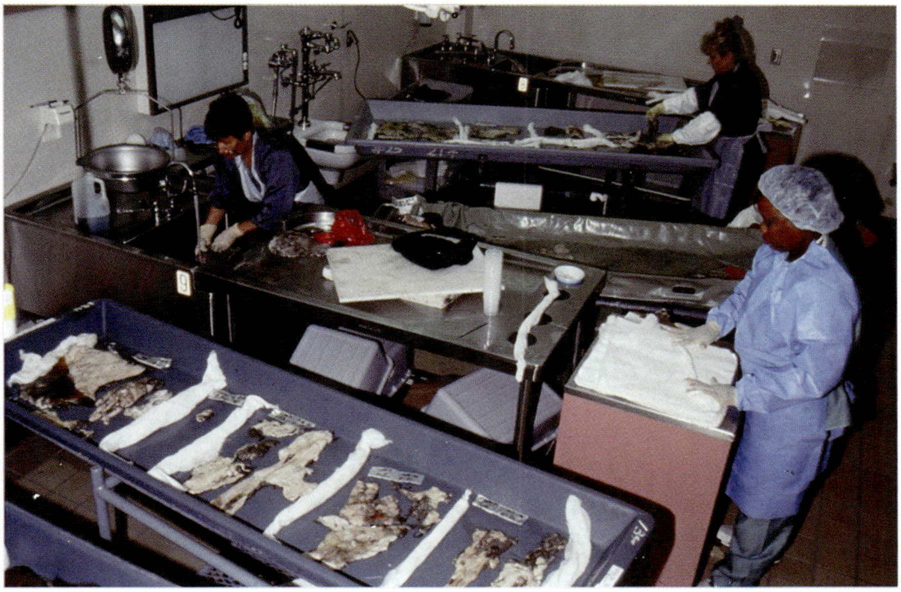

Figure 11.6b Valuejet remains at the Miami Dade Medical Examiner Morgue. (Courtesy of the Miami Dade Medical Examiners office. Used with permission.)

Figure 11.7a Burial crypts (Hurricane Katrina).

in tent cities (Figure 11.9), set up just for this purpose, with portable power, morgue, storage, dining, communication, and staffing facilities, all in the same compound. Add to this the necessity to provide personal living space for DMORT staff which varied from the inside of large trailer trucks, to half-destroyed hotels without electricity, to old warehouses converted for the occasion.

Figure 11.7b Displaced caskets (post-Hurricane Ike).

Figure 11.8 Filling station (post-Hurricane Katrina).

Compare that with the crash of a Chalk seaplane in Miami, with 20 people aboard, when all identifications were made within a day by the regular staff of three odontologists. This old airplane broke up in the air and fell into the water in Government Cut, in sight of many beachgoers at the south end of Miami Beach. Coast Guard and local responders were unable to save anybody. Most of the persons on board were from the Bahamas, returning home after Christmas shopping in Miami. The remains were

Figure 11.9 Morgue tent and storage area (post-Hurricane Katrina).

recovered immediately, except for one body which was recovered days later. All remains were transported to the Miami Dade Medical Examiner Department morgue where the identifications were made the same day, with the assistance of family and neighbors from the Bahamas. Dental records confirmed the identifications (Figure 11.10).

Figure 11.10 Chalk disaster dental examination. (Courtesy of the Miami Dade Medical Examiners office. Used with permission.)

Facial Approximation

12

Facial reconstruction might be more accurately defined as facial approximation. The process whereby a face is constructed on the bare bones of a skull is as much artistic as it is scientific. There may be sufficient clues as to the makeup of the individual from the scene where the body was found. Dress size, other clothing, and undergarments may indicate gender and body type. It is also important to note the type of clothing in order to determine the climate at the time of death, for example, heavy wool clothing, gloves, or shorts. Hair will not decompose, but it may go missing after a while. Skin tags may be available to determine color and racial types. Jewelry can determine socioeconomic status. Eyeglasses, hearing aids, canes, and condition of the teeth and supporting bone could be important indicators of age. The skull and other skeletal parts may produce clues as to ancestry or ethnic origin as well as gender. Measurement of long bones will suggest stature.

The process of facial approximation will be guided by many charts that suggest tissue thickness in different locations. The skin over the forehead is closest to the underlying bone, and the thickness of the cheek, as determined by the buccal fat pad and musculature, is quite variable. According to the racial characteristics, the lips may be thick or thin and the nose may be broad or narrow. Age will often determine the smoothness or furrowed nature of the surface of the skin.

Jack in the Woods

In this case we have an unknown person whose likeness has been approximated by clay reconstruction from the skeletonized remains. His necklace, with a Swiss Army knife and a medallion, lies limp around his skeletonized cervical vertebrae. There is a knitted wool hat with a Nike logo and a pair of eyeglasses by his side. Left in the woods in the Ocala National Forest in Central Florida and found in 1999, he still remains unknown.

The reconstruction process involves mounting the skull in an appropriate setting, so that the location is mobile but the skull is fixed, and then the setting of erasure plugs about the skull to determine tissue thickness (Figure 12.1a). Once tissue depth is established it is time to add the clay in the appropriate thickness (Figure 12.1b) until all the finishing touches have been applied, and the known possessions have been placed, to complete the artist's conception of this person's appearance (Figure 12.1c).

A second case illustrates a clay approximation with different clues. This person's remains were found in a box in the north section of Miami. Hair sample, skin tags, and clothing were available to suggest that this was a medium-build white female with dark hair, perhaps 25–35 years old (Figure 12.2a). Tissue depths were determined by chart and depth markers placed about the skull (Figure 12.2b) and clay was added in layers until depth markers were covered. The correct lip position is such that the teeth will be exposed to further assist in any identification. The finishing phase is very artistic. This involves skin lines, eyebrows, hair style, and color. In the female figure this can vary widely

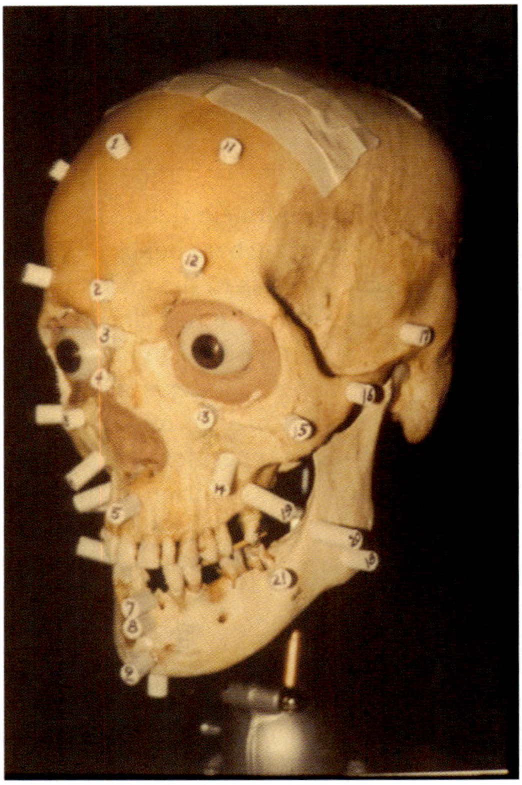

Figure 12.1a Clay restoration – beginning.

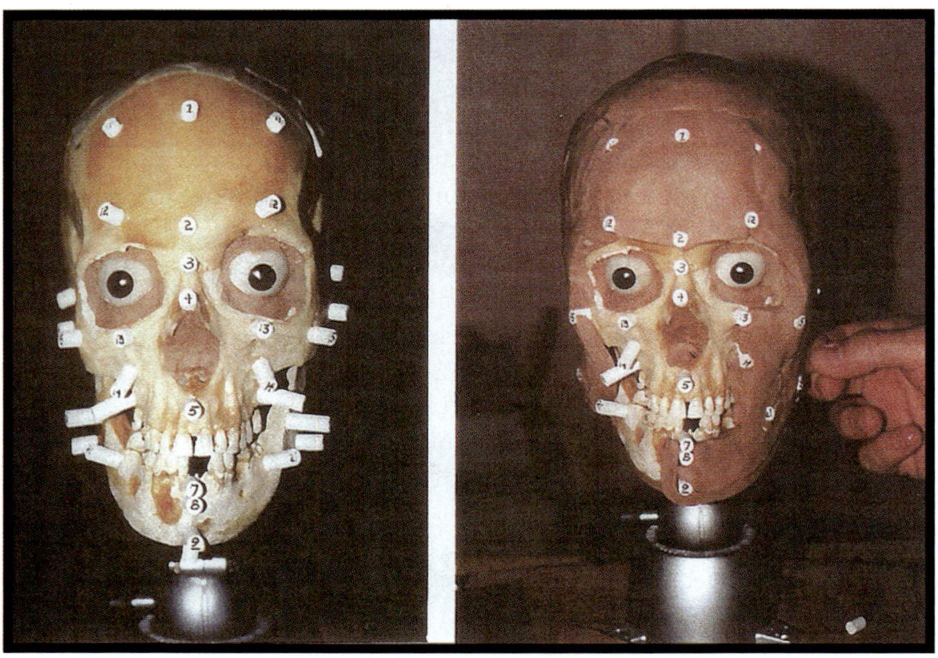

Figure 12.1b Clay restoration – progress.

Figure 12.1c Clay restoration – final.

(Figure 12.2c). In an attempt to visualize the person, a two-dimensional representation is often requested, and that sketch is then presented in the newspaper for further distribution and possible identification. This is usually accomplished by the police artist who may not have any knowledge of the three-dimensional product in clay (Figure 12.2d). Both of these cases are still considered active as no positive identifications have been made to date.

A very important element in the forensic facial approximation process is age progression. The time of discovery of the remains may disclose the approximate age of the individual, but in cases where the face of the perpetrator is to be created, the time between the act and the present time must be taken into consideration. When a child is missing, photographs are very important. However, if much time has elapsed from the date of missing/abduction, then changes associated with age must be a consideration in the two-dimensional facial creation.

When it comes to three-dimensional (clay) reconstruction, Betty Pat Gatliff of Norman, Oklahoma (http://www.skullpturelab.com) presents courses annually in basic and advanced sculpting. In the two-dimensional realm, Karen T. Taylor of Austin, Texas (http://www.karenttaylor.com) has authored many books on the subject.

Photographic modification of existing photographs has undergone dramatic changes in the past few years. Manual painting and tracing have been replaced by electronic enhancement led by Adobe Photoshop and other software programs. One quick example of photographic enhancement is to take the postmortem photograph of the damaged physiognomy of an unknown victim, and demonstrate the value of electronic software to create what that face might have looked like, for the purpose of identification (Figure 12.3). The manipulation of the tissue and color is still in the hands of the operator.

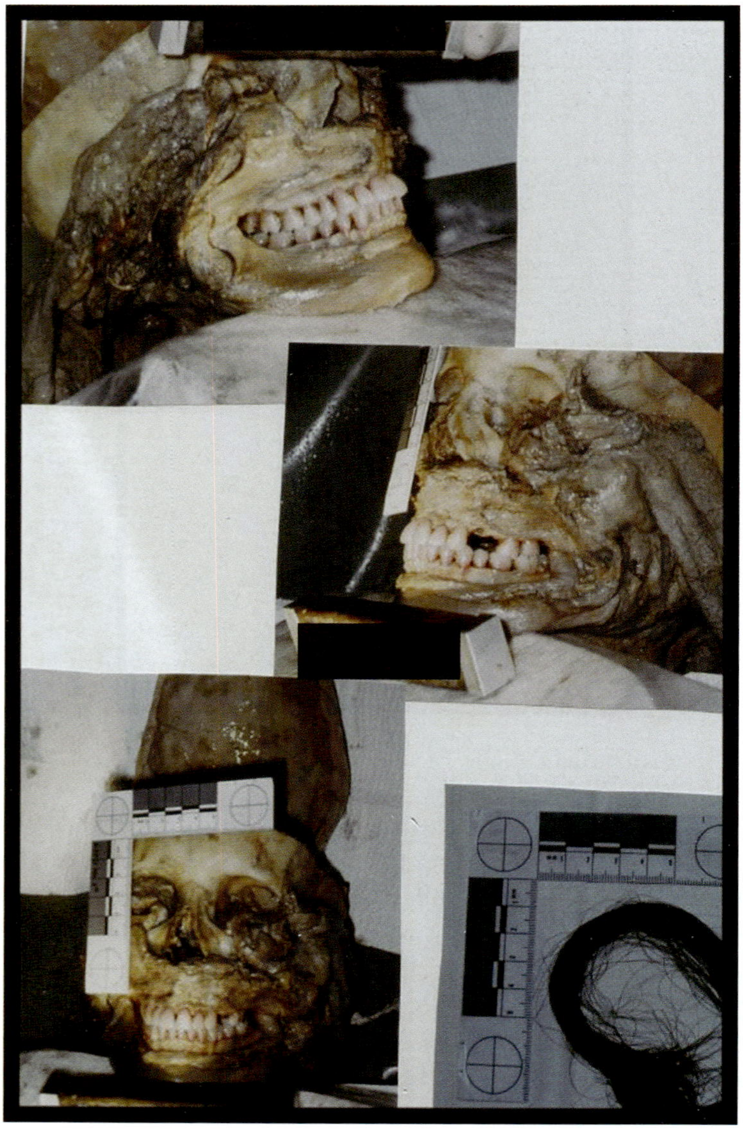

Figure 12.2a Unidentified female remains. (Courtesy of the Miami Dade Medical Examiners office. Used with permission.)

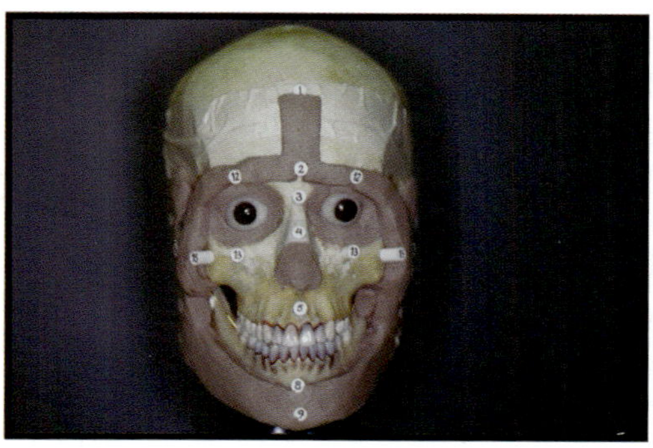

Figure 12.2b Partial clay restoration.

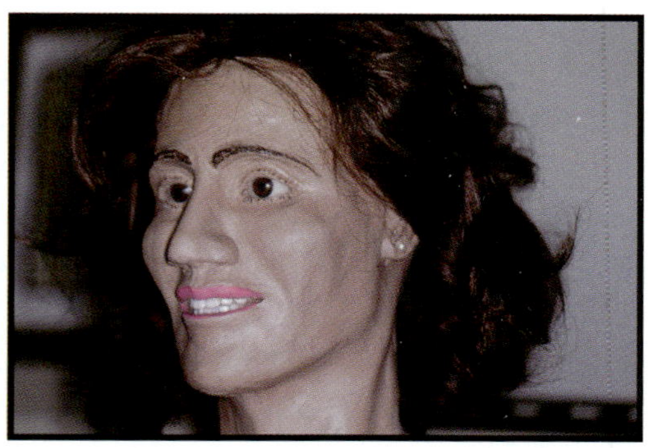

Figure 12.2c Clay restoration – final.

Police seek ID of woman found in canal

Police have developed a composite sketch to help them identify a woman found Oct. 29 in a North Central Dade canal.

Her body was in a cardboard box, bound with duct tape and rope, floating in a canal behind a residence in the **13900 block of Lake Placid Court.**

The victim was described as a white woman between the ages of 25 and 35, five feet two inches tall, with a slight build. She had dark brown, shoulder-length hair, plastic dental fillings and a slightly deviated septum.

Anyone with information or who can identify the victim is asked to contact Detective C. Strose of the homicide bureau at (305) 471-2400 or Crime Stoppers at (305) 471-8477 (TIPS).

SKETCHES OF WOMAN: With two hair styles.

Figure 12.2d Newspaper article on unidentified female. (Courtesy of the *Miami Herald* and the Miami Dade Police Department. Used with permission.)

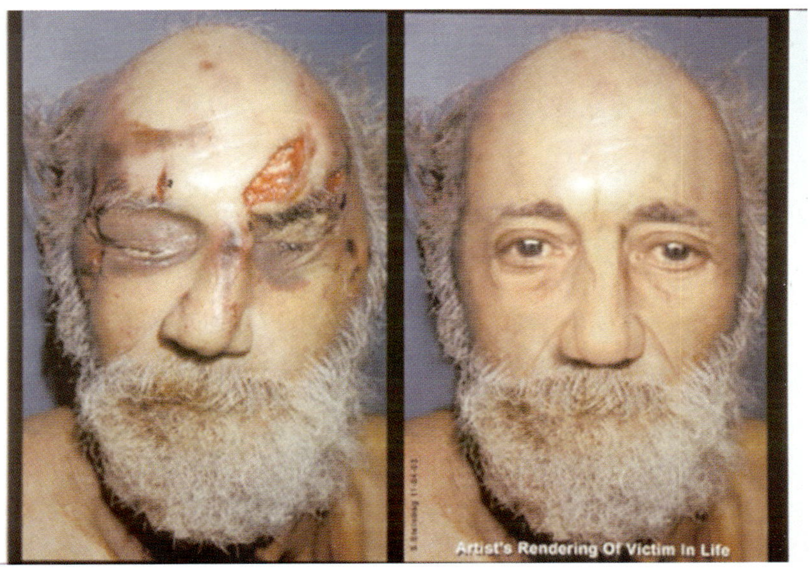

Figure 12.3 Photographic reconstruction. (Courtesy of the Miami Dade Medical Examiners office. Used with permission.)

Approximation of facial characteristics on a bare skull is still an art, even though practiced on a computer. There are computer programs that will laser-scan the skull and then refer to a database, which is based upon ethnic, gender, genomic, and syndromic characteristics. The value of this procedure is only as good as the database, which is presently under development in many areas. If you are working in China, it will produce predominantly

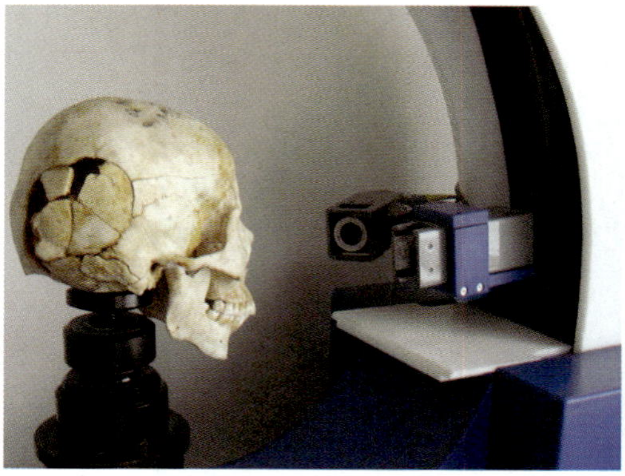

Figure 12.4a Laser 3D scan of skull.

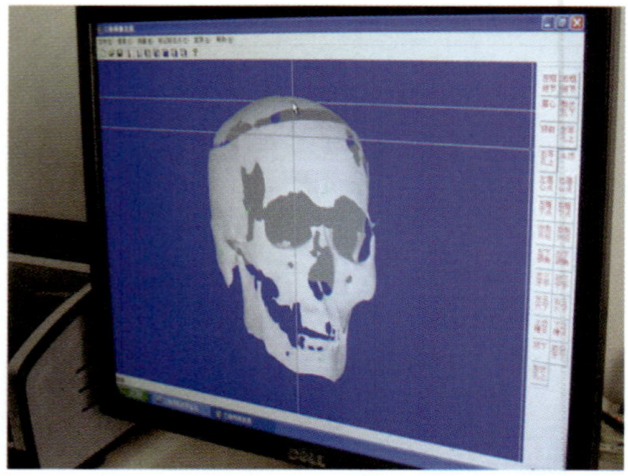

Figure 12.4b Computer-generated recreation of skull.

Oriental facial features (Figure 12.4a,b). In Texas, it will be quite different. If you are comparing teeth as in ADIS (Automated Dental Identification System), the computer will assist but not make a positive identification due to the large differential between antemortem and postmortem radiography. If you are comparing faces, the biometric analysis depends upon the database for comparison. The purpose of the comparison may vary from criminal to the identification of a missing person. The database has many shortfalls. Some may say that the program is simply "under development." Others may say that it is unscientific and unacceptable. In any case, it is another weapon in our identification tool chest.

Odontoglyphics—Bitemarks

13

Introduction

An odontoglyphic or a bitemark is produced by the voluntary action of teeth being forced into a softer object. Bitemarks can be left by humans, animal, insects or sea life.

Background and Case Histories

State v. Doyle (Texas, 1954)

A piece of cheese left at the scene of a burglary was observed to have teeth marks. The bite out of the cheese found at the crime scene was compared to a bite out of a similar piece of cheese made by a suspect, Doyle. This 1954 Texas case, *State v. Doyle*, was the first "reported" bitemark case in the United States, where a bitemark was used to link a suspect to the crime. Dr. William Kemp, a Texas dentist testified that the bites in the two pieces of cheese were made by the same set of teeth (Figure 13.1). There were several significant points to this 1954 case. First, the police obtained the bitemark evidence from the suspect without a court order or search warrant. Secondly, a firearms expert and a dentist made a comparison of bitemarks in cheese without models from the defendant, Doyle. Third, on appeal the

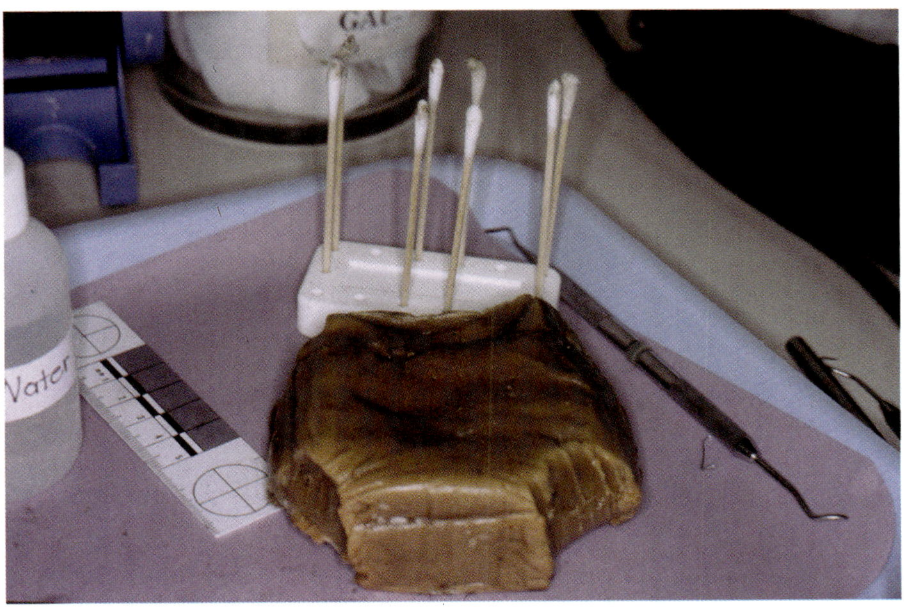

Figure 13.1 Cheese bite from scene with DNA. (Courtesy of RRS.)

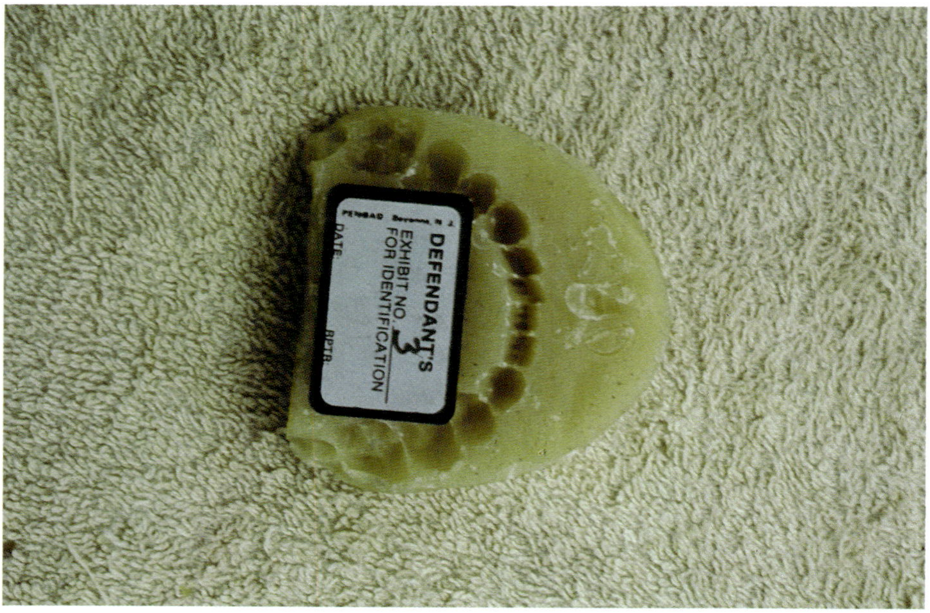

Figure 13.2 Beeswax bite. (Courtesy of RRS.)

defense argued that the "voluntary bite" in effect was a violation of his Fifth Amendment right for protection against self-incrimination. The court rejected this argument. It is interesting to note that a similar argument was made in *State v. DuBoise–Florida Sup Ct 1988.* In this case, the suspect, DuBoise, was asked to bite into beeswax (Figure 13.2). This gave an impression of his teeth, later used to compare to a bitemark on a homicide victim.

People v. Marx (California, 1975)

The *People vs. Marx* case in 1975 was the first bitemark case in California. It was described as "the gold standard for bitemark cases" by Souviron and "the seminal case for bitemark analysis" by Bowers. Why the gold standard or seminal case? There are several important reasons:

- First, the bite recorded the third dimension teeth marks indented into the nose (Figure 13.3a).
- Second, the bite records from the deceased were taken seven days after death, even after autopsy; embalming, and after exhumation had been performed.
- Third, the defendant Marx refused to voluntarily have impressions made of his teeth. He refused a court order. He was jailed for a period of approximately six weeks for contempt of court. He finally agreed to have impressions made.
- Fourth, Dr. Vale, Dr. Sognnaes, and Dr. Felando all participated in the analysis, "the team approach." Dr. Vale, the chief forensic odontologist in Los Angeles elicited the aid of two of his colleagues.
- Fifth, three-dimensional molds were made of the bite on the nose (Figure 13.3b) and test bites were made in materials such a frankfurter, an arm, and a volunteer nose using the dental casts of the suspect's teeth. Test bites were compared with the three-dimensional molds of the teeth and the nose bite (Figure 13.3c).

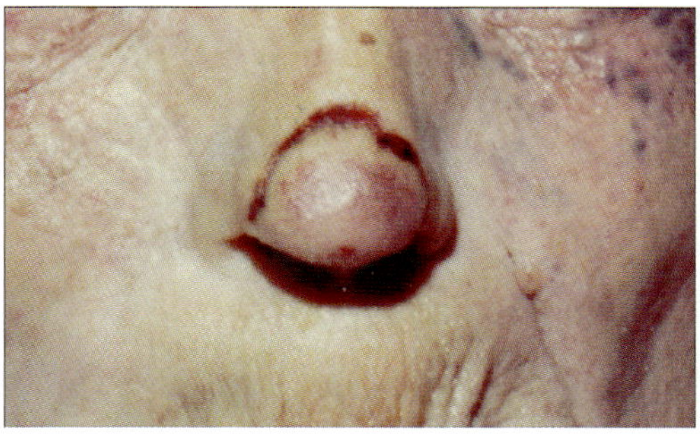

Figure 13.3a Bite mark on nose, homicide victim. (Courtesy of Dr. Jerry Vale.)

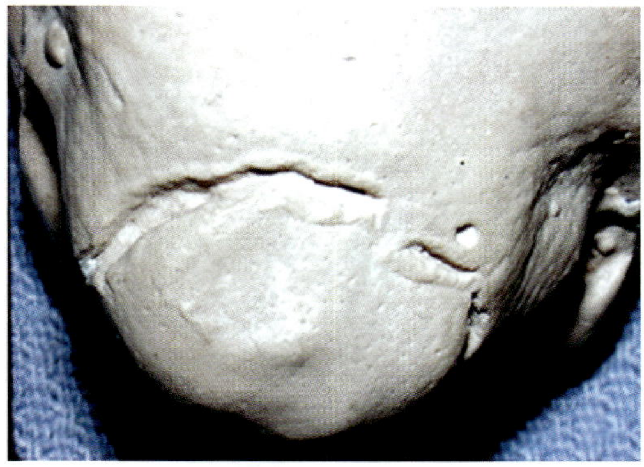

Figure 13.3b 3D model of bite on nose. (Courtesy of Dr. Jerry Vale.)

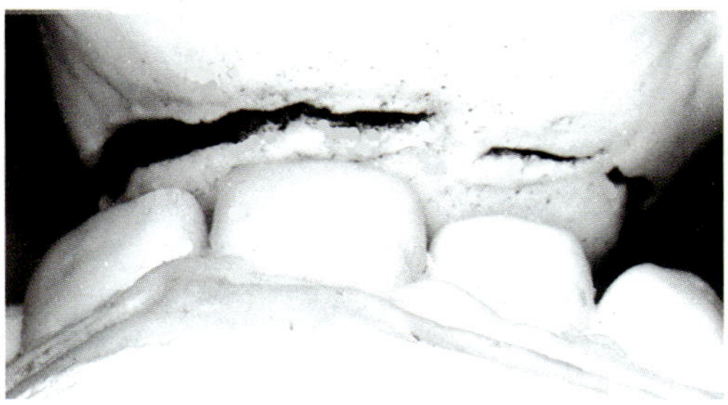

Figure 13.3c Suspect's dental model on 3D model of nose. (Courtesy of Dr. Jerry Vale.)

- Sixth, admissibility of bitemark evidence was accepted for the first time in California under the Frye rule even though this evidence had not been "generally accepted in the scientific community."

At trial each of the three odontologists testified to the high degree of similarity with the defendant's teeth and the bite on the nose of the deceased. Walter Marx was found guilty of the charge of involuntarily manslaughter.

State v. Bundy (Florida, 1979)

This was a significant case for several reasons. It was unique because: (a) the bitemark was left by a serial killer; (b) the case had national significance because of the high profile of Ted Bundy (Figure 13.4) and the fact that the killings had taken place from Washington State across the country to Florida State University; and (c) Bundy, the law student, attempted to provide his own defense. (A lawyer who represents himself has a fool for a client.)

There were several similarities between the 1975 California Marx case and the 1979 Theodore Bundy case. Both were the first bitemark cases in their states. A search warrant was used to get impressions and photographs of Bundy's teeth (Figure 13.5). This was based on the fact that the court order was used in the Marx case and a search warrant provided a better opportunity to avoid a "contempt of court" refusal by Bundy. The team approach was used in both cases. In the Florida case Dr. Levine, Dr. Sperber, and Dr. Campbell

Figure 13.4 Ted Bundy. (Courtesy of RRS.)

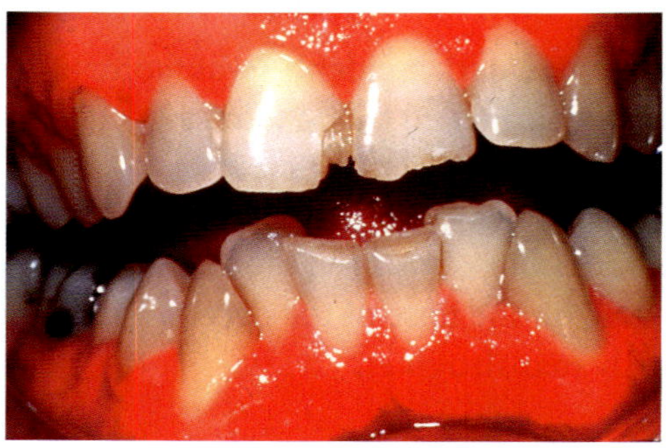

Figure 13.5 Ted Bundy's teeth. (Courtesy of RRS.)

independently came to the same conclusions as Dr. Souviron. Both bites recorded excellent teeth marks in the skin. The suspects in both cases had a distinctive tooth arrangement.

Ted Bundy was tried for the double homicide of the two Chi Omega sorority sisters. Because of the high press coverage in Leon County, Florida, the trial was moved to Miami and Bundy was found guilty. He was sentenced to death by electrocution for each of these two murders. This case is discussed in detail later in this chapter.

Odontoglyphics—Bitemarks

What is a bitemark? It is a pattern left when teeth are actively, voluntarily pressed into a soft material. It is not to be confused with a tooth mark. Teeth marks are different. A tooth

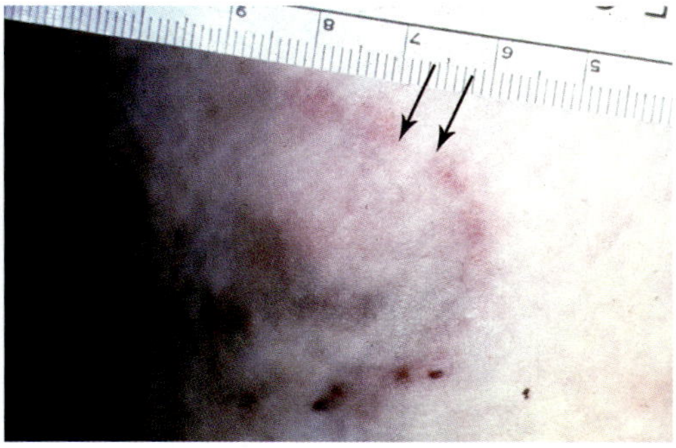

Figure 13.6a Bite mark showing diastema. (Courtesy of RRS.)

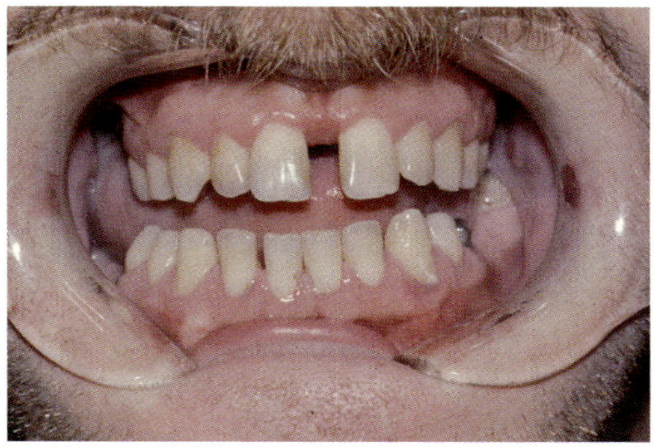

Figure 13.6b Suspect's teeth. (Courtesy of RRS.)

mark is a pattern left when teeth or a tooth are forced into an object, an involuntary act. Pattern injuries left by teeth that are not bitemarks are, for example, teeth embedded into a dashboard, steering wheel, and the like as a result of a high-velocity impact. Another example of tooth marks, not bitemarks, is when one strikes a blow to the face and the fist strikes the teeth leaving an injury pattern. Another example is if the deceased has a removable dental prosthesis and it happens to be out of the mouth and under the body it will leave "teeth marks" not a bitemark. In this case the false teeth of the victim were near the body and the police investigators thought they may have left the "bite." The bite shows a large gap (Figure 13.6a) and thus the false teeth were ruled out. The suspect will have a large space between his two centrals. Weeks later the police arrested a suspect (Figure 13.6b); his teeth fit the bitemark.

Not to be confused with a tooth mark, a bitemark is left by a biter (animal, human, or insect) and is an active, dynamic, and voluntary act. In the case of a human bite both arches usually leave a mark, but not always. The dynamics of the event will determine the variables of the pattern. The movement of the victim, the biter, juxtaposition of clothing or other objects, and the area of the body bitten all can and will influence the bitemark injury. Bitemarks can be found on anything bitten from food at a crime scene, to on the victim or on the attacker, and in some cases both. For the odontologist, the most significant bite is that of the mark or marks left by the attacker on the victim or the victim on the attacker or both. Less frequent is the bite found on inanimate objects such as food at the crime scene (Figure 13.7a). Everything from a cigar holder to a styrofoam cup has yielded bitemark evidence that has been used in the prosecution of a crime (Figure 13.7b).

Variables in Bitemarks

The variables in bitemark pattern injuries are infinite. It is impossible to list all of the possibilities but just consider a few. The dynamic of the biter and of the victim, the area of the body, the clothing, the force of the bite or bites, the vertical opening of the mouth, the amount of tissue bitten, the action of the tongue, the duration of the bite, bleeding, autopsy distortion, positional distortion, and postmortem changes are all potential variables that can affect the bite pattern. When one takes into consideration all the variables of the teeth that inflicted the bite, it introduces a whole new dynamic. The teeth can change, can be removed, or altered in position or shape by a dentist or by the biter himself. With these

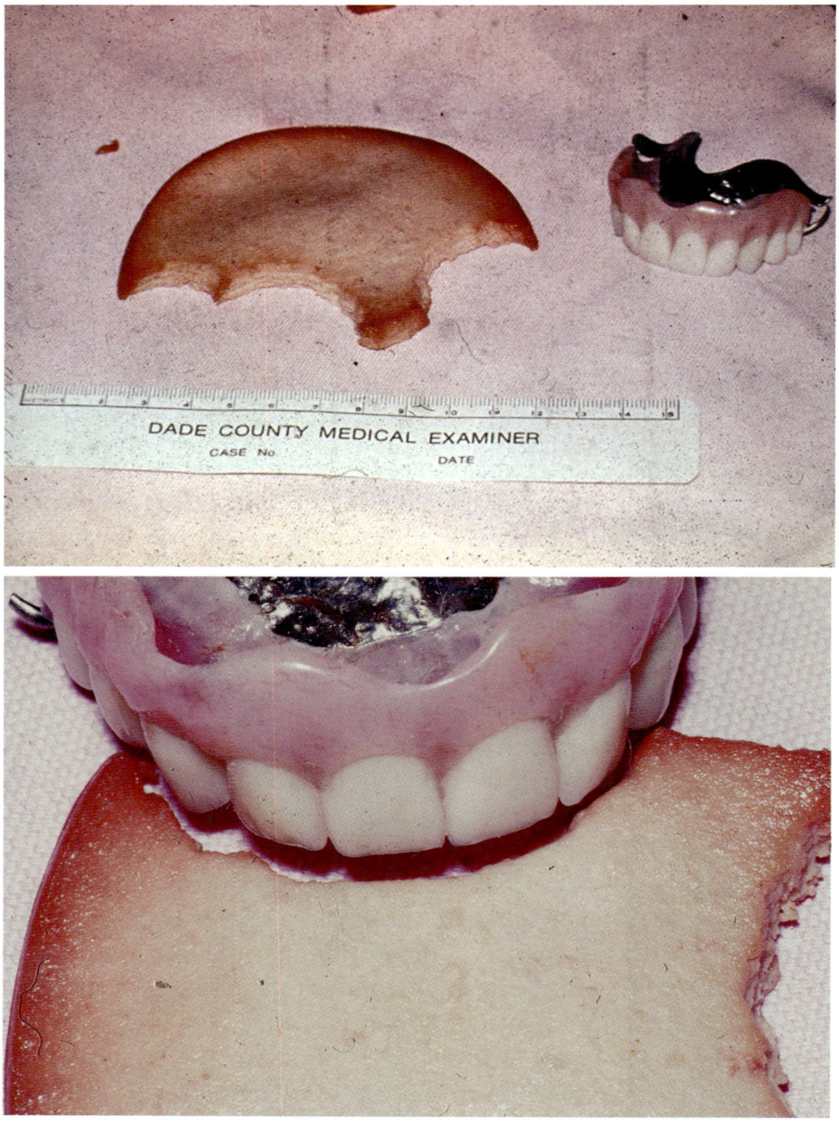

Figure 13.7a Bologna with bite imprint. (Courtesy of the Miami Dade Medical Examiners office. Used with permission.)

tremendous amounts of variables how can it ever be said that a suspect inflicted a bitemark to the exclusion of everyone else?

The observation by Dr. Joseph Davis (chief medical examiner emeritus of Miami Dade County Florida) that the "specificity of the evidence is inversely proportional to the variables" answers the previous question. **It can't!**

Fingerprints and DNA have far fewer variables than a bitemark and are thus far more specific when it comes to identification of a suspect from a large population group. The obvious conclusion then is that bitemark evidence is of no value. When using bitemarks to make an identification of a suspect from a large population group the preceding statement does have some merit but, "Don't throw the baby out with the bath water." What can bite marks do that a fingerprint and DNA cannot do? There are at least ten very significant differences:

Figure 13.7b Bite marks on cups. (Courtesy of the Miami Dade Medical Examiners office. Used with permission.)

- A bitemark can show and demonstrate pain.
- A bitemark can be offensive as well as defensive.
- A bitemark usually demonstrates violence.
- A bitemark may produce a permanent injury, the loss of an ear, finger, or nose. It elevates a simple battery (third-degree felony) to aggravated battery, a (second-degree felony) that carries a much longer prison sentence.
- A bitemark may, in certain cases, be distinctive in both class and individual characteristics and may yield a dental profile of the biter, that is, his or her dental arrangement, spaces, turned or missing or broken teeth.
- A bitemark can, in some cases, help to determine the age of the biter (child vs. adult).
- A bitemark or marks can be aged (fresh, healing, scar-old). In cases of child or elderly abuse, multiple bites over time will show a pattern of abuse, not just a single episode.
- A bitemark may give a clue as to when it occurred in relation to the time the victim died. If the third dimension or indentations are present, as in the Marx case, the bite more likely than not was inflicted during the fatal event or shortly thereafter. The indentations of a bitemark will not last on a live victim because of the vital reaction, that is, skin rebound, swelling, bleeding, and so on.
- A bitemark may give information as to the position of the biter and victim when the bite was inflicted. It may provide an investigative opinion as to the circumstances of the event.
- A bitemark may or can yield salivary DNA to help with the identification of the suspect.

Nevertheless, the bottom line for the forensic odontologist, the ME/C, the police investigators, the prosecutor, and the defense attorneys is, "Did she or he make the bite?"

The authorities want to know the answer "beyond a reasonable doubt." It is the forensic odontologist's most difficult challenge: Who made the bite? When was the bite made and to what level of certainty can a suspect be excluded or included? The rest of this chapter will, it is hoped, provide some of the answers—through scientific analysis, techniques, rationale, and circumstances—to the bottom-line questions Who made the bite? When was the bite made and how sure are you?

Bitemark Classification

The types of human bitemarks can vary greatly; they can be offensive, defensive, self-inflicted, or consensual. The wound, regardless of type, can be classified as human or animal. Animal bites are discussed later in the text but human bites in skin can be classified based on severity.

Class I: The pattern is diffuse. No individual tooth marks are identified. There may be one or both arches marking (Figure 13.8). It may appear as a diffuse bruised ring and may be of little or no evidentiary value for matching to a suspect (Figure 13.9a,b). The Class I bite may not even be identifiable as a human bitemark, only a round pattern injury. However, it may be of great value in other regards such as saliva, DNA, arch forms, and so on.

Class II: This bite wound has both class and some individual characteristics. The arches upper (maxillary) and lower (mandible) can be identified. Specific teeth may be identified. A Class II bite may be used more for exclusion than for inclusion of a suspect (Figures 13.10 and 13.11).

Class III: This bite will show excellent tooth morphology in at least one arch. Specific teeth shapes and their position in the dental arch can be identified. This class of bitemark can produce a dental profile of the biter as in the Bundy case and will be used for both inclusion as well as exclusion (Figure 13.12). The third dimension or indentations may be present and can help estimate the time the bite was inflicted in relation to the time of death (Figure 13.13).

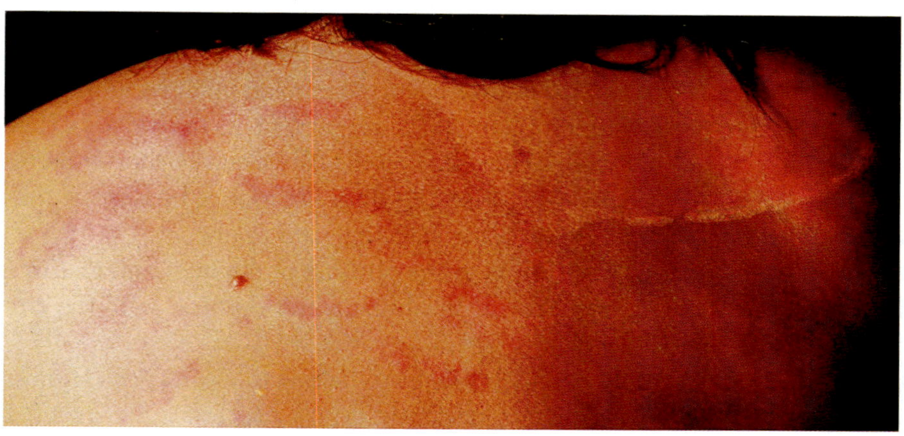

Figure 13.8 Class I bite: multiple bites. (Courtesy of RRS.)

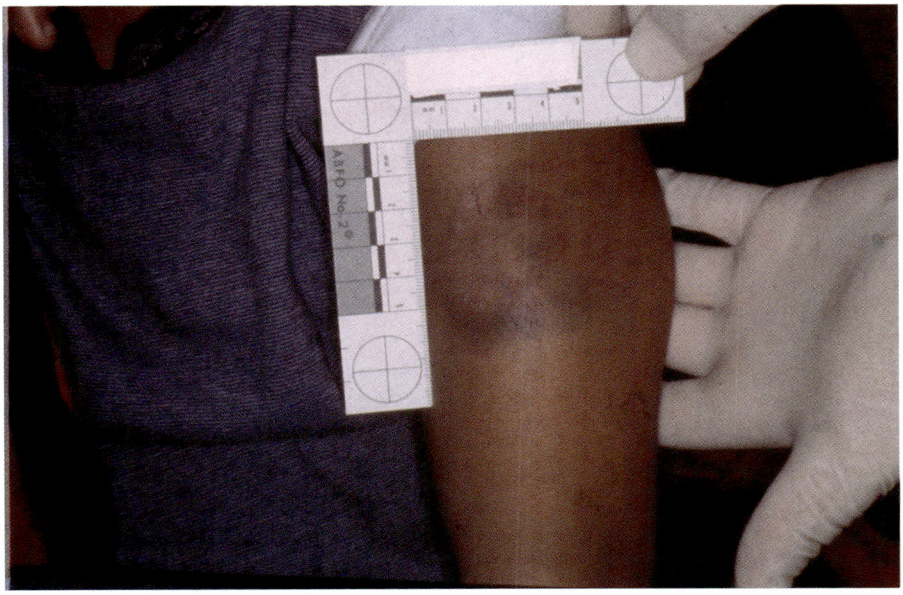

Figure 13.9a Class I bite: bite mark on arm. (Courtesy of the Miami Dade Medical Examiners office. Used with permission.)

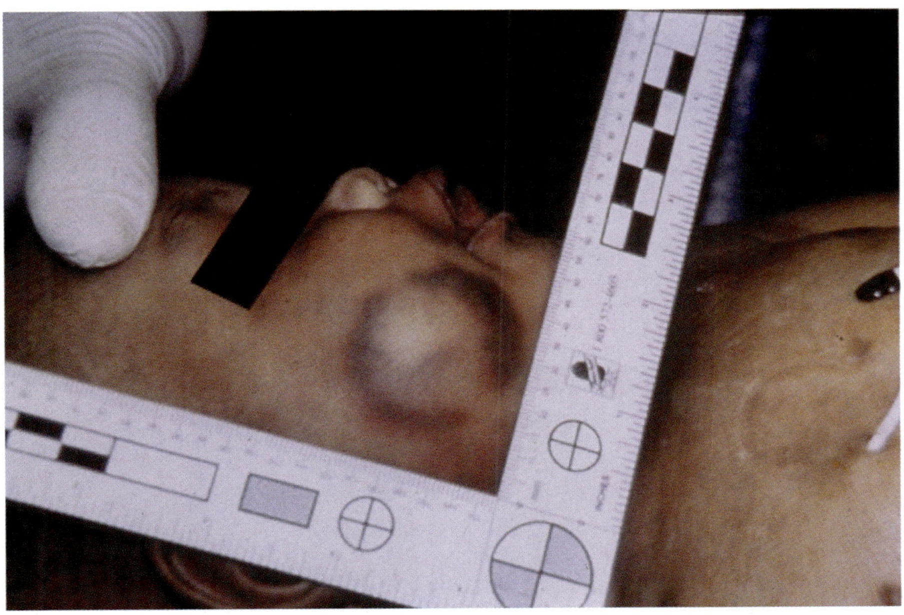

Figure 13.9b Class I bite: bite mark on cheek. (Courtesy of RRS.)

Class IV: This bite will be an incision or possibly an excision of the tissue. Blood is present on the surface and DNA may be contaminated. This class of bite is difficult if not impossible to get a profile of the teeth that caused it. However, a Class IV bite will almost always produce a permanent injury or disfigurement (Figure 13.14): the loss of a finger or an ear (Figure 13.15), or a permanent scar.

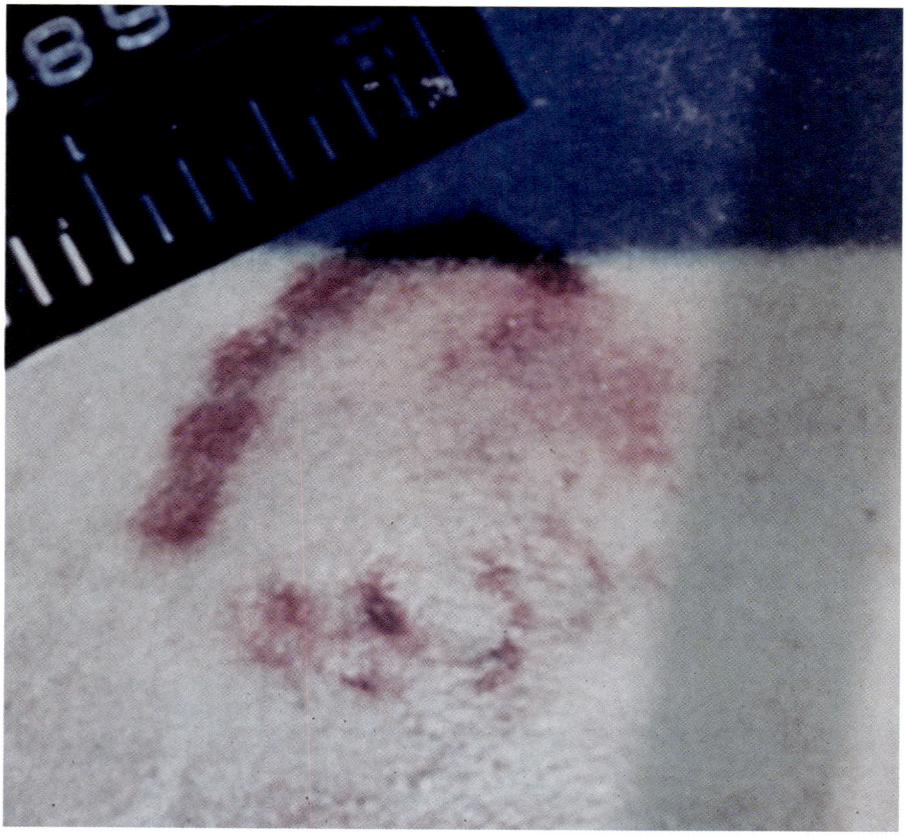

Figure 13.10 Class II bite. (Courtesy of RRS.)

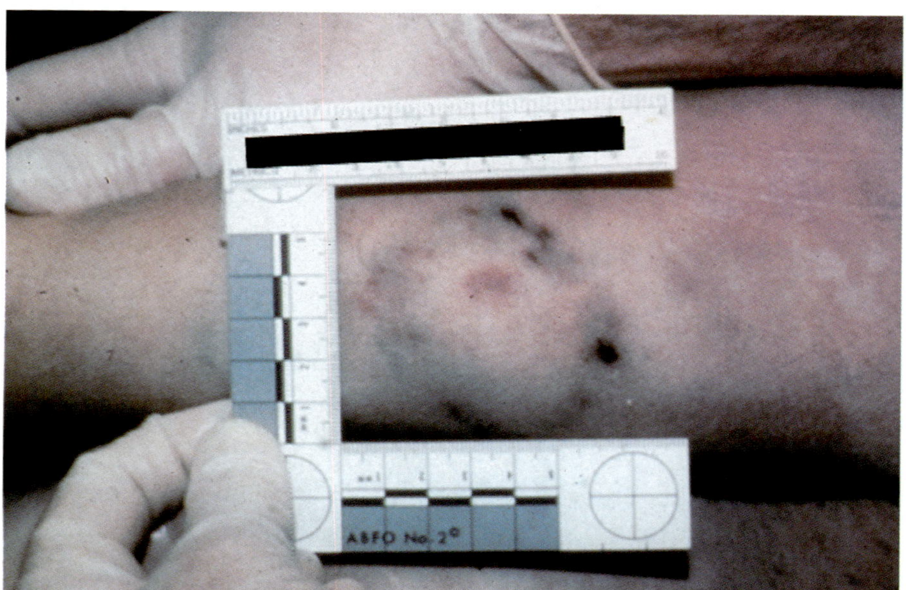

Figure 13.11 Class II bite. (Courtesy of RRS.)

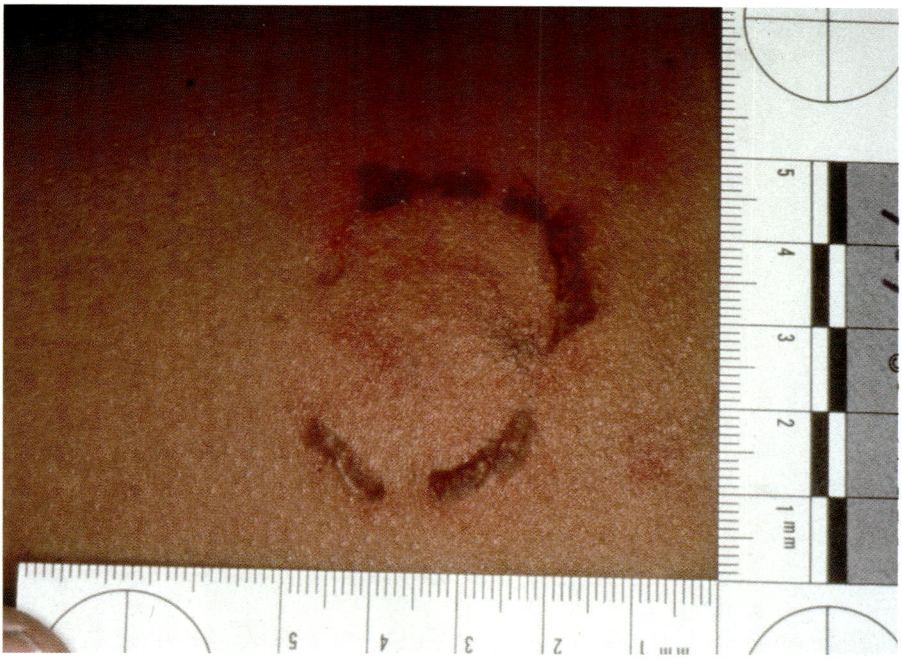

Figure 13.12 Class III bite. (Courtesy of RRS.)

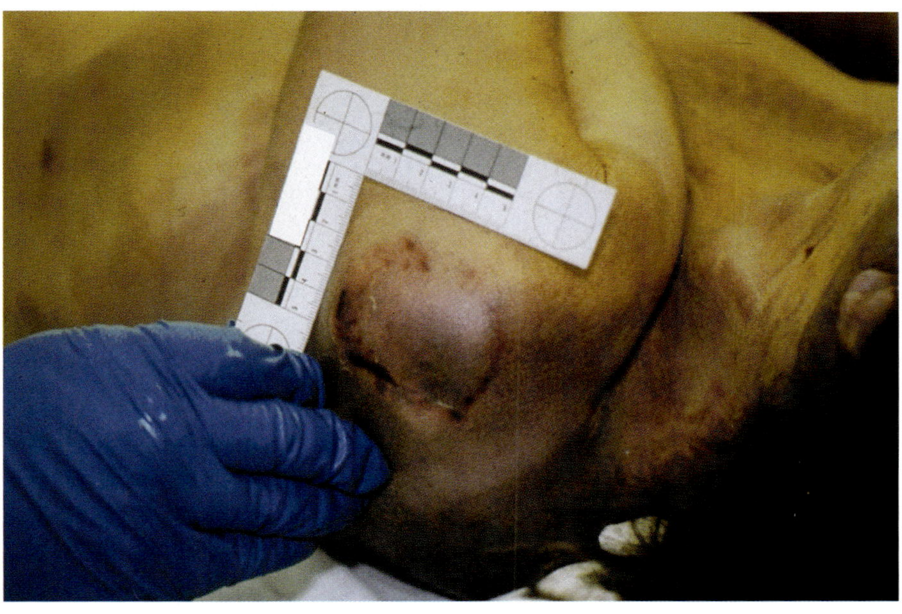

Figure 13.13 Class III bite. (Courtesy of RRS.)

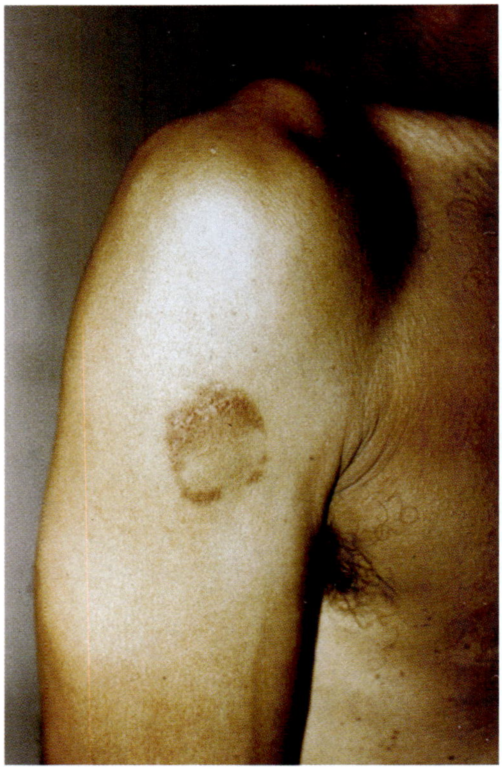

Figure 13.14 Class IV bite: one-year-old bite scar. (Courtesy of RRS.)

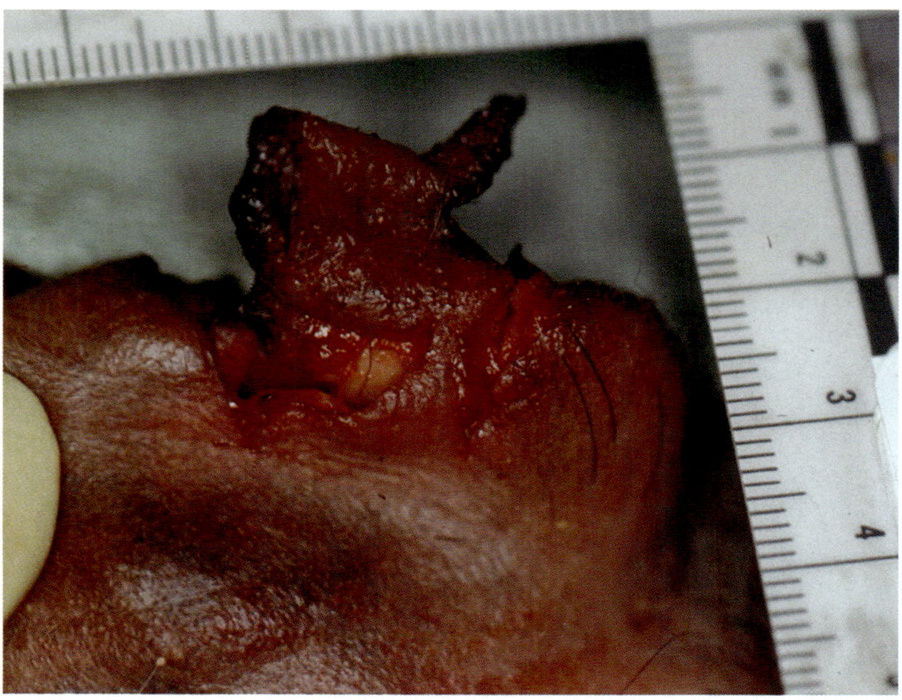

Figure 13.15 Class IV bite: on ear (avulsion). (Courtesy of the Miami Dade Medical Examiners office. Used with permission.)

Bitemark Evidence Collection and Preservation

If we are to assume the odontologist is the primary investigator of the bite wound, then there is a sequence of events that usually takes place and a protocol to follow in order to obtain the best possible evidence. However, oftentimes the evidence has been gathered by others not familiar with the proper protocol for bitemark evidence collection. Mistakes can produce less than ideal material with which to work. The ideal sequence is as follows:

- The Scene: A crime scene investigator (CSI) usually will discover the bitemark. The body is photographed. The bite is photographed with and without a ruler, preferably the ABFO#2 scale. DNA is recovered from the wound. The odontologist is called and advised of the circumstances of the event, usually by a police officer or a medical examiner investigator. The odontologist may be requested to go to the scene. He should observe and record the bitemark and document circumstances surrounding the body (Figure 13.16).
- The Morgue: The body is logged into the morgue and photographed. The DNA is collected if it has not been done at the scene. The odontologist and forensic photographer document the wound. The odontologist will analyze the bitemark and determine if a profile of the biter's teeth can be made, classify the bitemark, and may draw or trace the bite (Figure 13.17a,b). The bite is dusted with fingerprint powder, photographed, and lifted with a gel lifter (Figure 13.18). The bitemark with the fingerprint powder present is recorded and preserved with polyvinylsiloxane (PVS) impression material. From the impression of the bite, a stone or plastic model is made which would be a positive reproduction of the bitemark. The non-invasive procedures have been completed and now, if indicated, the tissue can be removed. This can be incisional (Figure 13.19a–c) or total excision. Microscopic studies may be performed on the incised portions (a bitemark biopsy) or, if totally

Figure 13.16 Crime scene. (Courtesy of RRS.)

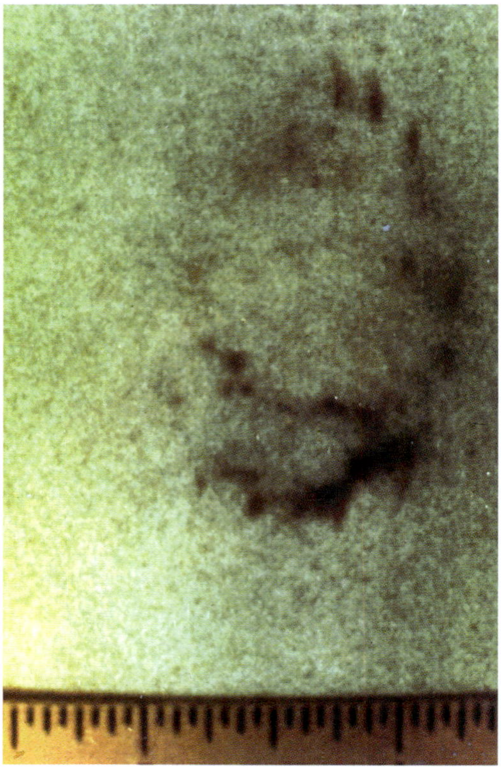

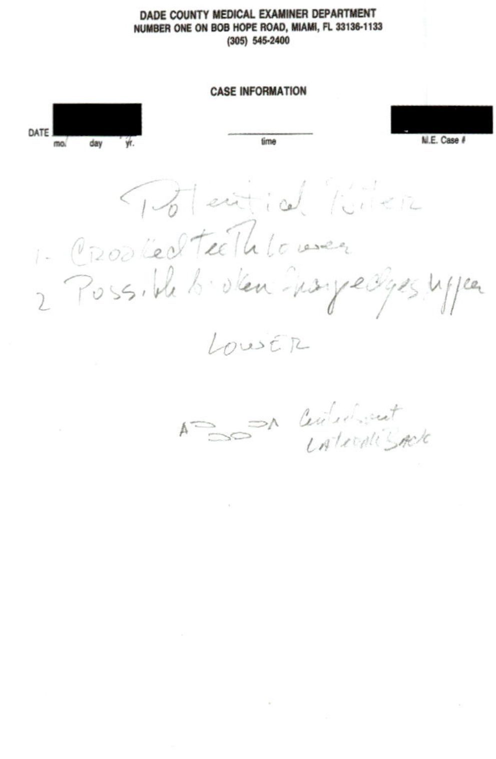

DADE COUNTY MEDICAL EXAMINER DEPARTMENT
NUMBER ONE ON BOB HOPE ROAD, MIAMI, FL 33136-1133
(305) 545-2400

CASE INFORMATION

DATE [redacted] mo. day yr. ______ time [redacted] M.E. Case #

Potential Biter
1- Crooked Teeth lower
2 Possible broken edges upper
LOWER

Central
Lateral Back

Figure 13.17 (a) Bite. (b) Biter's profile. (Courtesy of the Miami Dade Medical Examiners office. Used with permission.)

removed, the bitemark is transilluminated, photographed, and may be further analyzed microscopically and in some rare cases a scanning electron microscope may be used. The tissue is preserved in 10 percent formalin and refrigerated for possible future analysis.

After the conclusion of the analysis, the odontologist may be asked to produce a written report. At this stage of the investigation the report should be clearly documented as a preliminary investigative document (Figure 13.20).

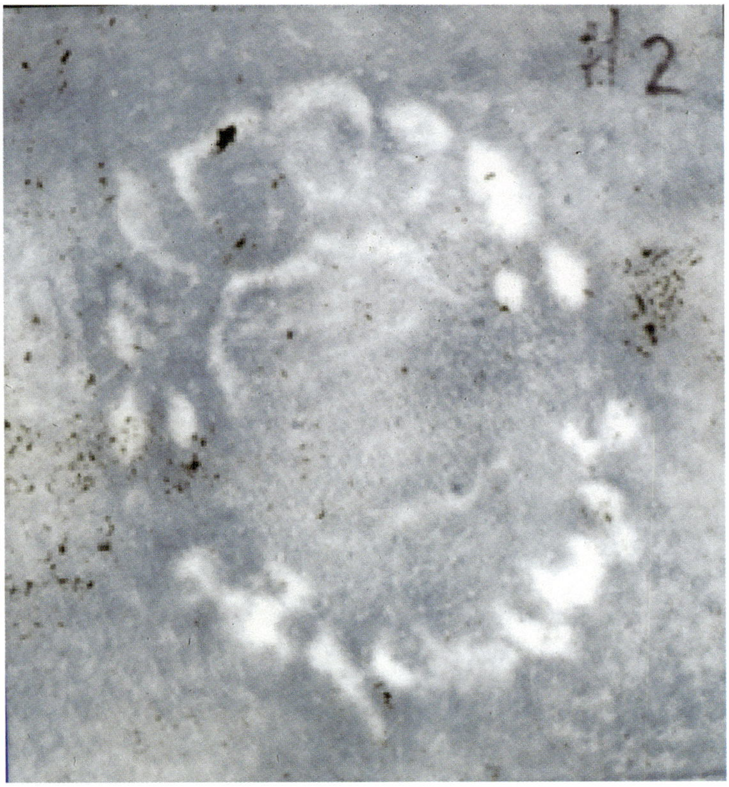

Figure 13.18 Gel lifter bite print. (Courtesy of the Miami Dade Medical Examiners office. Used with permission.)

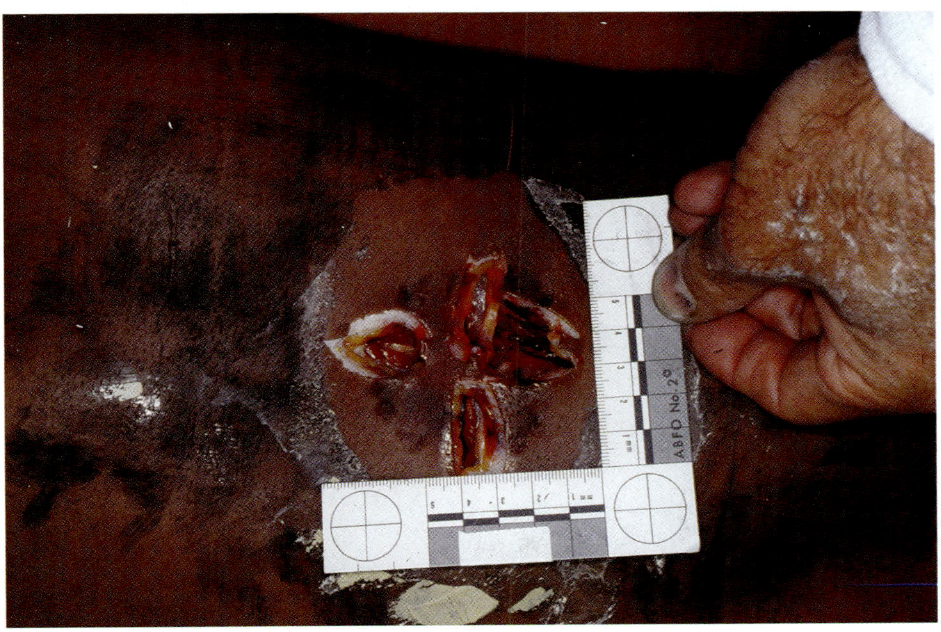

Figure 13.19a Incisional biopsy. (Courtesy of the Miami Dade Medical Examiners office. Used with permission.)

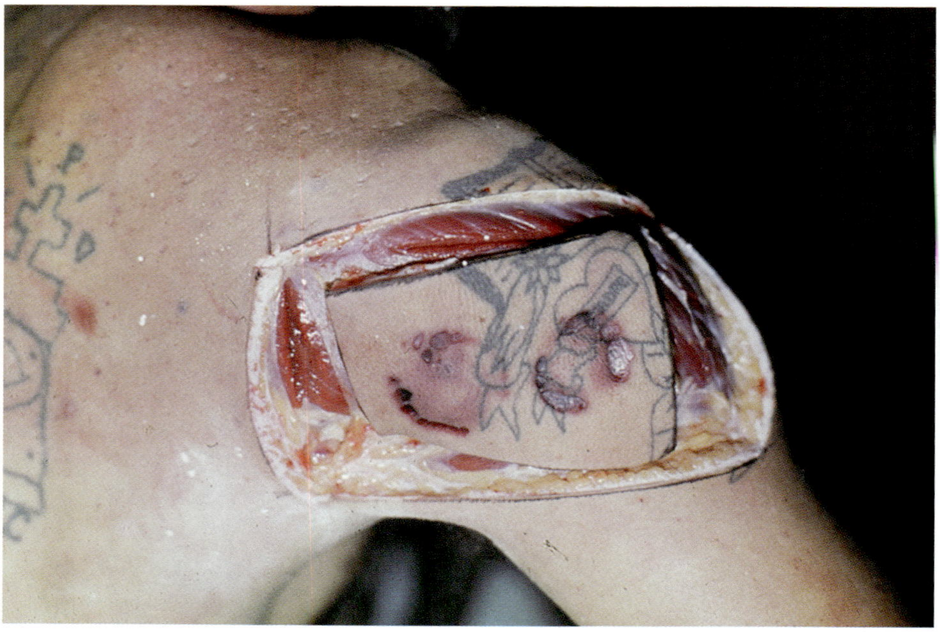

Figure 13.19b Excisional biopsy. (Courtesy of the Miami Dade Medical Examiners office. Used with permission.)

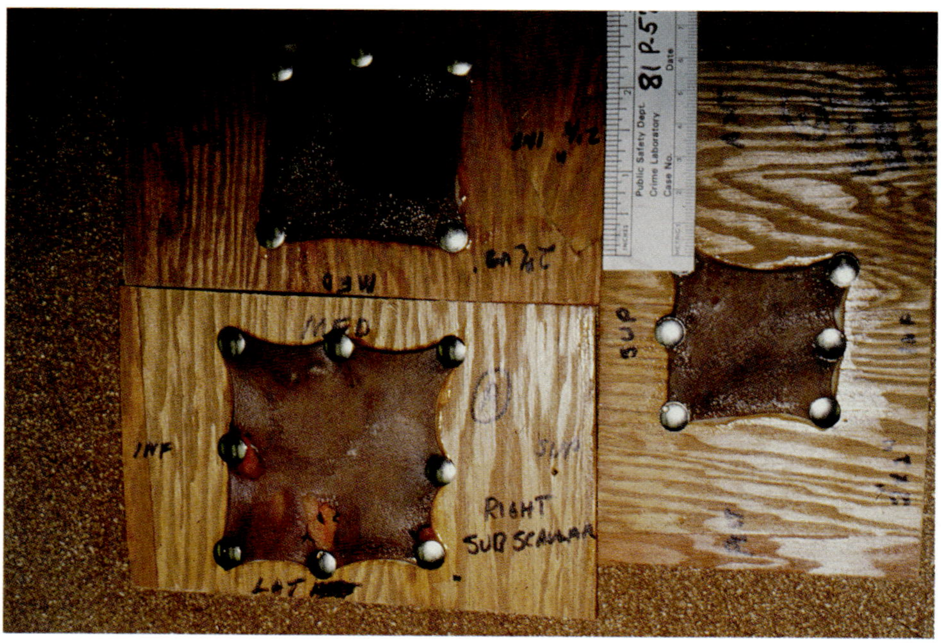

Figure 13.19c Excisional biopsy extracted tissue. (Courtesy of the Miami Dade Medical Examiners office. Used with permission.)

MIAMI-DADE COUNTY, FLORIDA

MEDICAL EXAMINER DEPARTMENT
NUMBER ONE ON BOB HOPE ROAD
MIAMI, FLORIDA 33136-1133
(305) 545-2400

April 25, 2006

Detective James D. Murray
451 NW 70th Terrace
Plantation, FL 33317

RE: Case ;
Consultation Case#

Dear Detective Murray:

On Monday April 24, 2006 I had an opportunity to review the package of information forwarded to me by yourself with specific attention to the pattern injury on the left arm of the white female. This pattern injury has class characteristics of a bite mark but it lacks individual characteristics. The close up of this injury with the morgue case # shows clearly that there are two opposing semi circular arches which is consistent with a bite mark. However, because of the fused nature of the bruising this pattern would serve little value in matching to a suspect. It may be of some value for exclusion of a suspect.

If you need any additional information of if I may be of further service please do not hesitate to contact me.

Sincerely,

RICHARD R. SOUVIRON, D.D.S.
Associate Medical Examiner
Chief Forensic Odontologist

RRS:nb

Figure 13.20 Investigative correspondence documentation. (Courtesy of the Miami Dade Medical Examiners office. Used with permission.)

The Scene

It is rare for the odontologist to go to the scene where there is a homicide with bitemark evidence. However, the odontologist is often called to the "scene" where a living victim has a bitemark. A bitemark on a living person is ephemeral. The changes occur rapidly with time. Photographic documentation of the injury should be accomplished as soon as possible. The victims are usually first seen at emergency rooms, rape treatment centers, children's hospitals, or government/private treatment facilities, that is, nursing homes or police departments. The odontologist should be familiar with the collection, preservation, and documentation procedures for DNA recovery, along with the proper chain of custody protocol. The DNA collection kit makes for an easy, accurate, and defensible protocol to follow. The odontologist should have this material with them as part of their routine bitemark evidence collection kit (Figure 13.21).

Photographs of the scene are extremely helpful to the odontologist and should show the body, the surrounding area, the pattern injuries before any manipulation, and a complete photographic documentation of all body trauma with and without a scale. The presence of insects on the body, especially ants can explain injuries that mimic

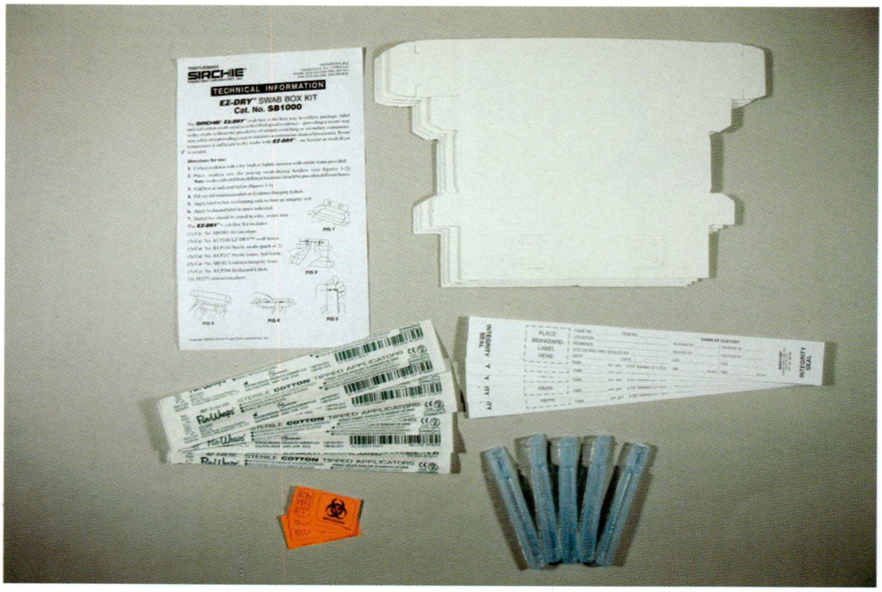

Figure 13.21 DNA collection kit. (Courtesy of the Miami Dade Medical Examiners office. Used with permission.)

bitemarks. Likewise, jewelry, medical devices, and medical intervention therapy all may produce pattern injuries that may mislead the investigator. Emergency room treatment, hospital therapies, and autopsy manipulation should be documented photographically and reviewed by the odontologist. Without all of the scene photographs and other prior records the analysis of the bitemark may produce a false or misleading opinion.

Morgue Photography

When the odontologist is called to the medical examiner facility to perform a bitemark evaluation, the protocol is much more in depth because the victim is deceased. When called to a rape treatment center, emergency room, nursing home, or hospital usually the victim is alive but traumatized and is or has been receiving medical treatment. Then DNA recovery, photograph, and history of the event are all that can be done. However, in the morgue, more time is available. Forensic photographers are sometimes available to assist with specialized photographic techniques. ALS (alternate light source), UV, IR (infrared) black and white and color photography, ambient light, and digital photography are all techniques that will aid with the future analysis of the pattern injury. The photographs should be taken both with and without the ABFO#2 scale.

A photographic protocol should include an overall body and a close-up photograph of the bitemark. It is important to document both dental arches individually with a scale when the bitemark is on a curved surface such as an arm or hand. Body position can change the configuration of the bitemark. Prepare in advance for the challenge by photographing the different possible positions, such as arm up, down, bent, or outstretched. The forensic photographs of the entire procedure from autopsy to bite printing, impression, excision, transillumination, and microscopy often provide the best means of analyzing and documentation. In most cases the odontologist has only the photographs of the bitemark with which to work. This puts him at a disadvantage because without scene photographs, autopsy photographs, and knowledge of the circumstances of the event his opinions will be compromised.

The Bite Print

Bitemark printing is helpful in adding another dimension to the analysis process. Dusting the bitemark with fingerprint carbon powder using the magna brush seems to work best in our studies (Figure 13.22). Here the third dimension (indentations) if they are present are enhanced and recorded both by photography and by lifting the printed bite with a gel lifter or fingerprint card. How sweet it is to see the imprint of the tooth or teeth with their lingual anatomy and obvious indentations. When present this information can raise the level of certainty of the comparison to or the exclusion of a suspect. The bite printing has been found to enhance the PVS impression of the bitemark (Figure 13.23). The next step in the collection of evidence is the bitemark impression.

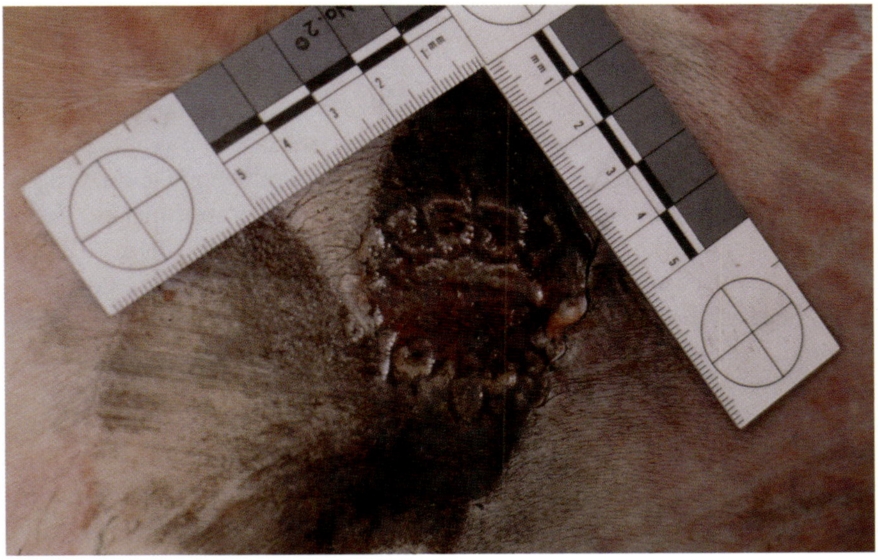

Figure 13.22 Fingerprint dusting for bite print. (Courtesy of the Miami Dade Medical Examiners office. Used with permission.)

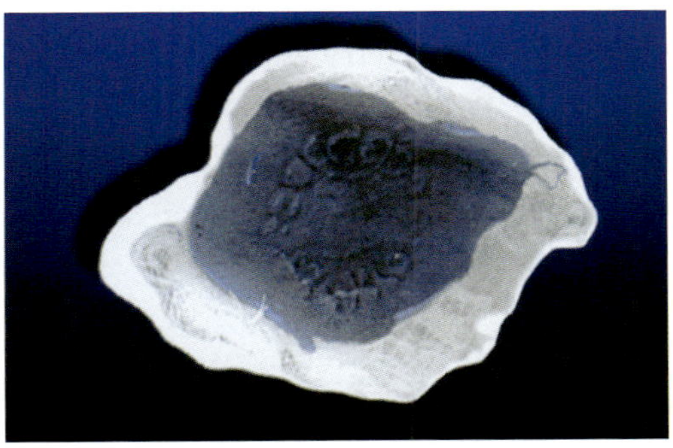

Figure 13.23 Polyvinylsiloxane impression of printed and dusted bite mark. (Courtesy of the Miami Dade Medical Examiners office. Used with permission.)

Bitemark Impressions

Following the dusting and lifting of the bitemark or pattern injury an impression should be made. The technique of choice is to leave some of the fingerprint powder over the wound and, using the PVS dispensing gun, spread the material completely over the wound and well beyond the margins. While still flowable, use staples, paperclips, or gauze to act as a retention vehicle for the stone backing. If the body has been in the storage locker (37 degrees Fahrenheit) the impression material will take an extra amount of time to set up. The same will be true for the stone backing. To decrease the setting time use a hot towel over the PVS and stone or, if available, a hair dryer. When the impression material and stone have set, the impression is removed with the stone attached to form a perfect "negative" of the wound. Now, a countermaterial such as dental stone will give a positive model of the bitemark. In some cases, a PVS model can be produced where you need a flexible model or in some cases an acrylic (plastic) model may be produced where a hard nonbreakable model is desirable.

Tissue Removal

In cases of a bitemark on the deceased it may be important to preserve the wound for future analysis both macro- and microscopically. The medical examiner or homicide detective may request this procedure to be done. In our jurisdiction, the body is the property of the medical examiner who will then determine if tissue removal is appropriate. The odontologist should never remove the wound without proper approval by the medical examiner and then only if common sense dictates. The concern of the family should be considered and if the bite is on the face, cheek, or other visible body part one might err on the side of caution and not remove the tissue. The question is, if all other evidence has been gathered properly, is the tissue removal really essential?

If the wound is to be totally excised a frame of some type should be used to secure the tissue. The odontologist usually constructs an acrylic frame as a retaining ring. Other devices can work as well, such as a knitting or needlepoint frame. The frame is glued to the tissue using cyanocacrylate (superglue). The retaining ring is sutured to the skin. The ring is then marked for identification and orientation (head, toe, right, left and ME case #). A scalpel is used to incise the tissue well outside of the retaining ring and sutures. The tissue is carefully separated from the underlying fatty layer and once removed, the donor site is photographed. The underside of the tissue (wound) is photographed. The tissue can be preserved in 10 percent formalin and refrigerated. Freezing the tissue has been shown to be a poor alternative for preservation. The tissue, once removed, can be transilluminated (Figure 13.24).

Summary

Preserving the Bitemark

1. Scene photography: orientation and scale.
2. DNA collection.
3. Morgue examination, bite orientation, biter's profile, investigative opinions.

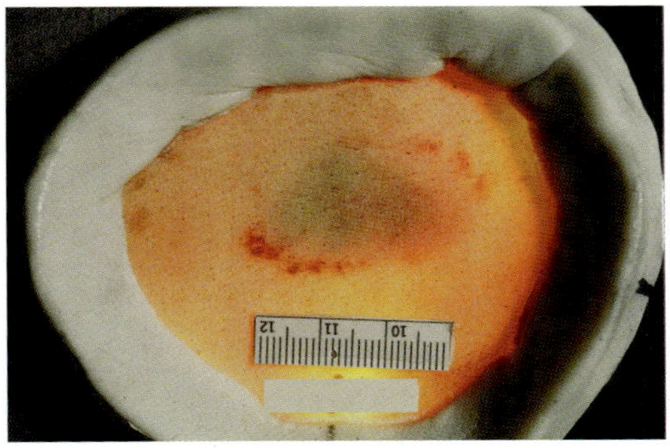

Figure 13.24 Transillumination of excised bite mark. (Courtesy of the Miami Dade Medical Examiners office. Used with permission.)

4. Photography: alternate light, IR, digital, UV, ambient color with and without ABFO scale photography.
5. Dusting and lifting the bite print.
6. Impression and model construction of the bitemark.
7. Tissue removal: excisional or bitemark biopsy (incisional).
8. Store the tissue in 10 percent formalin and refrigerate.

Under normal circumstances where the bitten victim is alive items #5 and #6 are not usually performed. Items #7 and #8 are never performed on a live individual.

Analysis of the Bitemark

There will be times when the odontologist is asked to give opinions regarding the bite wound without knowledge of a suspected biter. If he cannot make an intelligent evaluation of the evidence without a set of teeth to compare, how can he possibly be objective and scientific when asked to include or exclude a potential suspect? He can't. The analysis of the bite without a suspect occurs or should occur with every case from its inception. The questions that beg answers are: is the pattern injury a human bitemark or trauma that mimics a human bitemark? Ant, roach, or unknown insects, scrapes, drags, all have been identified as being human bites and shockingly matched to a suspect. Even more disturbing, convictions have been obtained with these mendacious opinions.

If the wound has been identified as a human bitemark it may be a Class II bitemark or Class III bitemark. If it is a Class II bitemark the odontologist should be able to opine as to the location of the upper and lower arches, the position of the biter in relation to the victim, and possibly the general overall tooth arrangement, in general, not specific terms, such as protruding teeth and so on (Figure 13.25) without any examples of a possible suspect's teeth.

If the wound is a Class III bitemark the odontologist should be able to opine as to all Class II identifiers and in addition give a dental profile of the biter (Figure 13.26a,b). Does the biter have spaces between some teeth, rotated teeth, broken or chipped, or missing teeth? Is the bite from an adult or child? If the wound shows a clear third dimension (indentations) then one could or may determine that the bite had been made near the time of death. Furthermore, the bitemark may show signs of having been made through clothing.

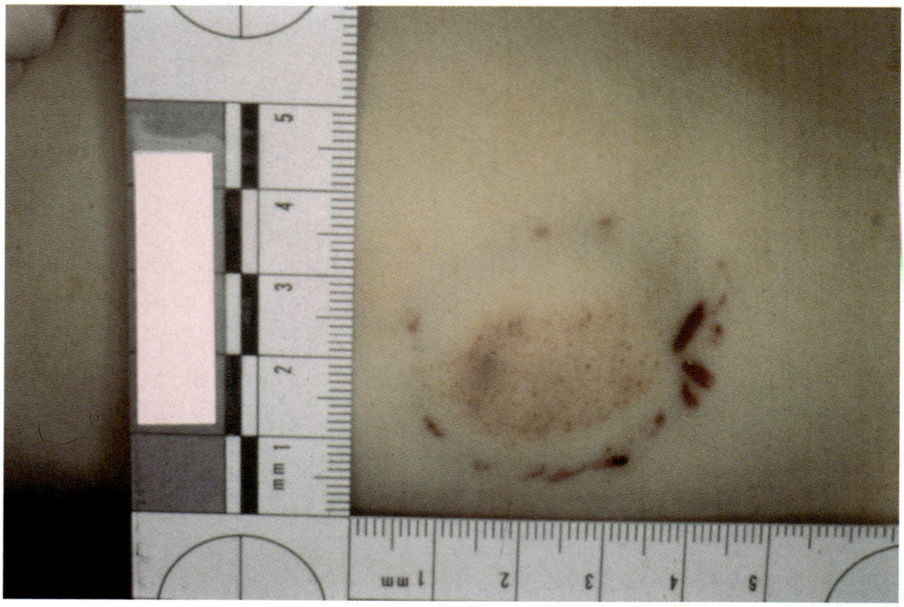

Figure 13.25 Class I upper arch, Class II lower arch. (Courtesy of the Miami Dade Medical Examiners office. Used with permission.)

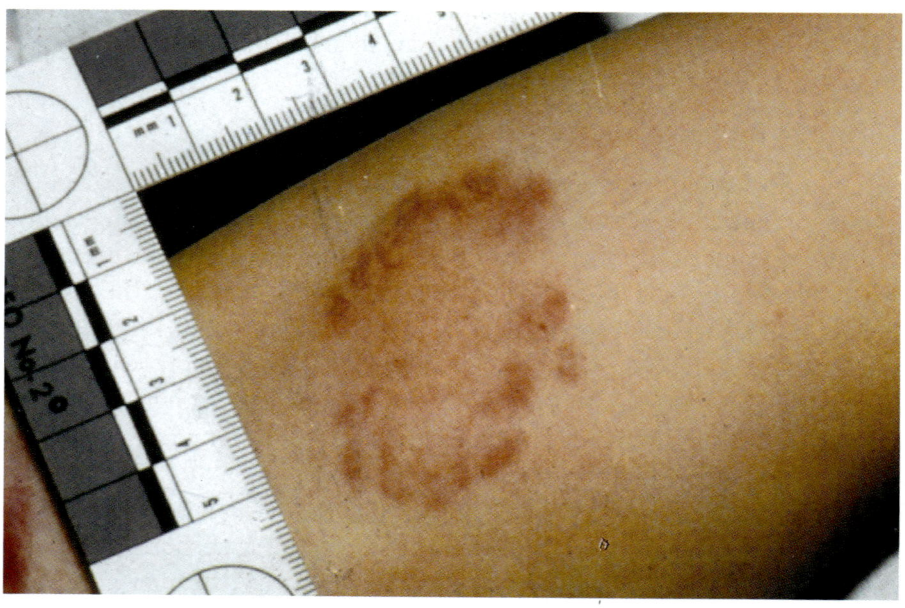

Figure 13.26a Class III bite. (Courtesy of RRS.)

The analysis of a Class IV bitemark, incisional or excisional, is very difficult and it is best to say that this was made by teeth as opposed to some other source (Figure 13.27).

To summarize, the analysis should always be done prior to having the dental cast, photographs, or description of a suspect. The bitemark analysis opinions are for the most part investigative but in certain unique circumstances they can be evidentiary. Investigative opinions are just that: subject to change or modification with new information or more extensive testing.

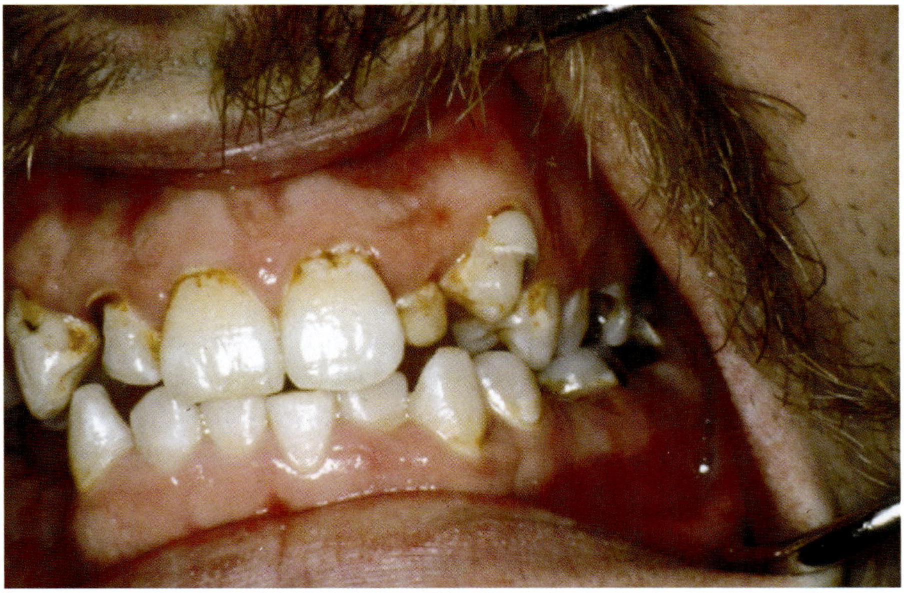

Figure 13.26b Biter's teeth. (Courtesy of RRS.)

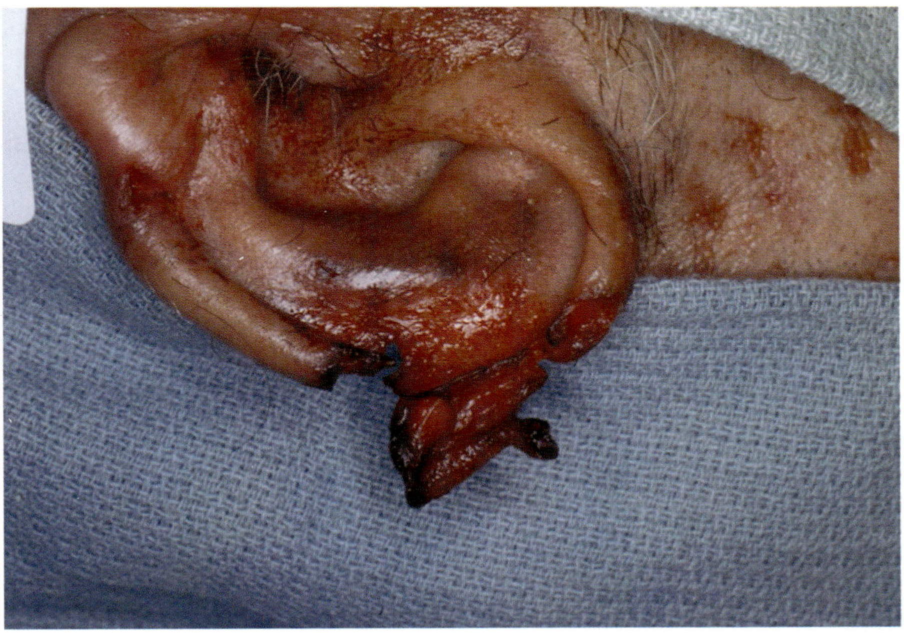

Figure 13.27 Class IV bite on ear. (Courtesy of the Miami Dade Medical Examiners office. Used with permission.)

Obtaining Bitemark Evidence from a Suspect

The odontologist who examines the bite wound may or may not be the one to take the records from a suspect. It is the opinion of this author that it is preferable that the most experienced odontologist obtain the records from the suspect because if there are errors, omissions, poor records, poor impressions, bite registrations, or a flaw in the chain of custody, the case can be severely or irreparably damaged. It is a good idea to have an assistant (dentist) when the records are taken from the suspect. The suspect, if he is aware that his teeth may have left a bitemark, can alter or remove his teeth. Thus, confidentiality is very important in all bitemark cases, but especially a homicide case.

Search Warrant or Court Order

In order to obtain a search warrant or court order probable cause is necessary. The analysis of the bite wound can provide probable cause; that is, photographs of the suspect's teeth are similar to the configuration of the bite (Figure 13.28). Once the warrant is issued the records should be obtained as quickly as possible for the reasons mentioned above. The teeth can be altered or removed if the suspect is aware of the bitemark evidence.

A warrant or court order to obtain records from a suspect should contain at least five requests:

1. Photo of the defendant and his teeth
2. Dental history: present treatment and oral exam (check for mobile teeth, recent extractions, etc.)
3. Dental impressions
4. Bite records
5. Requests for the use of reasonable force if necessary

Is reasonable force necessary? Not in this author's opinion. However, on several occasions the suspect had refused to submit to the order or warrant because it did not authorize the use of necessary force. The penalty for refusal was contempt of court and jail. Well, the suspect is already in jail. The authorization for the use of force has always defused the problem and the suspect has cooperated (Figure 13.29).

In certain cases voluntary consent is given for "persons of interest" to give bite exemplars; see *State v. Doyle 1954* and *Florida v. DuBoise 1987.* This can be a problem with violation of the individual's right against self-incrimination and should only be carried out with the prior approval of the agency in charge: police, prosecutor, medical examiner, and so on. It should also be mentioned that on occasion the odontologist may be asked to take buccal swabs for DNA analysis. If so, it should be specified in the court order and is a special request not usually the purview of the odontologist.

Comparison Analysis

The specificity of the opinion depends upon the variables of the evidence. Another way of saying the same thing is the level of certainty is inversely proportional to the variables. There are basically two types of opinions that can be expressed by the odontologist when reporting on the analysis and comparison of bitemark evidence. They are:

1. Investigative opinion: fluid non-specific, possible or probable, more likely than not.
2. Evidentiary: The final conclusion arrived at using the scientific method; to a reasonable degree of medical/scientific certainty.

METROPOLITAN DADE COUNTY, FLORIDA

MEDICAL EXAMINER DEPARTMENT
~~NUMBER ONE ON BOB HOPE ROAD~~
MIAMI, FLORIDA 33136-1133
(305) 545-2400

July 11,

ASA Sally Weintraub
1350 NW 12th Avenue
Miami, FL 33136

RE: State of Florida vs. [redacted]
Victim-
Case #

Dear Ms. Weintraub:

On I had the opportunity to examine Trooper at my office and take records of several bite marks located on her body

HISTORY

According to the history provided by Detective Stone and Lt. Michael Hughes (Florida Highway Patrol) and Miami Dade Crime Scene Technician T.C. Carroll, at approximately 2:00 AM on was attacked while transporting a prisoner in her patrol car. She was bitten on the right arm and in the left face. Detective Carroll advised me that he had taken photographs at approximately 5:00 AM on approximately 3-4 hours after the bite occurred.

INJURY PATTERNS

Bite mark injuries were identified on the left jaw area at approximately the angle of the mandible. A second bite mark was located in approximately the tricep area of the right arm. The bite was a tooth to skin type injury. Photographs were taken of the pattern injuries along with a acetate tracing of the wounds. The orientation of the bite wounds in my opinion is as follows. The bite on the left facial area would indicate the lower teeth marking inferiorly, the upper teeth marking superiorly. The lingual aspects of the upper anterior teeth recorded in the skin. The arm bite would indicate that the upper teeth marked to the outer aspect with the lower teeth marking towards the inner aspect.

The dental profile of the biter would indicate that the upper anterior teeth were straight with the two centrals probably longer than the laterals. In the lower jaw the bite would indicate that there is a possible rotation of the lower anterior teeth as related to the cuspid. The cuspid appeared to be prominent in the lower right. Subsequent to the initial examination in approximately March of I had an opportunity to review the evidence taken and one to one photographs were produced from the slide. These photographs were of both the original pictures taken by Detective Carroll and by the photographs taken by myself some four days post trauma.

Figure 13.28 Probable cause report. (Courtesy of the Miami Dade Medical Examiners office. Used with permission.)

How does one arrive at one or the other of these opinions? The variables of the bitemark, the dynamics, and the changes have been discussed previously in this chapter. Likewise, the biter's teeth are changeable, can be removed or modified in position or shape. With so many variables, is it possible to make an identification of a suspect? Possibly. Can a suspect be eliminated? Possibly.

At the end of the day the investigative agency will want to know: Did she or he make the bitemark? Yes or no? This requires an evidentiary opinion. Be very careful and follow the guidelines when you attempt to answer this question. The analysis of the bite followed by the comparison to a suspect or suspects is a thought-provoking

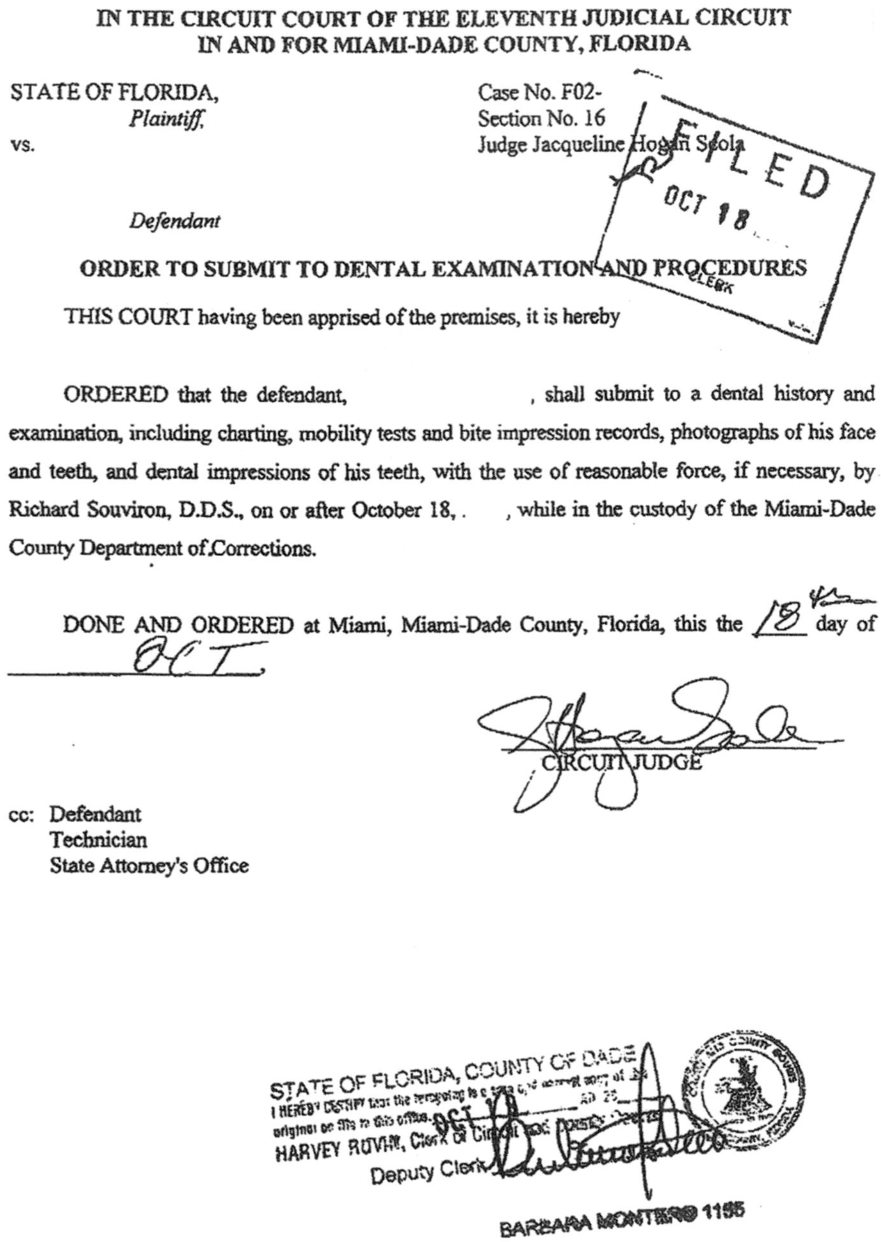

IN THE CIRCUIT COURT OF THE ELEVENTH JUDICIAL CIRCUIT
IN AND FOR MIAMI-DADE COUNTY, FLORIDA

STATE OF FLORIDA,
Plaintiff,
vs.

Defendant

Case No. F02-
Section No. 16
Judge Jacqueline Hogan Scola

FILED
OCT 18
CLERK

ORDER TO SUBMIT TO DENTAL EXAMINATION AND PROCEDURES

THIS COURT having been apprised of the premises, it is hereby

ORDERED that the defendant, , shall submit to a dental history and examination, including charting, mobility tests and bite impression records, photographs of his face and teeth, and dental impressions of his teeth, with the use of reasonable force, if necessary, by Richard Souviron, D.D.S., on or after October 18, . , while in the custody of the Miami-Dade County Department of Corrections.

DONE AND ORDERED at Miami, Miami-Dade County, Florida, this the 18th day of OCT.

CIRCUIT JUDGE

cc: Defendant
Technician
State Attorney's Office

STATE OF FLORIDA, COUNTY OF DADE
I HEREBY CERTIFY that the foregoing is a true and correct copy of the original on file in this office.
HARVEY RUVIN, Clerk of Circuit and County Courts
Deputy Clerk
BARBARA MONTERO 1195

Figure 13.29 Court order. (Courtesy of the Miami Dade Medical Examiners office. Used with permission.)

and time-consuming process. The examiner should have as much information as possible for comparison analysis. This should include but not be limited, necessarily, to the following:

- Circumstances of the event, a history
- Scene photos of the victim and injury
- Accurate and multiple photographs of the injury or injuries
- Life-size photos ALS, UV, IR

- Dusted and printed bitemark
- Impressions of the bitemark
- Tissue itself for analysis both macro- and microscopically

This, of course, rarely happens but the odontologist is expected to ask the authorities to produce these items or permit the odontologist to have access to be able to produce the material himself.

Can a bite produce a positive identification from an unknown large population group? **No.** However, from a known or limited group, if all suspects except one are eliminated, the remaining suspect can be identified by the process of elimination. This, of course, assumes that you have a bite that would classify as a Class II or Class III bitemark. Of equal or greater significance is the elimination of a suspect as being the biter. This can be much more definitive than the inclusion. Again, this depends upon the quality of the evidence (the bite): a Class II or Class III bite and the investigative information such as scene photographs, circumstances of the event, and quality and type of the photographic documentation.

Multiple and varied techniques have been described for the comparison of the injury to a suspect's teeth. These include overlay transfers, metric measurements, computer or video comparison, direct manual overlay of models, test bite pattern comparisons, and so on. The techniques, their production, and their use have been discussed in great detail in other texts. All of the comparison techniques—metric, digital, manual, photographic, and video,—and the respective conclusions drawn from them are dependent upon the quality of the evidence and the known variables. All conclusions should be subject to a peer review, consultation, and independent second opinion. DNA samples taken from a bitemark will or may produce a positive ID from an unknown population but a bitemark cannot. With that said, bitemarks can be and have been very helpful in the investigation and successful prosecution of a crime, first in eliminating a suspect as having left the bite, then showing and being able to demonstrate to the authorities how a set of teeth could have produced the bitemark. In a courtroom, the odontologist may be able to demonstrate by comparison techniques how the teeth fit the bite, but more importantly, unlike DNA and fingerprint evidence, the trier of fact, the jury members, can physically perform the techniques of comparison themselves. Juries have in the past and will in the future use life-size photos (one-to-ones) of the bitemark and the models of the suspect's teeth along with test bites and digital acetate transfers to concur with or reject the opinions of the odontologist. The use of bitemark evidence by the jury to arrive at their own conclusion is one of the reasons bitemark evidence is so powerful. One should be especially conservative in presenting the evidence in court. Mistakes in the analysis and interpretation of pattern injuries have resulted in several very serious miscarriages of justice.

Materials Left at the Crime Scene That May Contain Bitemarks

Materials left at the crime scene, primarily food, vary greatly from an apple to yucca (a root from the yucca plant very popular with Hispanic populations especially in South Florida). A review of the literature would indicate that apples left at crime scenes along with cheese are the most common foodstuffs found with bitemarks. Food materials with bite marks are documented in the literature and in court records. Harvey had documented cases of food with bitemarks in England and Scotland, among other places. A bite in an apple left at a crime scene in Nova Scotia in 1924 is the first recorded bitemark case in Canadian courts. Likewise, a bite left in cheese was used to convict Doyle, the first reported bitemark case (1954) in the United States.

Bitemarks in food found at crime scenes in modern times will produce two major pieces of evidence, DNA and tooth marks. Collection, preservation, and analysis of the DNA, although costly and time consuming, will produce positive exclusion or inclusion of a suspected biter. Bitemark analysis of bites in food may be of value for exclusion but rarely produce identification to the exclusion of a large population group. With this said, there are always going to be exceptions. For example, if the investigative authorities have limited the potential suspect pool, a higher level of certainty is possible. The fewer in the suspect group, the higher is the level of exclusion or inclusion.

A bite in a piece of cheese may show and record not only class characteristics (the arch size, tooth arrangements) but may show individual tooth characteristics (chips, fractures, etc.; see Figure 13.1). Other material may not provide this type of detailed information. However, an apple, one of the most commonly reported foodstuffs found at crime scenes, will or may show overall class characteristics of the biter and some individual tooth arrangements (a crooked or missing tooth, rotated, spaces or gaps between teeth), but not the detail of individual teeth characteristics as may be seen in cheese.

Although the literature documents a long history of teeth marks or bites left in food or other materials, the discovery of the material depends solely upon the expertise of the investigative authorities. Preservation, analysis, and comparison opinions usually are the responsibility of the odontologist. Preservation of bites in most objects including skin, food, and non-foodstuffs (basically everything) is accomplished by photography. The same photographic protocol is used for saving bitemarks in non-skin material as in skin. Of course, there are going to be variables but one should always document the evidence photographically first. DNA recovery will require contact with the material or even destroying the material. Use common sense when dealing with fragile or perishable materials. In real-life situations some irreversible mistakes have been made in the transportation and preservation of foodstuffs. Some examples are:

- Chewing gum with teeth marks was mailed to the odontologist in waxed paper placed in an envelope. The marks were destroyed when the envelope was processed by the post office.
- An apple with multiple bitemarks was refrigerated but decomposed before trial.
- A cookie (moon pie) with a bitemark was found at a crime scene of a triple homicide. It was placed in an evidence bag with red evidence tape and stored in the refrigerator at the morgue. Prior to discovery deposition (duces tecum) the moon pie was missing. An extensive investigation was conducted and it was discovered that one of the forensic morgue technicians had eaten the moon pie. Fortunately, the bitemark evidence had also preserved photographically. Strange things happen in this field.
- Bologna with bitemarks was discovered at the scene of a homicide. The material was photographically documented and impressions taken (see Figure 13.7a). The evidence was destroyed when the impressions were taken and the impressions were of no value. Photographs preserved the evidence which was later presented at the trial by the odontologist (State of Florida v. Roy Allen Stewart). The judge at a subsequent trial referred to this odontolgist as a bologna expert.

To summarize, all bitemark evidence is best preserved photographically. Photography before and after DNA recovery and always before any manipulation of the material is, or should be, the standard procedure. Once the material with the bitemark evidence has been photographed, then bite printing, impressions, preservation, and storage of the material may prove helpful in documenting and preserving the third dimension (indentations). It may also destroy the material. Care should be taken and consultation with the investigative authorities is strongly advised prior to any manipulation of the evidence that may result in its destruction.

Animal Bites

Without question the dog is the most common culprit of animal bites on humans. Eyewitness testimony is the most common means of identification and documentation of the injuries. With this said, there are going to be incidences for a variety of reasons when the evidence is going to require analysis and the opinion of an odontologist.

Although rare, dogs may be implicated in a homicide where the only witness is the dog. With no witnesses to the event the forensic analysis and the circumstances of the event will provide a scientific answer to the cause and manner of death: maybe. An example of the "maybe" is the death of a seven-year-old white female in the basement of her home in Ontario, Canada. The original autopsy reported the manner of death as homicide: multiple stab wounds. Even though a pitbull was present in the basement at the time, dog bites were ruled out as a cause of death. The mother was charged with the homicide and incarcerated. Two years later, a second autopsy was performed on the exhumed body by a second pathologist for the Crown. The pathologist (not the original pathologist) opined that there was a combination of dog bites and stab wounds. After four years the prosecution dropped all charges against the mother because "there was no longer proof that death was caused by stab wounds." The mother has subsequently sued all concerned on the prosecution team for negligence—the amount—several millions of dollars (Canadian). This case has been reported in the press both written and electronic and in the textbook, *Bite Mark Evidence*, by Dorion.

Several cases of dog bite deaths and injuries have occurred in Florida. One similar to the Canadian case was the mauling of a 12-year-old white female by two German Shepherds. The child's medical condition (spinabifida) prevented her from talking and although she survived the attack she was unable to assist the investigators. The mother was charged with the attack, not the dogs, because an emergency room nurse made the statement to the police, "I don't know what caused the injuries but they were not produced by dogs." The defense enlisted the aid of Miami Dade County Chief Medical Examiner Dr. Joseph Davis, the Deputy Chief Medical Examiner Dr. Ema Lew, the odontologist Dr. Richard Souviron, and a veterinarian, a total of over 150 years experience. The conclusion was that all injuries were produced by dogs. Charges were dropped against the mother but the damage had been done.

The documentation of dog bite injuries and the offending species have been documented in the press. According to the Miami Dade County Animal Control, 992 dog bites were reported in 2007. The number-one offending species—the terrier—108 reported cases out of the 992. The pitbull was last on the list of nine species. The reason: the pitbull is outlawed in Miami Dade County. Ownership carries a $500 fine and confiscation of the dog. However,

Broward County, the next county north of Miami has no such law and the pitbull was by far the number-one offender with 182 reported bite cases out of a total of 616.

From California to Texas to Florida and throughout the United States and Canada dog bites can be fatal. As tragic as this is, the misdiagnosis of dog bites, specifically referring to them as human-produced stab, laceration, or puncture wounds, will exacerbate the tragedy by directing the death investigation to a suspect rather than the dog. These mistakes can be prevented in the absence of eyewitness by following an investigative protocol:

1. Examine the suspected animal for blood and visible traces of evidence from the victim such as clothing.
2. Gather DNA from the animal's mouth, lips, hair, claws, and so on.
3. As soon as possible, take the animal to a veterinarian to induce vomiting.
4. Analyze the vomitus for tissue, clothing, and foreign objects to compare to the victim.
5. Quarantine the animal as soon as possible. Collect the feces and analyze for bone tissue, clothing, and foreign objects to compare to the victim.
6. Take dental impressions of the suspected animal's teeth. Produce a plastic (acrylic) model.

Note: From experience stone models are difficult to produce because of the small six anterior teeth and the long canines. The models in stone will have bubbles and the teeth fracture easily. This is not the case with an acrylic model.

7. Test the animal for rabies especially if the victim survives the attack.

If a protocol such as the above had been followed, the tragic arrests that took place in Canada and Florida could have been avoided.

Pattern Injuries That Can Mimic Bitemarks

The odontologist often is called to evaluate a pattern injury on the deceased that may resemble a human bitemark. A presumptive diagnosis (an investigative opinion) may have been made by a first responder, homicide investigator, forensic nurse, or medical examiner. The question that needs an answer is what caused the pattern on the body. The odontologist must be cautious and circumspect in his or her evaluation of all injuries, but especially bitemarks. Knowing the circumstances of the event and reviewing scene photographs, knowing about the medical intervention, if any, along with the times, location, temperature, animal and insect possibilities, as well as eyewitness statements, are all or some of the information that is included in the overall knowledge that is part of the circumstances of the event. Misinterpretation of a pattern injury as being a human bitemark and conversely misinterpreting a bitemark (such as dog bite) as stab wounds will always carry serious consequences. If the odontologist is confronted with a pattern injury that cannot be readily recognized as a human bitemark she would be wise to give an investigative opinion such as, "I don't know what caused it," or, "More analysis needs to be done before I can arrive at an opinion."

Avoiding mistakes in interpretation of pattern injuries can be accomplished by careful analysis of the pattern, knowing the circumstances of the event and consultation with

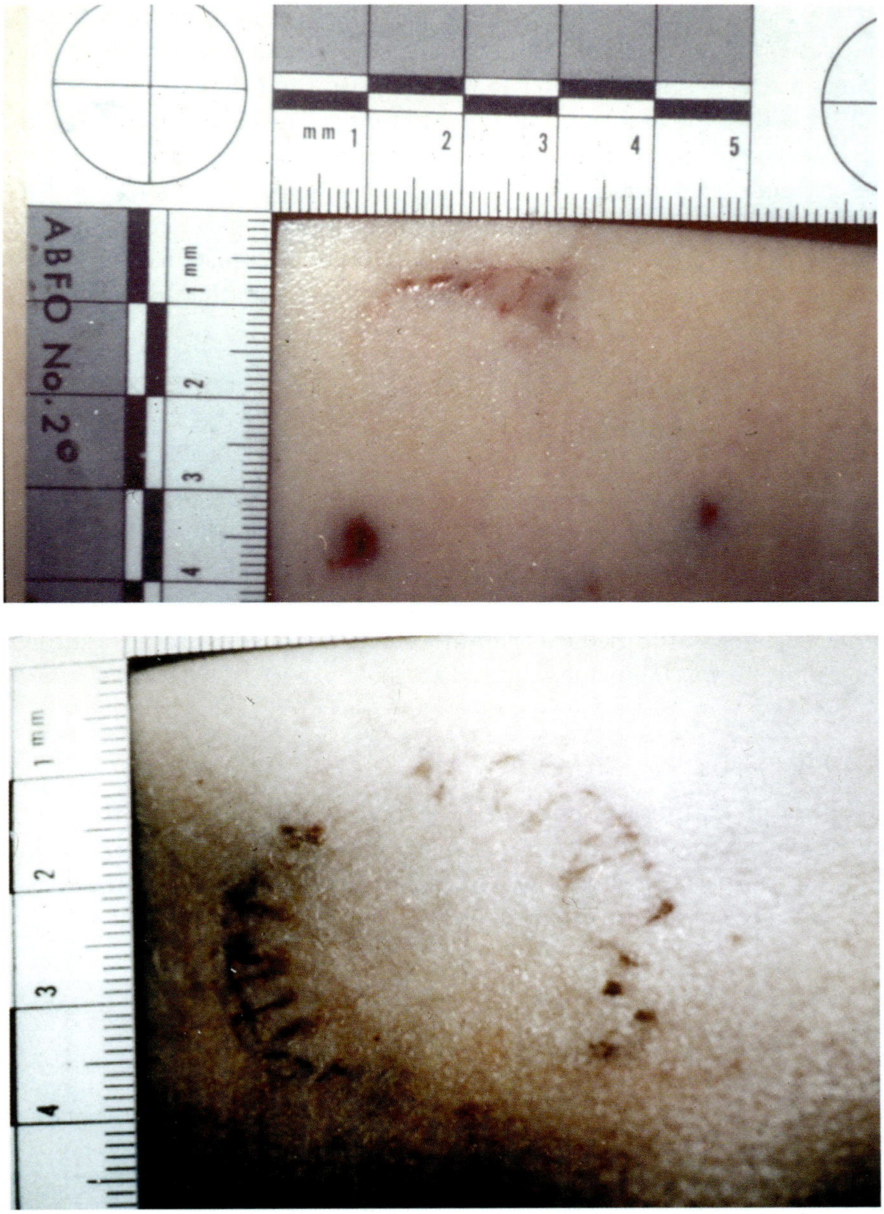

Figure 13.30 Pattern injury and a bitemark. (Courtesy of the Miami Dade Medical Examiners office. Used with permission.)

other people involved, such as the police, hospital personnel, medical examiner, and other odontologists. The mistake of designating a pattern injury as a human bite will almost always lead to the "slippery slope" of matching to a suspect. The consequences are tragic for everyone but especially for the innocent suspect and his or her family. Prevention of a misdiagnosis of pattern injury is first to admit the obvious. If the pattern does not have obvious class and individual characteristics of a human bitemark your opinion must be either it is not a human bitemark or you don't know what made it.

One example is the pattern injury of unknown origin left where other injuries are obvious human bitemarks (Figure 13.30). Another example is the case of *Mississippi v.*

Brewer, where a misinterpretation of pattern injuries on the body of the deceased as being a human bitemark or bitemarks and then matched to the suspect (Mr. Brewer) led to his conviction and a death sentence. After 13 years in prison and 10 years on death row, he was eventually cleared, found innocent, and released from jail by DNA evidence and the tireless work of the defense team in Mississippi and the Innocence Project attorneys. There are several other cases of misinterpretation of pattern injuries as being human bitemarks but this case should be analyzed carefully because it is a classic example of compounding of mistakes in analysis, interpretation, lack of knowledge of the circumstances, or ignoring them, and providing an opinion based only after the dental molds of the suspects were provided to the odontologists.

Circumstances of the Event-Brewer Case

A three-year-old female, Christine Jackson, was abducted from her home while the babysitter (Kennedy Brewer, a 21-year-old black male) was asleep. The child was raped and the body dumped in a creek and later found in a pond in a rural heavily wooded area of Mississippi. The body was in the water over 20 hours. The weather was warm. The date was May 3, 1992. At autopsy, the medical examiner ruled the cause of death was drowning and the manner of death was homicide (Figure 13.31a,b).

Wound Analysis

The odontologist for the prosecution opined that there were 19 human bitemarks on the body. Five could be matched positively to only one suspect, Mr. Brewer (Figure 13.32). Models were made of the four suspects and only one, Mr Brewer, had a space (diastema) between his two front teeth. By overlooking the circumstances and ignoring the fact that there was tissue

From the Air

Figure 13.31a Scene from air. (Courtesy of RRS.)

Before Body Remover

Figure 13.31b Body in pond. (Courtesy of RRS.)

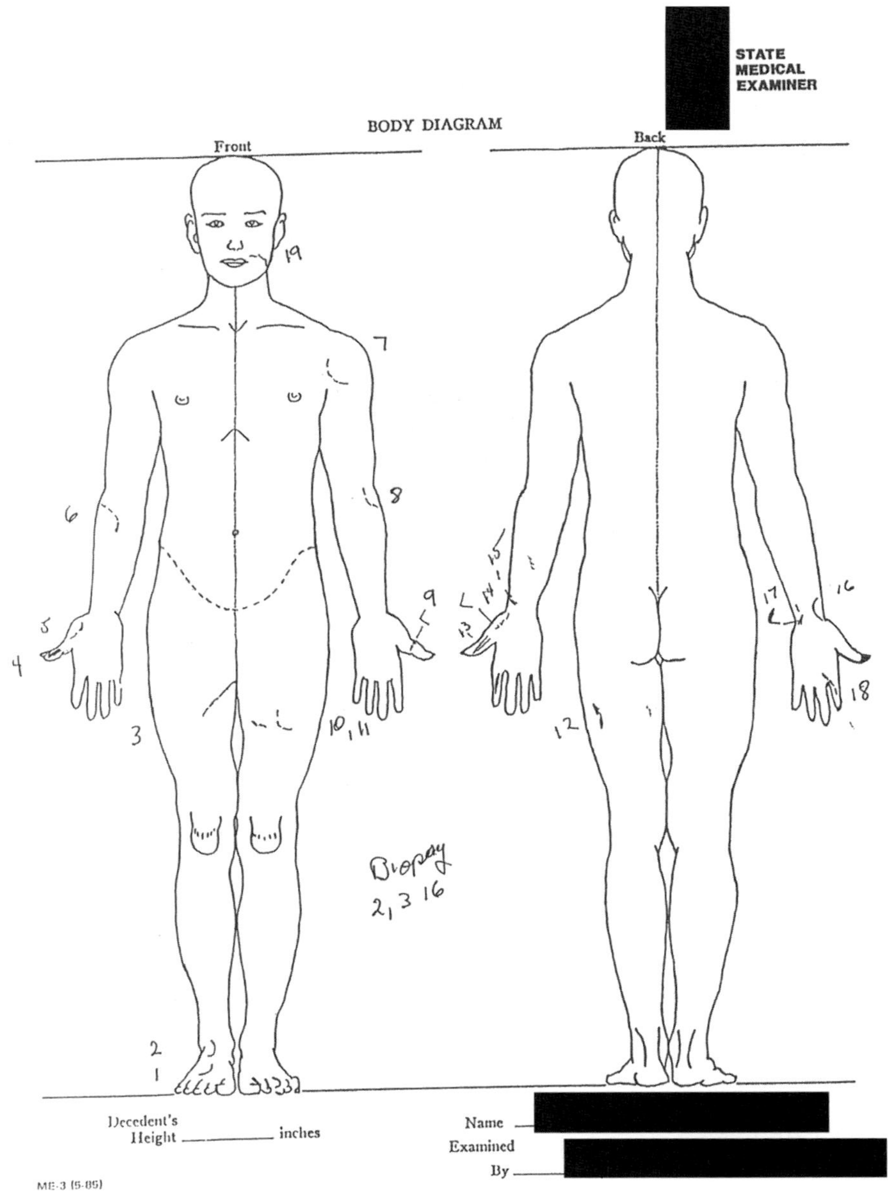

Figure 13.32 Diagram, false bites. (Courtesy of RRS.)

sloughing, early decomposition, and insect and aquatic predation, an irreversible misdiagnosis was made. None of the 19 pattern injuries that were thought to be human bites, and none of the five "positive" Brewer bites were analyzed by incisional or excisional biopsy. None were correctly diagnosed as aquatic bites, fish, crawfish, turtles, or insect activity or tissue sloughing from decomposition.

Comparison to a Suspect

The tragic error of diagnosing a pattern injury as a human bitemark and comparing to a suspect is further compounded by the fact that the investigation of other possible suspects

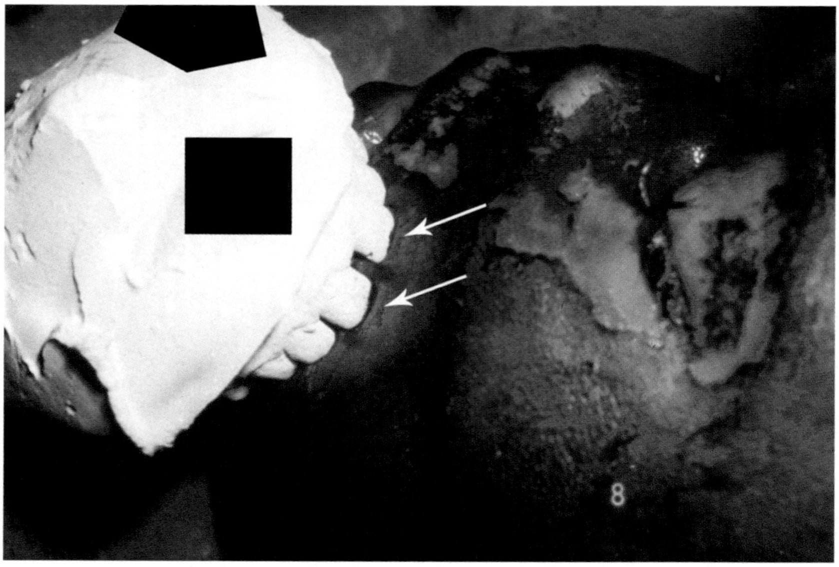

Figure 13.33 Suspect's dental model on body. (Courtesy of RRS.)

is stopped and the guilty party is spared prosecution. There can be very few circumstances where a suspect can be matched to a bite pattern "indeed and without doubt." In this case, out of 19 false bitemarks, none showed any sign of being made by lower teeth, only by the two upper centrals (Figure 13.33). Common sense tells you this is not possible. How can 19 bites be made with only the upper two or three front teeth and no lower teeth marking? Insane (Figure 13.34)!

Of the five "positive" human bitemarks, only Mr. Brewer's teeth were involved and then only his two front incisors. There were no other methods of comparison except to apply the models to the body in the morgue. There were no consultations with any other odontologist by the prosecution expert. On the other hand, the defense odontologist obtained the independent opinion of two other odontologists and three medical examiners, all of whom agreed that none of the 19 marks were made by human teeth and all were obvious signs of tissue sloughing, and insect and aquatic animal (fish, crab, and crawfish) activity (Figures 13.35 and 13.36).

Conclusion

In 2007 and 2008 DNA samples from the deceased child Christine Jackson and in a similar case, Courtney Smith, were found to be from the same person, J. A. Johnson. Mr. Johnson confessed on February 5, 2008 to both murders. He further stated that he did not bite either of the children. He also stated that "I am not crazy." Mr. Brewer was freed after many years of incarceration.

Errors in Bitemark Interpretation

Some of the more common pattern injuries occur as a result of medical intervention. They can mimic a bitemark when one does not know the circumstances and is limited to photo-

MICHAEL H. WEST
Deputy Medical Examiner Investigator
FORREST COUNTY MISSISSIPPI

P. O. Box 15846
Hattiesburg, MS 39402

Business: (601) 264-2474
Residence: (601) 264-1422

Diane Brooks
DMEI Noxubee Co.
Rt. 4 Box 115-6
Macon, MS 39340

May 14, 1992

RE: Christina Jackson

Dear Diane,

On 5 May 92, at the request of Dr. Steve Hayne, I did travel to the Rankin Co. morgue. I examined the remains of one Christina Jackson, a black female DOB 5-21-88. She had been raped and sodomized. It was decided to hold her body until the weekend and examine it then.

On 8 May 92 Noxubee Co. Sherif Dep. Bud Permenter brought four suspects to my office for Dental impressions. They were Kennedy Brewer 21y/o black male, Gloria Jackson 24y/o black female, Dwayne Graham 17y/o black male and Leshone Williams 15y/o black male.

On 9 May 92, I returned to the Rankin Co. Morgue to examine and compare the Dental study models to the remains of Christina Jackson. Nineteen (19) human bitemarks were found and compared to the dental study models.

OPINION

The bitemarks found on the body of Christina Jackson are peri-mortem in nature.

The bitemarks found on the body of Christina Jackson were indeed and without doubt inflected by Kennedy Brewer.

If I can be of any further assistance in this matter, please feel free to contact me at home or office. A statement for my fee is enclosed, please remit upon receipt.

Sincerely,

Michael H. West BS DDS ABFO DMEI SCSA

cc: SO
DA

Figure 13.34 Odontology report. (Courtesy of RRS.)

graphs of only one area. If the odontologist is given only a single close-up photograph of a pattern injury he or she should never opine as to its origin without knowing the circumstances of the event and requesting all photographs from the scene to medical treatment to autopsy. Occasionally the odontologist is requested to examine a questionable pattern injury in the morgue. If there are no scene photographs, no information regarding medical intervention, and no history of the events, then mistakes in interpretation can and will occur. Pattern injuries on the living become equally problematic because the pattern will change rapidly with time. A bitemark on a living person is always ephemeral, especially on children. All bitemarks on living individuals will change dramatically with time and with medical intervention and treatment. However, in some cases the detail of a bitemark may

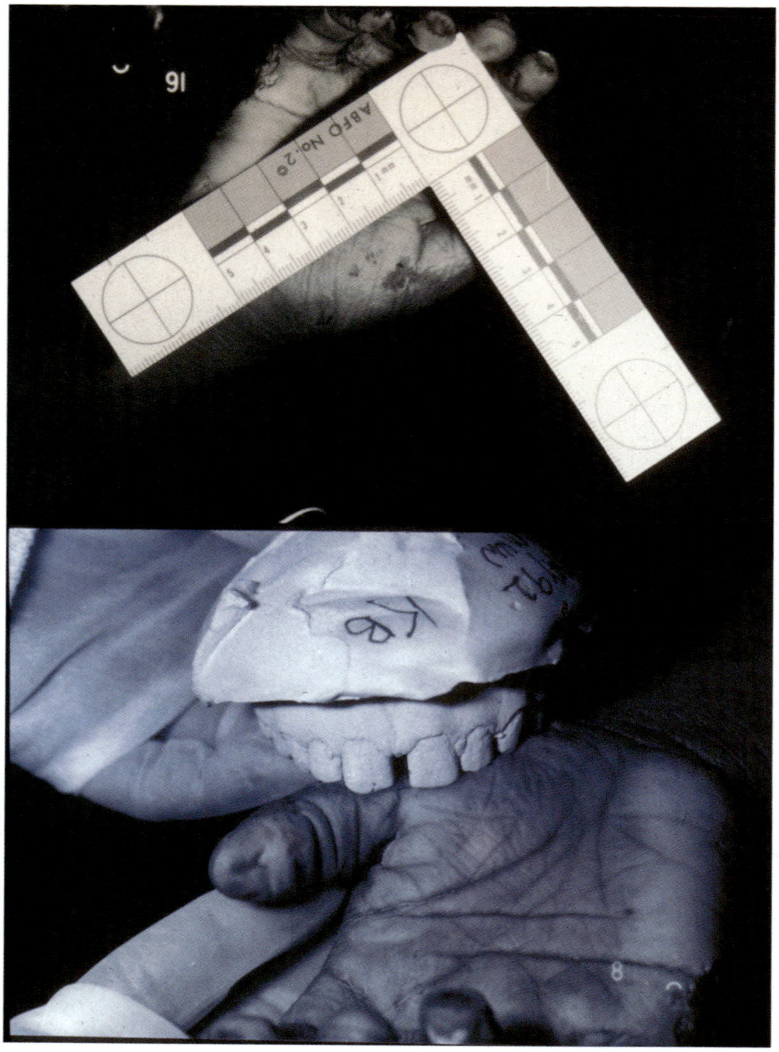

Figure 13.35 Teeth over pattern energy. (Courtesy of RRS.)

be enhanced with time. Where possible, it is a good idea to get photographs of the bite as soon possible and then document it photographically over a period of time. Always document the day, date, and time when the photographs were taken.

One cannot always depend upon the victim to provide an accurate account of the cause of the injury. In cases of severe trauma, the victim often has no memory of the event. In the case of children they may not be able to talk or describe the perpetrator because of their age and the possible fear factors. In the case of spouse abuse the fear factor and emotional considerations may prevent an accurate account of the injuries. Some witnesses, and victims, may also have reasons to lie. An example is the case of a white female beaten and reportedly bitten several times, but she survived her attack. During and subsequent to her hospitalization she informed authorities of the circumstances of her abduction by five men, and their assault on her. She identified who bit her, where, and how often. She had numerous bites and non-bite pattern injuries. An experienced odontologist "matched" the bites on two different areas of her body to two different suspects out of the five identified

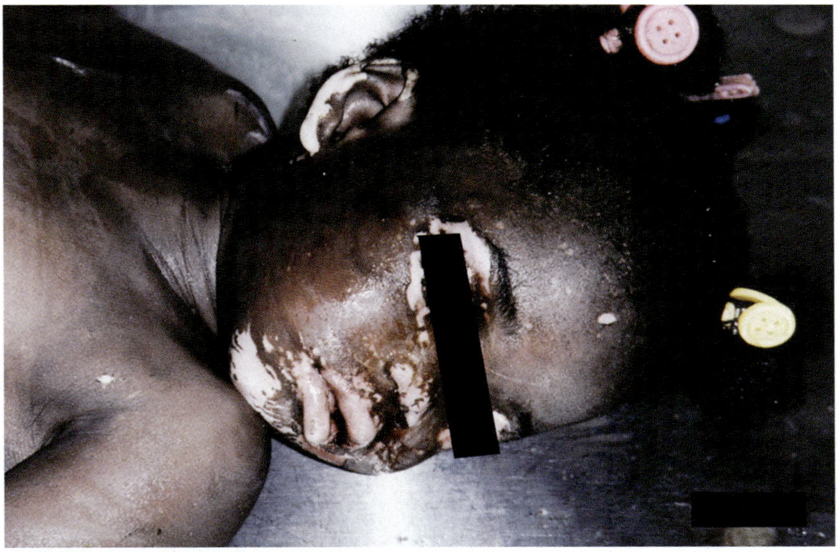

Figure 13.36 Teeth over pattern injury. (Courtesy of the Miami Dade Medical Examiners office. Used with permission.)

attackers. His report contained unsupported and unscientific numbers of probabilities in relation to the world population, that is, one in 4.3 billion. At trial, both men were convicted and sentenced to long prison terms.

Approximately 10 years later, after numerous motions by the defense attorneys and new "discovered" evidence, the cases were set for retrial. One defendant was released without a trial, based on lack of evidence. The other was given a new trial and acquitted by a jury of 12, based in part on the original misinterpretation of the bitemarks. How could this have been prevented? If the authorities had informed the odontologist of all the circumstances, such as: the victim had lied regarding the identification of her abductors, and the details of the assault given by the victim and the perpetrators of the bite were not accurate. Also, the odontologist should have been more careful and conservative in his attempts to "make a match" of the suspects to the bite pattern to the exclusion of everyone else in the world.

Another example of the importance of knowing the circumstances and being thorough in the analysis of the pattern occurred in a rural North Florida community. A witness to the attack and the victim herself both had reasons to mislead the authorities. The victim and her witness described the vicious attack in which the attacker cut her with a razor, bit her breast, and burned her breast with a cigar. The circumstances indicated both a possible racially and politically motivated event. An odontologist was consulted by the police. He reviewed the photographs and opined that the pattern injury on the breast was not a human bitemark and that the burn was not from a cigar but from a penny (Figure 13.37). Note the outline of Lincoln's head on her breast. A major tragedy was avoided in this case because the investigative authorities provided the odontologist with the facts and not theories. It is important to remember that the "victim" may have reason to give false and misleading information to the authorities.

Pattern injuries on the living that mimic bitemarks are most commonly the result of some form of medical treatment whether from the first responder or from the emergency room. One cannot always depend upon the victim's statement. In the case of young children, injuries or infection such as ringworm, diaper rash, or any number of dermatological diseases

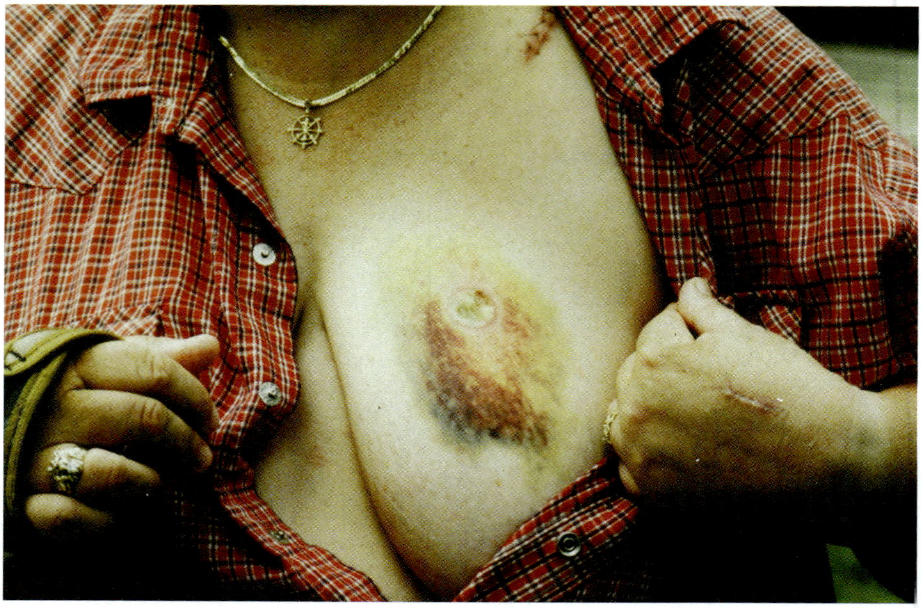

Figure 13.37 Pattern injury, self-inflicted (burn). (Courtesy of RRS.)

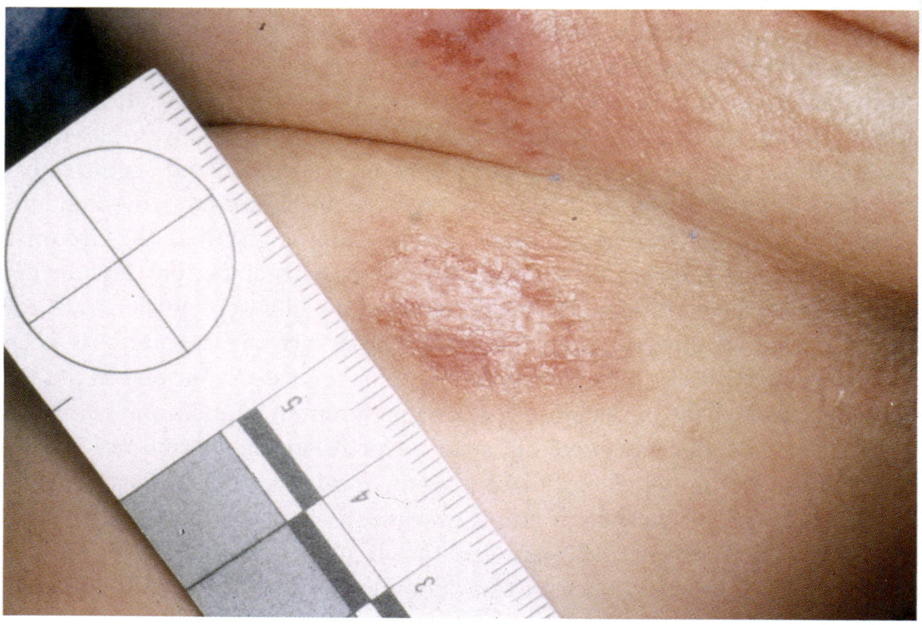

Figure 13.38 Diaper rash misdiagnosed as a bite mark. (Courtesy of RRS.)

may produce a lesion resembling a bitemark. In this case (Figure 13.38) a 17-month-old child had round lesions located on her external genitalia and inner thigh which were mistakenly diagnosed by an odontologist as bitemarks. These "injury patterns" were then subsequently matched by the odontologist to the teeth of a male family friend. When second and third odontologist opinions were obtained both, independently, ruled out the lesions as bites and were determined to be a form of dermatitis. The charges against the male suspect were dropped by the authorities but the damage had been done.

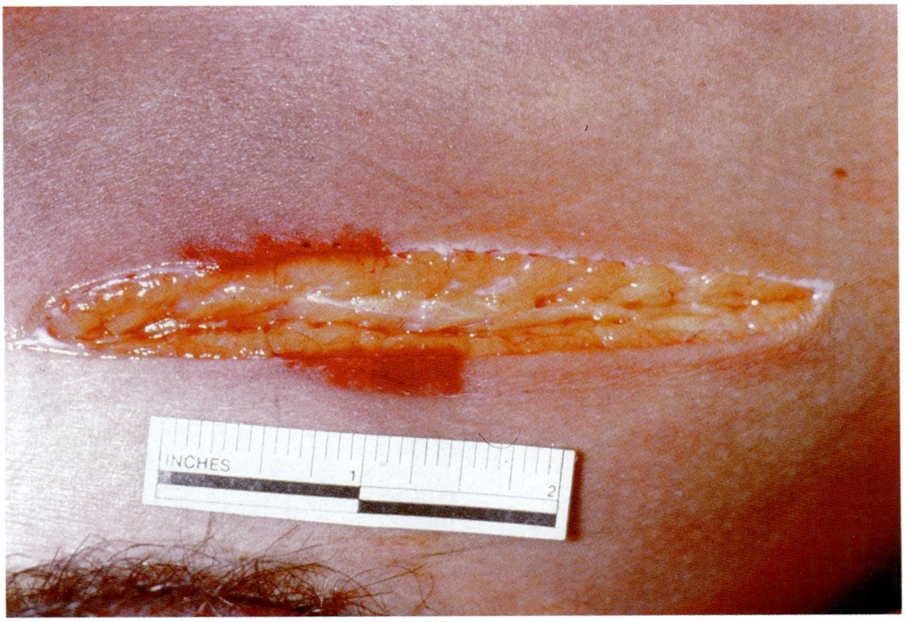

Figure 13.39 Incision through pattern injury. (Courtesy of the Miami Dade Medical Examiners office. Used with permission.)

The most common source of pattern injuries on the deceased, when the body is left unattended and exposed to the elements, is insect activity and animal predation. Insects produce bite patterns that have been misinterpreted as human bitemarks. Feeding by ants, roaches, and the like begins almost immediately after death, depending upon the circumstances: location, weather, soil, and body conditions. Bodies left in the water are fed upon by aquatic life, fish, crabs, turtles, and crawfish. Further complicating and producing pattern injuries is the decomposition factor as well as location and weather. Postmortem insect, ant, and roach activity on a body produces surface patterns that can be differentiated from a bitemark by several means: first, by an incision through the pattern and the analysis of the subcutaneous wound. A human bite is a compression injury and produces subdermal changes that are visibly different from surface activity from insects or an abrasion (Figure 13.39). An incision through the area should quickly show the distinction. Second, a tissue wedge similar to a biopsy followed by microscopic analysis will confirm the original investigative opinion. Had either of these two tests, that is, incision and microscopic examination, been performed in the Kennedy Brewer case there would have been scientific proof that the pattern injuries were, in fact, surface lesions and not human bitemarks.

Misinterpretation of pattern injuries as being human bitemarks on the deceased has led to conviction in several very high profile cases. Specifically, two of the most notable cases are the Tony Keko case from Southern Louisiana and the Duncan case from Northern Lousiana. The Keko case was covered by international television, specifically, the BBC and ABC's *Night Line* in 1995. Mr. Keko was charged and convicted of killing and biting his ex-wife. The only link that showed violence connecting Mr. Keko to the homicide was the pattern on the right shoulder of the victim. It was not noticed or documented at autopsy but a subsequent review of autopsy photographs by an odontologist found what he opined was "suggestive" of a possible human bitemark.

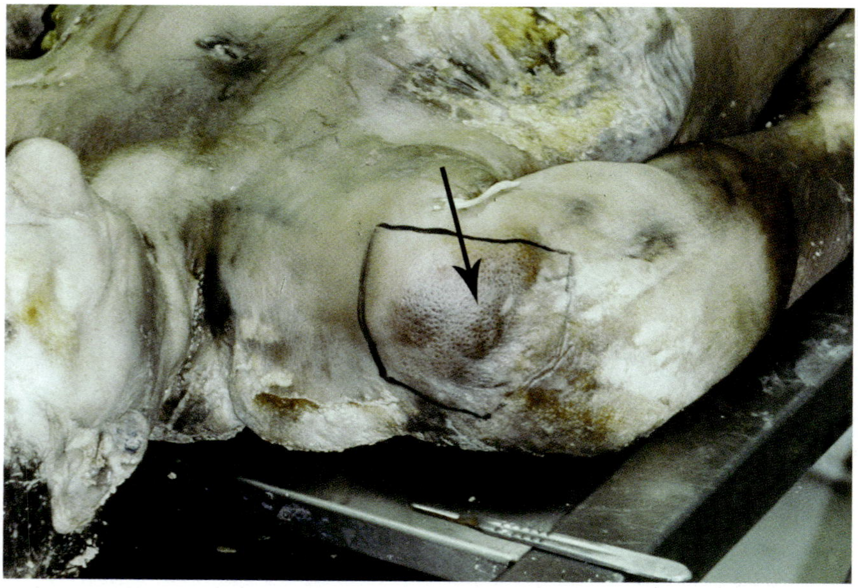

Figure 13.40a False bite mark. (Courtesy of RRS.)

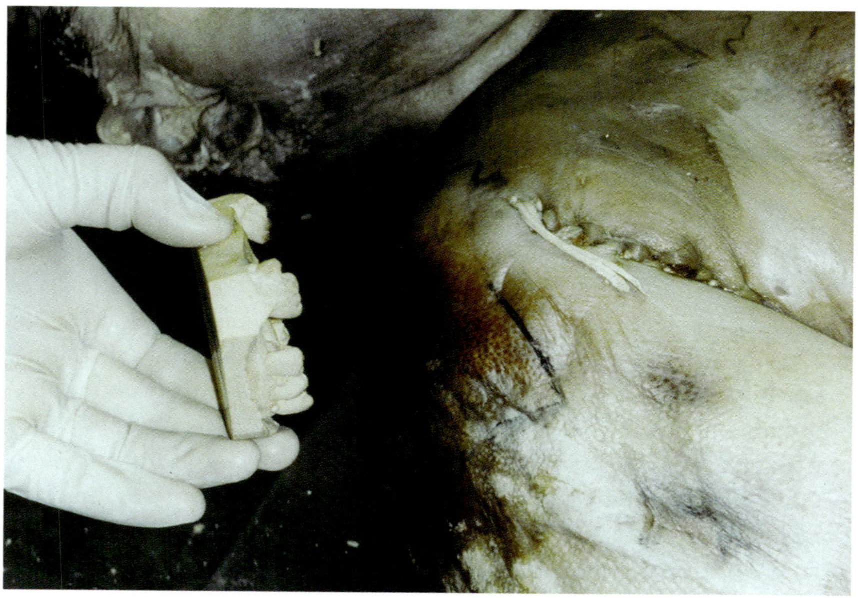

Figure 13.40b Teeth fitting to false bitemark. (Courtesy of RRS.)

The embalmed body was exhumed some 14 months later and was photographed using "special video and alternate light" photography. The right shoulder revealed what in the mind of the odontologist was a human bite (Figure 13.40a,b). Even more unbelievable was that it was left by only the lower right cuspid and premolars of Mr. Keko. No upper teeth and no lower front teeth made any marks. The prosecution sought and obtained an independent second opinion from an odontologist who stated that the pattern injury was not a human bitemark and stated that neither Mr. Keko nor anyone else could possibly be matched to the pattern on the right shoulder. Nevertheless, the prosecution proceeded to try Mr. Keko

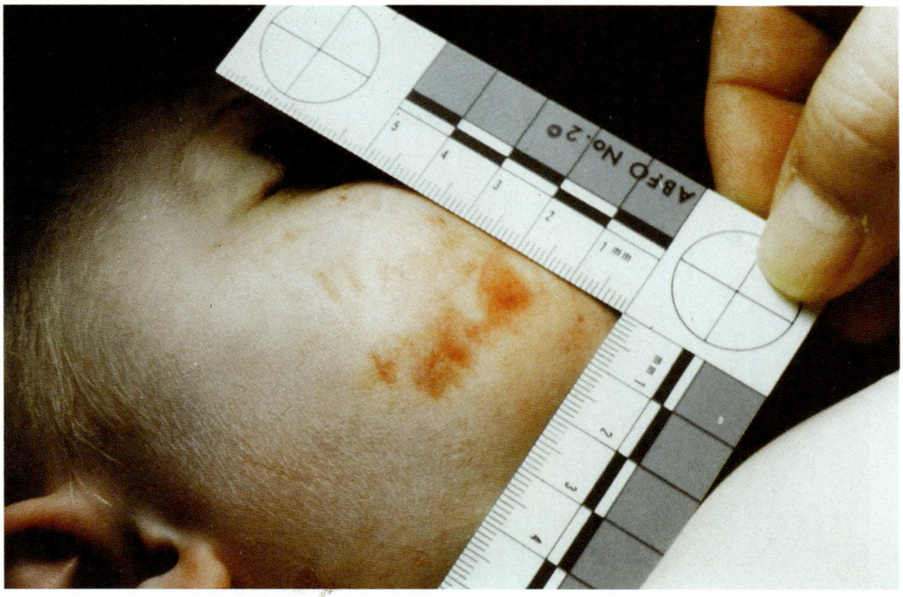

Figure 13.41 Facial abrasions from tape called human bite mark. (Courtesy of RRS.)

using the original odontologist and the "flawed bitemark opinion." The opinion of the second independent odontologist was ignored. The defense experts (two odontologists) opined that there was no bite, and even if there was, it was anatomically impossible to have produced the mark in the manner in which the prosecution dentist alleged. Based largely upon a "positive match" indeed and without a doubt, by the prosecution odontologist, Mr. Keko was given a life sentence. The defense filed numerous motions and the case became the focus of a science gone bad. The judge granted a new trial under the eye of international television. The prosecutor, without a credible bitemark expert, did not refile the case. Mr. Keko was ruined financially but after two years of incarceration he was set free.

A case of hospital intervention with the odontologist having no knowledge of the circumstances of the event is documented in the Louisiana Duncan case in which a five-year-old child was found "drowning" in a bathtub. She was transported to the emergency room of a local hospital; resuscitation attempts were made but the child subsequently died. The medical examiner noted injuries on the body that were consistent with sodomy and possible rape. The odontologist was called to evaluate pattern injury on the side of the individual's face (Figure 13.41). The odontologist had not examined any scene photographs and was not aware of the total circumstances of the event. The autopsy photographs were all that were available for him to evaluate. The odontologist should have asked for more details regarding the circumstances of the event and certainly should have asked for any photographs that were available from the prior medical intervention team. The odontologist opined that the pattern injury on the side of the face and possibly on the elbow and ear were human bitemarks and in fact were left by none other than the only suspect in the case, the boyfriend of the mother.

The defense odontologist testified that there were no human bitemarks on the child anywhere and specifically the ones documented as bitemarks on the face were more likely then not made by the tape holding the intubation tube (Figure 13.42). If the original odontologist had had an opportunity to see the photographs from the emergency room with the

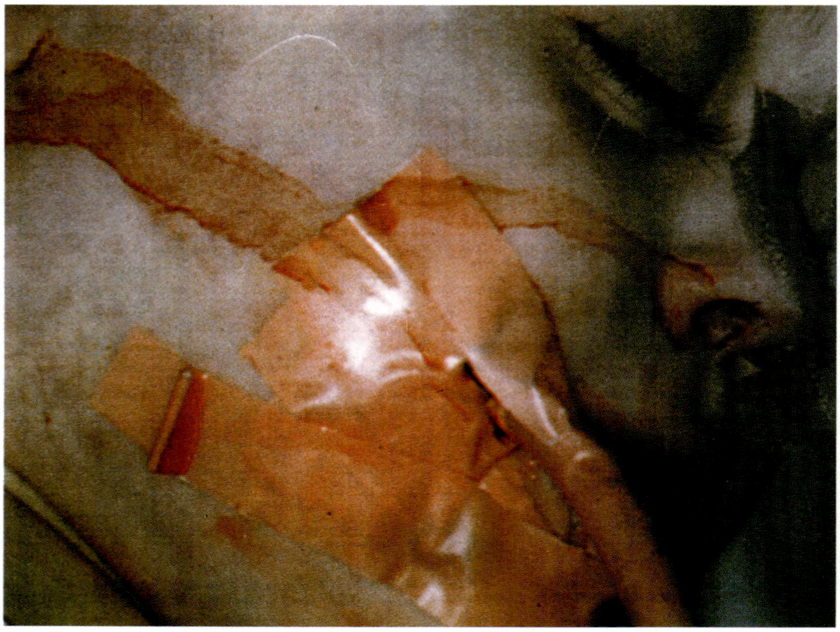

Figure 13.42 ER tape on face, body in hospital. (Courtesy of RRS.)

The News-Star

NLU's Dominique Hadley

SUNDAY, APRIL 5, 1998

Bite marks 'perfect match,' dentist testifies

■ Prosecution rests in trial of Jimmy Christian Duncan, accused of killing toddler

By ANDREW STANDARD
Staff Writer

CRIME
Justice system

Figure 13.43 Newspaper article: suspect's teeth matched to facial abrasions. ("Bitemarks 'perfect match', dentist testifies". Copyright the *News-Star*, Sunday, April 5th, 1995. Used with permission.)

tape in place and knowing the circumstance of the event, he may not have opined that the marks at autopsy were human bitemarks. They obviously were marks left when the tape was removed from the face (Figure 13.43).

Misinterpretation of pattern injuries as being human bitemarks have led to tragic conclusions. It is impossible for the investigator—whether the pathologist, medical examiner, or forensic dentist—to always determine the cause of the pattern injury. Complete knowledge of the circumstances of the initial event and the subsequent intervention by the first responders, emergency room and hospital treatment, transportation, autopsy trauma, and so on, as well as time, temperature, and location of the body are all necessary pieces of evidence to consider in interpreting a pattern injury. Interpretation of pattern injuries, whether bitemarks or otherwise, cannot be properly made in a vacuum. Mistakes in interpretation of pattern injuries can be corrected if the evidence has been properly collected and preserved.

The odontologist is best advised to know all the circumstances of the event, be circumspect, cautious, and seek independent second opinions. Always be conservative before giving an evidentiary opinion. Note the difference between an investigative opinion versus an evidentiary opinion. To this end the American Board of Forensic Odontology (ABFO) has in the past provided a voluntary bitemark proficiency test. In the future, all diplomates will be required to take a proficiency test in bitemark evidence evaluation every five years in order to be recertified. Ongoing research in the field of bitemark evidence and postgraduate education has advanced the science of bitemark interpretation and identification. There is still more training that needs to be done and more work on scientific methods, such as those listed in this chapter, to prevent the tragedies of the past.

The Expert Witness

14

Introduction

If the forensic odontologist practices the specialty long enough she or he will be summoned to give expert testimony in a courtroom. This can be an intimidating experience and is not the place for one who is timid and or easily angered. The courtroom is a place where the truth is sought. In many courtrooms above the judge's bench is a sign that reads, "We who labor here seek only the truth." When a witness is sworn in by the clerk of the court he will be instructed to either raise his right hand or place his left hand on the Bible and raise his right hand and swear to "tell the truth, the whole truth, and nothing but the truth, so help you God." No one has ever said "no" to the oath, to my knowledge.

There have been cases where a witness has lied. A witness that lies while under oath has committed an act of perjury. Perjury carries very serious consequences for not only the witness but for all the parties involved in the proceedings: the attorney, plaintiffs or defendant, the state (prosecution), and the jury. The best advice that can be given to the expert witness in any legal proceeding is to always tell the truth. The attorney who engages your services wants to know the truth. The judge and more importantly, the jury, want to know the truth. A quote from Sir Walter Scott (1771–1832) says it best: "Oh what a tangled web we weave—when first we practice to deceive."

The forensic odontologist will be involved in both civil as well as criminal cases. In criminal cases you may be required to present evidence and expert opinion as to the identification of a victim and the age, especially with children. Bitemark evidence is by far the most challenging and will be the most frequently requested criminal testimony from the forensic odontologist. The reasons are numerous but it boils down to the fact that bitemark evidence can be subjective, therefore controversial, especially as to the identification of the perpetrator of the bite. In civil cases or tort cases the expert witness is to give opinion testimony about causation, damages, and permanency of an injury or injuries. Determining a deviation from the standard of care and the proximal cause of an injury are opinions rendered in malpractice or standard of care cases. The litigation involves money to compensate the plaintiff for the loss. This is a major difference from a criminal proceeding, where the defendant-suspect may lose his liberty or even his life.

Civil Proceeding

There are many differences between civil and criminal proceedings both for the attorneys and the forensic odontologists. There are also many similarities. Civil cases are tort cases and in their simplest form are all about damages and money as compensation for injury. The forensic odontologist will usually be asked to review both personal injury cases and standard of care issues (dental malpractice). There are many other issues the forensic

Fla. Std. Jury Instr. (Crim.) 8.3 ASSAULT AND BATTERY

8.3 BATTERY
§ 784.03, Fla.Stat.

To prove the crime of Battery, the State must prove the following element beyond a reasonable doubt:

Give 1 or 2 as applicable

1. [(Defendant) **intentionally touched or struck** (victim) **against [his] [her] will.**]

2. [(Defendant) **intentionally caused bodily harm to** (victim).]

Lesser Included Offenses

BATTERY — 784.03			
CATEGORY ONE	CATEGORY TWO	FLA.STAT.	INS. NO.
None			
	Attempt	777.04(1)	5.1

Comment

This instruction was approved in 1981.

Figure 14.1 Legal definition of Battery (Florida statute).

odontologist may be asked to review and evaluate, such as insurance fraud, Medicare and Medicaid issues, dental practice act violations, grievance committee issues, and many variations from this list.

The personal injury issues that the forensic odontologist will usually be asked to review are slip and fall, auto accidents (MVA), assaults, batteries (can be both civil and criminal; (Figures 14.1–14.3), and work-related injuries (workers' compensation and standard of care issues). The dental injuries resulting from the accidents and trauma involve not only the teeth but the jaws, muscles, nerves, temporomandibular joints (TMJ), and the function of all of the above: the occlusion. The forensic odontologist is asked by the attorney requesting his or her service to evaluate causation. Was the event, the MVA, fall, battery, or job injury, the direct or proximal cause of the injury? Were there pre-existing conditions that contributed to the injury or was the event the proximal cause of the condition and complaint? The next question to be determined by the dentist (forensic odontologist) is what are the damages, if causation of the injury can be related to the proximal traumatic event?

As an example, you are asked to evaluate an individual who fell while at a supermarket. The claim is for dental injuries and a TMJ disorder. Objective testing reveals no temporomandibular joint dysfunction, only subjective complaints of pain when the jaw is in function. The dental condition shows moderate to advanced periodontal disease with a pre-existing anterior bridge that is mobile. Did the fall cause the mobility or is the mobility a result of the periodontal disease? Without objective evidence of a temporomandibular joint disorder, does the problem exist? It is the duty of the dental expert to be able to answer these questions and further determine if the claim is legitimate. If there is objective evidence of an injury, what are the damages and are they permanent?

ASSAULT AND BATTERY Fla. Std. Jury Instr. (Crim.) 8.4

8.4 AGGRAVATED BATTERY
§ 784.045, Fla.Stat.

To prove the crime of Aggravated Battery, the State must prove the following two elements beyond a reasonable doubt. The first element is a definition of battery.

1. (Defendant)

   [intentionally touched or struck (victim) **against [his] [her] will].**
   [intentionally caused bodily harm to (victim)**].**

Give 2a or 2b as applicable.

2. (Defendant) **in committing the battery**

   a. **intentionally or knowingly caused**

      [great bodily harm to (victim)**].**
      [permanent disability to (victim)**].**
      [permanent disfigurement to (victim)**].**

   b. **used a deadly weapon.**

Definition. Give if 2b alleged.
A weapon is a "deadly weapon" if it is used or threatened to be used in a way likely to produce death or great bodily harm.

Figure 14.2 Legal definition of Aggravated Battery (Florida statute).

There will be occasions when the forensic odontologist is involved in a civil bitemark case. These occur primarily with dog bites but may also involve human bitemarks. A human bitemark may be an example of a civil case in domestic abuse and a criminal case with battery. A Class III or Class IV bitemark where an ear, finger, or other body part is incised or excised resulting in a permanent injury can often be both criminal and civil. The biter (attacker) may be acquitted in the criminal case but guilty in the civil court with monetary damages being awarded. The forensic odontologist may be consulted in the case where a child is bitten severely while in the care of other than the parent, such as daycare, summer camp, babysitter, and so on. The questions for the forensic odontologist are: was the bite inflicted by an adult or by another child? Is this an old bite or a fresh bite? Is there a single bite or multiple bites? Who made the bite? It should be remembered that it is not always possible to answer all of these questions and furthermore the standard in civil cases is not as strict as in a criminal case. In a civil case the standard is "more likely than not—over 50 percent—probable." In criminal cases the standard is higher: "reasonable certainty—beyond reasonable doubt."

The dog bites are far more frequent in occurrence than human bites and are often determined by eyewitness. But occasionally the forensic odontologist will be called to help determine that the injuries are dog bites in the absence of an eyewitness or if the victim is deceased or if the witness testimony may be less than candid, that is, secondary gain. It may be important to determine which dog did the biting or differentiate a dog bite from another

Fla. Std. Jury Instr. (Crim.) 8.2 ASSAULT AND BATTERY

8.2 AGGRAVATED ASSAULT
§ 784.021, Fla.Stat.

To prove the crime of Aggravated Assault, the State must prove the following four elements beyond a reasonable doubt. The first three elements define assault.

1. (Defendant) **intentionally and unlawfully threatened, either by word or act, to do violence to** (victim).

2. **At the time,** (defendant) **appeared to have the ability to carry out the threat.**

3. **The act of** (defendant) **created in the mind of** (victim) **a well-founded fear that the violence was about to take place.**

Give 4a or 4b as applicable

4. a. **[The assault was made with a deadly weapon.]**

   b. **[The assault was made with a fully-formed, conscious intent to commit** (crime charged) **upon** (victim).**]**

If 4b is alleged, define the crime charged.

Definition. Give if 4a alleged.

A weapon is a "deadly weapon" if it is used or threatened to be used in a way likely to produce death or great bodily harm.

Give if 4a alleged.

It is not necessary for the State to prove that the defendant had an intent to kill.

Figure 14.3 Legal definition of Aggravated Assault (Florida statute).

animal or other type of injury, that is, stab wound, or infectious disease, among others. In the case where a dog has been declared a dangerous animal, such as the pit bull, or if the dog has bitten before (the one-bite theory) then the bite or bites by a dangerous dog under Florida Statue #767.11, 767.13, 777.011 (Figure 14.4) can be a third-degree felony. A single bite by a "dangerous dog" is a misdemeanor whereas multiple bites are a third-degree felony. The forensic odontologist may be required to analyze the wounds on a victim that has been bitten by a "dangerous dog" and determine if all the injuries are from single or multiple dog bites. Thus the case can be criminal or civil depending upon the opinion as to single or multiple bites. This is a very heavy responsibility and critical to the dog owner, the dog, and the victim.

Standard of Care Issues—Dental Malpractice

The standard of care issue is the most difficult civil case for the evaluating dentist. They must determine the injury, proximal cause, extent of damage, permanency, and if there

West's F.S.A. § 767.11

West's Florida Statutes Annotated Currentness
Title XLV. Torts (Chapters 766-774) (Refs & Annos)
Chapter 767. Damage by Dogs (Refs & Annos)
➡767.11. Definitions

As used in this act, unless the context clearly requires otherwise:

(1) "Dangerous dog" means any dog that according to the records of the appropriate authority:

(a) Has aggressively bitten, attacked, or endangered or has inflicted severe injury on a human being on public or private property;

(b) Has more than once severely injured or killed a domestic animal while off the owner's property;

(c) Has been used primarily or in part for the purpose of dog fighting or is a dog trained for dog fighting; or

(d) Has, when unprovoked, chased or approached a person upon the streets, sidewalks, or any public grounds in a menacing fashion or apparent attitude of attack, provided that such actions are attested to in a sworn statement by one or more persons and dutifully investigated by the appropriate authority.

(2) "Unprovoked" means that the victim who has been conducting himself or herself peacefully and lawfully has been bitten or chased in a menacing fashion or attacked by a dog.

(3) "Severe injury" means any physical injury that results in broken bones, multiple bites, or disfiguring lacerations requiring sutures or reconstructive surgery.

(4) "Proper enclosure of a dangerous dog" means, while on the owner's property, a dangerous dog is securely confined indoors or in a securely enclosed and locked pen or structure, suitable to prevent the entry of young children and designed to prevent the animal from escaping. Such pen or structure shall have secure sides and a secure top to prevent the dog from escaping over, under, or through the structure and shall also provide protection from the elements.

(5) "Animal control authority" means an entity acting alone or in concert with other local governmental units and authorized by them to enforce the animal control laws of the city, county, or state. In those areas not served by an animal control authority, the sheriff shall carry out the duties of the animal control authority under this act.

(6) "Animal control officer" means any individual employed, contracted with, or appointed by the animal control authority for the purpose of aiding in the enforcement of this act or any other law or ordinance relating to the licensure of animals, control of animals, or seizure and impoundment of animals and includes any state or local law enforcement officer or other employee whose duties in whole or in part include assignments that involve the seizure and impoundment of any animal.

(7) "Owner" means any person, firm, corporation, or organization possessing, harboring, keeping, or having control or custody of an animal or, if the animal is owned by a person under the age of 18, that person's parent or guardian.

CREDIT(S)

Laws 1990, c. 90-180, § 2; Laws 1993, c. 93-13, § 2. Amended by Laws 1997, c. 97-102, § 1156,

Figure 14.4 Dangerous dog statute (Florida statute).

was a deviation from the standard of care by the practitioner: malpractice. In all cases the evaluation must be based on facts, objective evidence, circumstances of the event or events, as well as testimony from the plaintiff and from the defendant dentist. Always error on the side of caution and be open to changing your opinion if new facts or evidence are discovered. The evaluating dentist must always keep in mind that the plaintiff is seeking monetary compensation for the injuries and therefore may have reason to be less than candid, or to be mendacious or hyperchondriacal in describing the claimed injuries.

However, there are cases where the treater (practitioner) has stepped over the line. The damages may be severe or even fatal. As the evaluator, you must determine the extent of damage, the cost of repair if possible, and the degree of permanency. An obvious example of a deviation from "The Standard of Care" is the treating dentist who uses a procedure or medication that is determined to be dangerous. An example is an endodontic procedure using N2 or paraformaldehide or using IV anesthesia without the proper training and license.

Then there are the errors of omission that can be as serious as the errors of commission. An example is performing endodontics without the use of a rubber dam. The patient swallows, or worse yet, aspirates the file. Then there is the omission of premedication (antibiotics), when required, especially for the patient with heart valve damage, possibly resulting in infection, subacute bacterial endocarditis (SBE), and possible death of the patient. Premedication for the patient with prosthetic joints or other medical condition is the responsibility of the treating dentist and is the standard of care that must be met. If not done (omitted) then there is a breach of the standard of care and the resulting damage is the responsibility of the treating dentist. The patient's physician should be consulted in these circumstances.

There are cases where the outcome is poor and the treater, the practitioner, has done nothing below the standard of care. The standard of care is defined as "what a reasonable practitioner of similar training and experience would have done under the same or similar circumstance." The bad result of a procedure does not always equate to malpractice. It is the duty of the reviewing dentist to determine causation and then based on all the facts establish if there was a deviation from the standard of care. Even more difficult and challenging is to determine how the deviation resulted in the damages. Assume a treating dentist removed a lower wisdom tooth and the jaw fractured. Was this malpractice? The answer can be yes or no depending on the circumstances and the facts prior and subsequent to the event. The main point to keep in mind is that a bad result is not necessarily malpractice. A thorough, accurate, and comprehensive evaluation of the facts, circumstances, and testimony of all parties are necessary before a final opinion can be reached as to causation, deviation from the standard of care, and damages.

The Expert for the Plaintiff

The legal procedure for the expert witness in a typical standard of care or malpractice case is that you are requested to evaluate the case by a defense or plaintiff attorney to determine causation, damages, and any deviation from the standard of care. The plaintiff attorney will initiate suit based on "pre-suit discovery." If hired by a plaintiff attorney you will be given "facts" based on the plaintiff statements to his attorney and records, x-rays, and materials from the defendant dentist as well as records from the subsequent treating dentist. You must carefully evaluate this material knowing there are always two sides. Carefully review the evidence, the treating dentist records, x-rays, medical reports, hospital records, and so on. All these records will be furnished by the plaintiff's attorney in pre-suit. There are several answers you can give to the plaintiff attorney:

- There are damages but no deviation from the standard of care.
- There is a deviation but minimal damages easily reversible and repairable.
- There is a deviation from the standard based only on the records and plaintiff's statements.

AFFIDAVIT OF RICHARD R. SOUVIRON, DDS

STATE OF FLORIDA)
:ss
COUNTY OF)

COMES NOW the Affiant, Richard R. Souviron, DDS, under oath and deposes and says as follows:

1. My name is Richard R. Souviron, DDS. I am a dentist licensed to practice medicine in the State of Florida. Attached hereto is my curriculum vitae which fairly and accurately reflects my education, training, background and experience.

2. At the requests of attorneys [redacted] and [redacted] I reviewed records which reflect the dental care provided to a patient by the name of I was asked to review these records to determine whether or not there are reasonable grounds to believe that the medical records of , DMD, presuit statement of facts executed by the patient dated January 19,

3. It is my opinion, based on a reasonable degree of medical probability and/or certainty, and based on the records that I have been provided with, there are reasonable grounds to believe that the dental care and treatment rendered by to this patient represented a deviation from the prevailing professional standard of care. In particular, it appears that failed to utilize a "rubber dam", or similar item, for infection control during the procedure.

4. It is my opinion within a reasonable degree of probability and/or certainty that the patient suffered some injury as a result of failure to utilize a "rubber dam" or similar device for infection control. This would include, at the very least, the patient contracting a pericardial infection.

Figure 14.5a Pre-suit affidavit: plaintiff (page 1).

Next for the plaintiff's expert witness comes the pre-suit affidavit. This legal document is what initiates the suit against the defendant dentist and is based only on the pre-suit information. It is subject to change if new information is provided. The plaintiff expert dentist is now on record and must defend his position with facts and be prepared to testify under oath both at deposition and possibly trial (Figure 14.5a,b). A plaintiff expert in dental malpractice cases should never give her deposition until she has had the opportunity to review the defendant dentist's deposition and plaintiff's deposition as well as the defense expert's deposition. There

Affidavit of Richard R. Souviron, DDS
Re:
Page Two

5. No opinion rendered by me has ever been disqualified in any Court of any jurisdiction to my knowledge. I have never been found guilty of fraud or perjury in any Court in any jurisdiction nor have I ever been accused of such.

FURTHER THE AFFIANT SAYETH NOT.

______________________________ DDS
RICHARD R. SOUVIRON, DDS

SWORN TO AND SUBSCRIBED before me by RICHARD R. SOUVIRON, DDS, on this 25th day of April, who is personally known to me or who produced the following photo identification ______________________________, and who did/did not take an oath.

NOTARY PUBLIC STATE OF FLORIDA
Kathy E. Findley
My Commission DD338062
Expires September 22,

Kathy E. Findley
NOTARY PUBLIC, State of Florida
Printed name of Notary:

Cert. No. ____________________

Figure 14.5b Pre-suit affidavit: plaintiff (page 2).

are always exceptions, but it is only fair to know what the defendant dentist has to say before you as the plaintiff expert give a final opinion. There will surely be cases where your opinion as to the defendant dentist will change 180 degrees based on your colleague's testimony.

The defendant in a malpractice case should remember that the plaintiff expert cannot by law, discuss the case beforehand with the defendant dentist. It is also important to remember, as the defendant, that the pre-suit affidavit is subject to change and modification with the discovery of new evidence. In cases where there is an obvious deviation, but the damages are not permanent and are repairable, the attorney will usually work out a settlement of money to the plaintiff. However, there are cases where the offer to settle is too high or the defense feels there is cause to proceed to trial. Then the case will go to a jury. On rare occasions, especially in federal court, it may be a bench trial where there is no jury, just the judge.

The Expert for the Defense

The defense expert is called to evaluate the case after suit has been filed. The legal process has begun. The malpractice insurance carrier usually has several law firms it

AFFIDAVIT

STATE OF FLORIDA
COUNTY OF DADE

BEFORE ME, the undersigned authority, this date personally appeared Richard Rafael Souviron, DDS, who, after being duly sworn, deposes and says as follows:

1) I am a dentist duly and regularly engaged in the practice of general dentistry. I am board certified in forensic odontology and by the National Board of Dentistry. My professional qualifications are attached hereto in the form of a curriculum vitae.

2. My address is:
Richard R. Souviron, D.D.S.
336 Alahambra Circle
Coral Gables, Florida 33134

3. I am familiar with the prevailing standard of care for dentists, including the standard of care applicable to the care and treatment rendered by D.D.S. to

4. In forming my opinion I have reviewed and relied upon the following records: Office records of D.D.S., P.A. a/k/a Dental Care, which include the records of and pertinent imaging studies.

5. I have also considered the following information: the Notice of Intent to Initiate Litigation for Medical Malpractice provided by , Esquire, and the Affidavit of D.M.D.

6. Based upon the foregoing, it is my expert opinion, within a reasonable degree of dental probability, that , D.D.S. did not deviate from the standard of care in his care and treatment of . It is my opinion that Dr. , D.D.S. appropriately and timely provided care to including recommending that she receive veneer crowns on teeth #8 and #9. Subsequently, the

Figure 14.5c Pre-suit affidavit: defendant (page 1).

uses to defend their insured. They will pick the defense firm, but you as the defendant should be involved in this process and you should be given a choice. Unfortunately, this is not always the case. The defense expert, the defense attorney, and occasionally the defendant dentist will (depending on the defense attorney and insurance adjuster) discuss opinions, meet and conference prior to any written reports, depositions, or trial. A defense expert will have access to the same records, x-rays, charts, and other material reviewed by the plaintiff expert. The defense expert may be, and often is, requested to appearance did not satisfy Ms. and he appropriately recommended porcelain crowns for teeth #8 and #9. The porcelain crowns for teeth #8 and #9 were done appropriately. The preparations on #8 and #9 do not appear to be over reduced and the biological width of teeth #8 and #9, as well as the gingival margins, appear to be well within the standard of care. Consequently, I disagree with claimant's expert, D.M.D. and believe that Dr. complied with the standard of care in his care and treatment of

7. I have never been disqualified from rendering any expert opinion in any court of law to the best of my knowledge.

FURTHER AFFIANT SAYETH NAUGHT.

DDS

RICHARD RAFAEL SOUVIRON, DDS

SWORN TO AND SUBSCRIBED before me this 13 day of September,

NOTARY PUBLIC STATE OF FLORIDA
MARIA HERNANDEZ
MY COMMISSION # DD 290552
EXPIRES: February 12,
Bonded Thru Budget Notary Services

Notary Public
My Commission Expires:

Personally known ✓
Produced Identification

Figure 14.5d Pre-suit affidavit: defendant (page 2).

draft a report documenting his opinions. The report should contain but not be limited to the following:

- Who requested his services?
- When were his services requested?
- List of materials reviewed.
- History provided by both the plaintiff and the defendant dentist.
- The injury.
- The causation, if any, procedure performed or omitted.
- His opinion based upon his training experience and facts of the case.

This report is presented to the requesting party. It may be the defense attorney or the insurance adjuster, and on rare occasions the judge may request a written opinion. The plaintiff expert is in a much different position from the defense. He is rarely requested to draft a report but is required to sign the affidavit in pre-suit. The plaintiff expert witness may be asked to draft a report of his findings but usually he will provide his final opinion at his deposition. These opinions are given only after he has had the opportunity to read the defense expert's opinion and always after reading the defendant dentist deposition with his explanation of the events and any mitigating circumstances. The plaintiff attorney will or should have conferences with his expert several times prior to his deposition and certainly prior to trial.

In cases that involve federal employees or their spouses or children the dental malpractice is adjudicated in federal court. The testimony may be either before a jury or bench trial. If it is a federal civil action, there is usually a bench trial, but if it is criminal it is going to a jury, especially a capital murder case. Insurance fraud cases involving dental issues can be tried in either state or federal courts. The facts of the case will determine where it is adjudicated. Medicaid cases are going to be federal. The type of fraud cases usually are cases involving filing a false claim for services, that is, services not done or claiming a procedure of greater value than actually performed. The dentist expert for both the defense and the plaintiff must produce his past record of court appearances and testimony from the prior five years when in federal court. For some experts it may be very difficult to produce such detail of all civil case testimony, but it is essential for criminal cases when in a federal court.

The Deposition Duces Tecum

A standard of care case (dental malpractice) is usually initiated by a patient's complaint to her attorney followed by the pre-suit discovery and an expert witness affidavit. Then the legal process begins for the defense. There may be defense pre-suit statements, unsworn, taken of the defendant dentist by his insurance adjuster or attorney but rarely of the plaintiff and never of the plaintiff's expert witness unless approved by the plaintiff and the plaintiff's attorney. In tort cases such as the slip and fall, motor vehicular accident, assault or battery, and the like, there is no requirement for the pre-suit affidavit. The plaintiff's expert witness is usually the treating dentist but the plaintiff's attorney may want a second expert involved to testify regarding causation, damages, necessary treatment, and future costs for maintenance.

The defense, usually an insurance carrier attorney, will have the case reviewed by an expert in the field. The examination by their expert is called an IME (Independent Medical Examination) and is to help the defense attorney understand the extent of injuries, causation, or proximal cause, and treatment required to "make whole." In some states this exam is called a court-appointed exam but the object is the same: it is a defense exam. The examiner does not treat the patient, does not make any recommendations for treatment, and should not discuss the findings with the plaintiff (the injured party, or the plaintiff attorney). With approval of the court the examination may be videotaped or taken down verbatim by a court reporter. The plaintiff attorney is going to want to know how much time the doctor actually spent examining the patient, what was said, and how the examination was conducted.

If you are asked to perform an independent medical evaluation be prepared for a court reporter or videographer to be present. You should be notified in advance if this is to be videotaped but not necessarily that the plaintiff attorney and or a court reporter are to be present. The defense counsel wants to know the truth. Is the injury real? Is it related to the accident in question? Is the injured party being overtreated? Is the plaintiff (injured party) forthright, candid, and accurate in her description of her injuries?

Following the independent medical examination, the defense attorney and insurance carrier will want an in-depth written report. This report is very important and it is usually very lengthy. It covers the materials that you have reviewed prior to the examination, the examination itself, your findings of the examination, any conflict between what was stated

EXPERT WITNESS INTERROGATORIES

1. Please state the name and last known address and telephone number of any and all expert witnesses that you expect to call to testify as expert witnesses at the trial of this cause, and as to each, please state with specificity:

   a. The subject matter on which he/she is expected to testify;

   b. The substance of the facts and opinions to which he/she is expected to testify; and,

   c. A summary of the grounds for each opinion that he/she holds.

   d. Any and all materials, documents, literature, texts, etc., relied on, and/or referred to, etc., in formulating the opinion(s).

   e. Any tests; destructive, non-destructive or otherwise; analysis, etc., performed in formulating your opinion(s).

2. Please state the fields of expertise of any and all expert witnesses whose name(s) appear(s) in your answer to Interrogatory 1 above and set forth the professional education, training and experience held by each expert witness and a brief summary of his/her qualifications including professional society and association memberships, professional degrees and academic or professional honors.

3. Please attach a curriculum vitae or professional resume for each expert witness you expect will testify at trial.

4. Please state whether or not any or all of the expert witnesses whose name(s) appear(s) in the answer to Interrogatory 1 above have prepared any kind of written report; and, if so, please state the date of the report, and the name and last known address and telephone number of the person who currently has custody and control of the report.

5. Please attach a copy of any written reports referenced in interrogatory 4 above.

6. Please state whether or not any or all of the expert witnesses whose name(s) appear(s) in the answer to Interrogatory 1 above, have/has ever testified on behalf of clients represented by your attorneys in his case; and, if so, please state the number of times, the date upon which the testimony was given and the case styles, and numbers and Court identifying information with regard to each occasion.

Figure 14.6a Expert witness interrogatories (page 1).

by the plaintiff versus what was in the medical records, and a summary of the medical records followed by your opinion.

The treating dentist as well as the defense expert will be required to give opinions under oath, which is the deposition. They will, more likely than not, be served with a list of expert witness interrogatories prior to their deposition but surely before trial testimony (Figure 14.6a,b). The deposition is designed to obtain information from the expert witness

7. Please state whether any or all of the expert witnesses whose name(s) appear(s) in your answer to Interrogatory 1 above have been provided with any kind of written report or factual summary and, if so, please state the name and last known address and telephone number of the person who currently has custody and control of the report.

8. Please state the general litigation experience of any and all expert witnesses whose name(s) appear(s) in your answer to Interrogatory 1 above and set forth for each expert witness named:

    a. the percentage of work performed for plaintiffs and the percentage of work performed for defendants.

    b. the expert's involvement as an expert witness in terms of percentage of income derived from serving as an expert witness, percentage of hours spent serving as an expert witness and number of hours spent serving as an expert witness.

9. Please state, within the last three (3) years, all cases in which any expert witness whose name(s) appear(s) in the answer to Interrogatory 1 above, testified. For each case named, for identification purposes, please state the name of the expert witness who testified, the case style, the case number, the Court, and all dates testimony was given.

10. Please state, for each expert witness whose name(s) appear(s) in the answer to Interrogatory 1 above, the amount of compensation charged for services rendered in the pending case. For each expert witness named in Interrogatory 1, please specify:

    a. the rate per hour for review of documents, research and investigation, deposition testimony and trial testimony;

    b. the amount reasonably expected to be charged for all services rendered in the pending case.

Figure 14.6b Expert witness interrogatories (page 2).

whether he is a treating physician, the defense, or the plaintiff expert witness. The *duces tecum* (*subpoena duces tecum*) means to "take the thing," get all the facts and as much testimony under oath for trial as possible. Another object of the deposition is for the attorney to have a possible tool for impeachment at time of trial if the testimony differs and at the very least to be able to show a jury that the witness is not consistent in his or her testimony. An expert witness should prepare for the deposition testimony as if it were going to be trial testimony. In fact, if you don't appear live at trial, your testimony will be read to the jury as if you were there.

Thorough preparation by both the plaintiff and defense expert witness cannot be overemphasized. You will be asked to produce all your records and certain ones may be marked as exhibits for later introduction into the court record at trial. The deposition will consist of a direct examination and cross-examination depending upon which side sets the deposition. For example, if the opposing counsel sets the deposition it is usually a deposition *duces tecum* and is for discovery. What do you have? To what are you going to testify? What are your opinions? He will want to see how you look, how you answer his questions, and where your weaknesses are so he can attack them at trial. You may or may not be asked any questions on cross-examination by the attorney that hired you. If, on the other hand, you are set for a deposition by the attorney that hired you, it is usually because you're not going to testify live at trial. Your direct deposition testimony will be in great detail similar to trial testimony starting with your education, experience, awards, honors, publications, and so on, and followed by what you reviewed, when you reviewed, time spent, fees charged, and your opinions. You will have a very lengthy direct testimony and usually the same on cross-examination as if it were at trial in front of the jury. You must be prepared!

In a tort case, the treating practitioner will only have to give testimony about causation and need for treatment, conditions present that she found, diagnosis and treatment plan, and future care, as well as costs for present and future treatment. The treating dentist may be asked to give a disability rating to the injured party. The disability rating is an estimate and may be based on guidelines published by the American Medical Association, *Guides to the Evaluation of Permanent Impairment* (orthopedic guide to disability).

The defense expert will be called to evaluate but not treat the plaintiff. The IME or defense exam is usually performed after the expert has had an opportunity to review the records, usually voluminous, including all treating physicians' reports, emergency room reports, police reports, and, in the dental case, prior as well as subsequent treating dental records. These records should be read in detail and abstracted or notes taken of important findings. An example would be a finding of a pre-existing condition that is now claimed as having occurred as a result of this accident. Another example of the importance of prior records is the case of a pre-existing treatment plan for corrective procedures that is the same as or similar to what is related to this accident. Perhaps the prior recommended treatment was necessary, the condition diagnosed, but the treatment was never done. Subsequently, there is an accident and now this treatment is being performed as having been caused by the accident. Knowing what is in the records is part of the foundation to be able to tell "the whole truth."

If your deposition is to be used at trial in place of your live testimony, it is usually by videotape. You should be advised in advance so you are prepared to dress appropriately and have your workplace or office in proper shape. It may be necessary to give your deposition in the attorney's office for various reasons, but usually with your permission. If, as the expert witness, you are hired to review and testify about a case from another town or even another state, your deposition will be taken in a place of your convenience. On the other hand, the trial testimony will be in the city and state where the accident occurred. You will be subpoenaed to trial and should be prepared to travel. The attorney who hired you will make arrangements for transportation, hotel, meals, and so on. She will confer with you prior to your taking the stand and make every effort to see that you are comfortable. The deposition is different. It is at your place and time of convenience in most civil cases, but can be different in criminal cases. The role of both the defense and plaintiff expert witness is very important to the outcome of the case and the litigators depend upon you for accurate and truthful testimony. The deposition is a tool used to help prepare the attorney for mediation or for trial. Settlements are often structured, based upon expert witness testimony at the deposition.

The criminal case can be much different from the civil. Some states do not have the pretrial deposition. The opposing attorney will have to hear your testimony at trial for the first time. In other jurisdictions you may be interviewed by the opposing counsel over the telephone or a telephonic deposition may be taken. In all cases you will be given advance notice by subpoena or otherwise when your deposition or conference with the opposing counsel will take place. You should prepare well in advance and confer with the prosecutor or defense attorney before giving a deposition or confer with the opposing counsel. Remember, what you testified to in deposition or in a phone conference can and will be used by opposing counsel at trial. In a criminal trial the expert witness is to appear live especially when giving testimony for the state. The deposition is used to help structure a plea agreement or as a tool to impeach at trial, but not as a substitute for live testimony, as is often done in the civil cases.

The Civil Trial

The expert witness should expect all cases he or she is asked to review to go to trial and prepare accordingly. In most cases there will be voluminous amounts of material to be reviewed. This material usually includes many long depositions from the parties involved. There will be expert witnesses for defense and plaintiff and these may be numerous. For example, in a motor vehicular accident, the plaintiff may have been treated by an oral surgeon, endodontist, TMJ expert, and so on. All will give deposition testimony. The defense will have an equal number of examining experts. In standard of care cases the plaintiff will have as experts the subsequent treaters and they may be numerous. There will be, as well, independent expert witnesses who will document all treatments as necessary and causally related to the malpractice. The plaintiff expert witness will further state that the charges were reasonable and the treatment appropriate and necessary.

The defense will produce their own experts who will try to mitigate the cost, the treatment, and the injury. The defense expert should be able to state that the treatments, although necessary, are not related to the claimed malpractice nor was the alleged malpractice procedure performed below the standard of care. Although the results of the procedure may not be ideal, no dentist can guarantee a perfect result every time on every patient. That is not a reasonable expectation.

Trial preparation is critical to both the plaintiff and the defense. The attorneys for both sides spend numerous hours in preparation. The expert witness should do the same. The jury verdict is usually final and is based in large part on the testimony of the expert witness. Preparation is a key part to being an effective witness and this point cannot be overemphasized. The five Ps, "Prior Preparation Prevents Poor Performance," applies to all phases of life but is especially critical in the case of the expert witness in his or her effectiveness at trial.

Direct Testimony—Plaintiff Expert

Direct testimony is usually fairly easy for a prepared witness. You will be asked your training and experience and qualifications as an expert. However, if you have ever been disqualified in a court of law for your previous testimony you may be disqualified in this case.

This fact may have been concealed from the plaintiff or the defense attorney. If you have any "baggage" you should disclose it to your counsel long before the trial.

The line of questioning usually proceeds similarly to the deposition. What have you reviewed and when did you review it? What have you charged for your services for review of the material and what are your charges for your appearance here today? A well-prepared expert will be able to answer these questions without hesitation, forthrightly, truthfully, and unapologetically. Most important he should be able to justify and document the number of hours spent in his review, the number of pages of records reviewed, and number of deposition pages read, as well as pages of abstracts produced and the literature research done.

The plaintiff attorney will have the expert explain his opinion and his reasons and the process followed in arriving at these opinions. There may be jury aids used by the expert to help the jury understand the issues. As an example, in a motor vehicular accident or other trauma case there may be photographs of the scene or the plaintiff in the hospital. These are usually introduced to the jury in order to explain and illustrate the extent of damages. In a malpractice case the plaintiff has the burden of proof and the expert must have the jury understand the extent of damage, the procedures done, or the omission of procedures that caused the damage, and the treatment necessary for repair. He will also be asked to discuss the amount of discomfort and time required to repair the damage as well as the future costs and conditions that may be required for proper maintenance. The legal term used is "to make the person whole."

Direct Testimony—Defense Expert

The defense expert on direct examination will be asked the same questions as the plaintiff expert including the number of times she or he has given testimony for the defense. This line of questioning, as well as fees charged, is often done in cross-examination if not covered thoroughly on direct testimony or if answered poorly or inaccurately. Both sides will try to address these questions—fees and prior testimony—in direct testimony. The defense expert will be asked on direct to explain how this treatment or condition was not related or caused by the alleged trauma, and explain to the jury the lack of basis in fact for the subjective complaints of the plaintiff. An example is the complaints by a plaintiff of a painful temporomandibular joint injury but there is no objective evidence. Another example is the complaint that teeth were lost, abscessed, moved out of position, or fractured by the traumatic event. However, prior records, that is, x-rays, photographs, and the like, can demonstrate that the condition may have existed prior to the trauma.

In the case of malpractice the defense expert will give testimony to refute the plaintiff's expert or mitigate the damages. If the plaintiff has exaggerated or been less than candid, is mendacious or hyperchondriacal in his sworn testimony, the defense expert witness should be able to explain this to the jury in a forthright and believable manner. As an example, the plaintiff claimed the dentist did not explain the need for the extractions and now he is suffering loss of function in eating and embarrassment when smiling. However, in the time since the alleged malpractice the plaintiff has made no attempt to have the corrective procedures done nor has the patient/plaintiff returned to a dentist for any treatment of this "terrible" condition over a time period of several years. Another example is the plaintiff's complaint that the necessary treatment agreed to and paid for did not provide satisfactory results. The plaintiff changed dentists and as of trial has not done any corrective work. The original treatment plan and treatment were within the standard of care but not necessarily ideal because of cost or prior existing conditions. In cases such as these two examples the jury will usually find for the defendant, a defense verdict.

Cross-Examination

The cross-examination of the expert witness in civil cases can be extensive, embarrassing, humiliating, frustrating, and occasionally anger producing. The well-prepared, self-confident, and truthful expert will be able to handle the best cross-examination and in some cases even "turn the tables" on the attorney. The areas that will be challenged on cross-examination include, but are not limited to, your experience (number of times testified for the defense or plaintiff) to try to demonstrate that you are a one-dimensional expert. Another area of challenge is your testimony outside your area of expertise. Never let yourself get into this trap. Your prior testimony in other cases or in your prior published papers and texts may contradict your testimony in this case. Then there is the attempt to impeach by quoting your prior sworn testimony in previous court cases or in your deposition in this case. Here it is most important that you are prepared. You must be familiar with and have total recall of your deposition testimony in this case and know what you have published previously. When challenged by the opposing attorney on your prior testimony or your publications, always have it produced for you to review on the stand. To help his case, the opposing attorney will take your statements out of context or, in the case of a publication, that are outdated. All opinions, especially in texts, journals, and other publications will change or be modified with time. This is true not only for your publications but for all authors.

The next area of challenge in cross-examination is the fees charged. Be prepared to explain fees, show the time spent and volume of reading done by the number of pages, x-rays reviewed, dental and medical records, conferences, and depositions. The more prepared you are, the easier it is to justify your fees. Remember, everyone in the courtroom is getting paid except the jury, and the jury understands.

Both the plaintiff and the defense expert witness will be challenged extensively regarding their opinions. If you have been truthful, consistent, and fair it will be hard to discredit your testimony. Always admit the obvious, don't be afraid to admit mistakes, hopefully not serious and not numerous. Always be respectful of the jury and address your answers, when appropriate to the jury. Look at them. Don't try to fake it by always looking and answering to the jury. It is not natural. Be respectful of the opposing attorney. He really does not dislike you, only your testimony.

The next area of cross-examination for both the plaintiff and defense expert is their opinion in regard to causation, damages, permanency, costs, and so on. In a malpractice case the plaintiff expert will have to explain the deviation and how it relates to the causation and damages. The previous example of the lower third molar extraction and subsequent broken jaw is a good example of yes and no answers. The plaintiff expert will state that there was excessive force used, not adequate informed consent, and improper follow-up care. All causation, deviation, and damages should be explained, documented, and illustrated to the understanding of the jury. From the defense expert, the consent was documented in the record or consent form signed by the patient. The procedure was medically necessary and performed in the proper manner and excessive force was not used. The fracture was a known consequence or complication of the procedure. The diagnosis and subsequent treatment were proper and timely. Every case is different. In a similar case the author (RRS) acting as a defense expert was able to show by the records that the fracture actually occurred five days after the extraction and furthermore, the actual tooth was available to show the jury the roots which were fused and conical. No excessive force was necessary to remove the tooth. The verdict was for the defense.

Following cross-examination of the expert witness, there may be one or two questions by the plaintiff attorney: redirect. The redirect of the plaintiff expert witness will focus on some points during cross-examination and likewise recross-examination will focus on his answers to redirect. These same procedures are used for all witnesses and give each side one last chance to "rehabilitate" a witness or drive home his or her conclusion. The attorney asks the questions and plans his strategy in advance and modifies it as the case progresses. He has to "think on his feet" and "go with the flow." The expert witness has to prepare for the questions in advance, know how to answer what surely will be asked and be able to think and recall under pressure. He will be sworn to tell the truth and must answer all questions truthfully. It is the responsibility of the attorneys to get the "whole truth" to the jury. An expert witness, when answering a question truthfully you may not be giving the "whole truth." You must play by the rules. Example question to the plaintiff expert witness:

Q. Did Ms. Jones' temporomandibular joint condition require a second operation after the first temporomandibular joint surgery?
A. Yes.
Q. Did the oral surgeon do malpractice?
A. No.

The whole truth is the first procedure may have been done prematurely and without enough conservative treatment. This information is up to the defense attorney on cross-examination to get from the plaintiff's expert witness. The defense's expert witness will address this same issue on direct. It is hoped that the jury will get the complete, true, and full understanding by the end of the testimony.

Expert Witnesses Do's and Don'ts

Do

- Dress well in business attire
- Be objective and analytical
- Be truthful, forthright
- Be thorough
- Be accurate
- Be prepared
- Be self-confident
- Be cool and relaxed
- Be serious and realize the seriousness
- Talk to the jury
- Be humble
- Admit a mistake

- Leave the court after your testimony
- Use language that can be understood by the jury
- Answer only the question asked but explain answers if necessary

Don't

- Rush to conclusions
- Be influenced by the requesting attorney, agency, or circumstances
- Be an advocate
- Be sloppy in a report or in your dress
- Be evasive in answering questions or timid when asked a question
- Be humorous or make jokes
- Sit in on any other part of the trial
- Use words where you don't know their meaning
- Talk over the jury's head, too technical
- Be condescending
- Argue with the attorney
- Volunteer information beyond what was asked
- Lose your temper
- Wear a lot of jewelry or flash the Rolex

Expert Witness in Criminal Cases

The forensic odontologist will meet challenges in criminal cases much different than in a civil case and should be prepared for the increased pressure especially where bitemarks are involved. As a rule when the forensic odontologist is called upon to give testimony in a criminal case he or she will be subject to a much stronger, lengthier, and more grueling cross-examination than in a civil case. The reports, the preparation, case review, research, and experiments are far more in-depth and time consuming, as a general, rule than in civil cases. The exception is if called to give testimony regarding body identification and even here where the evidence should be pretty much straightforward you may have to sustain a rigorous cross-examination. It should be remembered, and can't be emphasized strongly enough, that in civil cases it is all about the money, but in criminal cases it involves the liberty and possibly the life of the defendant, a much more serious situation. You bet!

Types of Cases

The majority of case work for the forensic odontologist involves body identification. Here the evidence is usually straightforward and a report usually satisfies the defense and the prosecution as to the identity of the individual. The forensic odontology identification is usually "stipulated to" and the odontologist gives no further testimony. Occasionally body identification is not straightforward. In some homicide cases the perpetrators will go to extreme lengths to prevent the identification of their victim. The removal of the head, destruction of the teeth, and incineration of the body are methods that have been used by criminals to

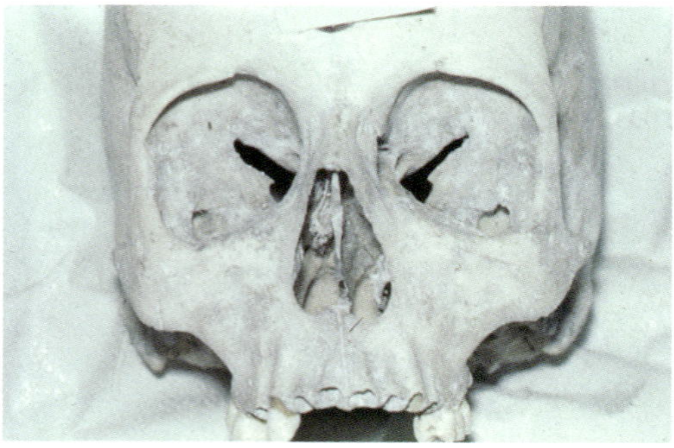

Figure 14.7a White female skull (frontal view). (Courtesy of RRS.)

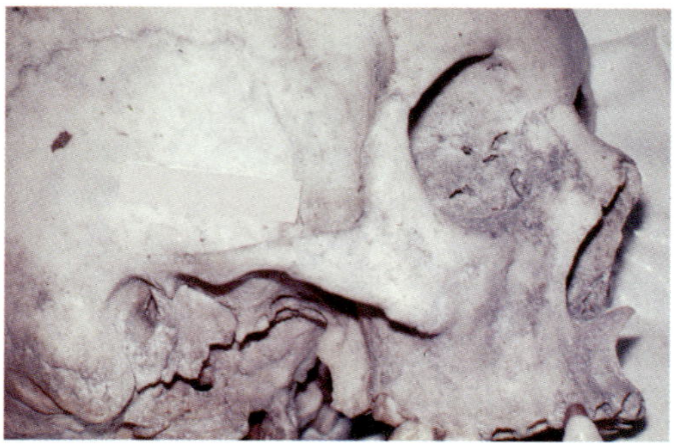

Figure 14.7b White female skull (lateral view). (Courtesy of RRS.)

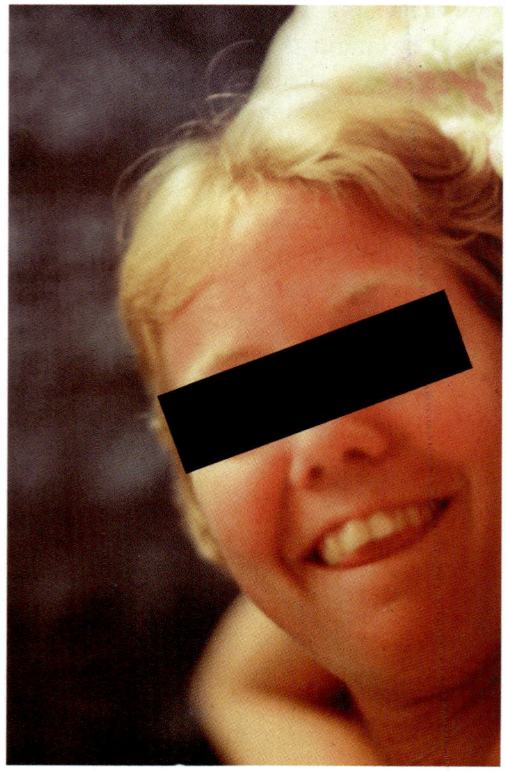

Figure 14.7c Smiling photo antemortem match. (Courtesy of RRS.)

prevent identification of their victims. The forensic odontologist may be asked to perform identifications where only a single tooth remains or where there are no antemortem dental records. These types of cases are far from straightforward. In cases where there are no antemortem dental records available, the identification may be made by the forensic odontologist when comparing a smiling family photograph of the deceased prior to death with the postmortem, anterior dental arrangement. If a full or partial set of the victim's teeth exists postmortem and dental records of the victim are found, there still is the challenge of making a match. All cases are not easy and the body identification in a criminal case may be subjected to extensive cross-examination and lengthy legal arguments.

The forensic odontologist should be prepared to give an opinion regarding the age, race, and sex of the unknown victim in addition to the identification. The best example of this is the skull of a victim that is discovered without any other body parts. It is a challenge to determine the identification and circumstances of the event. All agencies are called upon to help answer these questions. The anthropologist, medical examiner, and forensic odontologist all participate in determining the age, race, and sex of the unknown skull. The forensic odontologist may be able to provide an opinion as to what a dental profile would look like, even if no anterior teeth are present (Figure 14.7a–c).

If the skeletonized victim is a child with mixed dentition consisting of some deciduous and some permanent teeth, a dentist can usually give an age estimate within a plus or minus six-month range. This information may be used not only to determine the age, but it has been used to prove evidence of prolonged abuse or starvation of the victim. Not only

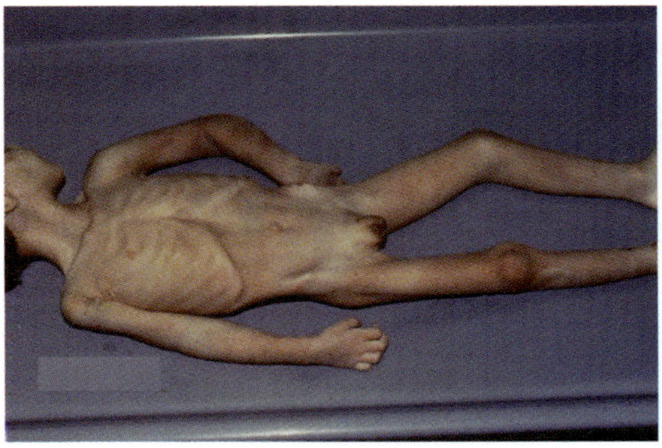

Figure 14.8a Long-term child abuse. (Courtesy of the Miami Dade Medical Examiners office. Used with permission.)

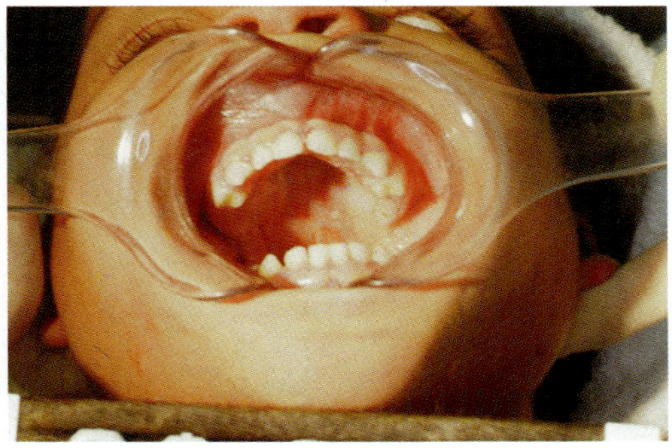

Figure 14.8b Delayed dental development (2 years behind normal). (Courtesy of the Miami Dade Medical Examiners office. Used with permission.)

will the development of the teeth be years behind the normal child of that age but the tooth itself may be deformed (Figure 14.8a,b).

The straightforward routine body identification may constitute the majority of cases for the forensic odontologist and are certainly very important, but the real challenge comes where the unusual occurs. The forensic odontologist is challenged not only to help with the identification but also to assist in the determination of age, race, sex, dental profile, growth, and development. The forensic report and the trial testimony will require research, literature review, careful preparation, and documentation. Consultation with the medical examiner and a second opinion from an independent forensic odontologist (blind opinion) is recommended in these difficult, unusual, challenging, and controversial cases. It is well advised for the forensic odontologist to be cautious, circumspect, and conservative before giving a final opinion in body identification cases where there is not complete and irrefutable material to make a comparison.

In addition to body identification the forensic odontologist will be called upon to give opinion testimony in criminal cases involving assault and/or battery. The definition of battery is the unlawful touching of an individual (see Figures 14.1–14.3). The loss of teeth from an aggravated battery will produce a permanent injury to the victim and will require the testimony of a dentist. The questions will involve the extent of damage, the force required, and the cost to repair as well as future problems and costs as a result of the damage. As in a civil case the forensic odontologist will be asked to give an opinion as to "pain and suffering" and the extent of permanency. The teeth may produce injury to the person striking another in the mouth, not a bitemark but a tooth or teeth mark. An example is where the attacker claims the victim's teeth were broken from a fall but not a blow to the mouth yet teeth marks are documented on the fist of the defendant. The forensic odontologist would be called to give testimony not only of the extent of the injury to the victim but to the origin of the "marks" on the defendant's hand (Figure 14.9).

Not all criminal cases involve violence. The victim is not always dead or injured. The forensic odontologist may be called to give testimony in criminal cases involving some type of dental fraud. The "victim" may be the United States government or a private insurance company. The forensic odontologist will be required to review dental records and cross-reference these with the records submitted to the insurance company or to Medicare/Medicaid. She may be required in some cases to conduct an independent

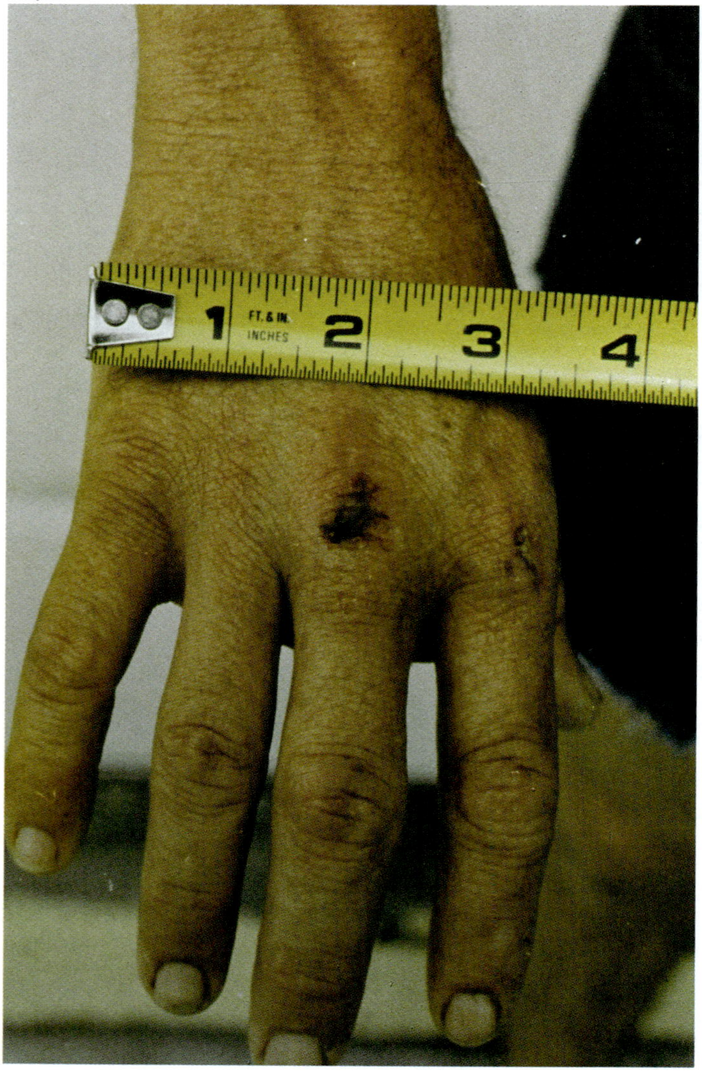

Figure 14.9 Teeth marks on fist of suspect from homicide victim. (Courtesy of the Miami Dade Medical Examiners office. Used with permission.)

medical examination (IME) on the patient to evaluate the claimed procedures. Were the procedures done? Were they done properly? Were the billing and coding of the procedures accurate for what was found in the patient's mouth? If the procedures were not done or were billed improperly, there may be fraud. If criminal charges are filed by the carrier, the case can either be in state or federal court. If the insurance carrier is private but a national company the case can be in federal court because the fraudulent act crossed state lines and involved the U.S. mail. The prosecution will be handled by the U.S. Attorney's Office in that jurisdiction and the investigation will be by the FBI. The case will go to federal court and the defendant, if guilty, may face prison or loss of licenses to practice as well as a monetary fine.

The cost to defend a criminal fraud case is very expensive and the penalties are severe. The defense costs are not covered by malpractice insurance and will have to be paid "out of pocket." When the forensic odontologist is asked to provide assistance to the prosecution or defense in a dental fraud case the same advice is applicable as in any criminal case. The defendant's liberty and livelihood are at stake. Be thorough, cautious, circumspect, and conservative. Above all, be honest and truthful in your evaluation.

Bitemark Testimony

Although all criminal cases are very challenging to the expert witness, the forensic odontologist's most challenging type of case is the bitemark case. The evidence collection and preservation are important to the forensic odontologist for his evaluation and interpretation of the bite wound. Oftentimes the forensic odontologist is not the one collecting, observing, and preserving the bitemark, but is going to be the one who goes to court and gives testimony that may result in the conviction of an individual. From the viewpoint of the prosecution, the bitemark evidence is very powerful forensic evidence. The odontologist, who is giving testimony for the prosecution, must be very careful not to get trapped on a "slippery slope" and give an opinion or opinions beyond what is justifiable by the evidence. As pointed out in Chapter 13, bitemarks are ephemeral and if not recorded properly and in a timely manner may be of little value in forming a dental profile of the biter or giving an evidentiary opinion as to a perpetrator.

Truly, the burden of analyzing a bitemark and giving an "investigative opinion" as well as an "evidentiary opinion" rests on the prosecution expert. There have been tragic consequences in the past where the prosecution expert made the mistake of giving an investigative opinion as an evidentiary one. When it comes to comparing a bite wound left in flesh to the teeth of a suspect, this evidence takes a secondary role to DNA and fingerprint evidence. The interpretation of a bitemark is difficult and is limited by a number of factors outside the control of the prosecution expert (the forensic odontologist). There is a certain degree of subjectivity to bitemark evidence and the expert should evaluate this evidence with an open mind, cautiously, and in depth. A "blind" second opinion or multiple second opinions from other qualified experts are excellent tools to employ prior to giving the evidentiary opinion, the final opinion.

The heavy responsibility of providing an opinion in a bitemark case that may result in a defendant losing his liberty or possibly his life, can not be overemphasized. An error or errors by the prosecution expert not only may result in the conviction of the innocent but the truly guilty party goes free. Errors by the prosecution expert will result in very serious consequences to the expert. A malpractice claim and monetary damages are the least of the consequences of an error. The reputation and public damage to the expert along with his or her internal grief and the knowledge of the consequences to the defendant can be devastating. In the future as the justice system sorts out this problem the expert may be subject to criminal prosecution for giving incorrect opinions. The burden on the expert for the prosecution is a heavy one and not to be undertaken lightly.

Prosecution Expert Testimony

Once the odontologist has reviewed, analyzed, and formulated an investigative opinion, usually for the medical examiner or police agency, the case is presented to the prosecutorial agency for a decision whether or not to proceed against the defendant. The decision is up to the prosecutor, not the expert witness. If the case is to proceed, usually there is more evidence than just a bitemark. How much of the other circumstantial evidence should the expert know? This is a question that is debated at length among forensic odontologists. Are the circumstances of the event important? Are the autopsy findings as to cause and manner of death, the DNA, and fingerprint results helpful for the expert odontologist to know? If the bitemark evidence is of sufficient quality and the dentition of the defendant unusual the expert may give an opinion as to a comparison with a high level of certainty. The highest level is reasonable medical or dental certainty or beyond reasonable doubt. More likely than not is a lesser degree of certainty: over 50 percent. The expert's opinion and the basis of this opinion will be put under oath by means of a subpoena for deposition prior to trial, a discovery deposition by the defense.

If the testimony is not taken prior to trial by means of a deposition, then the testimony will be taken under oath at the time of trial. Some states do not have discovery depositions by the defense even in a capital murder case. The defense is expected to provide its own expert and the defense attorney is to discredit or refute the prosecution expert's opinion on cross-examination. The defense expert in a bitemark case rarely sees the actual victim or the actual bitten tissue. In cases where the defendant bit the deceased, rarely is an exhumation performed in order to see the actual bitten tissue but it has occurred. In a bitemark case where the victim is alive, the defense may have an opportunity to observe the actual wound and obtain the records firsthand. More often than not, the defense expert is asked to look at the evidence secondhand and after the expert for the prosecution has opined as to the level of certainty in the comparison of the bitemark to a defendant's teeth.

It is the responsibility of the defense expert to educate the attorney as to the errors, if any, in the prosecution's expert analysis, techniques, and opinions. Because bitemarks do not rise to the level of certainty of DNA and fingerprint for comparison purposes, the defense expert must point out what the areas of deficiency with bitemark evidence are in general and then focus specifically on the case at hand. In all criminal cases the burden is on the prosecution to prove "beyond a reasonable doubt" that the defendant is guilty. The defense must show only a "reasonable doubt." The expert witness is only responsible to tell the truth and answer only the questions asked of him or her truthfully. The defense expert does not have the burden of the prosecution expert. A mistake by a defense expert will not result in an innocent person losing his life or liberty, but could result in a guilty party going free. She will not, however, suffer the public embarrassment and humiliation that an error by the prosecution expert will endure. Errors by the defense expert will almost never result in a malpractice suit being brought against the defense expert.

Following pretrial discovery by the prosecution and defense, whether by deposition, conference, or otherwise; and if there is no plea bargain, the case goes to trial, usually by a jury but occasionally by just the judge (bench trial). The prosecution and defense experts must be prepared. The burden is on the prosecution (state expert) to show the jury the facts in a manner they can understand. The forensic odontologist will prepare jury aids in the form of overlays, photographs, enlargements, dental casts, video, and numerous other types of presentations. The job of the prosecution is to present the facts truthfully and explain the forensic evidence so that a lay person can understand it. The language used between forensic odontologists may seem basic and simple but not to the jury. The prosecution expert will present his testimony in an orderly manner and usually prearranged by the prosecutor. As in all cases the expert witness will be asked to state her qualifications including education, training, organizations, publications, and so on. Giving false or exaggerated credentials may lead to disqualification or at the very least a fertile ground for the defense cross-examination. The defense expert should be expected to help the defense attorney point out the weaknesses or misstatements of the state's expert qualifications.

Following qualification of the expert witness, the prosecutor will lead the expert with questions regarding what she has reviewed, when and where it was reviewed, and the opinions reached. On occasion the prosecutor will not ask for an opinion until the end of direct examination. The expert will be asked to explain and show the jury using exhibits, the details of the bitemark evidence and the areas of concordance with the defendant's teeth. She will be asked her charges, time spent, and materials reviewed. Be prepared to answer truthfully. Have a list and documentation of time and charges. Avoid vague, apologetic, and timid answers to charges (fees) and time. Do not give false (lowball) estimates of your fee; it will be used against you on cross-examination.

The cross-examination of the prosecution expert by the defense will be grueling, intense, and sometimes insulting. It is designed purposely to anger and frustrate the prosecution witness. The well-prepared and self-confident expert can handle cross-examination and even turn it in his favor. The expert is usually allowed to answer the questions and explain his answers. Listen carefully to the question asked, it usually starts with "Do you have an opinion?" Then the question, "Do you have an opinion?"; Answer, "Yes. Then give your opinion. A favorite question on cross-examination is the type of question, "When did you stop beating your wife?" Think before you answer these trick questions; use them to your advantage.

The defense will try to exaggerate any weakness in your evidence or your testimony including your fees. Question: "How much are you being paid for your testimony here today?" The inference to the jury is supposed to be you are testifying for money. The truth is you are being paid for your work and time just like he is. The key point in cross-examination is not to lose your cool. Take your time and think before you answer. Listen to the complete question; don't interrupt, even if you know what the question is going to be. An effective technique after you are asked a controversial question is to take a long pause and then say, "That is a good question. I am glad you asked it." How do you think that makes the attorney doing the cross-examination feel when he knows he just asked the wrong question? An example is a frequently asked question on cross-examination, "Did you and the prosecutor discuss this case while you were at lunch?" Answer: That is a good question; yes. Question: "What did you discuss?" (Note: A golden rule for all attorneys is never to ask a question of an expert witness to which you don't know the answer, an open-ended question.) Answer: "Well, we discussed what an attentive jury we have and how they are taking notes. It is the best jury that I have ever testified in front of." The attorney will try to stop the answer but usually the judge will allow the expert to finish the answer.

Another major cross-examination tactic for the defense attorney taking on the prosecution expert is to get him or her to admit to possibly having made a mistake. When the answer is no or, "I am reasonably certain of my conclusion," the cross-examination may continue along this line with more of the same: "Could you be wrong? Could you have made a mistake?" When the repeated answer is no, the attorney has accomplished one of two objectives. First, if the answer to any of his questions is yes then he has, on closing argument to the jury, the ability to show that the state's witness could be wrong and there is reasonable doubt the defendant did not leave the bitemark. Second, if the answer to his, "Could you be wrong," "Could you have made a mistake," questions, is no, he is going to show that you are not believable, arrogant, or an advocate. In his closing arguments you, as the expert, are in his trap. If you know in advance what is happening to you, you may be able to turn the tables. You may be able to answer, "I am only human and can make a mistake but in this case I realize the importance of my opinion and have put in much time and study before reaching my conclusion. I am reasonably certain." You may be asked after several no answers to the question, "Did you make a mistake or could have made a mistake?" "Doctor, you never make a mistake, do you?" Answer: "Oh yes, I make a lot mistakes. Just ask my wife!" End of cross-examination.

As the expert for the state in criminal cases it is important to remember that the jury is focused on forensic evidence; science equals truth and you are a scientist presenting scientific evidence. But the interpretation of the science is opinion. The attorney for the defense must show by his cross-examination of you and or his expert that the state's position is subject to error or at the very least does not rise to the level of "beyond reasonable doubt."

The forensic odontologist in a bitemark case will be hammered on cross-examination by a good defense attorney. He will try to show that your testimony in this case differs from one that you did years ago. He will have done his homework. Have you? You must always be consistent and truthful in all your testimony, from past to present. Another important point to remember is never to agree that any text is authorative or you agree completely with any other expert or even your own and previous publications written years ago as authoritative today. You may be shown an article published on your subject of testimony during cross-examination and asked if you agree with the passage. If you have done your homework you will be familiar with the article and can answer in context of the whole not just this specific area. If you are not familiar with the article you are permitted to say so, or you can read it while on the stand before you answer.

Be cautious and take your time before your answers on cross-examination. Remember the record being made of your testimony will be read by attorneys, judges, and the press. All capital cases are appealed and years later your answers on cross-examination will be documented in the final opinions. The record does not reflect the tone, gestures, or volume of the attorney during cross-examination. There are many incidences where the defense attorney will shake his head, stick his finger in your face, or even shout the question at you to cause anger or confusion just to "rattle you" and to get an answer to this and future questions that you would not make if you were calm. Stay cool and in control. You can state, for the record, that the attorney is yelling and shaking his finger, before you answer the question. This now puts the question and answer in proper context.

Following your cross-examination the state will have the opportunity to "redirect" and will usually have no questions of you if you did a good job on cross-examination. The prosecutor may ask only one question, so be prepared for this question. "Did the defendant leave the bitemark?" Answer: "Yes, in my opinion, to a reasonable degree of medical certainty." The defense may or may not do a recross-examination but it is limited to the state's questions on redirect. Be prepared. You may be asked, "What do you mean by reasonable medical certainty?"

The cross-examination of the state's expert witness in criminal cases, specifically involving bitemarks, is the most intense, difficult, and grueling of any case you will ever be involved with. Your statements may contribute to the defendant being sentenced to death or to life in prison. This is an awesome responsibility for any forensic expert and should be undertaken with caution and thoroughness. Your testimony can only be as good as the evidence that you have to work with and in bitemark cases can never be "absolute" or "indeed and without doubt." Never ever give as "science" or "fact" numbers or degrees of certainty of a match, such as one in four billion, that no one else in the world could have left the bitemark. Bitemark evidence has its place in the criminal justice system in many other ways than matching a suspect to a bitemark. There are many advantages to bitemark evidence, however, such evidence should be used to augment a positive identification by fingerprint or DNA. Bitemarks will not give a positive identification out of an unlimited population group. Bitemarks can be used most effectively to eliminate a suspect as having left a bitemark. The forensic odontologist can only give an opinion to a reasonable degree of medical or dental certainty. The jury has the ultimate responsibility to give weight to the bitemark evidence after hearing direct and cross-examination of the state's expert, the direct and cross-examination of the defense expert, and the closing statements by the state and the defense attorney.

Defense Expert Testimony

After the state has completed its case, "the state rests." Now the defense has its turn to present its own expert. The forensic odontologist who is asked to review the case material for the defense will usually not have the same opportunity as the state's expert. She should review all the same material as the state's expert with the exception of the bitemark on the deceased. She should review but not be limited to the scene photographs, autopsy photographs, and reports from all agencies, medical examiner, police, and labs. If depositions were taken she should review these in detail, especially those of the state's expert forensic odontologist, taking notes and abstracting the depositions. It is the role of the defense expert to help the defense attorney with any and all information about the state's expert that will help him on cross-examination. Her training, experience, prior cases, publications, previous testimony, and statements to the press, any and all information will be helpful to the defense.

If the defense expert, after a thorough review of the evidence and statements of the state's expert, should agree with the final opinion, she can still be helpful to the defense, although she probably will not take the stand. Many times the defense will not use the expert at trial but will obtain specific points for his cross-examination of the state's expert. However, if the defense expert can find an error or a difference of opinion with the state's expert as to the alignment of arches, tooth position, tooth arrangement, time of bite in relation to death, and so on, she will most likely be called to give testimony at trial. The defense expert usually will not prepare trial exhibits for several reasons. First, cost: the defense is usually limited as to cost and has to get the court's permission to pay the expert. The defense is usually restricted to a very limited budget. The exception is if the defendant can afford to pay the cost of the expert, the jury aids, displays, and videos. Most of the defense attorneys are not familiar or comfortable with presenting their expert's displays. The general rule is that they use the state's displays, charts, and photographs to prove a defense point.

The direct examination of the defense expert witness is much the same as the state's: qualifications; CV; what, when, and where the materials were reviewed; the fees charged; and opinions and detailed explanation to the jury of the differences of opinion with the state's position and their reasons. A series of questions and answers regarding the lack of subjectivity, specificity, and variations in bitemarks, skin, teeth, and points of concordance are all very important points for direct by the defense expert witness. Usually the defense expert does not hear any testimony prior to giving his. The court invokes the "rule" preventing the experts from hearing each other's testimony. The experts, state and defense, are instructed by the courts not to discuss the case with anyone except the attorneys. Furthermore, the court may prevent your discussing the case or your testimony until the jury reaches a verdict. This order is exactly what it says. In high-profile cases the press is always present to get your take, but if there is a "gag order" by the court you are not allowed to speak to them. On the other hand, the press and TV may be allowed in the courtroom. The decision is up to the judge in most cases.

The pressure on the expert witness for the defense is not as great as on the state's expert witness because the defense has only to show some "reasonable doubt." Again, the prepared, calm, and truthful witness is hard to discredit on cross-examination. The state will attempt on cross to have the defense expert criticize the state's witness, his techniques, his research, and experience, but most of all his opinions linking the defendant to the bitemark. The defense expert should be aware in advance for the potential questions on cross-examination and have the answers. It is a good rule never to criticize the witness on the other side personally or professionally but it is fair game to criticize his opinions and techniques. The attorneys, however, will look for any possible opportunity to attack the witness in almost any way and may go so far as a personal attack, but this is the exception.

The usual cross-examination of the defense expert by the prosecution is an attempt to show the jury that he is biased because of previous testimony, his publications, statements made about this case, and the number of times he has been hired by the defense. The fees charged will be attacked usually with the question, "How much are you being paid for your testimony?" The obvious outcome is to make the witness look like a "hired gun." If you are prepared to provide documentation of the time spent in preparation and can produce records to prove it, the attack stops. The cross-examination of the defense expert is usually shorter and far less aggressive than that of the prosecution expert. In fact, in some cases the state will have no cross-examination. This can be very frustrating for the defense expert and the inference to the jury is that your direct testimony was so weak it did not need to be challenged or that your statements on direct will help prove the state's case. The state will use certain portions of your direct testimony during closing arguments to bolster their case. They do not want to give you the possibility on cross-examination to repeat your direct testimony or to give more emphasis to your strong points of disagreement with the opinions of the state's witness.

The strong tactic for the defense attorney is the cross-examination of the state's witness. The prosecuting attorney is the opposite. His strong tactic is the direct testimony of his witness. Many times the state's witness can actually help the effectiveness of his direct testimony by his answers on cross-examination. The defense expert has the same opportunity on cross-examination but if no questions are asked he is denied the opportunity.

Following the testimony of the prosecution witness the state rests its case. The defense follows and at the conclusion of its case, it rests. The state has the right to provide more testimony in rebuttal. The state may recall its expert to rebut certain points that were introduced by the defense or the state may call a different expert to provide testimony or to "back up" certain statements made by the state's witness during direct testimony. In any event the rebuttal witness is subject to the same intense cross-examination by the defense attorney as during the state's case. The cross-examination here is limited to the area of rebuttal testimony but often will go into previous testimony. The judge will control the scope of testimony on rebuttal both direct and on cross-examination.

Once the state and defense have concluded their respective presentations of evidence, the case is summarized to the jury during closing arguments. The expert witness should never attend closing arguments but would learn a lot if he could. Transcript of the closing arguments is one way to learn what was said. Comments about the witness and the witness's testimony can be very humbling or insulting. The best way to learn and see closing arguments is if the proceedings are televised. A word of caution to the expert, especially in criminal trials: if you should attend the closing arguments in person the attorney on the opposing side will point you out to the jury and emphasize the point that you are not just an impartial scientific witness but an advocate with a vested interest in the outcome.

Conclusion

The role of the expert witness in criminal, as well as in civil cases, is to provide facts and give expert opinions to help the jury reach a fair and just verdict. In civil cases the jury is to determine fault, pain, and suffering and permanency, and to award monetary compensation to the plaintiff. In a criminal case the jury will determine guilt or innocence and in capital cases recommend a sentence of life or death, an awesome responsibility to be undertaken very seriously. The expert witness does not have the same responsibility as the jury but nevertheless should realize that the opinions given will be used by the jury or judge to make the final determination of guilt or innocence. An expert needs to be fair, thorough, truthful, accurate, and prepared in order to give the jury the best possible understanding of the issues and her opinions. Remember that you are an expert and are responsible for your testimony. If you give false, prejudicial, or grossly negligent testimony you may be held liable in the future. You may have to stand trial and justify your testimony, which is a very sobering prospect, especially in criminal cases. Think before you act. Always be truthful, conservative, objective, and scientific in your final opinions and you will be a good expert witness.

Psychological Consequences

15

Death is inevitable, but represents emotional consequences to all those who observe it and its consequences. Religious custom is centered on the beginning and the end of life. Nothing is more mystifying. As a medical examiner or forensic odontologist conducting an autopsy, you are among the few and privileged to attend to the needs of the person who is no longer alive. What are these remains and how do we deal with them? It is important to understand the emotional as well as the physical components. To disregard the elements of either will result in damage to the examiner that in some cases is permanent, and in other cases just passing. The mere appearance of bodily remains is anathema to many. When you add the odors and the sometimes brutal fragmentation or decomposition, it can become a deadly cocktail.

Before accepting a position as a practicing forensic odontologist, it is important to pass an initiation test. A visit to the morgue is mandatory. The sights and smells of the morgue are akin to no other earthly place. Few have seen death and fewer still have witnessed the visual and olfactory trauma after death.

The sterile atmosphere of the room, from sink to ceiling, is in sharp contrast to the sanguine exposure of the body's interior organs. What was before, will never be again, and yet it will speak to us of myriad times, past and present, if only we learn to understand its language.

The difficulty lies in maintaining one's professional attitude. Emotion can overcome education and science. Viewing the human body in its various agonal stages, from fresh to decomposed to skeletal (Classes I, II, III), requires a steady hand and mind. As important as this attitude may be in the individual cases, it can be multiplied hundreds or thousands of times when dealing with mass disaster. In addition, the morgue is the office, and as professionals, we have been admonished many times, "Do not bring your work home." This means physically as well as mentally.

No one who responds to an individual dental autopsy or a mass disaster event is unaffected by it. Feelings of sadness, grief, and anger may be considered normal reactions to such an abnormal event. There is a certain compulsion not to leave the area until all the work is finished, and yet, many try to overcome these feelings with dedication and commitment, while others even deny the need for rest and recovery.

The signs telling you that you may need stress management are:

Difficulty communicating
Difficulty remembering instructions
Difficulty maintaining balance
Difficulty making decisions
Limited attention span
Unnecessary risk taking
Tremors/headaches/vomiting
Impaired hearing and vision
Disorientation or confusion
Difficulty concentrating
Loss of objectivity
Easily frustrated

Refusal to follow orders
Increased use of drugs/alcohol
Clumsiness

Stress is an important element which leads to distress. There are "Things to Do" to control stress within the first 24–48 hours:

For responders:

Have periods of appropriate physical exercise alternating with a period of relaxation.
Structure your time and keep busy.
Don't label yourself "crazy."
Talk to people, friends, and family unaffiliated with your work
Be aware of numbing the pain with drugs or alcohol.
Maintain as normal a daily schedule as possible.
Spend time with others.
Help your co-workers by sharing feelings and checking on how they are doing.
Give yourself permission to feel rotten and share your feelings with others.
Keep a journal.
Do things that feel good.
Don't make any big life changes.
Make as many daily decisions as possible.
If someone asks you what you want to eat, answer right away even if you are not sure.
Get plenty of rest.
Recurring thoughts, dreams, and flashbacks are normal; don't fight them.
Eat well-balanced and regular meals, even if you don't feel like it.
Expect the unexpected; try not to be surprised.
Do not depend on medication for relief.
Try yoga and other similar meditation systems.

For family members and friends:

Listen carefully.
Spend quiet time with the traumatized person.
Offer assistance and a listening ear.
Reassure them that they are safe.
Help them with everyday tasks: cleaning, cooking, and minding children.
Give them private time.
Don't take their anger personally.
Don't tell them, "Lucky it wasn't worse."
Tell them you are sorry such an event has occurred.

If the time comes when you or your family feel that there has not been any upward progress, do not be afraid to seek professional assistance. Post Traumatic Stress Disorder (PTSD) may occur after such events as a mass disaster, a single autopsy, or the battlefield in Iraq. There is no telling when the ugliness of distress will raise its twisted limbs and attack. After each incident of mass disaster there is a period when all members are gathered together and "debriefed." This is usually conducted by a professional and it is a group endeavor in an attempt to return to normal lives again.

Professional Organizations 16

AAFS

"The American Academy of Forensic Science is a multi-disciplinary professional organization that provides leadership to advance science and its application to the legal system. The objectives of the Academy are to promote education, foster research, improve practice and encourage cooperation in the forensic sciences." The AAFS was first organized in 1948 as a non-profit professional society. It is devoted to the improvement, the administration, and the achievement of justice through the application of science to the process of law. For 60 years the AAFS has served its nearly 6000 members in eleven different sections representing the entire panoply of all sciences in the legal system. The United States, Canada, and 52 other countries worldwide are represented. In addition, it publishes the *Journal of Forensic Science*, which is an internationally acclaimed scientific journal. As the world's most prestigious forensic organization it serves as a resource to the public at large for the most recent information and research in the field of forensic science.

The eleven sections in the AAFS are:

- Criminalistics
- Digital and Multimedia Sciences
- Engineering Sciences
- General
- Jurisprudence
- Odontology
- Pathology/Biology
- Physical Anthropology
- Psychiatry/Behavorial Sciences
- Questioned Documents
- Toxicology

In the Odontology section, memberships are available as a Student Affiliate, Trainee Affiliate, Associate Member, Active Member, and Fellow of the Academy. There are very strict requirements at each level. The annual meeting is held during February at different locations throughout the United States.

You may obtain detailed membership and annual meeting information at the website http://www.aafs.org or contact:

Anne Warren, Executive Director
410 North 21st Street
Colorado Springs, CO 80904
719.636.1100
awarren@aafs.org.

ASFO

The American Society of Forensic Odontology is the largest organization representing all those interested in forensic odontology worldwide. It is not necessary to belong to any other organization, or to have any qualifications or references, other than an interest in forensic odontology. Student applications are welcome. The ASFO annual meetings are held for one day in conjunction with the AAFS meeting.

The ASFO publishes the *Manual of Forensic Odontology*, which is in its fourth edition and available online. As part of their mission they have research grants available to encourage and stimulate investigation in forensic odontology. Membership application, registration for meetings, current courses in forensic odontology, and dues payment are all available online at the website. Information may be obtained from the website http://www.newasfo.com or:

Dr. Bruce Schrader, Executive Director
13408 No. Research Boulevard, Suite B
Austin TX 78750
director@asfo.org.

IAI

The International Association for Identification was formed in 1915 and is the oldest and largest forensic science organization in the world. There are 60 divisions worldwide and many training sessions and meetings are conducted independently through these associations. Many disciplines including fingerprints, firearms, tool marks, and odontology are active within the organization.

Members receive a subscription to the *Journal of Forensic Identification*. Its professional membership is involved in the investigation and analysis of crime scenes, collection and examination of evidence, and biometric identification. Forensic odontology plays a major role in the process of identification. Because the teeth and dental restorations are among the most everlasting elements in or on the body, they are often the last great hope to establish identification. In a closed population, even a single tooth may be sufficient to establish identification.

Further information may be obtained from their website at http://www.theiai.org or:

Joseph Polski
International Association for Identification
2535 Pilot Knob Road, Suite 117
Mendota Heights, MN 55120-1120
651.681.8566.

ABFO

The American Board of Forensic Odontology is the certifying body of forensic odontology. It was in 1976 that the Forensic Sciences Foundation received a grant to establish a credentials and certification board in the field of forensic odontology. Since that time 143 dentists have successfully challenged the Board examination. The ABFO qualifications and certification standards are very high and much time must be devoted to achieve this status. Today there are approximately only 100 active members throughout the world. Detailed information regarding application and requirements may be obtained at http://www.abfo.org or:

The American Board of Forensic Odontology
Forensic Sciences Foundation
410 North 21st Street
Colorado Springs, CO 80904-2798
719.636.1100.

Final Note

We cannot bring the deceased back to life, but we can bring a life back to the deceased.

Appendix

MIAMI-DADE COUNTY MEDICAL EXAMINER DEPARTMENT

Number One on Bob Hope Road
Miami, FL 33136-1133

(305) 545-2400 FAX (305) 545-2418

(BAR CODE LABEL)

REQUEST FOR FORENSIC ODONTOLOGY SERVICES

M.E. Case #_____________ Name______________________________(If Known) Race:_____ Sex:_____ Age:_____

To Be Completed By Forensic Investigator

Notification: Dentist Name: ______________________________ Date:_________ Time: _________

Morgue Tech______________________________ Date:_________ Time: _________

Investigator: Name: ______________________________ Dental Chart Copied: ☐ Yes ☐ No

Medical Examiner:__________________________ M.D.

To Be Completed By Forensic Odontologist

Teeth Charted: ☐ Yes No ☐ Comments:

Bite Mark Workup: ☐ Yes No ☐ Comments:

Dentures Taken: ☐ Yes No ☐ Comments:

Photos Taken: ☐ Yes No ☐ Number:______ ☐ Dig tal ☐ Film

X-rays Taken: ☐ Yes No ☐ Number:______ ☐ Dig tal ☐ Film

Impressions Taken: ☐ Yes No ☐ ☐ Maxilla: ☐ Mandible

Dental Records Available: ☐ Yes No ☐ ☐ Models ☐ Xrays ☐ Chart/narrative ☐ Photo/smiling, teeth

Confirmation: ☐ Yes No ☐ Comments:

Estimate: Age_________ Race_________ Sex_________

Dentist:______________________________________ D.D.S. Date__________ Time:___________

Please print name

____

Signature

Doctor, please complete this form and leave white copy with forensic investigations.
Yellow copy for your files.

118.01-42 4/02

Figure A.1 Request for forensic odontology services. (Courtesy of the Miami Dade Medical Examiners office. Used with permission.)

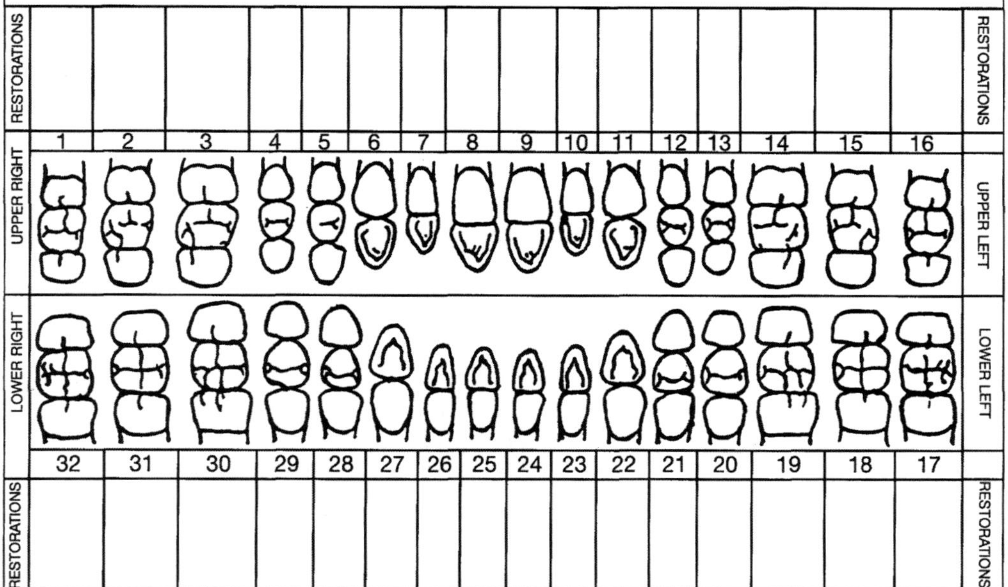

MIAMI-DADE COUNTY MEDICAL EXAMINER DEPARTMENT
Number One on Bob Hope Road • Miami, FL 33136-1133
(305) 545-2400
FAX (305) 545-2418

(BAR CODE LABEL)

RECORD IDENTIFICATION PROCESSING
DENTAL CHART

LAST NAME – FIRST NAME – MIDDLE INITIAL (or unknown number)	Age______ Race______ Sex______
Medical Examiner Case Number	Date__________________

Abreviations **(WIN ID)**

Primary Codes
M Mesial **O** Occlusal **D** Distal
F Facial **L** Lingual **I** Incisal
U Unerupted **X** Missing **J** Missing/Post Mort
/ (No Data) **V** Virgin (or root only-no crown)

Secondary Codes
A Annotation **B** Deciduous **G** Gold
T Denture Tooth **P** Pontic **Z** Temp/or Caries
H Porcelain **E** Resin **C** Crown
N Non-Precious **S** Silver Amalgam **R** Root Canal

THE FOLLOWING CONDITIONS WILL BE INDICATED IF PRESENT **(Describe in detail in Remarks section on other side)**

PATHOLOGY	CARIES	TONGUE	GINGIVAL RECESSION
ENAMEL FORMATION	UNERUPTED TEETH	FRACTURES OF TEETH	TORUS
EROSION	MALOCCLUSION	RETAINED DECIDUOUS TEETH	UNUSUAL APPLIANCES
ABRASION	SUPERNUMERARY TEETH	ABNORMAL INTERDENTAL SPACES	MALPOSED TEETH

PRINCIPAL ODONTOLOGIST (Print name and sign) License #________	**VERIFIED BY (Print Name and sign) License # ________**

118.01-43 4/02 WES 2u01

Figure A.2a Miami Dade County Medical Exaiminer dental chart (front). (Courtesy of the Miami Dade Medical Examiners office. Used with permission.)

DENTURES: Describe dentures including natural teeth replaced and teeth with retaining clasps. Show any numbers or letters appearing on the denture.

Annotations: (Any use of "A" must be accompanied by a notation on this chart together with the tooth number)
WIN ID standard notations are:

Abrasion	Apico	Cong Miss	Cyst	Hemisect	Impaction
Opacity	Ortho	Pedo	Pin	Post	Resorb
Retainer	RetroFill	Root Tip	RPD	Sealant	Silver Pt
SuperNu	Temp	Torus	Written Record Narrative		Date of X-rays

REMARKS: Describe pathology

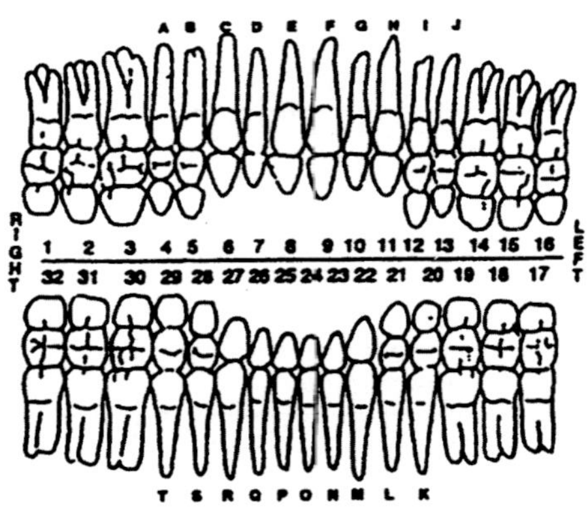

WES 2001

Figure A.2b Miami Dade County Medical Exaiminer dental chart (back). (Courtesy of the Miami Dade Medical Examiners office. Used with permission).

NCIC Missing Person File
Data Collection Entry Guide

Agency Case #_______________

NCIC Missing Person Dental Report

SECTION 1

Patient's Name: ____________________ Age at Disappearance: _____ NCIC #: ____________

Completed by: ____________________________ Date Completed: __________

Address: ____

Telephone #: __________________ Email Address: ____________________

X-Rays Available? ☐ Yes ☐ No Dental Models Available? ☐ Yes ☐ No Dental Photographs Available? ☐ Yes ☐ No

SECTION 2

DENTAL CHARACTERISTICS

Upper Right

01 (18)__________
02 (17)__________
03 (16)__________
04 (15)__________(A)
05 (14)__________(B)
06 (13)__________(C)
07 (12)__________(D)
08 (11)__________(E)

Upper Left

09 (21)__________(F)
10 (22)__________(G)
11 (23)__________(H)
12 (24)__________(I)
13 (25)__________(J)
14 (26)__________
15 (27)__________
16 (28)__________

(Numbers in parentheses represent FDI System.)

(Letters in parentheses represent deciduous dentition.)

Lower Right

32 (48)__________
31 (47)__________
30 (46)__________
29 (45)__________(T)
28 (44)__________(S)
27 (43)__________(R)
26 (42)__________(Q)
25 (41)__________(P)

Lower Left

24 (31)__________(O)
23 (32)__________(N)
22 (33)__________(M)
21 (34)__________(L)
20 (35)__________(K)
19 (36)__________
18 (37)__________
17 (38)__________

SECTION 3

DENTAL CODES

X = Tooth has been removed or did not develop
V = Tooth is unrestored or no information (Default Code)
M = Mesial Surface Restored
O = Occlusal/Incisal Surface Restored
D = Distal Surface Restored
F = Facial or Buccal Surface Restored
L = Lingual Surface Restored
C = Lab Processed or Prefabricated Restoration
R = Endodontic Treatment
/ = Tooth present but clinical crown missing (i.e., fractured)*

(*The codes V and / are used differently in the Missing Person Dental Report than in the Unidentified Person Dental Report.)

SECTION 4

DENTAL REMARKS

☐ ALL (All 32 teeth are present and unrestored) ☐ UNK (No dental information available)

____
____
____
____

Rev 2/06 30

Figure A.3a NCIC missing person dental report. (Courtesy of the U.S. Department of Justice.)

NCIC Missing Person File
Data Collection Entry Guide

Agency Case #________________

Dental Codes and Descriptions

Primary Dental Codes - *One or more codes must be entered for each tooth.*

Code	Description
V	Virgin. Default code for Missing Persons. Tooth is present or assumed to be present and unrestored. This includes unerupted teeth, such as wisdom or deciduous teeth. If no information is available for a particular tooth, this code should be used as it is assumed that all teeth are present (erupted or unerupted) and unrestored when they develop. This code is also used when a tooth has been restored but it is impossible to determine which surface has been restored (most common example of this is the location of a pit type filling on molars when it is impossible to determine whether the filling is on the facial or lingual surface). **Note: This code is used differently when coding dental characteristics for Unidentified Persons.**
	A portion of the tooth is remaining and treatment has probably been accomplished on the tooth but it is impossible to determine which surfaces have been restored. This code is most frequently used when a tooth has had an endodontic procedure accomplished and the clinical crown has fractured off. This code is seldom used in coding missing persons dental information. **Note: This code is used differently when coding dental characteristics for Unidentified Persons.**
X	Missing. Tooth has been extracted or is congenitally missing.
M	Mesial surface of the tooth has been restored.
O	Occlusal or Incisal surface of the tooth has been restored.
D	Distal surface of the tooth has been restored.
F	Facial or Buccal surface of the tooth has been restored.
L	Lingual surface of the tooth has been restored.

Secondary Dental Codes - *Cannot be used independently. Must be used in conjunction with Primary codes.*

Code	Description
C	Any laboratory processed restoration including crowns, inlays, onlays, and veneers. This code also includes prefabricated restorations such as stainless steel crowns, metal and acrylic temporary crowns, and porcelain processed veneers.
R	Root canal. Evidence is available to establish that an endodontic procedure has been started or completed.

Figure A.3b NCIC dental codes and descriptions (missing person). (Courtesy of the U.S. Department of Justice.)

NCIC Unidentified Person File
Data Collection Entry Guide

Agency Case #________________

NCIC Unidentified Person Dental Report

SECTION 1

ME/Coroner Case #: ________________ ________________ NCIC #: ____________

Completed by: _____ ________________ _________ Date Completed: _________

Address: ________________ ________________ ________________

Telephone #: ________________ Email Address: ________________ ____________

X-Rays Available? ☐ Yes ☐ No Dental Models Available? ☐ Yes ☐ No Dental Photographs Available? ☐ Yes ☐ No

SECTION 2 ***DENTAL CHARACTERISTICS***

Upper Right		Lower Right
01 (18)__________		32 (48)__________
02 (17)__________		31 (47)__________
03 (16)__________		30 (46)__________
04 (15)__________(A)	(Numbers in parentheses	29 (45)__________(T)
05 (14)__________(B)	represent FDI System.)	28 (44)__________(S)
06 (13)__________(C)		27 (43)__________(R)
07 (12)__________(D)		26 (42)__________(Q)
08 (11)__________(E)		25 (41)__________(P)
Upper Left		**Lower Left**
09 (21)__________(F)	(Letters in parentheses	24 (31)__________(O)
10 (22)__________(G)	represent deciduous	23 (32)__________(N)
11 (23)__________(H)	dentition.)	22 (33)__________(M)
12 (24)__________(I)		21 (34)__________(L)
13 (25)__________(J)		20 (35)__________(K)
14 (26)__________		19 (36)__________
15 (27)__________		18 (37)__________
16 (28)__________		17 (38)__________

SECTION 3 ***DENTAL CODES***

X = Tooth has been removed or did not develop	F = Facial or Buccal Surface Restored
V = Tooth is present and unrestored	L = Lingual Surface Restored
M = Mesial Surface Restored	C = Lab Processed or Prefabricated Restoration
O = Occlusal/Incisal Surface Restored	R = Endodontic Treatment
D = Distal Surface Restored	/ = Postmortem Missing or Not Recovered (Default Code)

(*The codes V and / are used differently in the Unidentified Person Report than in the Missing Person Dental Report.)

SECTION 4 ***DENTAL REMARKS***

☐ ALL (All 32 teeth are present and unrestored) ☐ UNK (No dental information available)

____

____

____

____

Rev 2/06 30

Figure A.4a NCIC unidentified person dental report. (Courtesy of the U.S. Department of Justice.)

NCIC Unidentified Person File
Data Collection Entry Guide

Agency Case #________________

Dental Codes and Descriptions

Primary Dental Codes - *One or more codes must be entered for each tooth.*

Code	Description
/	Default code for Unidentified Persons. Typically used when the tooth is not recovered. Also used when a portion of the tooth is remaining and it is impossible to determine if the clinical crown has been restored. **Note: This code is used differently when coding dental characteristics for Missing Persons.**
V	Virgin. Tooth is present and unrestored. This includes unerupted teeth such as wisdom or deciduous teeth. **Note: This code is used differently when coding dental characteristics for Missing Persons.**
X	Missing. Tooth has been extracted or is congenitally missing.
M	Mesial surface of the tooth has been restored.
O	Occlusal or Incisal surface of the tooth has been restored.
D	Distal surface of the tooth has been restored.
F	Facial or Buccal surface of the tooth has been restored.
L	Lingual surface of the tooth has been restored.

Secondary Dental Codes - *Cannot be used independently. Must be used in conjunction with Primary codes.*

Code	Description
C	Any laboratory processed restoration including crowns, inlays, onlays, and veneers. This code also includes prefabricated restorations such as stainless steel crowns, metal and acrylic temporary crowns, and porcelain processed veneers.
R	Root canal. Evidence is available to establish that an endodontic procedure has been started or completed.

Rev 2/06 32

Figure A.4b NCIC dental codes and descriptions (unidentified person). (Courtesy of the U.S. Department of Justice.)

406.135 Autopsies; confidentiality of photographs and video and audio recordings; exemption.--

(1) For the purpose of this section, the term "medical examiner" means any district medical examiner, associate medical examiner, or substitute medical examiner acting pursuant to this chapter, as well as any employee, deputy, or agent of a medical examiner or any other person who may obtain possession of a photograph or audio or video recording of an autopsy in the course of assisting a medical examiner in the performance of his or her official duties.

(2) A photograph or video or audio recording of an autopsy held by a medical examiner is confidential and exempt from s. 119.07(1) and s. 24(a), Art. I of the State Constitution, except that a surviving spouse may view and copy a photograph or video recording or listen to or copy an audio recording of the deceased spouse's autopsy. If there is no surviving spouse, then the surviving parents shall have access to such records. If there is no surviving spouse or parent, then an adult child shall have access to such records.

(3)(a) The deceased's surviving relative, with whom authority rests to obtain such records, may designate in writing an agent to obtain such records.

(b) A local governmental entity, or a state or federal agency, in furtherance of its official duties, pursuant to a written request, may view or copy a photograph or video recording or may listen to or copy an audio recording of an autopsy, and unless otherwise required in the performance of their duties, the identity of the deceased shall remain confidential and exempt.

(c) The custodian of the record, or his or her designee, may not permit any other person, except an agent designated in writing by the deceased's surviving relative with whom authority rests to obtain such records, to view or copy such photograph or video recording or listen to or copy an audio recording without a court order.

(4)(a) The court, upon a showing of good cause, may issue an order authorizing any person to view or copy a photograph or video recording of an autopsy or to listen to or copy an audio recording of an autopsy and may prescribe any restrictions or stipulations that the court deems appropriate.

(b) In determining good cause, the court shall consider whether such disclosure is necessary for the public evaluation of governmental performance; the seriousness of the intrusion into the family's right to privacy and whether such disclosure is the least intrusive means available; and the availability of similar information in other public records, regardless of form.

(c) In all cases, the viewing, copying, listening to or other handling of a photograph or video or audio recording of an autopsy must be under the direct supervision of the custodian of the record or his or her designee.

(5) A surviving spouse shall be given reasonable notice of a petition filed with the court to view or copy a photograph or video recording of an autopsy or a petition to listen to or copy an audio recording, a copy of such petition, and reasonable notice of the opportunity to be present and heard at any hearing on the matter. If there is no surviving spouse, then such notice must be given to the parents of the deceased, and

Figure A.5a Earnhardt Law (Florida statute, page 1).

if the deceased has no living parent, then to the adult children of the deceased.

(6)(a) Any custodian of a photograph or video or audio recording of an autopsy who willfully and knowingly violates this section commits a felony of the third degree, punishable as provided in s. 775.082, s. 775.083, or s. 775.084.

(b) Any person who willfully and knowingly violates a court order issued pursuant to this section commits a felony of the third degree, punishable as provided in s. 775.082, s. 775.083, or s. 775.084.

(7) A criminal or administrative proceeding is exempt from this section, but unless otherwise exempted, is subject to all other provisions of chapter 119, provided however that this section does not prohibit a court in a criminal or administrative proceeding upon good cause shown from restricting or otherwise controlling the disclosure of an autopsy, crime scene, or similar photograph or video or audio recordings in the manner prescribed herein.

(8) This exemption shall be given retroactive application.

History.--s. 1, ch. 2001-1; s. 1, ch. 2003-184; s. 1, ch. 2006-263.

Figure A.5b1 Earnhardt Law (Florida statute, page 2).

SUBPOENA DUCES TECUM WITHOUT DEPOSITION

To the Sheriff or any constable of said county

You are hereby commanded to summon: Dental records custodian of:
Dr. XXXXXXX YYYYYYYY
Address
Phone

And to have with you :

ANY AND ALL DENTAL HISTORY QUESTIONNAIRES, DENTAL HISTORY FORMS, MEDICAL HISTORY SHEET AND/OR PATIENT INTAKE SHEETS. RADIOGRAPHS ,MODELS, PHOTOGRAPHS, NOTE ON ATTENDANCE AND/OR TREATMENT INCLUDING WORK DONE AND PLANNED, CORRESPONDENCE, ATTACHED TO A COMPLETE PATIENT FILE INCLUDING ANY AND ALL SECTIONS OF THE FILE IN <u>ORIGINAL</u> FORM THAT YOU MAY HAVE IN YOUR POSSESSION REGARDING:

<u>PATIENT NAME (S)</u>

All conditions precedent to comply with HIPPAA in regard to the above mentioned person have been met as required by law.

Records may be mailed to :
Miami Dade Medical Examiner Department
Miami Florida 33136

Or transferred directly to a law enforcement agent.

Failure to comply with this order within 24 hours will result in contempt of court proceedings with attendant fine and imprisonment.

A true copy

_______________________________________Sheriff

_______________________________________ Seal __________Date

Receipt of records:

Received by________________________________ Date_____________

Figure A.6 Subpoena *duces tecum* without deposition. (Courtesy of the Miami Dade Medical Examiners office. Used with permission.)

EXAMPLE

MIAMI-DADE MEDICAL EXAMINER DEPARTMENT

Written Request To View Autopsy Photographs

I, the undersigned, in furtherance of my official duties, will be viewing autopsy photographs/videos for educational and training purposes only. The identity of the deceased shall remain confidential and exempt, and no reference shall be made in any way regarding the identity of decedents in any of the materials that I view.

____
Name [Print]

____
Signature

____
Date

Figure A.7 Request to view autopsy photographs. (Courtesy of the Miami Dade Medical Examiners office. Used with permission.)

MIAMI DADE COUNTY MEDICAL EXAMINER DEPARTMENT
Number One on Bob Hope Road
Miami, Florida 33136-1133
305-545-2400 305-545-2418(FAX)

Case No. ______________________________ Name ______________________________

Age__________ Race______________ Sex________ Height________ Weight________ Date / /

BITE MARK LOCATION

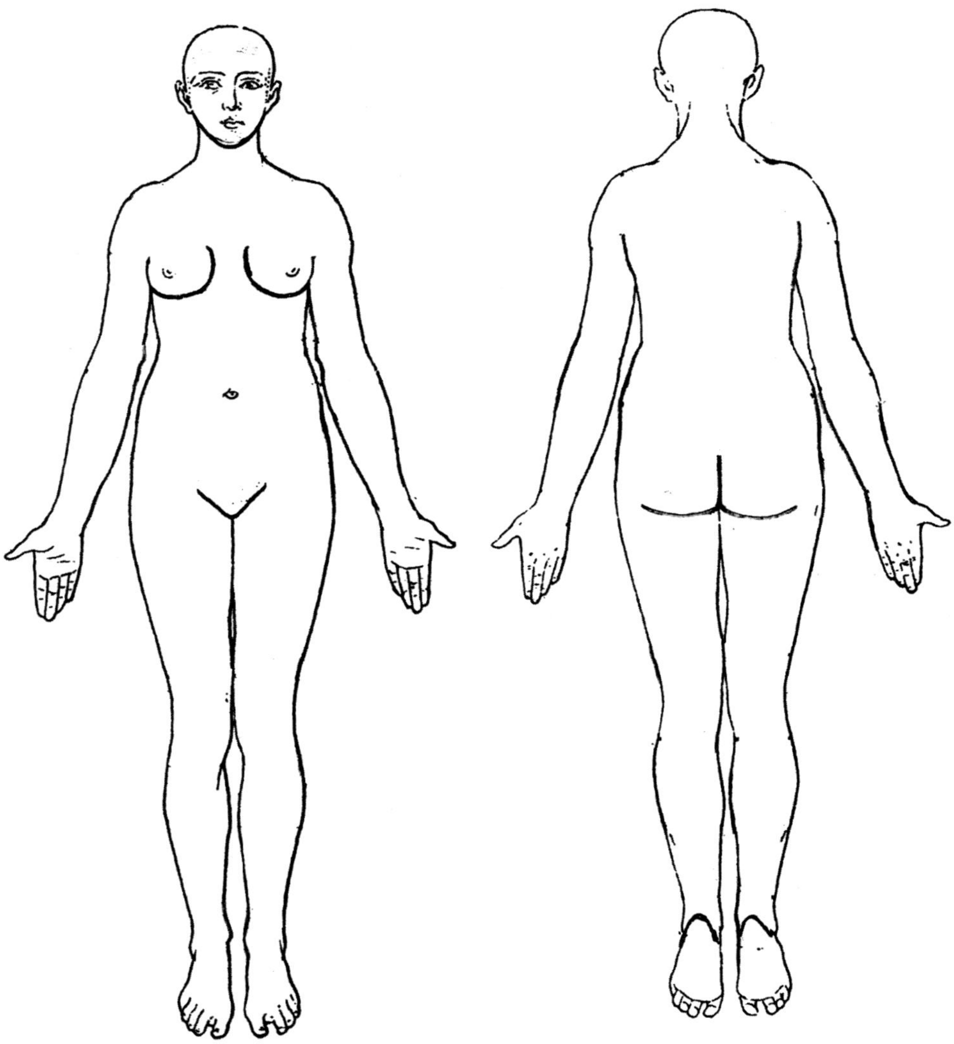

Figure A.8a Miami Dade Country Medical Examiner bitemark location chart, female whole body. (Courtesy of the Miami Dade Medical Examiners office. Used with permission.)

MIAMI DADE COUNTY MEDICAL EXAMINER DEPARTMENT

Number One on Bob Hope Road

Miami, Florida 33136-1133

305-545-2400 305-545-2418(FAX)

Case No. ______________________________ Name ______________________________

Age__________ Race__________ Sex________ Height________ Weight________ Date / /

BITE MARK LOCATION

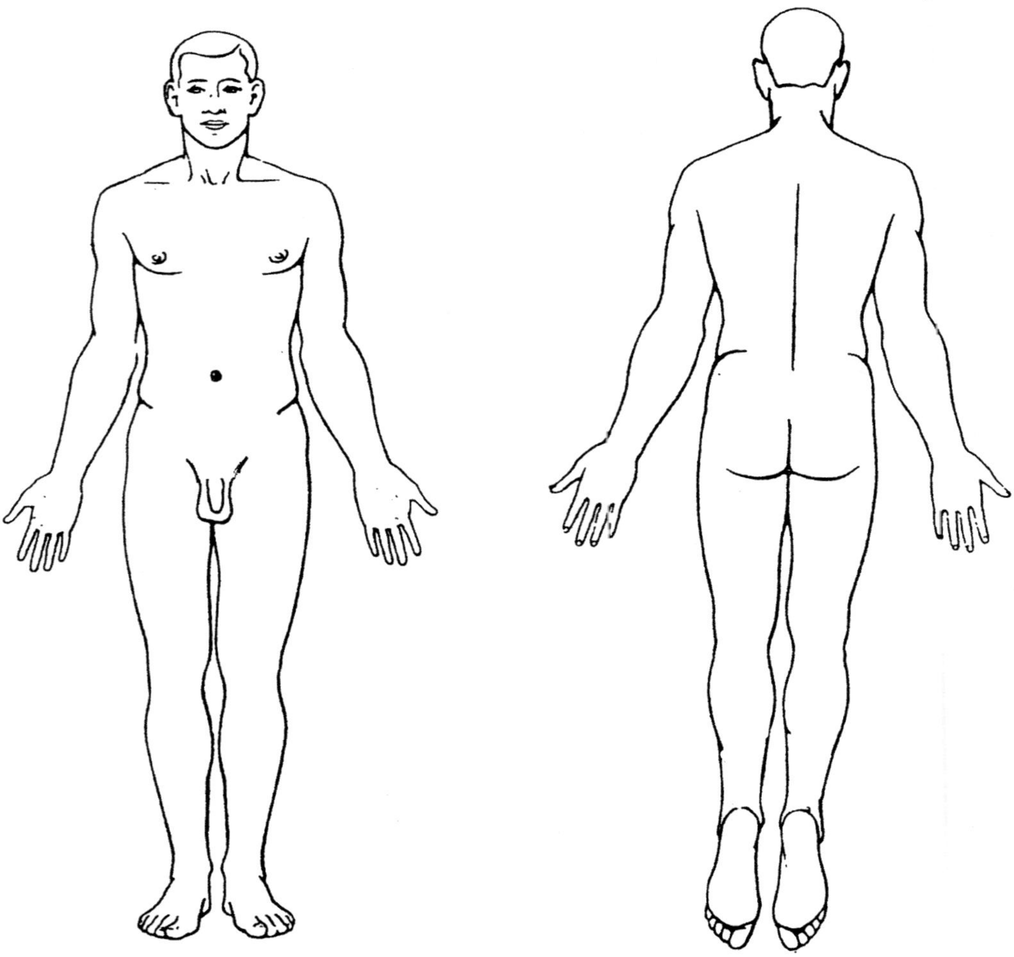

Figure A.8b Miami Dade Country Medical Examiner bitemark location chart, male whole body. (Courtesy of the Miami Dade Medical Examiners office. Used with permission.)

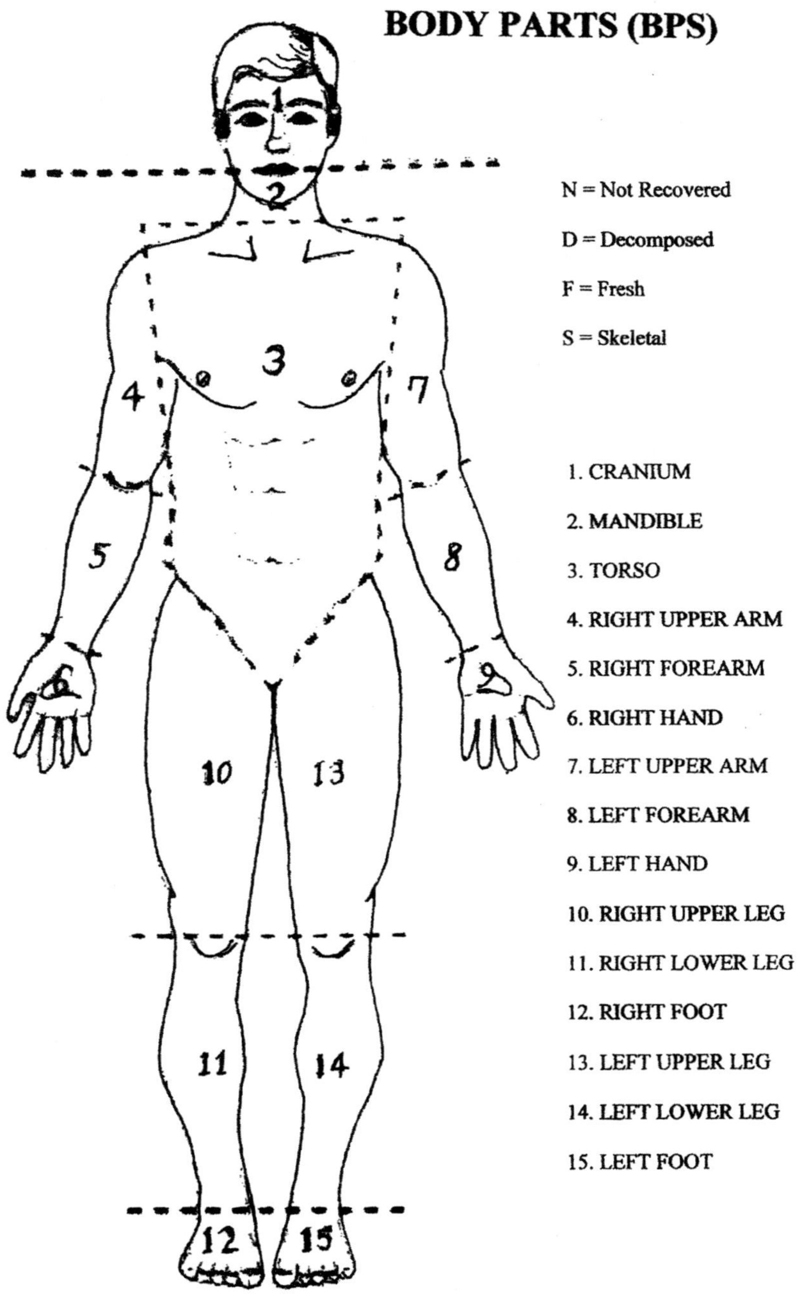

Figure A.9 Miami Dade Country Medical Examiner body parts chart. (Courtesy of the Miami Dade Medical Examiners office. Used with permission.)

Ante Mortem (yellow) **VICTIM IDENTIFICATION FORM** **F1**

MISSING PERSON

Family name : _______________ **No :** ________

Forename(s) : _______________

Date of birth : ☐☐ Day ☐☐ Month ☐☐☐☐ Year Male ☐ Female ☐

DENTAL INFORMATION		
76	**Missing Persons address** (see A1 item 10)	
77	**Missing since**	☐☐ Day ☐☐ Month ☐☐☐☐ Year
78	**Circumstances of the disappearance**	
79	**Dental information Obtained from family members and/or others** 01 Data in D2 item 45	1 ☐ No 2 ☐ Yes
DENTAL DATA PROVIDED BY		
80	**Dentist / Institution** Address Phone/E-mail Period covered DOCUMENTS filed with	From ______ To ______ ☐ Records ☐ X-rays ☐ Models ☐ Photos
81	**Dentist / Institution** Address Phone/E-mail Period covered DOCUMENTS filed with	From ______ To ______ ☐ Records ☐ X-rays ☐ Models ☐ Photos
82	**Dentist / Institution** Address Phone/E-mail Period covered DOCUMENTS filed with	From ______ To ______ ☐ Records ☐ X-rays ☐ Models ☐ Photos
Continued item no 86 (Item 83 - 85 in form PM only)		

Collected by	Signature / Date
Duty Title : Name : Address : Phone/E-mail :	

[(GB) Version 2002]

BINDING HOLES

BINDING HOLES

Figure A.10a Interpol victim identification form—missing person (yellow, page 1). (Courtesy of Interpol.)

Ante Mortem (yellow) **VICTIM IDENTIFICATION FORM** **F2**

MISSING PERSON

Family name : ______________ **No** : __________

Forename(s) : ______________

Date of birth : ☐☐ Day ☐☐ Month ☐☐☐☐ Year Male ☐ Female ☐

86	DENTAL INFORMATION in permanent teeth (Notify temporary teeth specifically)		
11			21
12			22
13			23
14			24
15			25
16			26
17			27
18			28

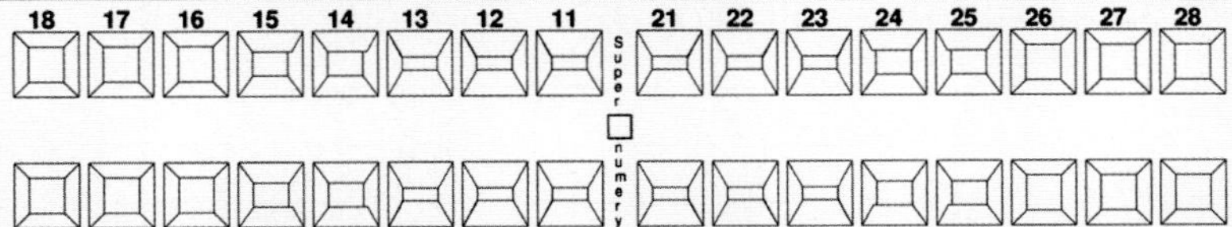

48			38
47			37
46			36
45			35
44			34
43			33
42			32
41			31

87	**Specific data** Crowns, bridges, dentures and implants	
88	**Further data** Occlusion, attrition, anomalies, smoker, periodontal status, etc.	
89	**X-rays available** Type, region and year	
90	**Further material**	
91	**Age at time of disapp.**	

[(GB) Version 2002]

BINDING HOLES

BINDING HOLES

Figure A.10b Interpol victim identification form—missing person (yellow, page 2). (Courtesy of Interpol.)

PostMortem (pink) **VICTIM IDENTIFICATION FORM** F1

DEAD BODY

Nature of disaster: **No**:

Place of disaster: *Sex unknown* ☐

Date of disaster: ☐☐ *Day* ☐☐ *Month* ☐☐☐☐ *Year* *Male* ☐ *Female* ☐

BINDING HOLES

DENTAL FINDINGS		
83	**In single cases** Site of recovery Recovery No. Date Police Agency Address Phone/E-mail DENTAL EXAMINATION Requested by (date) Performed at (date)	
84	**Material** 01 Jaws present	*Upper* 1 ☐ *Lower* 2 ☐ *Specimen taken?*
	02 Fragmentary remains	*Upper* 1 ☐ *Lower* 2 ☐ *Specimen taken?*
	03 Single teeth	*Specimen taken?*
	04 Other	*Specimen taken?*
	05 Location of specimen	
85	**Supplementary details** Condition of the body Condition of the jaws Injuries to - oral soft tissue - jaws - teeth Possible cause(s) of injuries Other details	

BINDING HOLES

Registered by Duty Title : Name : Address : Phone/E-mail :	Signature / Date

[(GB) Version 2002]

Figure A.11a Interpol victim identification form—unidentified person (pink, page 1). (Courtesy of Interpol.)

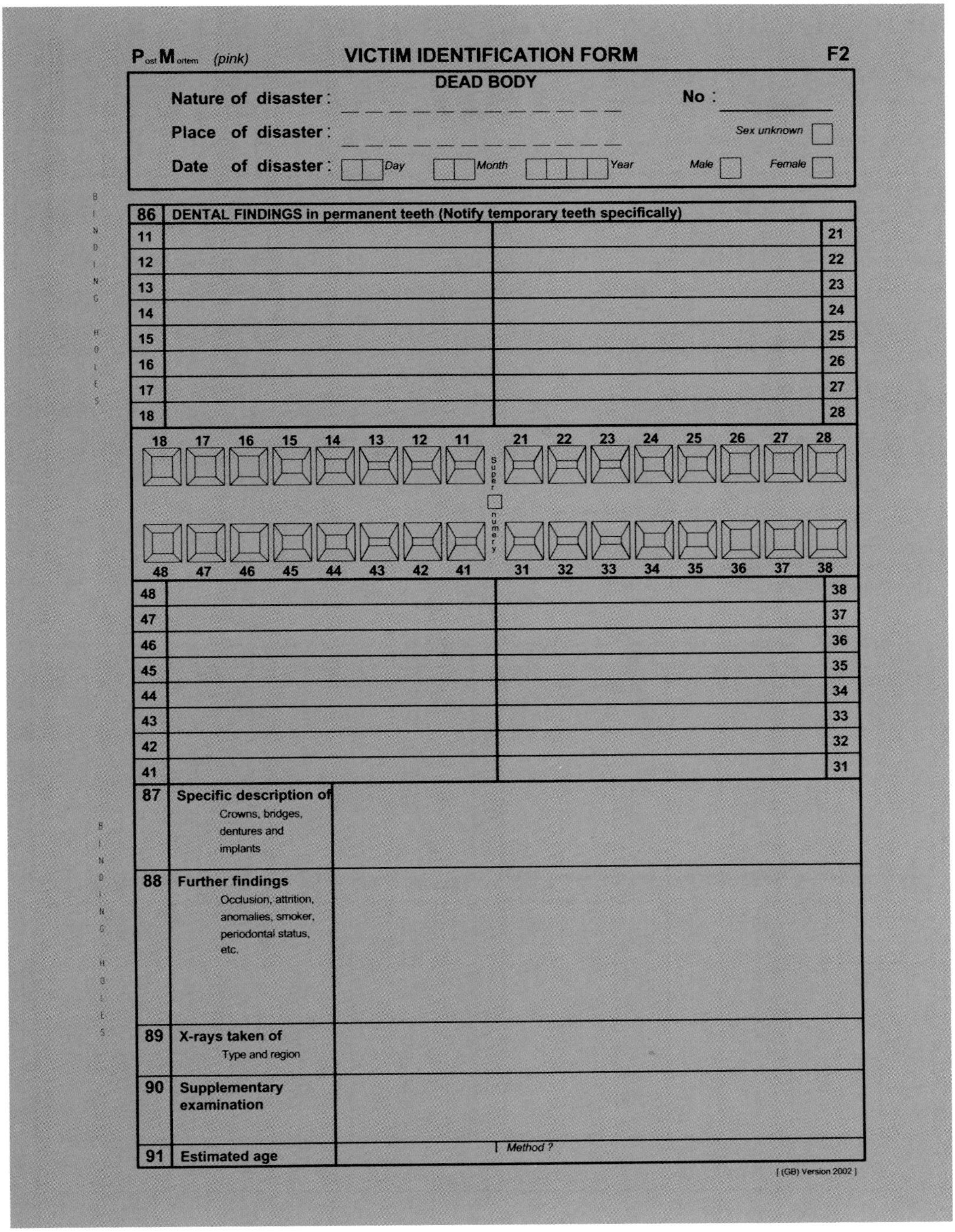

PostMortem (pink) **VICTIM IDENTIFICATION FORM** F2

DEAD BODY

Nature of disaster: ______________ No: ______

Place of disaster: ______________ Sex unknown ☐

Date of disaster: ☐☐ Day ☐☐ Month ☐☐☐☐ Year Male ☐ Female ☐

86	DENTAL FINDINGS in permanent teeth (Notify temporary teeth specifically)		
11			21
12			22
13			23
14			24
15			25
16			26
17			27
18			28

18 17 16 15 14 13 12 11 Supernumerary ☐ 21 22 23 24 25 26 27 28

48 47 46 45 44 43 42 41 31 32 33 34 35 36 37 38

48			38
47			37
46			36
45			35
44			34
43			33
42			32
41			31

87	**Specific description of** Crowns, bridges, dentures and implants	
88	**Further findings** Occlusion, attrition, anomalies, smoker, periodontal status, etc.	
89	**X-rays taken of** Type and region	
90	**Supplementary examination**	
91	**Estimated age**	Method ?

BINDING HOLES

BINDING HOLES

[(GB) Version 2002]

Figure A.11b Interpol victim identification form—unidentified person (pink, page 2). (Courtesy of Interpol.)

DENTAL CHARACTERISTICS INPUT DATA

Part 1 — To be completed by police authorities

NOTE: TO ASSIST THE POLICE IDENTIFICATION PROCESS, YOUR COOPERATION IS NEEDED TO OBTAIN ALL DATA PERTAINING TO THE DENTAL CHARACTERISTICS OF THE PERSON NAMED BELOW.			Date:
Surname:	Given name(s):	Sex:	Birthdates:
Police agency:			Investigator:
File number:	Facsimile number:		Telephone number:

Part 2 — To be completed by practitioner/dentist

INSTRUCTIONS

Maximum of seven (7) Dental Codes per tooth
M = Mesial, O = Occlusal, D = Distal, F = Facial, L = Lingual, C = Crown, R = Root Canal, U = Unknown, X = Missing, V = Virgin
(If X or V are used for a tooth, no other codes are permitted for that tooth.)

Unerupted teeth are to be identified as U=Unknown for Missing Persons.

[ ] represents new CPIC formats (Canadian Police Information Centre)
( ) represents vintage CPIC formats (FDI World Dental Federation)
{ } represents deciduous (Infant/childhood teeth)

Upper Jaw

RIGHT SIDE

[1]	[2]	[3]	[4]	[5]	[6]	[7]	[8]		[9]	[10]	[11]	[12]	[13]	[14]	[15]	[16]
(18)	(17)	(16)	(15)	(14)	(13)	(12)	(11)	C	(21)	(22)	(23)	(24)	(25)	(26)	(27)	(28)
			{55}	{54}	{53}	{52}	{51}		{61}	{62}	{63}	{64}	{65}			
								E								
								N								

C E N T R E

LEFT SIDE

[32]	[31]	[30]	[29]	[28]	[27]	[26]	[25]		[24]	[23]	[22]	[21]	[20]	[19]	[18]	[17]
(48)	(47)	(46)	(45)	(44)	(43)	(42)	(41)		(31)	(32)	(33)	(34)	(35)	(36)	(37)	(38)
			{85}	{84}	{83}	{82}	{81}	R	{71}	{72}	{73}	{74}	{75}			
								E								

Lower Jaw

Figure A.12a CPIC dental characteristics input form (page 1). (Courtesy of CPIC.)

Part 2 — Continued

DENTIST'S REMARKS (optional)

This section is to be used by the practitioner/dentist to include any pertinent remarks or comments that may assist the investigation.

DREM:
A maximum of 50 alphanumeric characters is allowed in this field.

PRACTITIONER/DENTIST

Surname: ______________________ Given name(s): ______________________

Address: ____

Telephone No.: ____________________ Date completed: ____________________

E-mail address: ____

X-rays available? Yes ____ No ____ If yes, were they provided? Yes ____ No ____

Dental photographs available? Yes _____ No ____ If yes, were they provided? Yes ____ No ____

Dental models available? Yes ____ No ___ If yes, were they provided? Yes ____ No ____

TO THE BEST OF MY KNOWLEDGE, THE INFORMATION PROVIDED IS ACCURATE. THIS INFORMATION IS PROVIDED FOR THE SOLE PURPOSE OF ASSISTING IN THE IDENTIFICATION OF THE PERSON NAMED ON THIS FORM.

______________________ ______________________
Signature Date

Part 3 — To be completed by police authorities

AUTHORITY:	DATE:	ENTERED ON CPIC BY:	DATE:

Figure A.12b CPIC dental characteristics input form (page 2). (Courtesy of CPIC.)

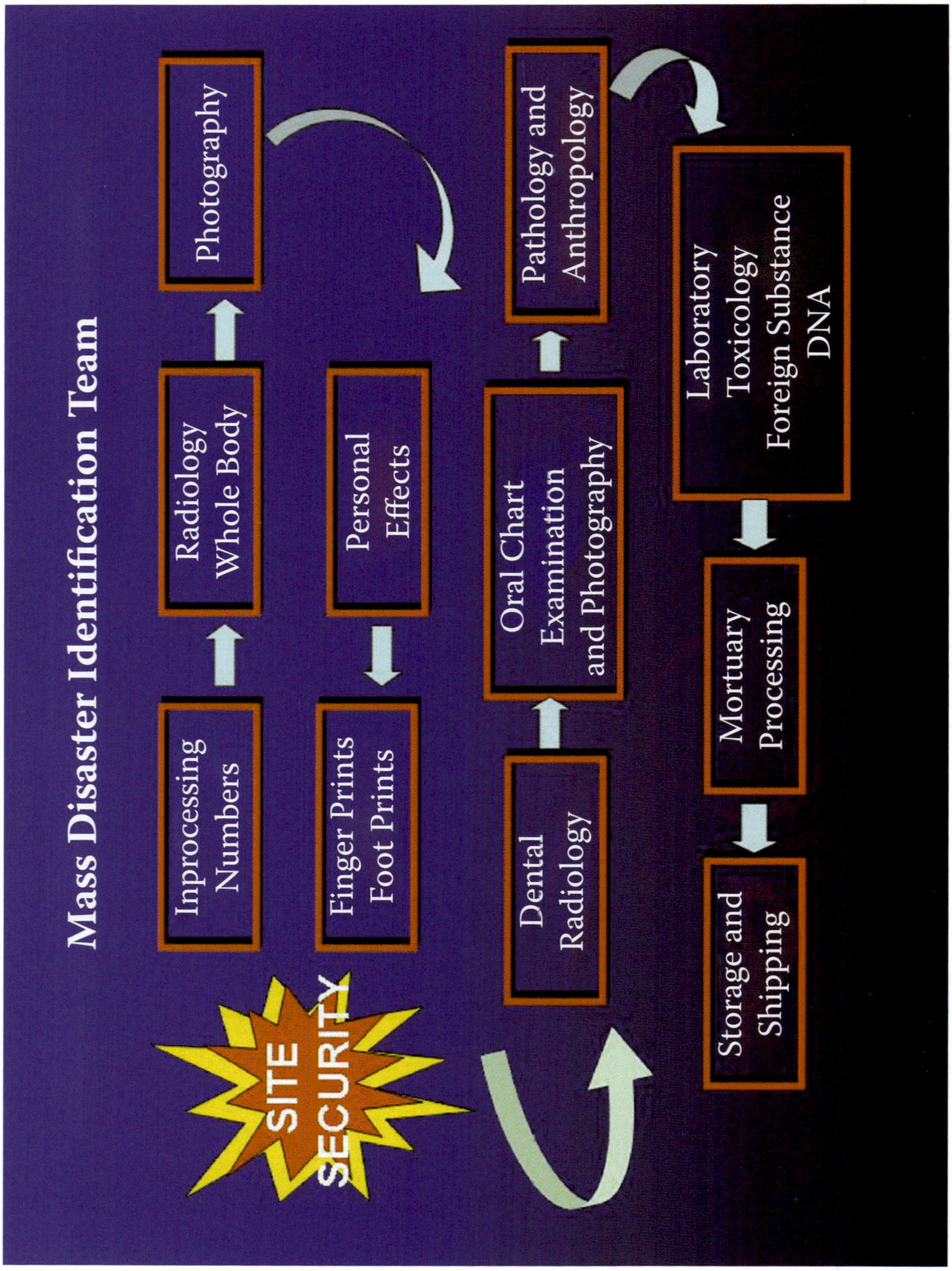

Figure A.13 Mass disaster identification team flowchart.

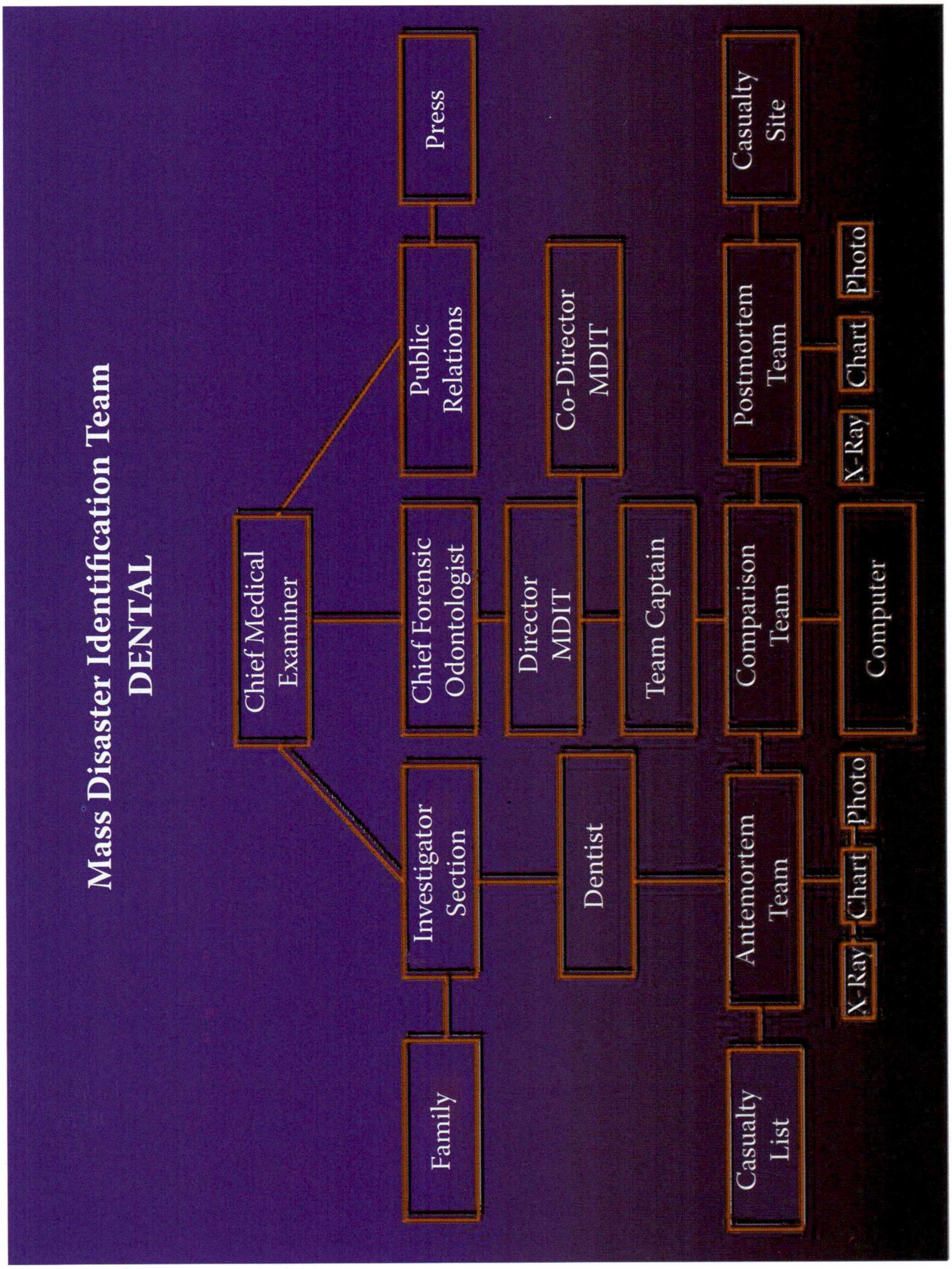

Figure A.14 Mass disaster identification team (dental) flowchart.

DMORT Antemortem Dental Record **ID#:** ____________

Last: ____________ First: ____________ MI: ____________

Date: ______ Sex: ______ Race: ______ Age/DOB : ____________

Height: _____ Weight: ____ Eye: ______ Hair: _____ Blood Type: _____

Team Member: ____________

☐ Confirm by: ____________

Type, Date and Number of X-Rays ____________

____

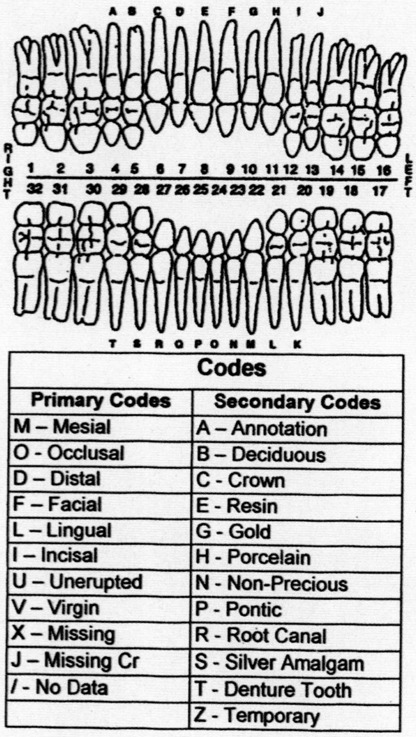

				Description	Code
1	18				
2	17				
3	16				
4	15	A	55		
5	14	B	54		
6	13	C	53		
7	12	D	52		
8	11	E	51		
9	21	F	61		
10	22	G	62		
11	23	H	63		
12	24	I	64		
13	25	J	65		
14	26				
15	27				
16	28				
17	38				
18	37				
19	36				
20	35	K	75		
21	34	L	74		
22	33	M	73		
23	32	N	72		
24	31	O	71		
25	41	P	81		
26	42	Q	82		
27	43	R	83		
28	44	S	84		
29	45	T	85		
30	46				
31	47				
32	48				

Codes

Primary Codes	Secondary Codes
M – Mesial	A – Annotation
O - Occlusal	B – Deciduous
D – Distal	C - Crown
F – Facial	E - Resin
L – Lingual	G - Gold
I – Incisal	H - Porcelain
U – Unerupted	N - Non-Precious
V – Virgin	P - Pontic
X – Missing	R - Root Canal
J – Missing Cr	S - Silver Amalgam
/ - No Data	T - Denture Tooth
	Z - Temporary

A: ____________
B: ____________
C: ____________

ID As: ____________

Comments: ____________

Figure A.15 DMORT antemortem dental record. (Courtesy of the National Disaster Medical Service.)

DMORT PostMortem Dental Record **ID#: ______________**

Date: ______ Sex: _______ Race: ______ Estimated Age: ____

Height: _____ Weight: ____ Eye: _______ Hair: ______ Blood Type: _____

Team member: ______________________

☐ Confirm: ______________________

Type, Date and Number of X-Rays ____________

____

Code	Description				
				18	1
				17	2
				16	3
		55	A	15	4
		54	B	14	5
		53	C	13	6
		52	D	12	7
		51	E	11	8
		61	F	21	9
		62	G	22	10
		63	H	23	11
		64	I	24	12
		65	J	25	13
				26	14
				27	15
				28	16
				38	17
				37	18
				36	19
		75	K	35	20
		74	L	34	21
		73	M	33	22
		72	N	32	23
		71	O	31	24
		81	P	41	25
		82	Q	42	26
		83	R	43	27
		84	S	44	28
		85	T	45	29
				46	30
				47	31
				48	32

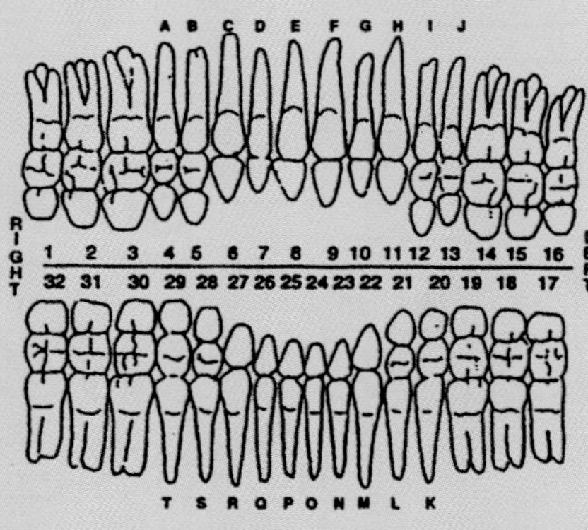

WinID Codes

Primary Codes	Secondary Codes
M - Mesial	A - Annotation
O - Occlusal	B - Deciduous
D - Distal	C - Crown
F - Facial	E - Resin
L - Lingual	G - Gold
I - Incisal	H - Porcelain
U – Unerupted	N - Non-Precious
V - Virgin	P - Pontic
X – Missing	R - Root Canal
J – Missing Cr MPM	S - Silver Amalgam
/ - No Data	T - Denture Tooth
	Z - Temporary

Comments: ______________________

A: ______________________
B: ______________________
C: ______________________

Body ID As: ______________________

Figure A.16 DMORT postmortem dental record. (Courtesy of the National Disaster Medical Service.)

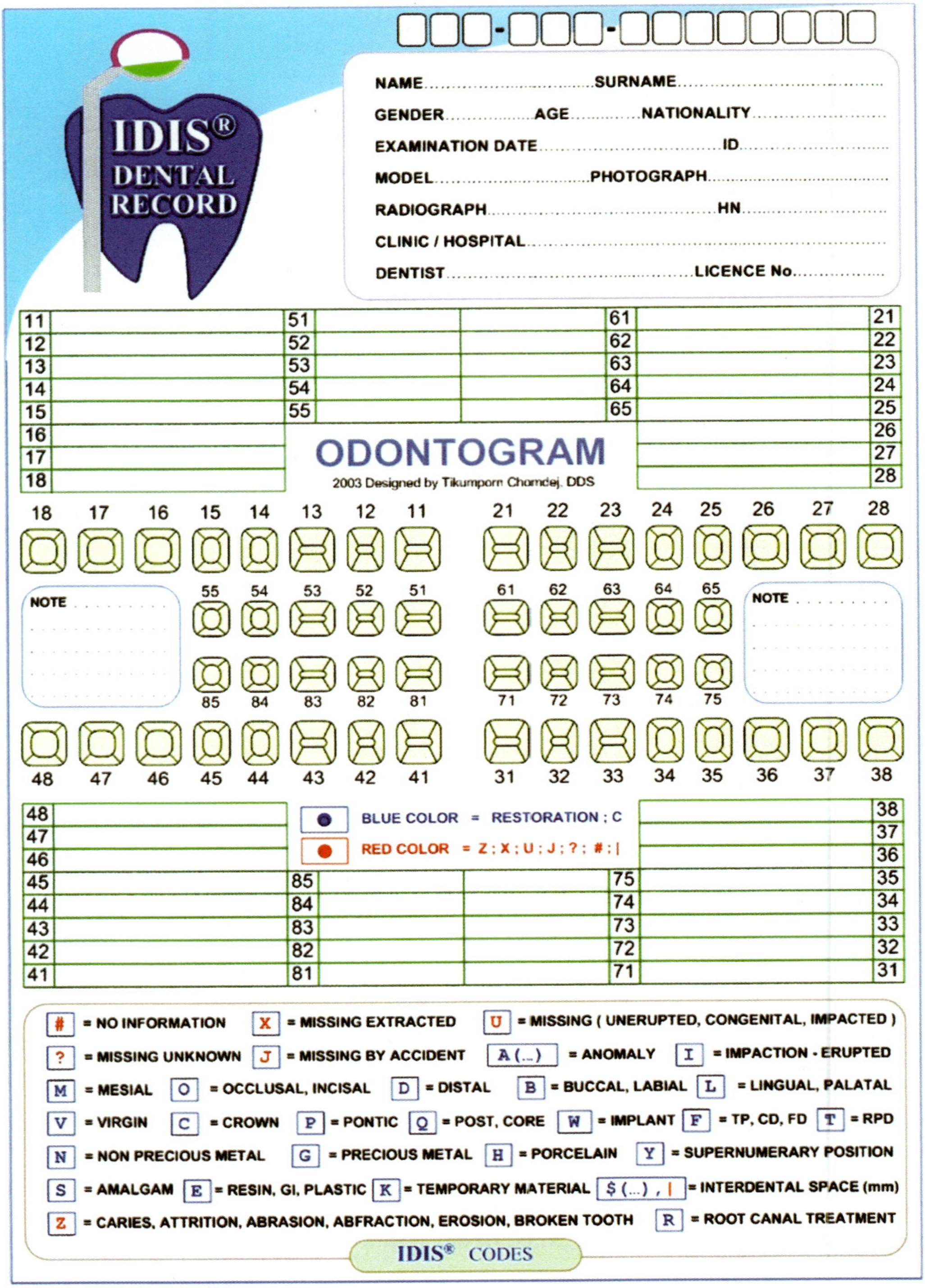

IDIS® DENTAL RECORD

NAME .... SURNAME ....
GENDER .... AGE .... NATIONALITY ....
EXAMINATION DATE .... ID ....
MODEL .... PHOTOGRAPH ....
RADIOGRAPH .... HN ....
CLINIC / HOSPITAL ....
DENTIST .... LICENCE No. ....

ODONTOGRAM

2003 Designed by Tikumporn Chomdej, DDS

18 17 16 15 14 13 12 11 21 22 23 24 25 26 27 28

55 54 53 52 51 61 62 63 64 65

NOTE ....

85 84 83 82 81 71 72 73 74 75

48 47 46 45 44 43 42 41 31 32 33 34 35 36 37 38

BLUE COLOR = RESTORATION ; C

RED COLOR = Z ; X ; U ; J ; ? ; # ; |

IDIS® CODES

\# = NO INFORMATION
X = MISSING EXTRACTED
U = MISSING (UNERUPTED, CONGENITAL, IMPACTED)
? = MISSING UNKNOWN
J = MISSING BY ACCIDENT
A (...) = ANOMALY
I = IMPACTION - ERUPTED
M = MESIAL
O = OCCLUSAL, INCISAL
D = DISTAL
B = BUCCAL, LABIAL
L = LINGUAL, PALATAL
V = VIRGIN
C = CROWN
P = PONTIC
Q = POST, CORE
W = IMPLANT
F = TP, CD, FD
T = RPD
N = NON PRECIOUS METAL
G = PRECIOUS METAL
H = PORCELAIN
Y = SUPERNUMERARY POSITION
S = AMALGAM
E = RESIN, GI, PLASTIC
K = TEMPORARY MATERIAL
$ (...) , | = INTERDENTAL SPACE (mm)
Z = CARIES, ATTRITION, ABRASION, ABFRACTION, EROSION, BROKEN TOOTH
R = ROOT CANAL TREATMENT

Figure A.17 IDIS dental record.

RELEASE AND WAIVER OF LIABILITY AGREEMENT
Miami Dade County Medical Examiner Department
Forensic Morgue Bureau

I,______________________________(print name) understand that as a visitor to the Miami Dade Medical Examiner Department I am not covered by County health insurance benefits or by County Workman's Compensation. I agree to display proper decorum and to assume full responsibility for my conduct. Since I may be exposed to various potential pathogens, I will wear protective clothing, including gown,mask,shoe covers and eye protection while in the morgue. Should I sustain any injury during my visit, I will immediately report the matter to the Morgue Bureau Supervisor.

Further, I , THE UNDERSIGNED HEREBY RELEASES, WAIVES, DISCHARGES, AND COVENANTS NOT TO SUE Miami Dade County, the Public Health Trust, and each of their officers and employees, all for the purposes herein referred to as "releasees", from all liability to the undersigned, his or her personal representatives , assigns, heirs, and next of kin for any and all loss or damage, and any claim or demands therefore on account of injury to the person or property or resulting in the death of the undersigned, whether caused by negligence of the releasees or otherwise while the undersigned is in or upon the facilities of the Miami Dade Medical Examiner Department or in any way arising out of a tour,visit or operation of that department.

THE UNDERSIGNED further HEREBY ASSUMES FULL RESPONSIBILITY FOR AND RISK OF BODILY INJURY, DEATH OR PROPERTY DAMAGE due to the negligence of releases or otherwise while in or upon the facilities of the Miami Dade Medical Examiner Department or while participating in a tour, visit or operation of that Department.

THE UNDERSIGNED further expressly acknowledges and agrees that the activities of the event can be dangerous and involve the risk of serious injury and/or death and/or property damage.THE UNDERSIGNED further expressly agrees that the foregoing release, waiver and indemnity agreement is intended to be as broad and inclusive as is permitted by the law of the State of Floida and that if any portion thereof is held invalid, it is agreed that the balance shall , notwithstanding, continue in full legal force and effect.

THE UNDERSIGNED HAS READ AND VOLUNTARILY SIGNS THIS RELEASE AND WAIVER OF LIABILITY AGREEMENT, and further agrees that no oral representations, statements or inducements apart from the foregoing written agreement have been made.

____ ________________
Signature Date

____
Print Name

Figure A.18 Miami Dade Medical Examiner Forensic Morgue Bureau release and waiver of liability agreement. (Courtesy of the Miami Dade Medical Examiners office. Used with permission.)

MIAMI-DADE COUNTY

Medical Examiner Department
Number One on Bob Hope Road
(1851 NW 10th Avenue)
Miami, Florida 33136-1133
T 305-545-2400

miamidade.gov

ADA Coordination
Agenda Coordination
Animal Services
Art in Public Places
Audit and Management Services
Aviation
Building
Building Code Compliance
Business Development
Capital Improvements Construction Coordination
Citizens' Independent Transportation Trust
Commission on Ethics and Public Trust
Communications
Community Action Agency
Community & Economic Development
Community Relations
Consumer Services
Corrections & Rehabilitation
Cultural Affairs
Elections
Emergency Management
Employee Relations
Empowerment Trust
Enterprise Technology Services
Environmental Resources Management
Fair Employment Practices
Finance
Fire Rescue
General Services Administration
Historic Preservation
Homeless Trust
Housing Agency
Housing Finance Authority
Human Services
Independent Review Panel
International Trade Consortium
Juvenile Assessment Center
Medical Examiner
Metro-Miami Action Plan
Metropolitan Planning Organization
Park and Recreation
Planning and Zoning
Police
Procurement Management
Property Appraiser
Public Library System
Public Works
Safe Neighborhood Parks
Seaport
Solid Waste Management
Strategic Business Management
Team Metro
Transit
Task Force on Urban Economic Revitalization
Vizcaya Museum And Gardens
Water & Sewer

{DATE OF LETTER}

{NAME AND ADDRESS OF INVESTIGATOR AND AGENCY}
Forensic Investigator
Miami Dade Medical Examiner Department
Number One on Bob Hope Road
Miami, FL 33136-1133

RE: M.E. # {CASE NUMBER}

Dear {INVESTIGATOR};
{DATE OF REQUEST FOR SERVICE}
{PLACE OF SERVICE}
{DATE AND TIME OF SERVICE}
{AUXILIARY PERSONNEL PRESENT}
{PROCEDURES}
Radiographs, Number and Type
Photographs, Number and type
Impressions/Models
Dentures
Special Procedures, eg, Jaw Removal
{NAME AND ADDRESS OF ANTEMORTEM DENTIST}
Records Provided , Patient Name , Dates, & Condition
{COMPARISON OF ANTEMORTEM AND POSTMORTEM RECORDS}
{CONCLUSION, ACCORDING TO ABFO ID GUIDELINES}
{DEGREE OF CONFIDENCE}
{ADDITIONAL INFORMATION TO VALIDATE OR INVALIDATE CONCLUSIONS}

Most sincerely,

{SIGNATURE}
{NAME}
{TITLE}
{AGENCY}

Delivering Excellence Every Day

Figure A.19 Miami Dade Medical Examiner Forensic Ontologist autopsy report.

Bibliography

American Society of Forensic Odontology. 2006. *ASFO Manual of Forensic Odontology*, 4th ed. Albany, NY: Impress Printing & Graphics.

Babitsky, S. and Mangraviti, J. 2003. *Cross Examination: The Comprehensive Guide for Experts*. Falmouth, MA: SEAK Inc.

Bell, G. 1993. Testing of the National Crime Information Center missing/unidentified persons computer comparison routine. *J. Forensic Sci.*, 38(1):13–22.

Bell, G.L. 2001. Dentistry's role in the resolution of missing and unidentified persons cases. *Dent. Clin. North. Am.*, 45(2):293–308.

Bowers, C.M. 2004. *Forensic Dental Evidence*, 1st ed. San Diego, CA: Elsevier.

Burns, K.R. 2007. *Forensic Anthropology Training Manual*, 2nd ed. Upper Saddle River, NJ: Prentice Hall.

Cantor, B.J. 1967. The role of the expert witness in a court trial. *Wis. Med. J.*, 66(1):21–22.

Chomdej, T., Pankaow, W., and Cheychumroon, S. 2006. Intelligent dental identification system. *Forensic Sci. Inter.*, 158, 27–38.

Clement, J.G. and Marks, M.K. 2005. *Computer-Graphic Facial Reconstruction*. Burlington, MA: Elsevier.

Cottone, J. and Standish, S.M. 1982. *Outline of Forensic Dentistry 1981*, Chicago, IL: Yearbook Medical Publishers.

Davis, J. 1993. Injuries due to animals. In Mason J., Ed., *Pathology of Trauma*, 3rd ed., pp. 227–241. London: Edward Arnold Publishers.

Davis, J. 2004. The role of the medical examiner/coroner/pathologist. In Dorion, R.B., Ed., *Bitemark Evidence*. New York: Marcel Dekker.

DiMaio, V.J.M. and Dana, S. 2007. *Handbook of Forensic Pathology*, 2nd ed. Boca Raton, FL: CRC Press.

Dorion, R.B. 1987. Transillumination in bitemark evidence, *J. Forensic Sci.*, 32(3):690–697.

Dorion, R.B., Ed. 2005. Bitemark Evidence. New York: Marcel Dekker.

Giles, E. and Eliot O. 1962. Race identification from cranial measurements. *J. Forensic Sci.*, 7, 236–238.

Goldman, A. 1995. Techniques for post mortem dental radiography. In *ASFO Manual of Forensic Odontology*, 3rd ed. Albany, NY: Impress Printing & Graphics.

Gustafson, G. 1966. *Forensic Odontology*, pp. 140–165. London: Staple Press.

Keiser-Nielsen, S. 1977. Dental identification: Certainty v. probability. *Forensic Sci.*, 9(2):87–97.

Lewis, C. 2002. WINID versus CAPMI4: Two computer-assisted dental identification systems. *J. Forensic Sci.*, 48(2):472.

Lorton, L. and Cornwell, K. 1990. System design for a computerized identification. In *Forensic Dentistry Workbook*, Dr. D. Averill, Ed. Austin, TX: American Society of Forensic Odontology.

Luntz, L. and Luntz, P. 1973. *Handbook for Dental Identification*. Philadelphia: JB Lippincott.

MacLean, D.F., Kogon, S.L., and Stitt, S. 1994. Validation of dental radiographs for human ID. *Int. Dent. J.*, 39, 1195–1200.

Maples, W.R. 1978. An improved technique using dental histology for estimation of adult age. *J. Forensic Sci.*, 23(4):764–770.

McGivney, J. 2007. WINID. Personal Correspondence.

Mincer, H., Harris, E.F., and Berryman, H.E. 1993. The ABFO study of third molar development and its use as an estimator of adult age. *J. Forensic Sci.*, 38(6):1524.

Mincer, H. 1995. Salvaging improperly exposed or incorrectly processed radiographs. In *Manual of Forensic Odontology*, Bowers, C.M. and Bell, G., Eds. Albany, NY: American Society of Forensic Odontology.

Moorrees, C., Fanning, E., and Hunt, E. 1963. Mean ages of tooth development, *J. Dent. Res.*, 42:1490–1502.

Moritz, A.R. 1981. Forensic pathology, then and now. *Amer. J. Forensic Pathol.* 2(4):299–308.

Morlang, W. 1986. Mass disaster management update. *CDA J.*, 14(3):49–57.

Nordby, J.J. 1992. Can we believe what we see, if we see what we believe? – Expert disagreement. *J. Forensic Sci.*, 37(4):1115–1124.

Pretty, I.A. and Sweet, D. 2001. A look at forensic dentistry. Part 1: The role of teeth in the determination of human identity, *Br. Dent. J.*, 190(7):359–366.

Pretty, I.A. 2003. The use of dental aging techniques in forensic odontological practice. *J. Forensic Sci.*, 48(5):1127–1132.

Pretty, I.A., Pretty, R.J., Rothwell, B.R., and Sweet, D. 2003. The reliability of digitized radiographs for dental identification. *J. Forensic Sci.* 48(6):1325–1330.

Rau, V.J. and Souviron, R.R. 1984. Dusting and lifting the biteprint: A new technique. *J. Forensic Sci.*, 29(1):326–330.

Rollins, C.E. and Spencer, D.E. 1995. A fatality and the American mountain lion: Bitemark analysis and profile of the offending lion. *J. Forensic Sci.* 40(3):486–489.

Rothwell, B.R. 2001. Principles of dental identification. *Dent. Clin. North Am.*, 45(2):253–270.

Shultz, J.M. and Espinel, Z. 2004. *Behavioral Health Awareness Training for Terrorism and Disasters*. Miami, FL: University of Miami Press.

Souviron, R.R. 2004. Animal bites. In: Dorion, R.B., Ed. *Bitemark Evidence*. New York: Marcel Dekker.

Souviron, R.R. 2004. Patterns, lesions and trauma mimicking bitemarks. In: Dorion, R.B., Ed. *Bitemark Evidence*. New York: Marcel Dekker.

Souviron, R.R. 2005. Forensic odontology. In: Dolinak, D., Matshes, E., and Lew, E., Eds. *Forensic Pathology, Principles and Practice*, pp. 605–629. Burlington, MA: Elsevier.

Souviron, R.R., Golden, G., Sweet, D., and Bowers, M. 2006. Medicolegal investigation of death. In: Spitz, W., Ed. *Forensic Odontology*, 4th ed., pp. 255–300. Springfield, IL: Charles C Thomas.

Spitz, W., Ed. 1993. *Spitz and Fisher's Medicolegal Investigation of Death*, 3rd ed. Springfield, IL: Charles C Thomas.

Stimson, P.G., and Mertz, C.A. 1997. *Forensic Dentistry*, Boca Raton, FL: CRC Press. Taylor, K.T. 2001. Forensic Art and Illustration, Boca Raton, FL: CRC Press.

Vale, G.L., Sognnaes, R.F., Felando, G.N., and Noguchi, T.T. 1976. Unusual three-dimensional bitemark evidence in a homicide case. *J. Forensic Sci.*, 21(3): 642–652.

White, T.D. and Folkens, P.A. 2005. *Human Bone Manual*. Burlington, MA: Elsevier.

Whittaker, D.K. 1990. The principles of forensic dentistry: Identification procedures. *Dental Update*, 17(8):386–390.

Wright, F. 1995. Postmortem considerations. *ASFO Manual of Forensic Odontology*, 3rd ed., pp. 9–13. Colorado Springs, CO: American Society of Forensic Odontology.

WEBSITES (Supplemental)

WIKIPEDIA	
Federal Bureau of Investigation	http://www.fbi.gov
American Academy of Forensic Science	http://www.aafs.org
American Association of Physical Anthropologists	http://www.physanth.org
American Board of Forensic Odontology	http://www.abfo.org
American Society of Forensic Odontology	http://www.asfo.org
Association of Firearms and Toolmark Examiners	http://www.afte.org
Forensic Entomology	http://www.forensicentomology.com
International Association for Identification	http://www.theiai.org
National Association of Medical Examiners	http://www.then ame.org
National Library of Medicine	http://www.ncbi.nlm.nih.gov/pubmed
Reddy's Forensic Page	http://www.forensicpage.com
Zeno's Forensic Page	http://www.forensic.to
BEST BET FOR FORENSIC ODONTOLOGY	http://www.forensicdentistryonline.com

Index

G

H

I

N

O

P

R

S

T

U

V

W

X